Breeding Endangered Species in Captivity

Conference Sponsors

The Jersey Wildlife Preservation Trust *Les Augrés Manor, Trinity, Jersey, Channel Islands, British Isles.*

The Fauna Preservation Society *c/o The Zoological Society of London, Regent's Park, London NW1 4RY, England.*

Breeding Endangered Species in Captivity

Edited by

R. D. Martin

Wellcome Institute of Comparative Physiology
The Zoological Society of London
Regent's Park, London

1975

ACADEMIC PRESS

London   New York   San Francisco

A Subsidiary of Harcourt Brace Jovanovich, Publishers

ACADEMIC PRESS INC. (LONDON) LTD.
24/28 Oval Road,
London NW1

United States Edition published by
ACADEMIC PRESS INC.
111 Fifth Avenue
New York, New York 10003

Library of Congress Catalog Card Number: 74–18526
ISBN: 0–12–474850–3

PRINTED IN GREAT BRITAIN
T. & A. CONSTABLE LTD., EDINBURGH

Contributors

BHATIA, C. L., *former Director, Delhi Zoological Park, New Delhi, India. (Present address: Conservator of Forests, Siwalik Circle, U.P. Dehra Dun, India.)*

BRAMBELL, Dr. M. R., *Curator of Mammals, Zoological Society of London, Regent's Park, London NW1 4RY, England.*

BRIDGWATER, D. D., *Minnesota State Zoological Gardens, St. Paul, Minnesota 55155, USA.*

BUSTARD, Dr. H. R., *Applied Ecology Pty. Ltd., PO Box 26, Woden, ACT 2606, Australia.*

CROWCROFT, Dr. W. P., *Chicago Zoological Park, Brookfield, Chicago, Illinois 60513, USA.*

DESAI, J. H., *Joint Director, Delhi Zoological Park, New Delhi, India.*

DUPLAIX-HALL, Mrs. N., *Editor, International Zoo Yearbook, Zoological Society of London, Regent's Park, London NW1 4RY, England.*

ERICKSON, Dr. R. C., *Assistant Director, Endangered Wildlife Research Program, Patuxent Wildlife Research Center, Laurel, Maryland 20811, USA.*

FRANCOEUR, Professor R. T., *Associate Professor of Experimental Embryology, Fairleigh Dickinson University, Madison, New Jersey 201 377-4700, USA.*

FYFE, R., *Canadian Wildlife Service, 10025 Jasper Avenue, Edmonton, Alberta T5J 1S6, Canada.*

HICK, Fräulein U., *Scientific Assistant, Aktiengesellschaft Zoologischer Garten Köln, 5 Köln-Riehl, Riehlerstrasse 173, Germany.*

HOMAN, W. G., *Curator, Phoenix Zoo, PO Box 5155, Phoenix, Arizona 85010, USA.*

HONEGGER, R. E., *Curator of Herpetology, Zoologischer Garten Zürich, Zürichberg-strasse 221, CH-8044 Zürich, Switzerland.*

HORSEMEN, D. L., *National Zoological Park, Smithsonian Institution, Washington DC 20009, USA.*

JACOBI, Dr. E. F., *Director, Stichting Koninlijk Zoölogisch Genootschap Natura Artis Magistra, Plantage Kerklaan 40, Amsterdam-C, Netherlands.*

JANTSCHKE, Dr. F., *Zoologischer Garten, 6 Frankfurt am Main 1, Alfred-Brehm-Platz 16, Germany.*

KEAR, Dr. J., *Avicultural Coordinator, The Wildfowl Trust, Slimbridge, Gloucester-shire, GL2 7BT, England.*

KINGSTON, W. R., *Hillcrest House, Belton, Loughborough, Leicestershire, England.*

KRISHNE GOWDA, C. D., *Curator, Sri Chamarajendra Zoological Gardens, Mysore, S. India.*

LA CROIX THROP, J., *Director, Honolulu Zoo, Wakiki Beach, Kapiolari Park, Honolulu, Hawaii 96815, USA.*

LANG, Dr. E. M., *Director, Zoologischer Garten Basel, 4000 Basel, Switzerland.*

MACFARLAND, Dr. C. G., *Director, Charles Darwin Research Station, Casilla 58–39, Guayaquil, Ecuador.*

MALLINSON, J. J. C., *Deputy Director, Jersey Zoological Park, Jersey Wildlife Preservation Trust, Les Augrés Manor, Trinity, Jersey, Channel Islands, British Isles.*

MANTON, V. J. A., M.R.C.V.S., *Curator, Whipsnade Park, Whipsnade, Bedfordshire, England.*

MARTIN, Dr. R. D., *Wellcome Institute of Comparative Physiology, The Zoological Society of London, Regent's Park, London N.W.1 4RY.*

MAYNES, G. M., *Department of Zoology, Monash University, New South Wales, Australia. (Present address: School of Biological Sciences, Macquarie University, North Ryde, N.S.W., 2113, Australia.)*

MERTON, D. V., *Fauna Conservation Officer, New Zealand Wildlife Service, Department of Internal Affairs, Private Bag, Wellington, New Zealand.*

PERRY, J., *Assistant Director for Conservation, National Zoological Park, Smithsonian Institution, Washington DC 20009, USA.*

PETTER, Dr. J.-J., *Sous-Directeur, Ecologie Générale, Muséum National d'Histoire Naturelle, 4 Avenue du Petit Château, 91 Brunoy (Essonne), France.*

RACZYŃSKI, Dr. J., *Mammal Research Institute, The Polish Academy of Sciences, 17–230 Bialowieża, Poland.*

REEDER, Dr. W. G., *Department of Zoology, Nolan Hall, University of Wisconsin, Madison, Wisconsin 53706, USA.*

SCHMIDT, C. R., *Zoologischer Garten Zürich, Zürichbergstrasse 221, CH-8044 Zürich, Switzerland.*

SCOTT, Sir PETER, *Hon. Director, The Wildfowl Trust, Slimbridge, Gloucestershire, GL2 7BT, England.*

STRAHAN, R., *Director, Taronga Zoo and Aquarium, Taronga Zoological Park Trust, PO Box 20, Mosman, New South Wales 2088, Australia.*

VAN BEMMEL, Dr. A. C. V., *Rijksmuseum van Natuurlijke Historie, Leiden, Netherlands. (Present address: Spinbollaan 30, Rotterdam 3012, The Netherlands.)*

VAN DEN BERGH, W., *Director, Royal Zoological Society of Antwerp, Kiningin Astridplein 26, Antwerp, Belgium.*

VOLF, Dr. J., *Curator of Mammals, Zoologicka Zahrada Praha 7, Czechoslovakia.*

WARLAND, Miss M., *c/o The Royal Bank of Scotland Ltd, 48 Haymarket, London SW1, England. (Formerly: Executive Officer, Survival Service Commission, International Union for Conservation of Nature, 1110 Morges, Switzerland.)*

WAYRE, P., *Hon. Director, The Pheasant Trust; Director, The Norfolk Wildlife Park, Great Witchingham, Norwich, Norfolk, NOR 65X, England.*

WEBER, E., *Animal Superintendant, Melbourne Zoological Gardens, Royal Park, Parkville, Victoria 3052, Australia.*

Foreword

Gerald Durrell

I am delighted that the Jersey Wildlife Preservation Trust, with the Fauna Preservation Society, could be joint hosts to the 1972 Conference on the Breeding of Endangered Species. I feel that this Conference was of the utmost importance since it is now vital that zoos all over the world assess their contribution to conservation and make clear the part that they are going to play in the conservation movement in the future. I think that to a very large extent most zoos will have to rethink their future policies, and so from that point of view it might be useful for me to set down here a short account of the establishment and purposes of the Jersey Wildlife Preservation Trust.

For many years I had felt that there was a need for more specialized zoological collections and, moreover, for collections of a kind that devoted their energies first and foremost to conservation. Then, in 1959, I established the Zoological Park in Jersey realizing that it would first have to become a viable concern as a simple zoo before it could branch out into doing more serious and important work. So for the first four years we were fully occupied with the establishment of the zoo, and then, when it was financially viable, I created the Jersey Wildlife Preservation Trust, which took over the property and the animal collection. The Zoo thus became the Trust's headquarters.

The Trust is a scientific, non-profit making organization, with a membership spread throughout the world. We started with a membership of 750 (mostly readers of my books) and this has now grown to the point where we have over 10,000 members spread all over the world. A sister organization has recently been created in the United States of America, which will not only assist us in our projects here in Jersey, but enable us to promote and assist captive breeding projects both in the U.S.A. and in various other parts of the world.

Over the years, many people I have talked to have had only a vague idea of the scope and importance of controlled breeding as a conservation tool and little idea of the necessity for it. It is interesting, therefore, to briefly review the history and present-day attitudes towards controlled breeding and our own aspirations in this field of conservation.

As we all know, all over the world there are various species of animal life which are in danger of extinction. Numerically, many of these have reached such a low level that they urgently need every form of assistance they can get if they are to survive at all. The reasons for their decline are many and various, but in almost all cases it can be traced directly or indirectly to the intervention of man. But, whatever the cause, unless help is forthcoming, we are going to lose a vast array of beautiful and fascinating creatures that share the world with us. So it is important that not only must their habitat be protected but, as a safeguard, what have been called "Zoo Banks" should be created. This means that a viable breeding *group* of these creatures should be given sanctuary in Zoological gardens or, preferably, a specially established breeding centre where, free from all the natural and unnatural hazards of existence (such as destruction of habitat, a failing food supply and so on) they can live and breed successfully. Then, when sufficient stocks have been accumulated and the species is safely established in a number of zoos and centres, one can start thinking in terms of reintroducing it into areas from which it has already vanished, or introducing it to help increase and strengthen wild populations whose numbers have become drastically reduced. This, in essence, is what controlled breeding is, and when one realizes that there are nearly a thousand forms of life in immediate danger of extinction, then one realizes the scope and urgency of the work.

The saving of species in this way is, of course, not a new idea. Thanks to this sort of breeding, we still have with us such creatures as the European and North American bison, the Père David's deer, the Hawaiian goose and so on. The list of successes is surprisingly long, and to a large extent more than justifies the use of this form of conservation. However, up until now this sort of rescue operation has only been tried in a vague and rather dilatory sort of way with a few species. No really concentrated effort has been made to turn controlled breeding from what was a series of haphazard experiments into a definite conservation tool.

It is, in fact, only comparatively recently that controlled breeding of threatened species as a means of conserving them has become even remotely respectable in the eyes of the dedicated conservationist. Even now it is an uphill struggle to persuade some of them that it is a valid line of defence to the conservation of species in the wild, and even now, if you mention it at some august gathering of conservationists, they tend to regard you as if you had advocated war, as an ideal form of population control.

But recently there have been signs of some sort of a breakthrough. In 1966 a conference was held at the San Diego Zoo entitled "The Role of Zoos in Wildlife Conservation". Sir Peter Scott was the Chairman, the following is an extract from his inaugural address:

> Some people say that no very rare animals should be allowed in zoos. I am totally opposed to that view. It is essential that people should be allowed to see animals, and especially rare animals, if they are to be concerned for their survival and to support world conservation. Furthermore, captive breeding can be a real safeguard for a species. When you think of the species which, say ten years ago, had never been bred in captivity, you realize the immense

progress that Zoos have made in the care of their animals. Those who now breed these animals have quite clearly demonstrated that in the long run it will be possible to breed almost any animal under good captive conditions.

Such a statement a few years previously would have been treated with scant respect, even coming from such an eminent source, for the hard-core conservationists considered that any idea of removing an animal from its natural habitat to protect it was heresy. An animal removed from its environment ceased to be an animal, according to this line of thought, and the fact that such an action might save the species (as it had done with the Père David's deer, the European bison and so on) was not taken into consideration. Gradually, however, the idea that captive breeding might be a useful weapon in the conservationists' armoury became, to a certain extent, reluctantly accepted.

However, the battle is not completely won. There are still conservationists who consider that controlled breeding is basically a bad thing and should only be considered as a last resort, or simply talked about but never employed. They seem incapable of seeing that it should be used alongside the more conventional conservation methods (saving of habitat, creation of reserves, etc.) as an additional safeguard. But unfortunately in the past—and to a large extent today—they do not seem to understand the simple fact that an antidote, to be effective, should be applied as soon as possible. Therefore, as soon as a species is proved to be on the wane, a captive breeding programme should be set up *automatically*, along with all the other methods of saving it. The situation should not arise, as it has done in the past, where conservationists are so fearful of being branded as zoo-keepers or worse, that they let the population of the species drop to such a low level that it then becomes a major decision as to whether you catch a sufficient number to create a breeding programme. If there are only 50 specimens of a creature left in the world, do you risk catching say, 10 per cent of them as a safeguard or do you stand by hoping they can recover unaided? It poses a nice problem in ethics which, of course, should not arise if controlled breeding is accepted and adopted early enough. But I have met so-called conservationists, mercifully only a few, who have actually told me that they would prefer an animal to become extinct rather than have it "languish" in captivity.

That the conservationists' arguments had a certain validity cannot be denied. Their attitude was that the majority of zoos were badly run and had never shown any ability or desire to assist conservation by indulging in controlled breeding programmes. Rather, by their profligate attitude of "there's plenty more where that came from", zoos had been a drain upon the wild stocks, depleting animal populations by capture to replace creatures which, by their bad management or carelessness, or both, had been killed. It is a very unfortunate fact that the conservationists were (and still are) right in this criticism. There were—and still are, unfortunately—many (far too many) badly run zoological gardens in the world with a high mortality and an extremely low breeding record among their animals, whose contribution (when it exists) to either conservation, scientific research or education is so minimal as to be almost non-existent.

Anyone who is not a hypocrite and has any knowledge of animal husbandry is forced to admit that, on the whole, one can count the really first-class zoos almost on the fingers of one hand, while the slovenly, ill-kempt third-rate zoos continue to exist, and what is worse, proliferate. Moreover, they have now been joined by a major enemy of wild life and conservation, in the form of certain Safari or Wild-life Parks which are nothing more than animal abattoirs in a sylvan setting.

Unfortunately, real and intelligent conservation efforts are still only confined to a comparatively small number of zoos. Many zoos have not the space (nor if they had would they be allowed to use it so "unproductively"), for the large breeding programmes of the sort needed for the intelligent establishment of worthwhile controlled breeding projects. There are far too many zoos paying vociferous lip service to conservation without doing anything valid; too many zoos who are still only anxious to display rarities and are not over-worried by the breeding results; too many zoos who still think of a rare animal in terms of gate money and publicity and not of its importance from a conservation point of view.

Unfortunately, it is by these bad examples that all zoological gardens are judged and condemned, which is a great pity for, in recent years, with major advances in zoological husbandry, the better run zoos are making a major contribution to both conservation and the public awareness of the necessity for conservation.

So it was—in the days before captive breeding was really recognized—that the Jersey Wildlife Preservation Trust came into being. It was a unique conception at the time and it still is. We are *still* the only organization in the world to dedicate all its energies and resources to controlled breeding programmes, in an effort to turn this method of saving endangered species from what has hitherto been a series of happy accidents, to a more exact, widespread and respected science. During this process we have always tried to make two points abundantly clear, but in an imperfect world one is so frequently misinterpreted or misquoted, so it surely cannot hurt to reiterate these points here.

First, and perhaps the most important thing to stress is that this Trust has never claimed—nor would it be foolish enough to claim—that captive breeding of an endangered species should take the place of conservation of that species in its natural habitat. We have always maintained that controlled breeding should be used "*as well as*", not "*instead of*" conservation in the wild.

Secondly, we have never claimed to be able to help *all* species currently in danger of extinction. Out of this long and melancholy list we can only aid a few, but we feel that even this is a worthwhile undertaking.

One of our chief aims, then, is to try to establish viable breeding colonies of a selected number of threatened species, generally the smaller and more obscure ones which tend to be neglected by zoological gardens and conservation schemes generally. Then, by establishing groups of them and studying them, we hope to learn something of their basic biology. Our ignorance of even some of the simplest facts about even the commoner animals is vast and lamentable, and it is only by knowing how a species functions that you can begin to evolve an intelligent conservation programme for it in the wild. Contrary to the belief held so tenaciously by some conservationists, there is a lot more to preserving a species or a group of species than simply buying and setting aside a chunk of land.

While we are establishing our breeding colonies, we are trying to create at the same time a favourable climate towards the whole concept of controlled breeding, to prove to people the urgent need for conservation generally and also to prove to the dedicated (but perhaps conservative conservationists) the viability of this particular form of conservation, used as an additional tool in his work.

It must be remembered that this Trust is not a Zoo in the accepted sense of the word, that is to say it is a breeding centre and not merely a showplace. This being so, we have many advantages over the average zoo and fewer disadvantages.

Our advantages are that firstly *all* our energies and finance can be spent on conservation, and, unlike the average large zoo, we are not concerned with maintaining a large and flamboyant collection of species, many of which are still comparatively common in the wild. As a breeding centre, it is our job to establish large breeding groups of a select number of species which urgently need help. The average zoo cannot—or perhaps will not—devote space to exhibiting such large quantities of the *same* creature. Our approach is different, and we find that people who visit us applaud rather than become bored by the *number* of species we have on display, when they understand our work.

As we are not an ordinary zoo, we can also free ourselves of many of the current zoo shibboleths and rules. For example, we can design our cages and enclosures for the needs of the animal, with the public as a secondary consideration. This means that we do not have to indulge in the type of cage and enclosure design so common in zoos today which can only be described as anthropomorphic architecture, edifices which delight and satisfy the visiting public but which are generally hopelessly inadequate for the breeding, conservation or control of the species incarcerated in them. In a word, we are not bound by the conventions that make so many zoos impotent in the conservation field. We are, if you like, a new sort of zoo. With luck, we may be groping our way towards a goal that all zoos in the future should aspire to, and we cannot relax, content to be (as so many in the past have been and so many today still are) merely stationary three-ring circuses contributing nothing to conservation, places visited by the unthinking population in the same spirit that their ancestors visited Bedlam.

Of course, there are many things we still have to learn. For example, will animals bred for many years under controlled conditions show genetic changes? Nobody can be dogmatic about this, but it is possible that, given a reasonable number of unrelated specimens to start with, this will give you a sufficiently strong gene pool. But what the ideal number is, we do not know as yet. However, there is a certain amount of hope to be gained from the fact that the golden hamster (extinct in the wild state as far as we know) has a world population probably numbering millions, and they originate from one gravid female found in Aleppo in 1925. So far they do not seem to be suffering from any genetic changes and it would be interesting to try and see if they could be reintroduced in the wild state. The same could be said of the Père David's deer.

This brings us to another point about which we are, at the moment, ignorant. What sort of reproduction programme must we evolve to train creatures, perhaps seventh or eighth generation born under controlled conditions, so that they *can* be reintroduced into the wild? So far this has only been tried with a few species, including the Hawaiian goose and the orang-utan, with mixed success. But it is early days yet and there is a lot of experimentation to be done. Reintroduction to the wild is made more complex, of course, by the likelihood that each species will have to have a special programme created for it. The future of controlled breeding bristles with questions of this sort, but it is precisely these challenges which make the task worthwhile.

I am afraid that we must face up to the fact that a vast number of species in our lifetime are going to become extinct in the wild state, and will—with luck—exist only under controlled conditions, if we set up programmes now. This is not an unnecessarily gloomy prognostication but a simple mathematical fact. Human growth is being allowed to continue almost unchecked. But even if one applied the most rigid growth limitations now, it would still take a great number of years before they had any appreciable effect. So, while we continue to propagate in a way that must be envied by the rabbit, the rat and the humble fruit fly, our demands on the natural world become greater. This simply means that in years to come there will be precious little room left for wild life, and unless we create reservoirs of them under controlled conditions, many species will vanish. Let us strive wherever possible to save habitat, and the creatures that live in it, but as a precautionary measure let us also set up breeding centres *now*.

It is to be hoped that as this Trust grows and prospers, it can act as a training ground so that in future similar breeding centres can be set up where they ought to be set up, in the natural habitat of the creatures concerned. But animal husbandry is an art, and it is just as difficult and complicated a one to learn as any other. You cannot hope to set up similar breeding centres in other parts of the world until you have trained staff who can run them. In this respect, we hope eventually to become what could be described as a training college. In addition, we hope that by our example we can add to the "respectability" of controlled breeding, and make conservationists use it as a means of aiding a species before a population drops so low as to make this unwise or impossible. If we can do all this, then this organization will have achieved what it was set up to do.

We realize that at the moment our work is only a small part of the whole complex machinery of conservation, but we feel it is important for three reasons. Firstly, no one else is doing it on the scale that we are; secondly, it is practical; thirdly, judged as a rescue operation, it is something that can—funds permitting—be done *today*, and with luck bears valuable fruit almost immediately.

Contents

Foreword *by Gerald Durrell* vii

Introduction *by R. D. Martin* xv

Breeding and Maintaining Reptiles in Captivity *by R. E. Honegger* 1

Breeding, Raising and Restocking of Giant Tortoises (*Geochelone elephantopus*) in the Galápagos Islands *by C. G. MacFarland and W. G. Reeder* 13

Note on the Management and Reproduction of the Galápagos Tortoise at the Honolulu Zoo *by J. La Croix Throp* 39

Captive Breeding of Crocodiles *by H. R. Bustard* 43

Breeding of Endangered Wildfowl as an Aid to their Survival *by J. Kear* 49

The Saddleback: its Status and Conservation *by D. V. Merton* 61

Breeding the Congo Peacock at the Royal Zoological Society of Antwerp *by W. Van den bergh* 75

Breeding Endangered Pheasant Species in Captivity as a Means of Ensuring their Survival *by P. Wayre* 87

Captive Breeding of Whooping Cranes at the Patuxent Wildlife Research Center *by R. C. Erickson* 99

Returning the Hawaiian Goose to the Wild *by J. Kear* 115

Conservation of Eagle Owls and other Raptors through Captive Breeding and Return to the Wild *by P. Wayre* 125

Breeding Peregrine and Prairie Falcons in Captivity *by R. Fyfe* .. 133

General Principles for Breeding Small Mammals in Captivity *by R. D. Martin* 143

Breeding the Parma Wallaby in Captivity *by G. M. Maynes* 167

Status and Husbandry of Australian Monotremes and Marsupials *by R. Strahan* 171

Note on the Breeding of the Eastern Native Cat at Melbourne Zoo *by E. Weber* 183

Breeding of Malagasy Lemurs in Captivity *by J.-J. Petter* 187

Breeding Marmosets in Captivity *by J. J. C. Mallinson* 203

The Breeding of Endangered Species of Marmosets and Tamarins *by W. R. Kingston* 213

Breeding and Maintenance of Douc Langurs at Cologne Zoo *by U. Hick* 223

Breeding Orang-Utans *by M. R. Brambell*   235
The Maintenance and Breeding of Pygmy Chimpanzees *by F. Jantschke*   245
Progress in Breeding European Bison in Captivity *by J. Raczyński*   ..   253
Breeding of Przewalski Wild Horses *by J. Volf*   263
Captive Breeding of the Vicuña *by C. R. Schmidt*   271
Breeding the International Herd of Arabian Oryx at Phoenix Zoo *by
W. G. Homan*   285
The Indian Rhino in Captivity *by E. M. Lang*   293
Breeding the Indian Rhinoceros at Delhi Zoological Park *by C. L. Bhatia
and J. H. Desai*..   303
Plans for Breeding Colonies of Large Mammals in India *by C. D. Krishne
Gowda*   309
River Otters in Captivity: a Review *by N. Duplaix-Hall*   315
Breeding Tigers as an Aid to their Survival *by A. C. V. van Bemmel*   ..   329
Captive Breeding of Cheetahs *by V. J. A. Manton*   337
A New Building for Small Cats *by W. P. Crowcroft*   345
Breeding Sloth Bears in Amsterdam Zoo *by E. F. Jacobi*   351
Experimental Embryology as a Tool for Saving Endangered Species *by
R. T. Francoeur*..   357
Captive Propagation—A Progress Report *by J. Perry, D. D. Bridgwater
and D. L. Horsemen*   361
A Cautionary Note on Breeding Endangered Species in Captivity *by
M. A. G. Warland*   373
Conclusions *by Peter Scott*   379
References   387
Index   399

Introduction

R. D. Martin

By way of introduction to this special collection of papers on the captive breeding of endangered species, the conference organizers suggested that it would be useful to bring together the salient points of the various speeches made to the conference, adding to these a personal assessment of the common themes which emerged. To the best of my ability, I have attempted to do this, and I hope that the comments which follow truly reflect the general consensus of the conference. This was the first international conference specifically devoted to the techniques of breeding endangered species in captivity and it was in many other respects a new departure in the history of captive management of wild animals. It is therefore very important that the main points should be carefully examined so that we can reach an appraisal of what has been achieved to date and of what remains to be achieved in the future.

Introductory addresses to the conference were given by His Excellency Air Chief Marshal Sir John Davis, Lt.-Governor of Jersey, and by the Right Hon. The Earl of Jersey. Following this, the Right Hon. The Marquess of Willingdon (President of the Fauna Preservation Society) provided a brief summary of the work and interests of the Fauna Preservation Society, pointing out that the conference really amounted in some ways to a "marriage" between Peter Scott and Gerald Durrell, symbolically combining efforts towards conservation in the field with attempts to maintain stocks of endangered species in captivity. Gerald Durrell and Peter Scott (now Sir Peter Scott), in their respective capacities as Director of the Jersey Wildlife Preservation Trust and Chairman of the Fauna Preservation Society, then outlined their own views on the prospects of maintaining threatened species in captivity. Many of the comments below originate directly from the speeches made by Gerald Durrell and Peter Scott, and care has been taken to ensure that their views are accurately represented. However, it would be tedious to make detailed quotations throughout this Introduction, and one can only emphasize that the text relies heavily on statements made at the meeting. Nonetheless, three quotations must be attributed to their authors straight away, as they so effectively set the scene for the basic interest of the conference—that of *conservation*:

> What an appalling indictment it is, what a disgrace to mankind, that the road to his so-called civilisation should be built on the memories of extinct species and species on the way to extinction.
>
> *The Right Hon. The Earl of Jersey*

Living species today, let us remember, are the end products of twenty million centuries of evolution; absolutely nothing can be done when the species has finally gone, when the last pair has died out.

Peter Scott

Let us feel a little shame that such a conference should be necessary at all.

Gerald Durrell

The first point that must be firmly made is that captive breeding should be regarded as an integral part of general conservation programmes, and not as a *substitute* for preservation of populations in the wild state. Nobody at the conference suggested that maintenance in captivity is in any way *preferable* to maintenance under natural conditions. The key word in the title of the conference is "survival". Gerald Durrell and Peter Scott expressed complete agreement that, in the struggle to preserve our dwindling heritage of wildlife, it is justifiable to use almost any means to save an animal species from extinction, and controlled breeding in captivity may in many cases provide the only hope for the survival of a species, at least during an interim period. Breeding of endangered species in suitable captive colonies should be regarded as an *insurance policy* (Erickson) which may in some cases simply provide security, but under special conditions might represent a last-ditch guarantee for avoiding extinction. This does mean, however, that any breeding centres acting as insurance bodies should be closely coordinated with those international bodies which are at present largely concerned with conservation of natural populations in the wild state, such as the International Union for Conservation of Nature (IUCN) and the World Wildlife Fund (WWF). As Moira Warland has suggested, a body such as the Survival Service Commission (SSC) Zoo Liaison Group of IUCN could provide a focal point for such coordination.

Various people concerned with conservation of animals in their natural habitats are understandably sceptical about the aims and prospects of various organizations (mainly zoos) which might participate in captive breeding programmes. Zoos themselves are largely responsible for such scepticism, since their record for animal breeding in captivity was scarcely impressive until comparatively recent times. Obviously, it is necessary to construct safeguards to ensure that zoos (for instance) do not deplete already threatened natural populations unless they can really contribute actively to the conservation effort. It is not sufficient that zoos and similar institutions should merely pay lip-service to the need for conservation. It is quite to be expected that people actively concerned with conservation in the field should be resistant to depletion of wild populations if the animals concerned are to be merely *displayed* and not effectively employed in captive breeding programmes. Here, it is essential that zoos, along with any other potential long-term breeding centres, should organize themselves in order to ensure that rare animals are only removed from the natural habitat in cases where viable breeding programmes can definitely be established. A strong organizing body could provide field conservationist agencies with the reliable assurances that they require.

It is sadly true that, until comparatively recently, zoos in general were neither noticeably concerned about conservation of animals nor particularly interested in breeding performance in captivity. This lack of interest in animal life *for its own sake* was further evident from the inappropriate cage conditions which were supplied in many zoos. It is still true that "good zoos" (that is, those which show a clear appreciation of animals in the fullest sense) are in a minority; but it is a growing minority, and one can only join Gerald Durrell in hoping that "in the fullness of time both bad zoos and their directors will become extinct".

The minority of "good zoos", together with a number of special scientific centres concerned with the breeding of wild animals, have nevertheless contributed significantly to a striking change in attitudes, conditions and results in recent years. It is particularly encouraging to note that many of the animal species discussed at the conference were, until recently, regarded as "impossible" to breed in captivity. Every year, in various zoos, more names are added to the list of species which have been effectively bred under artificial conditions. Indeed, it is in itself remarkable that many zoos now feel a sense of failure in maintaining a species in captivity until it has bred within their enclosures. The time is fast approaching when a zoo will be judged not by the variety of its exhibits, but by the range of species which have been bred there. This change is, in no small part, due to an increasing emphasis on "appropriate" cage conditions, which has primarily meant the provision of more *space*, but has also involved more attention to the specific natural requirements of each animal species. This, in turn, is related to the emergence of the science of *ethology* (the comparative study of animal behaviour) over recent decades, and the general realization that each animal species is naturally adapted to behave in certain characteristic ways in its natural surroundings. Catering for the natural behaviour of an animal species in captivity increases the likelihood that reproduction will occur, and at the same time it provides the public of any zoo with an attractive and instructive display. It is far better to see an animal *doing* something in a natural manner rather than simply standing still, or—still worse—carrying out the repetitive movements amounting to nervous tics which often emerge in close confinement. By paying attention to the natural requirements of animal species and by drawing upon the developing science of ethology, such pioneers as Heine Hediger of Zürich Zoo have sparked off a transformation process which must inevitably bring about a radical change in our concept of the "zoo". Quite apart from their contributions to a natural understanding of animals and to captive breeding success, "good zoos" are nicer places to visit!

It should be emphasized that the concept of breeding endangered animal species in captivity adds an entirely new function to those already served by zoos, and may lead to the establishment of special centres (perhaps associated with university departments). Historically, "zoos" began as stationary circuses, in which animals were displayed entirely for their curiosity value, with no attention to their natural requirements and certainly no concern for breeding successes. Improvements in the conditions provided in zoos have been accompanied by increased recognition of the responsibilities that zoos have both to their animals and to the general public. It is in the light of this new feeling of responsibility that the question of conservation in captivity should be judged, and hopefully more and more zoos will come to express this feeling of responsibility by actively associating themselves with the conservation movement and encouraging research which will provide basic information about the animal species in their charge. There is every reason for optimism about the future role of zoos in the general arena of animal welfare, in all senses of the term, and the papers collected in this present volume clearly illustrate the value of this new acceptance of responsibility.

If it is accepted that endangered species can reasonably be maintained in captivity, and that zoos and other institutions are both willing and able to establish the necessary programmes, one can broadly define the likely advantages of this initiative. In the first place, captive stocks can provide a kind of reservoir (a "wildlife bank") which would represent the necessary insurance policy against extinction in the field and act as a pool for eventual schemes of reintroduction into the natural habitat. Secondly, the pool of captive-bred specimens—if successfully managed in order to produce surplus animals—could eventually provide a supply source for captive installations of various kinds, thus reducing the depletion of natural stocks through orders from zoos. As Perry points out in his analysis of selected species maintained in captivity, zoos are still generally net consumers of wildlife, except where they specialize on particular species. From his data, it would seem that only 8 of 162 endangered species kept in captivity can be regarded as existing in "successful" breeding pools in captivity. Although it is possible to argue about the statistical details involved, it is doubtless true that zoos still have a long way to go, and we must listen to Peter Scott's warning that there is no room at all for complacency.

Zoos and similar institutions will have to pool their resources of knowledge and animal stocks in order to achieve the aim of successful breeding of significant numbers of endangered animal species. This will require an unprecedented level of mutual goodwill and readiness to seek appropriate advice for new programmes. The conference tended to think largely in terms of zoos, but there are other special institutions set up for the specific purpose of maintaining and breeding stocks of endangered species, and all of the organizations involved in this kind of work must combine forces, perhaps through the Zoo Liaison Group of SSC. There is certainly no justification nowadays for keeping single specimens of rare animal species in zoos merely for display if there is a reasonable chance of establishing breeding facilities elsewhere, and it is imperative that a much more flexible system of exchanges, loans and donations between zoos and related bodies should be constructed as a matter of urgency. At present such cooperation is largely a matter of individual initiative. For example, as part of the programme for captive breeding of the oryx (see Wayne Homan's paper), London Zoo made their single female available to the original Phoenix nucleus of two males and one female. Similarly, prior to the conference, London Zoo had arranged for Jersey Zoo to borrow a single male Sumatran orang-utan to set up a breeding pair with the lone Jersey female, and there is now a thriving baby male to bear witness to the wisdom of this arrangement. As a direct outcome of the conference, Chicago Zoo sent a single female spectacled bear to join a lone male at Jersey as a similar exercise. Such informal loans and exchanges must at least be greatly expanded, and if possible a more formal network of offers and information should be built up.

The central theme of the conference was, of course, the *breeding* of endangered species in captivity. However one should not overlook the fact that breeding installations (especially zoos) concerned with conservation have a far more important function—that of *education*. Indeed, in addition to the straightforward necessity of breeding endangered species in captivity, it is essential that rare animals should be *seen* to be bred as part of the conservation effort. In the struggle for public support for wildlife conservation, zoos have a central educational role to play in displaying rare animals and informing the public of their plight. If a particular zoo is able to maintain and display a given threatened species under conditions which reflect the animal's natural behaviour and its natural appeal, it could be argued that the educational value with respect to the conservation movement is considerable even without a breeding programme, provided that the zoos are not themselves contributing notably to the depletion of natural stocks. There is no doubt that any installation which is able effectively to display *and* breed endangered species can be regarded as making an important contribution to the conservation movement as a whole. This educational value of properly managed zoo collections is easily overlooked, as in Moira Warland's paper; but it should be given full credit in discussions of the usefulness of captive breeding, as was emphasized both by Peter Scott and by Gerald Durrell. On the other hand, it is equally important that the zoos themselves should be aware of their educational responsibilities and should make every effort to advertise the basic need for effective conservation in the natural habitat as the major task. The public may be more sympathetic to the question of conservation than many zoos seem to believe, and there is no reason why occasional "exhibits" should not simply consist of a large photograph and a sign saying: "Our single male rhino has been loaned to another zoo in order to set up a captive breeding colony, and we hope that we will eventually have several rhinos in a breeding colony of our own. Rhinos are extremely rare, and the Zoo Liaison Group is doing everything that it can to save this animal from extinction."

It should not be overlooked that endangered animal species in captivity can also permit education of a more specialized kind—actual scientific study of the animal and its general requirements in captivity. In any conservation programme, knowledge about all aspects of the biology of a given species can prove to be of value, and there is a continuing need for detailed zoological study of wildlife both in the wild and in captivity. Such study can also increase the likelihood of long-term maintenance and breeding successes in captivity, thus closing the circle of educational benefit. It is up to the zoos to make their collections available as far as possible for appropriate studies conducted by competent zoologists; but it is also up to the zoologists themselves to express the necessary interest in the general problem of captive husbandry of endangered species, and university departments should be expected to play their part in the overall scheme. Zoos can provide unique opportunities for observational study of exotic animals—particularly for the study of behaviour—and the universities should grasp these opportunities and make sure that the zoos are given the necessary feedback information.

Whatever the justification for captive breeding programmes, however, one must carefully avoid giving the impression that captive breeding can be conducted *instead* of conservation programmes in the wild. As Strahan reminds us in his paper on Australian mammals, "faunal conservation depends on habitat conservation". There is little point in maintaining captive colonies of threatened species if there is no accompanying attempt to preserve—or to reconstitute—the natural habitat. This does, however, highlight a particular flaw of "conservation in captivity", which is to some extent present even in conservation programmes aimed exclusively at action in natural habitat areas. It is somewhat unhealthy to emphasize the conservation of *single species*, since no animal occurs in isolation in nature. In the field, one must concentrate on the preservation of entire ecosystems, whilst with breeding programmes undertaken in captivity there must be artificial concentration on individual species dealt with as separate entities. This also brings in the question of "ugly species"—species which have no particular appeal at the emotional level but are nevertheless threatened with extinction and in need of active conservation measures. To be consistent, captive breeding programmes must also include species which may not be particularly pretty on display. For example, it could happen that a particular forest habitat is threatened with destruction and that two given animal species—one "attractive" and one "ugly"—need to be conserved in captivity as a temporary measure whilst appropriate steps are taken to set up a natural reserve area. Although, for various reasons, publicity about conservation is generally concerned with individual species, the actual problem involved is that of conserving the entire biological framework within which each species naturally occurs. In certain cases, therefore, it may prove to be impossible to return members of a captive colony of an animal species to the wild because there is no possibility of re-establishing a natural habitat area since certain other plant or animal species have become extinct. Thus, whilst maintaining breeding colonies in captivity as an insurance policy against extinction in the wild, the main effort should always be directed towards conservation of the natural habitat. There is therefore some justification for Moira Warland's suggestion that zoos should help to contribute to purchasing supports for habitat conservation in addition to purchasing wild animals for captive colonies. It would definitely be a great step forward if all zoos were to follow the example of the few and associate themselves more closely with the conservation movement, perhaps acting directly as fund-raising agents for conservation programmes. However, it should be noted that so far the zoos have not applied for funds to support any captive breeding programmes under the umbrella of the conservation movement, and that if zoos and similar institutions are able to set up breeding colonies of rare animals without diverting funds from conservation in the field, they will already be involved in a considerable financial contribution to conservation as a whole.

As a final point on the discussion of the need for captive breeding programmes, Strahan has pointed out that some animal species may *naturally* decline and become extinct, and that in some cases it may be possible to maintain in captivity animals which would otherwise have died out regardless of normal wildlife conservation schemes. There is, for example, some room for suspicion that some of the extinct large lemurs of Madagascar may have been victims of naturally-occurring climatic changes, though human activity may have contributed to their extinction. Although this is only a minor point in the broad spectrum of reasons for establishing captive breeding colonies of endangered species, it does underline the fact that such colonies may be significant in their own right, as well as in relation to actual conservation in the wild.

It has, of course, been suggested by some people that "natural extinction" could account for the disappearance of wildlife under all conditions, and this has even been used here and there as an argument against planned conservation. However, Peter Scott estimates that man has probably increased the rate of extinction of species by a factor of at least four over the last 200 years. This does admit the existence of a certain rate of natural extinction, thus adding weight to Strahan's comments, but it also places the blame for *most* recent extinctions squarely on human shoulders. Most of the 815 mammals and birds listed in the SSC "Red Book" are directly threatened in a variety of ways by man, and man alone can solve the problem of the increased rate of animal extinction.

Interestingly enough, the conference organizers and participants did not feel that it was necessary to discuss the reasons for conservation as such, and this is in itself an encouraging sign of the present rapid trend towards enlightened attitudes. The main questions raised were how the zoos could contribute to conservation, in association with similar bodies, and how far captive breeding could be regarded as a realistic support for conservation programmes. It is nevertheless instructive to examine the four basic reasons that Peter Scott listed for caring about the extinction of species in the first place:

1. Ethical, or moral, considerations.
2. Aesthetic appreciation.
3. Recognition of the fact that species represent the raw material of biological science.
4. Realization that, in many cases, there may be compelling economic reasons for establishing wildlife reserves.

Taking each of these reasons in turn, parallels can be found for the situation in captivity, provided that the major aim remains that of conservation of the species in the wild. Peter Scott cited a personal letter from Professor Dennis Gabor in which he said "I have never seen an elephant in the wild nor a blue whale, but it makes me feel better to know that they both exist." Many people may find it difficult to feel this sense of appreciation at a distance, and there can be no doubt that public display of endangered species usefully integrated into breeding programmes would enable far more people to appreciate the aesthetic and ethical values of conservation of wildlife in the natural habitat. But zoos must make it clear that they are no longer depleting wildlife stocks themselves, and that their major concern is to display the animals (as far as possible) in such a way that the importance of the natural habitat can be appreciated by the non-biologist.

Hence, a strong case can be made for breeding endangered species in captivity, and it is now necessary to turn to the practical problems involved. New programmes must be set up, and those rare animals which are already in captivity should be incorporated as soon as possible into organised breeding programmes. Even if certain species are not yet extremely threatened in the wild, establishment of joint breeding programmes would provide a valuable pool of experience and would in any case reduce the demand for further specimens from the wild. For example, Christian Schmidt shows in his paper on vicuña that, in this particular case, the species concerned is more effectively controlled in the wild than in captivity and that—given strict controls on exportation—the real problem is to prevent extinction of the vicuña in captivity! It is therefore advisable to breed as many species as possible in captivity, though obviously some central body (perhaps along the lines of the SSC Zoo Liaison Group) should establish the priorities for urgent action. Zoos have every reason to join forces and cooperate in the breeding of *any* animals in captivity, as all breeding successes can contribute directly or indirectly to this new role of acting as reservoirs—rather than consumers—of wildlife. The practical question of breeding those animals already in captivity is accordingly largely a question of organization and interchange among the zoos themselves. In this, the *International Zoo Yearbook* and similar publications can play a valuable coordinating role, especially in encouraging emphasis on rare species and on conservation in general, on the behaviour of animals in captivity, and on the pooling of information about animal maintenance and breeding. Centralized publications of this kind, which should be supported by all zoos and similar institutions, can encourage surveys of various types and act as a standard reference source for basic information. However, such centralization of information depends upon cooperation between the various zoos, and one can only hope that there will be increased progress in this direction. It is a sad reflection on the earlier attitudes of some zoos that the main sources of inaccuracy of surveys such as that conducted by John Perry lie in the inadequacies of reports returned by the zoos themselves, and those conducting surveys can only do their best within a limited range. Happily, information provided by zoos is becoming more regular and more reliable, and a sound basis for accurate surveys of zoo collections and their achievements is thus becoming available. Opinions about *studbooks* for individual species in captivity vary somewhat, but it is generally agreed that detailed records of breeding colonies should be maintained and, if possible, centralized in order to permit careful control of the genetic background to captive breeding. For reasons discussed below, it is essential that a careful check should be kept on the actual patterns of mating within each captive stock.

Perhaps the most difficult questions arose with respect to the task of actually reintroducing captive stocks into the natural habitat. Very few attempts have, in fact, been made to restock natural habitats with captive-bred specimens, and this is an area where much fundamental research is needed. It is, for example, necessary to collect detailed information about the long-term effects of maintaining breedings stocks in captive colonies, and a great deal of attention must be directed to the possible dangers of *inbreeding* and *unintentional selection* in small-scale captive colonies. One can, of course, proceed on the assumption that a maximum of genetic diversity should be maintained in any captive stock, but even then it is vital to exert careful control over the breeding management of any colony. Further, although it may be desirable to eliminate any obviously sickly individuals which may perhaps have undesirable genetic traits, there should be no explicit or implicit attempt to breed to a "perfect" type. Here, as with the natural situation, it is vital to think in terms of the population rather than the individual, and more effort should be directed to the prevention of inbreeding and artificial selection than to the elimination of genetic traits. In fact, as noted by Strahan, inbreeding may even represent a danger for small, natural animal communities, clinging on in the wild state, and any information which can be collected on the consequences of inbreeding would therefore be doubly valuable. For instance, Ernst Lang reports that of 20 known Indian rhino births, 11 have taken place in Basle Zoo. This intensive reliance upon a particularly successful zoo could easily lead to problems of inbreeding in a short space of time, and a careful analysis of progress of Indian rhino breeding could provide information and guidelines which will be of general relevance to maintenance of small captive colonies of rare species where space is an obvious limiting factor. Certainly, other zoos must rally round in situations, such as that existing with the Indian rhino, where a single zoo (however successful it may be) might eventually run into genetic problems.

The primary focus for research, however, concerns the actual process of restocking the natural habitat. There have been very few practical examples of reintroduction to the wild in cases where the animals concerned have actually been bred from adults maintained in captivity, and for the time being our experience seems to be largely restricted to birds (such as the Hawaiian goose, Swinhoe's pheasant and eagle owls). Yet these few examples do show that reintroduction is possible in practice, and Philip Wayre's account of the apparently successful release programme for eagle owls clearly shows how important it is to cater for the natural behaviour of each species when reintroduction is actually carried out. Restocking of the wild requires careful planning, expert supervision and long-term follow-up studies to ensure that the measures taken have been successful. We need many more projects involving a variety of species and many more years of follow-up study of reintroduced populations in order to assess realistically the prospects for captive breeding and subsequent release. This is certainly not an argument against such programmes, it is plainly an argument for carrying out more of them as soon as possible, whilst closely monitoring the effects. In any case, the act of reintroduction may itself contribute to the general aims of the conservation movement. Philip Wayre points out that reintroduction of Swinhoe's pheasant to Taiwan may have been a major contributory factor in encouraging legislation providing protection for more than 30 other birds and mammals.

There is, not surprisingly, a tendency to regard captive breeding and conservation in the field as two quite distinct operations; but various papers in this volume show that there are many gradations between these two extremes. One can, for example, transfer animals from one area to another (with closely similar habitat conditions which are less menaced by destruction) in order to increase the chances of survival. This was, for example, the case with the nine aye-ayes transferred to the island of Nossi Mangabe under the direction of Dr. Jean-Jacques Petter with the assistance of WWF. In other instances, animals may be maintained at an intermediate holding station in transit, and if the period in captivity becomes extensive under suitable conditions the threshold to captive breeding of endangered species may be crossed almost unwittingly. With birds (such as the whooping crane) or reptiles (such as Galápagos tortoises), it is possible to remove fertilized eggs from the wild, hatch them (hopefully with reduced overall mortality) and then release the offspring when they are able to fend for themselves relatively well. On another tack, full breeding and rearing in captivity may be used as a means of *supplementing* dwindling stocks in the natural habitat, thus to some extent side-stepping the genetic problems posed with small captive colonies. Indeed, there are many ways in which temporary or long-term maintenance and/or breeding in captivity can assist in conservation and every step in this direction deserves encouragement. The crucial point is that the zoos could gradually be transformed into sophisticated holding stations —with the added benefit of displaying the animals in their care—as opposed to their present role of terminal stations in the overall process of wildlife consumption.

A number of people at the conference, myself included, suggested that there is a pressing need for planned pilot projects—not necessarily using *endangered* species—designed to examine the various problems involved in captive breeding and subsequent release of captive-bred stocks in the wild. Such pilot projects, if appropriately studied, could provide detailed information about various fundamental aspects of small-group breeding and return to the wild, and this could provide a basis for general guidelines for zoos and similar institutions. To some extent, this idea of the "pilot project" has already been put into practice by Ray Erickson in his use of a relatively common species (sandhill cranes) as a "dummy run" for subsequent captive breeding and reintroduction of the rare whooping crane. It is noteworthy that the concept of captive breeding, in this instance too, initially met with resistance from various quarters, since it was probably felt that conservation in the field can be the only answer. But it is apparent that successful conclusion of the pilot project with sandhill cranes will do much to reduce this resistance, whilst at the same time providing a firm factual basis for the main scheme involving whooping cranes. However, it is essential that the genetic and other effects of captive breeding should be subjected to careful scrutiny in this and other projects. It is not in fact necessary, for some of the aspects involved, to conduct such scrutiny on actual captive breeding programmes; it would be more than useful to obtain appropriate information in cases where small numbers of wild-bred animals have been kept or reared in captivity and released in isolated areas of natural habitat, as with Galápagos tortoises (MacFarland and Reeder) and New Zealand island saddleback finches (Merton). When intensive studies have been conducted, at least with a small number of species, it will be possible to decide upon suitable standards for captive breeding programmes. Wayne Homan states that "75 oryx located in four separate centres should sufficiently establish this species in captivity". It is to be hoped that this is the case, but for the time being we have no real scientific basis to guide us in making such judgements, and this basis must be provided as a matter of urgency.

In conclusion, it can be said that captive breeding of endangered species *can* play an important accessory role in worldwide conservation programmes, but that much research and organization is required before this role can be effectively realised. There is certainly no room for complacency, and much hard work lies ahead, but the conference was undeniably extremely successful in that it established the common ground for accomplishing this task. The conference was also a landmark in that it has identified itself with a significant change in the attitudes and public image of the zoo world. Henceforth, a new level of concern for wildlife and active participation in conservation will be expected of zoos in general, and it is to be hoped that those zoos which are still straggling in the necessary transition from their earlier condition as "stationary circuses" will be prompted to change pace and catch up with the small band of pioneers. The display of wild animals in captivity can no longer be regarded as justifiable purely because of its curiosity value; zoos now have an obligation to educate by example, to show to the general public that concern for animal welfare is at the forefront and that this concern extends to conservation in the natural habitat as the primary problem. Far from acting as mere consumers of wildlife, zoos and other similar institutions must now act as a window to the world of wildlife under natural conditions—a world which is at present shrinking daily.

Breeding and Maintaining Reptiles in Captivity

R. E. Honegger*

INTRODUCTION

Reptiles are assumed to be standard animals for every major zoological garden, but in contrast to other zoo animals such as birds and mammals which have been bred successfully over several generations, the reproduction of reptiles over consecutive generations in captivity is still a novelty (see Table 1; Figs. 1 and 2). If the reasons for this are analysed, one discovers that the requirements for their care, breeding and rearing are still largely ignored:

1. Specimens have often been kept singly in collections, with no possible mates.
2. The patterns of sexual dimorphism of the species are not always known, resulting in difficulties in obtaining the proper mate.
3. The animals are unwittingly kept under conditions unsuitable for breeding, as the basic biological requirements are not always recognized.
4. Procuring the proper food for hatchlings is often extremely difficult, so that the total costs of incubation and raising the offspring are rather high.

The establishment of a breeding group may be a rather time-consuming and expensive process. With certain species only the young are imported, usually to save money on shipping costs, and often only one specimen is available.

SEXING TECHNIQUES

With most species of turtles it is not difficult to determine the sex; the form of the plastron, the length of the tail, and the shape of the claws on the front legs are the most useful criteria. It is important, however, to become acquainted with the relevant literature on a particular species, e.g. Legler (1960) on *Terrapene* and Moll and Legler (1971) and Carr (1952) on *Chrysemys* and *Pseudemys*. For various species of lizards there is distinct dimorphism of back and tail crest. The sex of various species of snakes may be determined by comparing counts of

* Curator of the Aquarium/Terrarium, Zürich Zoo, Switzerland. Support from the R. and R. Schlageter Fund, Zürich, is gratefully acknowledged.

belly scales or of tail length and width (Goin and Goin, 1962). The method of probing for the penis in the cloaca, as suggested by Schaefer (1934) and Zehr (1962), and elaborated on by Szidat (1968), is useful for determining the sex of live squamates.

TABLE 1. List of reptiles bred by zoos between 1960 and 1969, taking species listed in the *Red Data Book*, Vol. 3.* (Source: *International Zoo Yearbook*, Vols. 2-11, 1961-1971).

Pseudemys ornata callirostris South American red lined turtle	Washington, D.C., 1963, 1964
Gopherus polyphemus agassizzii Desert tortoise	San Diego, Tucson, 1963
Malacochersus tornieri Pancake tortoise	San Diego, 1962-1969 (Shaw, 1970)
Testudo radiata Radiated tortoise	Cairo, 1960; Zürich, 1962; Sydney, 1967
Pseudemydura umbrina Short-necked turtle	Perth, 1966, 1968, 1969
Sphenodon punctatus Tuatara	Auckland, 1965
Cyclura cornuta Rhinoceros iguana	San Diego, 1965, 1967, 1968; Miami Seaquarium, 1967, 1968; Miami Serpentarium, 1967
Cyclura macleayi caymanensis Cayman Island iguana	Kingston, Jan. 1966
Cyclura ricordii Ricord's grand iguana	Miami Serpentarium, 1960
Lacerta lilfordi Ayre Island lizard	Tel Aviv Univ., 1966
Heloderma horridum alvarezi Chiapan beaded lizard	Chiapas, 1964; Tuxtla, 1969
Heloderma suspectum Gila monster	San Diego, 1963
Varanus komodoensis Komodo Island monitor	Jogjakarta, 1968
Epicrates angulifer Cuban boa	Sofia, Bul., 1965; Havanna, 1967; Prague, 1969
Python molurus Indian python	Jaipur, Ind., 1961; Karachi, 1962, 1964 (?), 1965, 1966 (?); Tokyo, 1968; Fort Worth, 1969; Malton, GB, 1969; Silver Springs, Fla, 1969; Tokyo, 1969
Sanzinia madagascariensis Madagascar boa	London, 1961; Fort Worth, 1969; Washington, 1969

* For crocodiles see Honegger (1971).

FIGURE 1. Although various chameleon species are frequently kept by zoos, breeding successes are rather limited, and simply restricted to reproduction of imported gravid females. *Chamaeleo tigris* of the Seychelle Islands is one of the smallest of the genus. (Photo: Honegger.)

FIGURE 2. Keeping radiated tortoises, *Testudo radiata*, is almost a must for any reptile collection concerned about the "biggest and largest". However, captive breeding records of this unique species show that so far no serious efforts have been made to establish breeding programmes. (Photo: Honegger.)

With giant snakes, one can rely on the data provided by Lederer for *Eunectes notaeus* (1942), for *Python reticulatus* (1944) and for *Python molurus* (1956). In some reptile species the males shed their hemipenis and epidermis at about the same time. To date we have been able to find the tissue-like skin floating in the water basins of both *Dracaena* and *Eunectes* in our collection.

Sex determination in living crocodiles was rather difficult until a few years ago, when most methods still employed measurements such as head-length versus tail-length, that proved to be of little value, especially when no comparative data were available. Chabreck (1967) and Brazaitis (1969) have since described a practical method for determining sex in living crocodiles of various species. This simple method relies on manual probing for the penis in the cloaca of the male, and it is reliable for determination of sex in specimens over 75 cm in length.

Once the sex of a specimen has been determined, the individual can be marked by the scute-clipping method (Blanchard and Finster, 1933), the scale-clipping system, or the tattooing method (Woodbury, 1951). If only a few specimens are to be recognized, sketching the individual characteristics on the registration card will suffice.

It is obvious that more than one male and one female of any reptile species are necessary for a successful breeding programme. In general, the minimum requirement is for two males and three females. Species known to be highly territorial (e.g. geckos (Kastle, 1964) or chameleons) should be given special attention. The arrangement of the cage must be planned accordingly.

ENVIRONMENTAL FACTORS

Success in breeding reptiles depends on following guidelines similar to those outlined by Hediger (1965) for mammals. In short, this means that a wide range of conditions in a terrarium must be optimum if the species is to breed. It is not enough for animals to be fed regularly and to be kept in temperature-regulated and clean cages. If the animals are to breed, their specific requirements for temperature, light and relative humidity must be satisfied. Basic information on these factors can be found in the relevant literature.

SPACE

If we intend to maintain large species, such as rhinoceros-iguanas or other members of the genus *Cyclura*, or monitors (*Varanus*), it is extremely important that we offer them a terrarium with plenty of space and biological furniture, so that every member of the group is able to retreat during encounters between species. I fully agree with King (see Honegger, 1970a), who commented on the breeding potential of *Cyclura*: "Unknown, but probably not good, due to lack of sufficient space in most zoo exhibits." In setting up a breeding group of monitors, we also have to consider that they exhibit extremely space-consuming behaviour during pre-mating and mating activities (Hediger, 1962; Honegger and Heusser, 1969).

TEMPERATURE

Despite the fact that most reptile species kept in zoological gardens come from the tropics and subtropics, many of them—especially crocodiles, turtles and tortoises—are kept in outside terraria, at least during the summer, sometimes without additional heating. Extreme temperature variations favour eye and respiratory infections, and the specimens do not feed regularly or sufficiently. Taking this into consideration, it might be for this reason that the many radiated tortoises (*Testudo radiata*) kept in zoos all over the world rarely reproduce. As far as I know, *Testudo radiata* has only been bred at the Cairo Zoo and Sydney Zoo (Peters, 1969), at Zürich Zoo (Honegger and Schmidt, 1964) and by two amateurs in Switzerland (Schweizer, 1965). Nevertheless, some 20 radiated tortoises were imported into the U.S. by one person in the name of conservation in 1967 (Baudy, 1970).

Great care must be taken to heat the cages properly. Ideally, reptiles should be kept under thermal conditions allowing them to attain a preferred body temperature for at least a period of some hours during the day, so that their physiological processes are at an optimum. Since the thermal preference of reptiles is often near the upper lethal limit, specimens should be provided with burrows, dens, or climbing facilities for avoiding excess heat. Environmental temperatures should be similar to those in the wild, including daily and seasonal variation as with daylength and light intensity. Open-air enclosures during warm weather and temperature-controlled rooms during unfavourable weather have proved best for keeping and breeding Mediterranean tortoises (*Testudo graeca libera*, *Testudo hermanni hermanni*, *Testudo hermanni robertmertensi* and *Testudo marginata*—see Rohr, 1970). It is obvious that all terraria should have adequate ventilation, but no draughts.

LIGHT

Some snakes and the majority of geckos are nocturnal animals, whereas most tortoises and lizards, along with the other snakes, are diurnal. One should check on field studies in the available literature when arranging the lights in a terrarium for a particular species. Special care should be taken in setting up "mixed exhibits" so that noctural and diurnal species can live side by side without conflict. Nocturnal species can be displayed either in "red light cages" or simply in regular terraria with alcoves for hiding where they can still be observed by visitors.

Any modern terrarium should also be supplied with fluorescent bulbs, providing a maximum of light. Kauffeld (1969) comments on the use of UV-light, and he notes that "some lizards, notably the Iguanids and Agamids" require UV-rays, especially for the proper growth of the young. The importance of UV-rays for Iguanids and desert species has also been stressed by Pawley (1969). The same author states that more sensitive snakes, such as *Drymarchon*, *Spilotes* and *Dendroaspis*, definitely do not do so well when exposed to UV-rays, but he reports positively on the recovery of a lethargic mata-mata (*Chelys fimbrimata*) after it was exposed to a General Electric Sun Lamp (275 W) for 8 hours a day. The positive influence of "Vita-lite" (Vita-Lite (R) by Duro-Test Electric Ltd.) on lower vertebrates, especially the stimulating effect on their feeding, has been reported by Laszlo (1969). The quality of light is also of great importance to the plants in and near a terrarium. Generally speaking, one can judge from the plant life whether or not a vivarium is getting enough light.

RELATIVE HUMIDITY

Although reptiles are protected from dehydration by their cornified skin, one has to arrange for the proper relative humidity, especially for those species coming from tropical rain forests and neighbouring zones. We have learned that even typical desert dwellers such as both species of *Heloderma* prefer to retreat to slightly wet dens.

From observations of crocodiles both in captivity and in the wild we know that rain, regulated according to season and temperature, can also stimulate the animals' activity (Honegger, 1971). Here again, living plants chosen according to the species' habitat can indicate whether or not the relative humidity is correct.

FOOD

If we compare the food offered to reptiles kept in terraria with the food those species find in the wild, we may notice great discrepancies. In studying the food habits of the red-eared turtle *Pseudemys scripta*, for example, we learn that young in the wild are carnivorous and gradually become herbivorous. The carnivorous part of their diet consists of large numbers of various molluscs and insects (Moll and Legler, 1971), whereas the standard diet of captive emyid turtles is usually a mixture of minced beef, fish and vegetables.

If, for reasons of economy, snakes are fed only a diet of laboratory mice, rats and guinea-pigs, it is advisable to feed these prey animals carrots, wheat sprouts, or even grass before offering them to snakes. In our experience, animals prepared in this way are preferred to typically fed laboratory specimens. We prefer to offer freshly killed food animals to acclimatized snakes and monitors, thus avoiding possible injuries from the food animals and death from strangulation by other snakes (see Muller, 1970). In addition, freshly killed mice, rats and other rodents can be injected with multivitamin preparations, especially during the breeding period. For example, we enrich the food of *Boa constrictor* during the second half of the year, which is the period when it normally breeds (Honegger, 1970*b*).

The food for omnivorous lizards and turtles should be varied according to the season, and from time to time it should be enriched with vitamins and calcium phosphate. If possible, freshly collected insects, butterflies and moths should be offered during the appropriate season. Of course, such insects must not come from meadows treated with insecticides and the like.

Obviously, following these detailed guidelines for a well-balanced diet is of little value if conditions of light and heat are neglected.

BREEDING

There is a good chance that reptiles kept in biologically appropriate groups under optimal conditions will reproduce. With most diurnal species, copulation naturally takes place during the daylight hours, and when it occurs we prefer to close the relevant part of the reptile collection to the public to avoid any possible disturbance. This problem does not exist for nocturnal species, which usually mate at night. A keeper on the lookout will notice that copulation has taken place from changes in the cage.

FIGURE 3. As soon as all eggs are laid, the female *Python reticulatus* coils around them and broods them for about 100 days. During this time, the female only leaves the eggs in order to drink and to shed the skin. (Photo: Honegger.)

If daily inspection of the animals indicates that a female lizard or snake has increased in size or has stopped feeding, we recommend separating females of viviparous species into spare terraria, similar to those suggested by Pawley (1971). This eliminates losses from squeezing and feeding, as *Boa constrictor*, for example, may squeeze the young to death and lizards may feed on young. With oviparous species such as *Elaphae oxycephala*, the females are left in their regular cage to lay their eggs, and the eggs are then gathered immediately. With *Python reticulatus*, where the eggs are brooded, only those eggs lying outside the coils are gathered (Fig. 3). Each cage or terrarium should, of course, contain the proper nesting facilities (substratum) so that the eggs are not eaten or crushed by other inmates. Eggs laid in water should be gathered and kept separate from other eggs in the incubator. According to Legler (1960), *Terrapene ornata* eggs which had lain in water for 48 hours still hatched.

It is now known that optimal numbers of eggs and normal egg-laying behaviour in various tortoises can be achieved only at optimal cage or terrarium temperatures. At lower temperatures, the eggs remain in the oviduct where several layers of calcium may be added and, if so, an inflamed oviduct and serious difficulties in laying the eggs may result (Rohr, 1970).

All eggs should be marked on the top of the shell to indicate how they were lying in the nest. Individual clutches must be kept separate from the time of gathering to hatching to allow regular control of individual eggs. The length of the gestation period varies considerably with the different species of snakes (Joshi, 1967; Petzold, 1969a), and this is, of course, a factor, along with temperature and relative humidity, influencing the incubation time.

If, after some time, no mating or reproductive activity takes place, some changes should be made in order to identify the necessary conditions.

From our own experiences and those gained at Woodland Park Zoological Gardens, Seattle (Wash.), it is sometimes necessary to separate pythons that are regularly housed together. Keeping the separated animal on a different type of substratum (e.g. straw, leaves, etc.) may also induce breeding upon introduction to the group. Introducing new specimens can similarly induce breeding in some cases.

ARTIFICIAL INCUBATION

Various means of incubating reptile eggs have been described and all have proved to be about equally successful (Legler, 1956; Zweifel, 1961; Shaw, 1963; Kirsche, 1967; Zingg, 1968; Bustard, 1969; Petzold, 1969b). The Zürich Zoo uses a modification of the system first described by Zweifel (1961). The eggs are placed in plastic bags filled with a mixture of damp peat gravel or a mixture of two-thirds peat gravel and one-third sand. The bags are then slightly inflated and closed off with a rubber band, except for a small tube for air circulation. The individual bags are put in an incubator used for human babies (Fig. 4); the temperature is adjusted to between 26° and 30°C and the relative humidity is set at 75 to 79 per cent (Honegger, 1971). Regular control of the eggs is important. Eggs whose surfaces become wet and dirty, or on which a growth of fungus is visible, are best separated from the other eggs, thus avoiding spoiling of entire clutches.

Most reptilian eggs change size and weight during the period of incubation (Legler, 1960; Petzold, 1969a; Ernst, 1971). Eggs of *Terrapene ornata* (Legler, 1960) expand during the course of incubation, as do other reptilian eggs with flexible shells, e.g. *Chrysemys picta* (Ernst, 1971). We have noticed that *Python reticulatus* eggs change in shape and colour as well as in size and weight, a fact previously described by Lederer (1956) for *Python molurus*. A colour change was also noted with eggs of *Testudo carbonaria*, *Testudo hermanni* and *Varanus salvador*.

Special care should be taken to control the temperature and humidity in the incubator. Yntema's (1960) experiments with *Chelydra serpentina* show that even

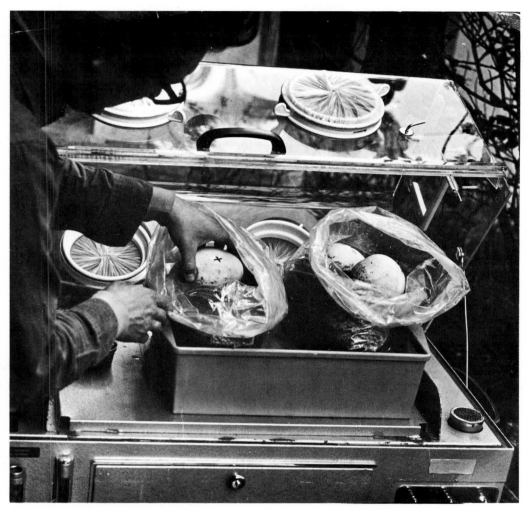

FIGURE 4. The Zürich Zoo uses an incubator designed for human babies to incubate reptile eggs. The eggs are placed in plastic bags filled with damp peat gravel, and are regularly examined. (Photo: Jurg Klages.)

a short decrease in temperature to 15°C resulted in malformations of the head, tail and extremities. Bustard (1969, 1971) demonstrated that 32°C is the optimal incubation temperature for *Crocodylus novaeguineae*. Eggs which were incubated at 23° or 26°C failed to hatch. At 38°C the hatchlings failed to emerge on their own, and, when removed by hand, showed deformed tails. Desiccated eggs of *Chrysemys picta* and *Chelydra serpentina* resulted in young with abnormalities;

eggs desiccated in the later half of the incubation period produced a higher percentage of abnormal young than eggs that were desiccated earlier (Lynn and Ullrich, 1950).

Progscha and Lehmann's report (1970) on *Sanzinia madagascariensis*, which gave birth to some deformed young, indicates that abnormalities of ovoviviparous species can result if the parent undergoes cold stress, for example, during shipping.

After hatching, the young reptiles are kept for a few days under thermal conditions similar to those in the incubator, i.e. until they have absorbed the umbilical sac. No attempt should be made to cut the cord. Later on, they are removed to small terraria with plenty of shelter and thus with a maximum of security. Food is offered at various intervals depending on the species. In feeding newborn snakes, it is best to wait for the first shedding of the skin. Nursery terraria must be cleaned regularly, as some species tend to be coprophagous. It is also vital for young reptiles to be given a bath from time to time to prevent dehydration.

One of the difficulties in breeding and raising reptiles is to procure food of the right size. Full-grown agamid lizards, for example, do well on a diet of vegetables, fruits, mice or chicken, and meat or fish, but hatchlings of some agamids need small insects, sometimes smaller than *Drosophila*. The appetite of reptiles varies greatly with their age (for Crocodiles see Corbet, 1959; Cott, 1961; Pooley, 1962; Pough, 1971).

Although several reptile hybrids are known (Mertens, 1950, 1956, 1964, 1968; Stemmler, 1971), it is not advisable to interbreed species, particularly in cases of endangered species, where a pure species pool is desired. If a mate for a specific subspecies is needed, the zoo should work out an exchange with a related zoo. In 1971, for example, the AAZPA initiated a project for crocodile exchange among its USA members, following some suggestions outlined at the Crocodile Conservation Meeting in New York in March 1971 (Honegger, 1971; Pooley, 1972). If it is impossible to obtain the proper subspecies as a mate, mating of related forms could be conducted for the sake of education.

In an earlier paper (Honegger, 1970a), I discussed the difficulties involved in breeding reptiles in captivity over several generations. It is most important that the keeper does not lose interest in an "easy to breed species", thus failing to give the special attention needed. For instance, over several generations, it has proved difficult to propagate *Gekko gecko*, a species which is still found in the wild and relatively easy to breed, and is thus common in terraria. Recently we have learned that it is possible to breed crocodiles under artificial conditions in natural surroundings, e.g. in the species' geographical range (Yangprapakorn *et al.*, 1971; Chabreck, 1971; Joanen and McNease, 1971; Pooley, 1971).

PREVENTIVE MEDICINE AND MEDICAL CARE

Many reptiles are infected with harmful parasites and bacteria both in the wild and in zoos (Kourany *et al.*, 1970). It is therefore of great importance to quarantine all specimens upon arrival.

Although it would be fanciful to believe that a quarantine period would eliminate all pathogenic germs causing death, the following reasons are convincing enough for establishing quarantine facilities:

1. New arrivals can adapt themselves to captive surroundings, without being infected by other cage-mates.

2. Ectoparasites can be eliminated.

3. Nematodes and cestodes can be controlled.

4. Specimens in which the faeces are found to contain dangerous forms of *Salmonella* (such as *S. typhi*, *S. typhimurium* and *S. enteritidis*) can be eliminated at once.

5. Although it is possible to control other species of *Salmonella* and *Amoebiasis*, it is impossible to cure specimens clinically of these infections.

Optimal quarantine facilities should be arranged as follows:

1. Spatial separation from the main reptile collection, preferably in a different building.

2. The keeper in charge should not be assigned to the main reptile collection.

3. All cages should be isolated individually.

4. All cages should be accessible to disinfection or, even better, sterilization.

5. Repeat checking of faeces is mandatory.

6. Treatment should be carried out only after a certain time has elapsed, to allow acclimatization of specimens.

Basic information on reptile disease and medical care of reptiles is to be found in Reichenbach-Klinke (1963), Ippen (1965, 1967, 1968, 1971) and Wallach (1969) to name only a few sources.

To eliminate possible infections and re-infections, all food (including mammals, birds, etc.) must be destroyed after it has been in the cage, even if it has been refused. In re-using left-overs one can transmit disease from one cage to another.

CONCLUSIONS

Most reptile species are presently kept under biologically inappropriate conditions in zoological collections and therefore rarely reproduce. This means that all institutions at present have to obtain their specimens from wild stocks.

Zoos and other institutions interested in the conservation of reptiles should therefore get together at once to work out an agreement to exchange specimens so that breeding groups can be established. If such an agreement cannot be reached, a statement should be worked out whereby the signing institutions agree: (1) To keep only those species for which they have adequate facilities, and (2) To provide optimal conditions for those species. Breeding farms should be established in the natural areas of distribution in order to produce specimens for zoos and possibly for rehabilitation, with the goal of establishing a stock sufficient to serve all institutions. The breeding of reptiles in captivity can provide important data needed for a better understanding of the species in the wild, and it can contribute to our relatively poor knowledge of reptilian biology. Nevertheless, it must be recognized that the conservation of endangered reptiles cannot be achieved simply by breeding them in captivity.

Breeding, Raising and Restocking of Giant Tortoises (*Geochelone elephantopus*) in the Galápagos Islands*

C. G. MacFarland and W. G. Reeder

INTRODUCTION

During the first six decades of this century, reports from scientific expeditions resulted in widespread acceptance of the idea that at least several, or perhaps most, races of the Galápagos Tortoise (*Geochelone elephantopus*) were extinct, and that virtually all surviving populations were imminently in danger of the same fate. It was also concluded that survival of the remaining races depended upon the establishment of breeding colonies outside of the Galápagos. Several expeditions in the 1920s and 1930s justified the collection of large numbers of tortoises for this purpose. Unfortunately, these notions are still widespread, especially among private collectors and even many zoo personnel, despite the total failure of most of these captive colonies to breed.

Field research conducted over the past ten years by the Charles Darwin Research Station and the Galápagos National Park Service, and the authors' investigations from August 1969 to November 1971, have significantly altered this bleak view of the status and survival potential of the tortoise populations. This paper briefly summarizes these findings and more extensively reports on the restocking programme now in operation in the Galápagos Islands. Except where noted, the data cover the period from 1965 to November 1971.

The value of attempting to preserve individual subspecies or races, rather than just the species, is frequently questioned. As is well known, the decision as to what constitutes a "species" or any of its sub-categories is very problemetical (Mayr, 1963; chapters 2–4), especially when dealing with insular populations, where the test of natural reproductive isolation or compatibility cannot be made. As a minimum, the following types of information about a set of subspecies or races are required in order to determine whether they represent apparently incipient species or are but local variants within a larger interbreeding population comprising a single gene pool: (1) the extent of their geographical

* Contribution No. 154 of the Charles Darwin Foundation for the Galápagos Isles.

isolation; (2) the extent of natural gene flow among them; (3) the existence of isolating mechanisms that prevent or reduce the full success of intersubspecific or inter-racial crosses (Mayr, 1963; chapter 5). In any given case, some or most of this information is usually lacking. Even with extensive data, however, it is virtually never possible to predict the future evolutionary course of a set of subspecies or races. In our opinion, the safest method is to preserve the subspecies or races intact and not to interbreed them in captivity.

Geochelone elephantopus is a case in point. The various taxa (taxonomic categories) differ in shape, colour and thickness of carapace, maximum size attained, and lengths of neck and legs. However, variation within any taxon (taxonomic category) is great and the differences among taxa are only statistical, at best. Assigning an individual specimen to a definite taxon is extremely difficult, though the range of possibilities often can be reduced to three or four taxa.

In the only major taxonomic treatment of the group, Van Denburgh (1914) assigned binomials to 13 of the taxa, leaving two unnamed because of insufficient material.* However, he consistently used the term "races" in discussing the 15 taxa, clearly recognizing the large amount of intergradation of morphological characteristics. The more recent interpretations regard all the taxa as subspecies of the single species *Geochelone elephantopus* Harlan 1827 (Hendrickson, 1966).

Whether the taxa are considered races, subspecies, or even species is a moot point. All are geographically isolated populations on separate islands or volcanoes, except for *G.e. vicina* and *G.e. güntheri*, which occur together on southern Isabela.† There is no evidence of ethological isolating mechanisms for any of the taxa; whether interbreeding would result in reduced fertility remains to be tested. However, because of the geographic barriers, the probability of natural interbreeding is minute. Since the taxa have evolved differences and certainly have been physically separated for a long time period (biologically speaking), they should be preserved individually. The extinction of any one taxon would be an irreversible loss of a unique form of life.

We accordingly use the term "race" for each taxon, primarily because no marked differences in structure exist among them.

STATUS OF TORTOISE RACES

A detailed report has been published elsewhere (MacFarland, *et al.*, 1974*a*, 1974*b*). Since much new information has made the most recent reports (Snow,

---

* The subspecific name *vandenburghi* is commonly used and accepted for the tortoises of Volcan Alcedo, Isabela; we continue with this usage. However, we note that, on the basis of the described location, De Sola (1930) almost certainly mistakenly applied the name to specimens of *G.e. güntheri* from Sierra Negra, Isabela.

† Perhaps eventually the *vicina* and *güntheri* taxa will be combined. Van Denburgh (1914) was unable to clearly distinguish them. Until 1925, no known physical barriers separated the two volcanoes. An extensive lava flow in that year partially separated them, but a large area on the southern coast of Isabela still remains as a potential pathway for interchange. The question requires further study.

1964; Perry, 1970; Thornton, 1971) outdated, a brief summary is necessary for an understanding of current conservation practices.

Fifteen races of *G. elephantopus* were originally described (Van Denburgh, 1914), ten from separate islands and one from each of the five major volcanoes of Isabela (Fig. 1). The massive decimation of these large populations by human

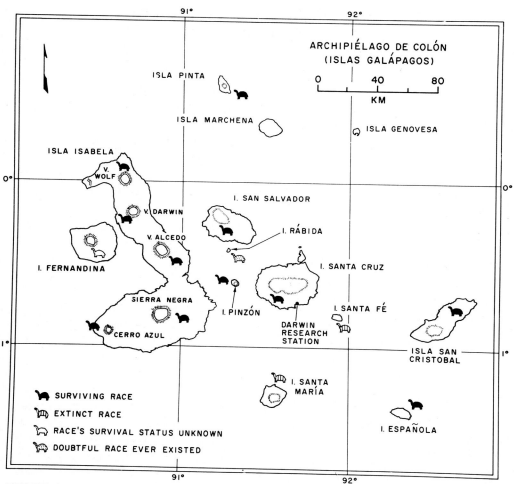

FIGURE 1. Map showing the distribution of the originally recognized 15 races of *G. elephantopus*.

exploitation has already been summarized in detail (Townsend, 1925; Slevin, 1959). During this century, various reports indicated that as few as two and perhaps many more races had been eliminated; the existence of some others was considered doubtful. However, these reports were based mainly on cursory visits to coastal areas. Extensive searches over the past ten years, especially in the islands' interior regions, have resulted in the rediscovery of several races thought to be extinct; the population sizes of most surviving races were found to be much larger than indicated by all previous estimates in this century (Van Denburgh, 1914; Bowman 1960; Eibl-Eibesfeldt, 1959 and 1961; Snow, 1964).

Eleven races have survived, in most cases due largely to the difficult terrain of the islands and the longevity of the tortoises. Two races are definitely extinct, and have been for more than a century. The other two races are enigmatic (see Fig. 1). The single specimen found on Rábida in 1906 was probably an artificial introduction, and there are no substantiated grounds for considering that a native race ever occurred there (see Snow, 1964 for detailed argument). The race of Fernandina almost certainly existed at one time. A single male was collected in 1906 and droppings of one were found in 1964. However, several searches in the past few years of areas considered to be prime potential tortoise habitat have not revealed further signs. A small population may still survive, isolated in one of the few small vegetated areas which have not yet been examined. Whatever the status of this race, its fate has been determined by natural causes (most probably vulcanism), because man has never exploited Fernandina and no introduced animals occur there (Perry, 1970).

The status of the eleven surviving populations is quite variable. All have been reduced in total numbers and the total area of habitat now occupied has decreased from the original range in most cases. For some races, these reductions have been extremely severe; for others, much less so.

Table 1 summarizes the status of each race. Population size estimates are based on numerous visits to, and extensive surveys of, the habitat of each population by personnel of the National Park Service and the authors. However, they are intended only as rough estimates. It has not yet been possible to utilize more accurate mark recapture techniques because of the large areas involved, the lack of detailed maps where terrain and vegetation are very heterogeneous, and lack of personnel. The estimates for *G.e. microphyes* and *G.e. becki* are the least accurate; each is based on only three visits. The estimates for small to medium-sized tortoises provide some indication of the success of population replacement. The number of tortoises permanently marked in each population primarily reflects the amount of effort expended, rather than the population size; marking efforts have been concentrated mainly on races considered most endangered.

Feral competitors and predators now pose the most severe threats to the tortoise populations. The presence and effects of these mammals vary considerably from one tortoise population to another. In Table 1, the ferals are divided into primary and secondary threats. The former are known either to destroy large numbers of tortoise eggs and/or young, or to limit severely the amount of available vegetation; the latter are either known to cause lesser amounts of similar damage, or are suspected of being predators or competitors. Black rats, cats, pigs and dogs all destroy hatchlings and very small tortoises. Pigs and dogs kill tortoises up to 25 lbs in weight and occasionally may destroy even larger ones. Pigs very efficiently destroy nests, and in some situations dogs do the same. Goats are the worst competitors, especially with young tortoises; donkeys and cattle may also compete for food.

TABLE 1. Status of 11 known, surviving races of *G. elephantopus*, November, 1971. Y = Young; N = Nests.

Race	Location	Number Marked	Population estimates		Primary threats		Secondary and potential threats
			Total	Small-med. sized	Feral animals	Stages affected	
hoodensis	Española	11	20–30	None	Goats	Y	—
ephippium	Pinzón	100	150–200	None	Rats	Y	—
chathamensis	San Cristóbal	213	500–700	Very rare	Dogs	N, Y	Rats
					Cats	Y	Goats
					Donkeys		
darwini	San Salvador	389	500–700	Very rare	Pigs	N, Y	Rats
					Goats	Y	Donkeys
porteri	Santa Cruz	1460	2000–3000	Moderate numbers	Pigs	N, Y	Rats
					Cats	Y	Man
abingdoni	Pinta	0	Very Small	?	Goats	Y	Donkeys
vicina	Cerro Azul	196	400–600	Very rare	Goats	Y	—
					Pigs	N, Y	Rats
					Dogs	Y	Man
güntheri	Sierra Negra	219	300–500	Rare except in one area (see text)	Cats	Y	Cattle
					Pigs	N, Y	Cats, Rats, Man, Goats, Cattle, Donkeys
vandenburghi	V. Alcedo	403	3000–5000	Numerous	Dogs	Y	
					?	?	Cats, Rats, Man, Donkeys
microphyes	V. Darwin	65	500–1000?	Numerous	?	?	Cats, Rats, Man, Donkeys
becki	V. Wolf	0	1000–2000?	Numerous	?	?	Cats, Rats, Man

Human exploitation is now a relatively minor problem. Settlers occasionally slaughter tortoises of the *porteri* and *güntheri* populations. Poaching, for meat and oil and of live tortoises for the international export market, occurs to a limited extent in certain coastal areas of the *vandenburghi*, *microphyes*, *becki*, *vicina* and *porteri* ranges.

The races can be divided into four groups based on their status, as follows (see Table 1).

(1) *hoodensis* and *abingdoni*. These two races have extremely small populations. The Española population has apparently not bred for years; the density is so low (ten females, two males found in the past 9 years) that the animals never meet. All tortoises found were old adults and the females had extensive lichen growth on the upper-rear portion of the carapace, an indication that no recent mating attempts had occurred (Hendrickson and Weber, 1964). The Pinta race has just been rediscovered (November, 1971), after several extensive searches in recent years had indicated no signs of living tortoises. One animal and signs of several others were found. The status of this race will require further investigation, but it is almost certainly similar to that of *hoodensis*. The vegetation of both islands has been extensively damaged by goats (see Weber, 1971 for details).

(2) *ephippium*, *chathamensis*, *darwini*, *vicina*, and *güntheri*. These populations are all reduced in size, and consist almost entirely of adults. Mating and nesting occur unimpeded. However, virtually none (or only extremely small numbers) of the young survive, due to predation on the young and/or nests by one or more feral mammal species. For example, the *ephippium* population on Pinzón consists of approximately 150 old tortoises; 64 per cent are mature females. In the past 10 years this population has produced several thousand hatchlings. Despite extensive searches, only a single 1-year old tortoise was found in this period. The *ephippium* nesting areas are littered with fragmented remains of hatchlings eaten by black rats, *Rattus rattus*. Although *güntheri* fits generally into this category, it deserves special mention. One population of the race, isolated (by human settlement) on the eastern part of Sierra Negra from the remainder, consists mainly of small and medium-sized animals. Few adults survive there, most having been killed by settlers in recent years. The only feral mammals in this area are goats.

(3) *porteri*. The main population of this race, in a tortoise reserve on the southwestern slopes of Santa Cruz, is quite large and contains moderately large numbers of small and medium-sized animals. However, several predators destroy large numbers of nests and young. Although not proven, it seems likely that recruitment is too low to replace adults lost by natural mortality and poaching. Probably, the population size is declining continually, though slowly. The other small, isolated population of the race, in the eastern sector of the island (Snow, 1964) now consists of only a few dozen tortoises. Its survival remains doubtful due to occasional human predation.

(4) *vandenburghi*, *microphyes* and *becki*. These populations are of large size and contain large numbers of small and medium-sized tortoises. Recruitment may be sufficient to maintain them as stable populations. However, present information is inadequate to provide conclusions regarding their status. Black rats and cats are present on all three volcanoes; their effects are unknown. Although this has not yet been demonstrated, the numerous donkeys on Volcán Alcedo may cause some nest destruction; their trails and dust wallows are present in tortoise nesting area.

Human exploitation of the tortoise populations has been notably decreased in the past few years, due to increased patrolling by the Servicio del Parque Nacional Galápagos, and more widespread education within the archipelago. Recent Ecuadorian laws prohibit both poaching and export of the tortoises from either the islands or continental Ecuador (MacFarland and Black, 1971). Enforcement remains a problem and more effective patrolling is required, especially in certain coastal areas of Isabela where most of the poaching occurs.

Ultimately, preservation of the tortoises, and the Galápagos environment in general, will require control, or elimination where possible, of the feral mammal populations. For most of these mammals, the only feasible method now available is systematic hunting. To date, the method has proved effective only with goats and pigs, and, for the former, only on the smaller islands. The National Park Service has eliminated goats from Santa Fé and markedly reduced their populations on Española, Marchena and Pinta. Similarly, pig populations have been reduced on San Salvador and Santa Cruz.

Where pigs are present, Park Service wardens protect tortoise nests with lava corrals, 1·5-2·0 m in diameter and 1 m high. The method has been almost 100 per cent successful in preventing nest destruction. Combined with effective control of pig populations by hunting, this method may prove to be sufficient for preserving certain races, e.g. *darwini* and *porteri*.

Systematic hunting requires frequent island visitation and great expenditures of manpower, time and funds. It is doubtful that the method could result in the elimination of either goats or pigs on the larger, more elevated islands with a diversity of vegetation zones. Judging from results on Cerro Azul, San Cristóbal, and Santa Cruz, the method is not feasible for controlling dogs or cats. Whether it would be effective against donkeys or cattle remains to be evaluated.

The possibilities of controlling or eliminating black rats, particularly on Pinzón, with anti-coagulant poisons or sterilization agents are currently under investigation.

BREEDING, RAISING, RESTOCKING PROGRAMMES

While additional control methods for feral mammals are being sought, the best interim preservation method is to raise young tortoises at the Darwin Research Station on Santa Cruz for eventual restocking of the native races.

The Darwin Station first initiated the programme in 1965, on a trial basis, with the *ephippium* population. Since 1968 the programme has been a co-operative effort between the Darwin Station and the Servicio del Parque Nacional Galápagos (part of the Dirreción de Desarrollo Forestal). Until very recently, the programme concentrated on only a few races because of lack of funds, personnel, and information concerning the status of some races; the data presented here reflect this concentration. Results from 1971 to 1972 are excluded, since data are currently being collected and analysed. Beginning with the 1972–73 breeding/nesting season, the programme will include all eight of the most endangered races, i.e., excluding only *vandenburghi*, *microphyes* and *becki*.

Two basic approaches are used. For the *hoodensis* population, which was reduced in size to the extent that mating was not occurring in the wild, a breeding colony was established at the Darwin Station. The same method is now being applied to *abingdoni*. For the races in which mating and nesting occur in the wild but feral predators destroy most of the nests and/or young (*ephippium*, *chathamensis*, *darwini*, *vicini*, *güntheri*), eggs are brought to the Station for incubation and raising of the hatchlings.

Since the *porteri* population is relatively large and therefore in less danger than most others, no concerted breeding and raising programme has been instituted. However, approximately 15–30 young per year-class are being raised in captivity for restocking of areas where poachers have depleted the population. These hatchlings derive from two sources: a small breeding colony at the Darwin Station (on display for visitors) and from nesting areas in the wild.

Breeding Colony Establishment

Over the past six years, one male and eight female *hoodensis* have been brought to the Darwin Station. The breeding enclosure is a large rectangular corral with lava walls measuring approximately 50 × 25 m; it is located in the typical coastal *Opuntia-Jasminocereus* forest of Santa Cruz. It contains a large cement water pool and abundant natural shade; mud wallows are present occasionally after heavy rains. The tortoises are fed a combination of natural foods (*Opuntia* pads and fruits, *Commelina diffusa*, various grasses), introduced plants (otoy or *Xanthosoma* and grasses) and occasional fruits and vegetables.

As in most races in the wild, mating in the *hoodensis* group occurred from December to August, the peak period being February to June. It was not necessary to separate the male from the females for any period in order to produce successful matings.

One of the most important aspects of a breeding enclosure is the provision of proper nesting sites. On the basis of our observations of natural nesting areas of the *porteri*, *ephippium*, *darwini*, *microphyes*, *vicina*, *becki*, *güntheri* and *chathamensis* populations, it is considered that the sites should have the following characteristics:

(1) The soil should be relatively fine and form an adhesive but workable mud when wetted by the copious urination of the female during excavation. The mud

facilitates digging, and results in a firm-walled and well-formed cavity, greatly reducing problems of cave-in. Sand or coarse, cloddy soils are improper substrates.

(2) Soil depth should be at least 25–40 cm and the surface area at least 3 sq. m in order to provide some freedom of movement for the female. Nest cavity depth is primarily determined by full extension of the female's rear legs, i.e., 25–35 cm depending upon racial and individual size variation.

(3) The soil should be rather vigorously tamped into place, layer by layer. This forms a solid working surface for the female, enhancing the excavation, and to some extent replicating natural sites.

The captive *hoodensis* females nested from late June to late November, approximately the same period as in wild populations of other races. Nesting

TABLE 2. Relationship of nesting success to soil type for and availability of artificial nesting sites for *G.e. hoodensis* in captivity at Darwin Station.

| Year | Artificial nesting sites | No. of females | No. nights attempted nesting/clutch laid | No. clutches laid | | |
				On surface	Natural sites	Artificial sites
1967–68	None	1	20–30[a]	2	0	—
1968–69	None	1	20–30[a]	2	0	—
1969–70	3; soil coarse and cloddy	2	10–30	2	0	2
1970–71	4; soil fine and clay-like	3	1–4, rarely to 12	0	1	7
1971–72	4; soil fine and clay-like	6	1–4, rarely to 10	0	1	7

[a] Not recorded accurately, approximate only.

attempts began in the late afternoon (1600–1800 h). Successful nesting required from 8 to 12 h. Except in rare instances, only one attempt per evening occurred.

During the 1967–68 and 1968–69 breeding seasons, the *hoodensis* females were not provided with artificial nesting sites; the few natural sites in the enclosure were small and surrounded by lava, lacking in depth and containing many obstructions (large stones); the soil was non-adhesive when wet. In 1969–70 three artificial sites were available, meeting the previously noted requirements, except that the soil was coarse and cloddy and thus had poor adhesiveness when wet. In 1970–71 four artificial sites were created using soil closely similar to that of natural nesting areas on Santa Cruz, and meeting all the previously noted requirements; the three 1969–70 sites were eliminated.

The lack of proper sites had marked effects (Table 2). During the first two breeding seasons, the females had great difficulty in excavating nest cavities.

They attempted to nest on successive evenings for long time periods, but obstructions and caving-in prevented nest completion; eventually the eggs were dropped on the lava surface of the enclosure. In 1969–70 almost all of the attempted nestings took place at the three artificial sites. However, caving-in was still a major problem resulting in long period of nesting attempts on successive evenings. Two nests were eventually made at these sites, but two clutches were also laid on the lava surface of the enclosure. During these first three nesting seasons, most eggs laid on the surface were destroyed by mockingbirds (*Nesomimus parvulus*) soon after being deposited. With the provision of proper soil type in the artificial sites (1970–71 and 1971–72), most nests were successfully

TABLE 3. Relationship of soil type of nesting sites to breakage or cracking of eggs during nesting, *G. elephantopus* (CDRS = Charles Darwin Research Station).

Race and location	Soil type of nesting sites	No. nests	No. eggs	% broken or cracked (No.)
Unspecified; San Diego Zoo (Shaw 1967)	sand	not stated, at least 3	44	66·0 (29)
hoodnesis (1969–70) CDRS	see Table 2	2	14	35·7 (5)
hoodensis (1970–71, 1971–72) CDRS	see Table 2	19	112	4·5 (5)
porteri (1969–70, 1970–71) in wild	natural nesting areas	55	520	1·2 (6)
ephippium (1969–70, 1970–71) in wild	natural nesting areas	54	252[a]	1·2 (3)

a The 54 nests contained a total of 259 eggs; 7 were broken in 3 nests when a second female nested at a site where another nest already existed.

constructed at those sites and the number of evenings of attempted nesting per clutch laid decreased greatly. The females which had demonstrated great difficulty in nesting during the first 3 years, as well as females new to the enclosure in either of the latter two breeding seasons, constructed functional nests without difficulty.

Poor quality soil also results in a large proportion of eggs being broken or cracked during nesting. Provision of artificial sites with proper soil results in low percentages of breakage and cracking, comparable to those noted for nests of other races made in the wild (Table 3). Breakage and cracking of eggs by the *hoodensis* females occurred during two parts of the nesting process: (1) just at the end of egg laying, when the females alternately inserted the rear feet, gently rearranging the eggs into more or less a single layer, and (2) during the first stages of covering the eggs with soil. When the soil was of poor quality, excessive caving-in resulted in insecure footing at these stages of the nesting process and damage to many of the eggs occurred. In wild populations of *porteri* and *ephip-pium*, the same behaviour patterns occur during nesting, but egg breakage or cracking is extremely rare. Apparently the same factors resulted in a high percentage of breakage and cracking on a sand substrate at the San Diego Zoo, although Shaw (1967) attributed it partly to the laying process, i.e. the eggs striking one another during laying. However, in both the *hoodensis* colony and *porteri* and *ephippium* in the wild, this factor was unimportant. The eggs are encased in a thick, gelatinous fluid which maintains connection with the cloacal opening, thereby slowing their descent and cushioning them on impact. Breakage or cracking due to striking another egg or the cavity floor occur rarely.

Egg handling

Excavation of the nests in the Darwin Station breeding enclosure is essential because of the high probability of egg damage due to nest interference, i.e. more

TABLE 4. Relationship of age at handling to fertility and hatching success of six clutches, *G.e. hoodensis*, 1970–71, in captivity.

Time between laying and handling (h)	No. eggs in clutch	No. definitely fertile	No. dead embryos	No. hatched	No. addled
9–12	6	2	1	1	4
15–18	5	4	0	4	1
15–18	1[a]	1	0	1	0
15–18	7	6	2	4	1
87–90	6	6	1	5	0
109–112	7	5	0	5	2

[a] 3 eggs in clutch, 2 broken.

than one nest being made at the same site. The surface of the enclosure consists primarily of lava, and only four artificial sites are available. In 1971–72, for example, seven of eleven nests were made at the same site.

Nests are usually excavated on the day following their construction. The eggs are weighed and measured in the laboratory and then placed in incubators. During these operations, the eggs are carried, in glass containers, a distance of approximately 200 m. The tops of the eggs are marked during excavation and they are carefully maintained in this same position throughout the handling process and incubation periods.

Fertility and hatching rates for six *hoodensis* nests, 1970–71, indicate no drastic damage to the eggs if they are excavated and handled during the first 109–112 h after being laid (Table 4). It seems unlikely that the handling process accounts for the four dead embryos; all were from several weeks to several months old at death. It is not possible to evaluate the 25 per cent (8) value for addled eggs, because no data are available from the wild for *hoodensis*.* It thus remains possible that handling resulted in the destruction of a small percentage of fertile *hoodensis* eggs.

The same marking, weighing, and measuring procedures are applied to eggs brought from natural nesting sites. They are transported in metal cans, with sawdust packing. However, the eggs are subject to considerable tilting during transport, first for 1–6 h by backpack over rough trails and then for 5–14 h in fishing boats.

TABLE 5. Relationship of age of eggs at transport to fertility and hatching success, *G.e. ephippiun* 1969–70 and 1970–71; data for undisturbed wild nests of *G.e. porteri*, 1969–70 and 1970–71 included for comparison.

Transport	No. nests	No. eggs	No. eggs excluded[a]	No. eggs incubated	% definitely fertile (No.)	% hatched (No.)	% dead embryos (No.)	% addled (No.)
G.e. porteri								
None	55	520	7	513	80·3 (412)	76·2 (391)	4·1 (21)	19·7 (101)
G.e. ephippium								
None	26	133	8	125	85·6 (107)	82·4 (103)	3·2 (4)	14·4 (18)
10–15 weeks old	16	71	13	58	82·8 (48)	74·1 (43)	8·6 (5)	17·2 (10)
7–9 weeks old	2	6	0	6	66·7 (4)	66·7 (4)	0 (0)	33·3 (2)
4–6 weeks old	6	29	3	26	50·0 (13)	19·2 (5)	30·8 (8)	50·0 (13)
0–2 weeks old	5	27	0	27	29·6 (8)	18·5 (5)	11·1 (3)	70·3 (19)

[a] Excluded for various reasons, i.e. broken in laying or by nest interference, or (for transported clutche broken by observer or found hatched in nest.

In order to evaluate the relationship of age at transport and addling, eggs from the *ephippium* population were brought to the Darwin Station for incubation at various ages (0–15 weeks). Transport was for 1–2 h by backpack and 5–6 h by boat. The younger the eggs at the time of transport, the greater the percentage of addling, or conversely, the lower the percentage which were definitely fertile (Table 5). Compared to the percentage addled for non-transported eggs in wild nests, these results strongly suggest that the transport process destroyed significant percentages of the younger eggs. Other possible factors, such as the time of laying during the nesting season (August–December) were eliminated by transporting eggs of varying ages at various times (October, December, January, February). When the eggs were transported at 10–15 weeks of age, at which time the embryos were well developed, the percentage definitely fertile

---

* Throughout this paper addled is defined as a liquified egg, i.e. either infertile or the embryo having died before attaining sufficient size to be detectable.

was little lower than for eggs left in the wild, and the percentage of dead embryos increased only slightly. Hatching occurred at 12–17 weeks of age, the variability being due to the time when the nests were made and the continually rising temperature of the macroclimate from August to March (see below).

This experiment with *ephippium* eggs demonstrates that it is feasible to maintain high fertility and hatching percentages if eggs are transported only late in their incubation period. This technique is now being applied to other tortoise races. Nesting areas are visited frequently (every 1 to 8 weeks); the age of a nest is determined in part by its degree of moistness, and by careful handling of eggs against sunlight.

Incubation

The incubators are constructed of wood, the interiors being cement-lined cavities measuring $58 \times 58 \times 50$ cm depth. The bottom of the cavity is filled with fine soil to a depth of 12 cm. The eggs are slightly embedded in this soil. Level with the eggs are two insulated wooden doors, one with a glass panel behind it for viewing, the other for access to the cavity. Above the soil is a 15 cm air space, then a corrugated asbestos sheet 0·3 cm thick supporting 9 cm of soil, then a 13 cm air space. The chamber is topped by a metal sheet (0·1 cm thick) with its exterior painted dull black (Fig. 2).

The incubators are naturally heated and continual humidity control is practised. The soil is lightly sprinkled with water when the eggs are first placed in the chamber. Thereafter, a bowl of water is maintained in the chamber throughout incubation. Aeration occurs every 2 to 3 days when the access door is opened for a few minutes. A mercury thermometer, readable to 0·5°C through the glass panel, measures air temperature inside each chamber. Incubator temperatures are not checked on a precise schedule. However, they were recorded at least once (often 2–4 times) almost every day from early July to the end of March, 1969–70. During any given month, temperatures were checked on numerous occasions at all hours from 0500 to 2000 h. While permitting no precise evaluation of temperature cycling, the ranges of temperatures for each month were established. Daily maxima usually occurred between 1700–1900 h, minima between 0500–0800 h. During 1970–71, incubator temperatures were checked less often, but the same trends appeared as in 1969–70.

Incubation periods in these chambers were quite variable, the length depending upon the time of nesting. Two major seasons occur in the Galápagos (see Bowman, 1961 for details): the garúa season (June-December) with frequent cloud cover and misty rain, and the hot season (January–May) with infrequent cloud cover, occasional heavy showers (only in some years), and intense solar radiation. A general warming trend occurs from August through March, the sharpest rise in temperatures occurring from mid-December through late March.

The data resulting from incubation of six *hoodensis* clutches in 1970–71 (Fig. 3) show that the earlier a nest is laid during the nesting season, the longer the incubation period. Changes in macroclimatic temperatures from July to March correlate well with these results; temperatures within the incubator chambers follow the same upward trend.

FIGURE 2. Front view of the naturally heated incubators at the Darwin Station.

As expected, incubation periods in the wild demonstrated the same relationship. For *porteri*, they varied from 250 to 110 days, for nests (N = 15) made from late June to early December; for *ephippium*, from 120 to 85 days for nests (N = 6) made from late September to mid-November.

Temperatures from natural nests of *porteri* and *ephippium* in the wild fell within the range of those measured in the Station incubators, but were much less variable (Fig. 4). The *porteri* eggs in the wild were subjected to temperatures near the incubator minimum, but no high temperatures; the reverse occurred for the *ephippium* eggs.* No evidence exists that the wider range of incubator temperatures causes egg damage, but more data are needed to evaluate this possibility.

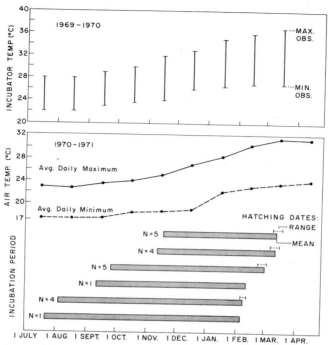

FIGURE 3. Dependence of length of incubation period on time during nesting season when nest is made; data for six *G.e. hoodensis* nests in incubators at Darwin Station; N = no. eggs hatched. Average daily temperature maxima and minima were taken at 2 m in a standard weather shield; monthly range for incubator temperatures (1969–70) established as indicated in the text.

Hatching and fertility rates

Fertility and hatching rates were high for eggs left *in situ* in wild nests of *ephippium* and *porteri* (Table 5). Since the eggs had not been disturbed, these percentages of addled eggs can be used as rough estimates of natural infertility rates.

Combined results for all eggs incubated at the Station, for the years 1966–67 to 1970-71,† demonstrate notably lower fertility and hatching rates and higher

---

* The *porteri* and *ephippium* nesting situations are considered typical of the range of conditions found among the tortoise races: The Santa Cruz nesting areas (*porteri*) have more total daily cloud cover at any given time of year than those on Pinzón (*ephippium*). Santa Cruz is one of the larger, wetter, more elevated islands; Pinzón is representative of the smaller, lower, drier islands.

† Data excluded for *ephippium*, 1965–66, because the number of eggs incubated was not recorded, and for two *hoodensis* nests, 1969–70, and two *hoodensis* nests, 1970–71, because eggs were clearly abnormal and infertile; i.e. very thin-shelled, ovoid in shape and enlarged.

percentages of dead embryos and addled eggs (Table 6) than for nests of *porteri* and *ephippium* in the wild (Table 5). However, most of the eggs incubated at the Station were those transported by boat from the *ephippium* and *darwini* populations. The eggs of *darwini*, and *ephippium* 1966–67 to 1968–69, were of unknown, but greatly variable, ages when transported; no special care was taken to transport them only late in the incubation periods. Also, the 1969–70 and 1970–71 *ephippium* eggs were used in the transport experiments described above. Transport damage almost certainly accounted for a large proportion of the dead embryos and addled eggs (Table 6).

Fertility and hatching rates from breeding colonies in zoos have been quite variable, but lower than at the Darwin Station. For 258 eggs (race(s) unspecified)

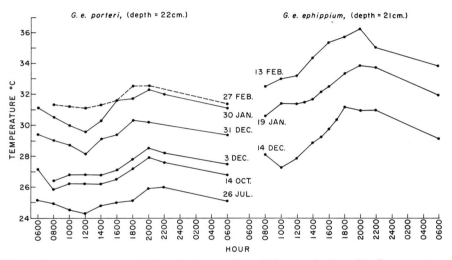

FIGURE 4. Temperatures, recorded by thermocouples, within nests in the wild. *G.e. porteri* nest made 20–21 June, 1970; *G.e. ephippium* nest made approximately 30–31 October, 1970.

at the San Diego Zoo, 10·42 per cent were fertile and 6·97 per cent hatched (Shaw, 1967); for 191 eggs of *vicina* at the Honolulu Zoo, 32·46 per cent were fertile, 31·10 per cent hatched (Throp, 1969). The reasons for these low rates are unknown. Throp notes that fertility rates were high in viable clutches but were zero in many others.

On the Galápagos, complete infertility or low fertility rates were rare for individual clutches of *ephippium* and *porteri* left *in situ* in the wild (Table 7).

Raising, mortality and growth

Young *G.e. ephippium* from the year-classes 1965–66 to 1967–68 were raised, until January, 1970 in large chicken-wire cages located just above sea level and 25 m inland from the high tide line. Because of the cage structure and surrounding vegetation, the pens received very limited solar radiation. At night throughout the year and during part of most days of the garúa season, the pens were exposed to strong, cool breezes. Water was provided *ad libitum*. Food consisted of green roughage, native grasses, *Commelina diffusa*, introduced grasses, and occasionally, partially-dried *Opuntia* fruits.

The 1968–69 *ephippium* year-class was raised in the laboratory; heat and light were provided 10 h/day by two 60–100W tungsten light bulbs, and no exposure

TABLE 6. Results of incubation at Darwin Research Station 1966–67 to 1970–71.

Race	Breeding/Nesting seasons	No. eggs incubated	% definitely fertile (No.)	% hatched (No.)	% dead embryos (No.)	% addled (No.)
ephippium	1966–67 to 1970–7	312	77·2 (241)	50·6 (158)	26·6 (83)	22·8 (71)
darwini	1970–71	118	61·0 (72)	37·3 (44)	37·3 (44)	39·0 (46)
hoodensis	1970–71	32	75·0 (24)	62·5 (20)	12·5 (4)	25·0 (8)
porteri	1970–71	17	35·3 (6)	35·3 (6)	0 (0)	64·7 (11)
chathamensis	1969–70	3	100·0 (3)	100·0 (3)	0 (0)	0 (9)
TOTALS		482	71·8 (346)	47·9 (231)	23·9 (115)	28·2 (136)

TABLE 7. Fertility rates of individual clutches left *in situ* in the wild, *porteri* and *ephippium*, 1969–70 and 1970–71 data combined; cf. Table 5; x̄ = mean, s = standard deviation.

Race	No. eggs incubated/clutch			No. clutches with % definitely fertile					
	x̄	range	s	0	1–24	25–49	75–50	99–74	100
porteri	9·3	5–16	2·6	2	2	3	11	18	19
ephippium	4·8	2–8	1·6	1	0	0	4	6	15

to cool breezes occurred. Food and water conditions were as for the previous groups.

In January 1970 all year-classes were moved to a new tortoise raising centre, constructed mainly with funds provided by the San Diego Zoological Society. All year-classes of 1969–70 and later, of all races, have been raised entirely within this centre. Each year-class of each race is maintained unexposed to sea breezes; a battery of six 100W tungsten light bulbs provides heat and light 10 h/day in one corner of each pen. Water is provided *ad libitum* 2 days/week; food is as previously described.

Between early 1966 and November 1971, 266 tortoises were hatched at the Station and 67 hatchlings were brought there from nests in the wild. Of the 333 young tortoises, 104 (31·2 per cent) had died by August, 1972. However, 3 per cent of the deaths resulted from accidents, e.g. killed by rats.

Most natural deaths, regardless of race or year-class, occurred during the first 9 months of life (Table 8). Mortality was apparently caused by digestive difficulties; food accumulated in the intestines, eventually resulting in infection and degeneration of the intestinal lining. Infrequent solar radiation and the cool

TABLE 8. Natural mortality rates and age and mortality relationships for the breeding and raising programme, CDRS, 1965–66 to August 1972; hatchlings which died accidently are excluded.

Race and year class	No. hatchlings	% mortality (No.)	Number died						
			0–3 mth	3–6 mth	6–9 mth	9–12 mth	12–18 mth	>18 mth	
G.e. ephippium									
1965–66	35	17·1 (6)	N/R	N/R	N/R	N/R	N/R	N/R	
1966–67	43	51·2 (22)	9	9	3	1	0	0	Seaside pens
1967–68	46	50·0 (23)	9	2	4	0	8	0	
1968–69	12	25·0 (4)	0	4	0	0	0	0	
1969–70	38	21·1 (8)	4	3	0	0	1	0	
1970–71	21	29·9 (6)	4	0	1	1	0	0	
G.e. hoodensis									Tortoise house or laboratory
1970–71	20	5·0 (1)	1	0	0	0	0	0	
G.e. porteri									
1970–71	20	10·0 (2)	0	1	1	0	0	0	
G.e. darwini									
1970–71	61	18·0 (11)	3	8	0	0	0	0	
TOTAL	296	27·7 (82)							

N/R = not recorded

winds at the seaside pens used earlier increased the frequency of such digestive problems.

In general, survival rates were markedly higher for those year-classes, regardless of race, raised from hatching in the tortoise centre or laboratory as compared to those raised in the seaside pens during the first 18 months or more of life (Table 8). Excluded from Table 8 are data from three races (6 year-classes) with extremely small sample sizes (3–7 hatchlings).

Figure 5 illustrates the growth rate for the first year-class of tortoises raised at the Station, *G.e. ephippium* 1965–66. Age was determined as the approximate median, because hatching occurred over a 3-month period from late December to late March. Unfortunately, the tortoises were not weighed at hatching. However, the average weight at hatching (79·7 g.; range, 56·8–101·8; s = 9·3) of the 1969–70 *ephippium* year class is given as an approximation. Curves for the other races and year classes raised in captivity are very similar.

Data on growth rates of young tortoises in the wild are very limited. During the first 8 months of life in 1971, two sets of wild young *porteri*, each consisting of four siblings, had average growth rates approximately 1·6 and 1·4 times greater than hatchlings of the same and other races raised at the Station.

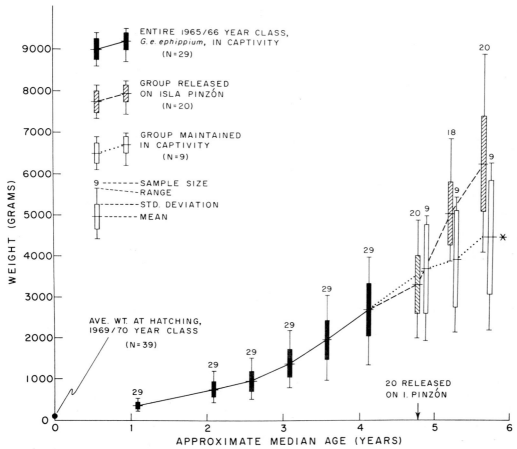

FIGURE 5. Growth curve for 1965–66 year-class, *G.e. ephippium* raised in captivity at Darwin Station. * Symbols for range and standard deviation shifted slightly to the right for clarity.

The low growth rates in captivity at the Station may be due primarily to the lack of natural solar radiation in the raising pens. Water is available in greater quantities than in the wild. Although the young receive primarily natural foods, a greater variety could certainly improve growth rates and probably reduce mortality. Very low mortality rates and high growth rates have been achieved at the Honolulu Zoo with young *vicina* which are fed lettuce, fruit, and Gaine's Dog Meal (Throp, 1972; personal communication). At present, dietary changes are being considered, and exterior balconies, where solar radiation will be available, are being added to each pen of the tortoise raising centre.

Return to the wild

Through August, 1972, a total of 302 young tortoises had been or were being raised at the Station, as follows: 148 *ephippium*, 25 *hoodensis*, 28 *porteri*, 71 *darwini*, 29 *vicina* and 1 *chathamensis*. Of these, 71 *ephippium* young have been returned to Pinzón.

Twenty of the 1965–66 *ephippium* year-class were released on December 11, 1970 in the eastern part of the upper, older crater of Pinzón. The release point is situated in a flat corridor, approximately 700 m long and 150 m wide, which lies between the steep, inner, eastern crater wall and sharply rising cliffs and boulders to the west. The corridor consists of large open areas of soil and others of mixed soil and rocks; the vegetation consists of scattered *Opuntia* trees, shrubs, and a variety of grasses and forbs. At approximately 280 m elevation, the area receives light rain frequently in the garúa season (June–December), providing fairly abundant grasses and forbs (e.g. *Commelina diffusa*, *Portulaca* sp.) and small quantities of water, which collects in pockets in rocks. In most years, Pinzón receives little or no rain in the hot season (January–May); however, when heavy rains occasionally occur, this area becomes covered with a dense growth of grasses and forbs, and numerous dry ponds are temporarily filled. Small quantities of fallen *Opuntia* pads are present in the area throughout the year.

Selection of this area for the first release was based on three criteria: (1) favourable moisture and vegetation characteristics (many other potential sites, e.g. nesting areas, are extremely dry and have sparser vegetation); (2) the area is part of the large eastern sector of the island from which tortoises had been eliminated by the cumulative depredations of buccaneers, fishermen and museum collectors; (3) black rats are present, as almost everywhere on Pinzón, allowing a test of whether they would harm the released young tortoises.

At release, the tortoises were almost 5 years old, weighed an average of 3·33 kg (range, 1·99–4·88; $s = 0·68$), and measured an average of 33·4 cm (range 27·8–38·2; $s = 2·7$) in curved length (see Van Denburgh, 1914, for definition). Nine individuals of the same year-class were retained in captivity for comparative purposes.

The young were watched for several hours immediately after release and for several days thereafter for 2–4 h per day. Their behaviour did not apparently differ from that of young wild *porteri*. Within a few minutes of release, they were feeding on several species of forbs, engaging in agonistic displays, and generally wandering over the area. Beginning with the first evening, they constructed the typical shallow night-time burrows under small shrubs or grass clumps in loose soil.

They were relocated, weighed, measured, and examined 1, 2, 5 and 10 months after release. No sign of rat attack or injury was detected. After 10 months in the wild, every individual had approximately doubled in weight.

Their growth rate was markedly higher than for the nine in captivity (see

Fig. 5). The mean weights for the two groups were not significantly different near the release date, but were so for the weights taken at 5 and 10 months after release (two-tailed *t*-test, $p < 0.4$, $p < 0.05$, $p < 0.01$, respectively).

Overall dispersal of the group was not great during the 10 months after release (Fig. 6). Although the total area of distribution was greater at each re-mapping period, little difference existed between 2, 5, and 10 months. In fact, after only 4 days, much of the dispersal had occurred. After 1 month, the

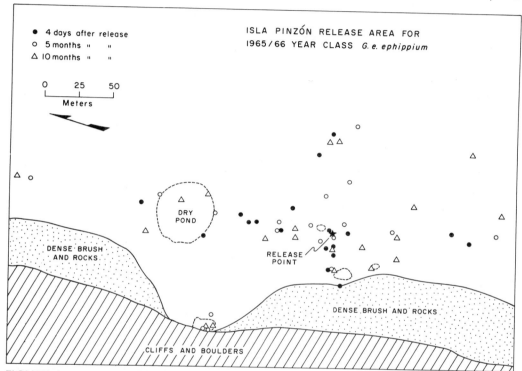

FIGURE 6. Distribution of 1965–66 *G.e. ephippium* young at 4 days, 5 months, and 10 months after release on Pinzón; N = 18, 18, and 20 respectively.

distribution pattern was more or less midway between that at 4 days and that of the latter three periods.

In general, the same individuals were found in the same part of the release area at the 1, 2, 5 and 10 month visits. The daily movements of individuals observed during these visits were usually restricted to an area of 400 sq. m or less.

This contrasted notably with the daily and longer term movements of wild *porteri* individuals of the same size in lowland nesting zones on Santa Cruz during the extremely dry hot season of 1970. They covered areas of up to 1000 sq. m daily while foraging and were found at locations up to 500 m apart from one month to the next.

The limited dispersal of *ephippium* young was possibly due to climatic conditions and the resultant abundance of vegetation on Pinzón during the 10 months. Heavy rains in early March provided a lush growth of forbs and grasses which were present from mid-March to late May. Forbs were moderately abundant during other months.

In October 1971, 51 additional young were released in three groups on Pinzón. Two groups, the nine remaining 1965–66 and the entire 1966–67 year-classes, were placed in dry nesting zones on the island's outer flanks. Dispersal and daily and seasonal movements of these groups will be compared to the 1965–66 group of 20. The entire 1967–68 year-class was released on the island's eastern side in an area similar to that of the 1965–66 group of 20. Their survival will provide a test of the ability of younger and smaller tortoises (N = 23; at release mean weight = 1·54 kg, range 0·90–2·35, s = 0·34; mean curved length = 21·2 cm, range 18·2–24·0, s = 1·47) to withstand black rats and environmental conditions.

DISCUSSION AND CONCLUSIONS

The preceding results emphatically demonstrate that, (1) for those races in which it is necessary, it is possible to establish functional breeding colonies of *Geochelone elephantopus* in the Galápagos Islands with only minimal care and effort; (2) with proper handling and incubation methods, high fertility and hatching rates can be maintained for eggs from breeding colonies and for those transported from nests in the wild, and (3) low mortality rates for young tortoises can be achieved with proper care during raising. Initial results indicate that survival rates of the young, after restocking, will be high.

Fertility and hatching rates for both artificially incubated clutches and wild nests show that there is no justification for the idea that Galápagos tortoises have not reproduced in substantial numbers in recent times or that they are now incapable of doing so (Shaw, 1967).

However, the programme faces numerous future tests and problems. Hatching rates and survivorship during raising can certainly be improved. Long-term survival rates and reproductive success of restocked tortoises remain to be evaluated. It may be necessary to raise the young of those races threatened by pigs or dogs to a relatively large size before releasing them in the wild. Complete elimination or substantial control of feral animals will be required, otherwise the current "nursemaiding" procedures for most or all of the endangered races will be required indefinitely. Estimates of the carrying capacity of the various islands or volcanoes and reproductive potential and mortality rates for the tortoise populations must be made in order to avoid overstocking.

There are numerous advantages to conducting such breeding, raising and restocking programmes in the Galápagos rather than establishing breeding colonies in North America, Europe or other locations. Natural climatic conditions and easily available natural habitat, food species, and nesting soils eliminate most of the reproductive, veterinary, dietary and special housing problems encountered in foreign locations. Costs are low and efficiency high: no long-distance transport of adults for breeding colonies and young for restocking is required; food and housing expenses are minimal. Since eggs for most endangered races can be brought in large numbers from the wild, total production of young is high for the time, effort and funds invested.

Inbreeding and genetic drift pose great potential problems for almost all breeding programmes with captive species, because the original parental generation usually consists of only a small number of individuals. Even the building up of a large colony of apparently "normal", interbreeding individuals from a small number of parents is not *prima facie* evidence that such genetic problems have not occurred. In such situations, the variability of the gene pool has certainly been reduced. Such individuals, though healthy and reproductive in the controlled artificial environment of a zoo, may have low or reduced survivorship and/or reproductive success after return to their native habitat.* For six of the eight endangered Galápagos tortoise races, these problems are being avoided by obtaining eggs from nests in the wild and then returning the offspring to their native populations. The attempt is being made to locate more adults for the *hoodensis* and *abingdoni* breeding colonies to increase genetic variability.

An additional significant advantage of conducting the raising and restocking programme in the Galápagos is its potential educational and public relations value. Guides demonstrate the various stages of the programme to visitors in the tortoise raising centre and at the breeding enclosures and incubators. In 1972, 4000–5000 tourists (approximately 15–20 per cent Ecuadorians) were expected to visit these facilities. A number of local inhabitants work within the programme, and many others visit the Darwin Station to observe its operation. Visitors are made aware that conservation of the Galápagos environment in general, and the tortoises in particular, is now the responsibility of the Ecuadorian National Park Service, and that the effort is being aided by the internationally supported Darwin Research Station, research by scientists, and the funds and interest of organizations and individuals from many parts of the world. The tortoise conservation programme thus serves as a prime example of what needs to be done to preserve what remains and to reclaim some of what has been lost or altered in the Galápagos.

We suggest that, perhaps in the majority of cases, such advantages would make it far more effective to invest most time, manpower, and funds in the establishment of education programmes, habitat and population status studies and breeding/raising centres for endangered species in or near their native habitats rather than in other locations. Of course, in some cases other factors make this impossible, e.g. warfare, other political problems, or virtual total habitat destruction. In such cases, a viable breeding nucleus in a safer location may be the main hope for preserving a species. However, we question whether

---

* Experiments testing survivorship and reproductive success in native habitats, of populations bred and raised in captivity from a small parental generation, are of immediate importance. A wide variety of vertebrate species should be tested and non-endangered species should be used.

the alternatives are seriously considered for many endangered species when breeding colonies are planned and established and funds raised, especially in North America and Europe. Whether some environmentalists, zoo personnel and animal suppliers like it or not, the survival of most endangered species and their habitats ultimately depends upon the interest and involvement of the people and governments of the native areas, albeit with international aid and cooperation in most cases. We suggest that more zoos and their sponsoring societies should follow the lead of the few, e.g. the San Diego and New York Zoological Societies, and begin expending a substantial proportion of their funds on the preservation of endangered species in their native habitats. Vast opportunities exist for sponsoring status surveys, ecological and ethological field studies, educational programmes, establishment of reserves, training of native personnel, and the construction of breeding/raising facilities for endangered species.

We do, of course, assert that effort should be made to establish successful breeding colonies with Galápagos tortoises already captive in zoos and private collections. They could serve the primary function of supplying tortoises to other zoos and private collectors on a world-wide basis. Although most zoos no longer attempt to obtain Galápagos tortoises from the islands or continental Ecuador, some private collectors still provide a market for illegal poaching and export activities. Captive-bred tortoises could help eliminate this market.

Unfortunately no completely accurate census of Galápagos tortoises in zoos and other collections exists. For 1971, the *International Zoo Yearbook* reported a total of 278 in 61 collections (Lucas and Duplaix-Hall, 1972). However, most collections contain only one to a few individuals and the race of most specimens is unknown. Cooperative exchange among collections will be necessary and racial lines should be kept pure, even if it requires excluding large numbers of unidentified specimens from breeding programmes. It would be most advantageous to return specimens of the extremely rare races, i.e. *hoodensis* and *abingdoni*, to the breeding colonies in the Galápagos in order to increase genetic variability. If only one or a few specimens of a less rare race exist in captivity, it would be most useful to return these to the natural populations in the Galápagos. The New York Zoological Society returned an adult *G.e. ephippium* female in 1971, an act which resulted in much publicity and goodwill both on the Galápagos Islands and in continental Ecuador.

Whenever breeding colonies can be formed with reasonably large numbers of captive adults of single races, such should be supported. As reported elsewhere in this volume, Jack Throp, Chairman of the Giant Tortoise Committee of the Wild Animal Propagation Trust is currently coordinating such a programme, and has had considerable success in breeding and raising *G.e. vicina* at the Honolulu Zoo. Of course, whenever significant numbers of tortoises are produced by breeding colonies of endangered races, such as the Honolulu *vicina* group, they could be used both for supplying collections and restocking of Galápagos populations.

ACKNOWLEDGMENTS

The authors' research was supported by the National Science Foundation, Grant No. GB-12256, and the National Geographic Society. Many individuals contributed much time and effort to these conservation programmes; in particular, we thank conservation officials Juan Black, José Villa and Basilio Toro and the wardens of the Servicio del Parque Nacional Galápagos, the personnel of the Charles Darwin Research Station, and Jan MacFarland and Tjitte DeVries. Funding for the work performed by the SPNG and Darwin Station came from many organizations and individuals, in particular the Government of Ecuador, the World Wildlife Fund, the New York Zoological Society, the San Diego Zoological Society, the Frankfurter Zoologische Gesellschaft and Mr. and Mrs. H. E. Hawkes.

Note on the Management and Reproduction of the Galápagos Tortoise at the Honolulu Zoo

J. La Croix Throp

An Agreement was entered into on 30 September 1971 between the City and County of Honolulu and the Wild Animal Propagation Trust to establish a permanent captive propagation programme for Galápagos tortoises in the Honolulu Zoo. At the present time the Zoo has 68 Galápagos tortoises, of which 52 were hatched in Hawaii. The original six male and five female tortoises of the breeding group were collected by Dr. Charles Haskins Townsend on Isabela Island in 1928. They are of the subspecies *Geochelone elephantopus vicina* (Fig. 1). It is believed that none of the tortoises was more than 3 years old at the time of collection.

The first egg was laid by one of the five female tortoises in 1951. It was found on the surface of the ground. The egg-laying female's age was approximately 24 years. Between the period of that first egg in 1951–66, 84 eggs are known to have been laid. Four were fertile, three hatched. Only one of the four lived to be an adult.

In 1966, a programme was begun to learn something of the propagation needs of the Galápagos tortoise. It was obvious that the Zoo had a potentially viable colony if we could just identify the hidden factors necessary to stimulate reproduction. At that time, the earth in the tortoise enclosure was hard packed and devoid of grass. The Zoo tortoises had been fed for years on a limited diet of cabbage and some fruit. Protein was almost non-existent in the foods which had been presented. A large cement pool included in the old compound was never used by the animals for anything more than drinking until recently, when it was filled with mud and water. Finally, the sexes were kept together continuously. Several changes were made in an effort to improve conditions that might affect reproduction. The enclosure was greatly enlarged to encompass a grassy paddock and grass was encouraged to grow in the old compound. This stimulated two activities: grazing and exercise.

The diet was further improved by adding a variety of coarse vegetation, such as pellets made of pineapple tops, alfalfa hay, palm leaves, banana tree trunks and their leaves and dog food. The tortoise faeces became firm and dry, and their odour was reduced.

A large mud-hole was dug and filled with water for the tortoises to lie in. The males frequently sleep in the pool all night. The females are most often seen in the mud during mid-afternoon. It is thought that the soft mud helps the animals to relax and might conceivably exert some effect on fertility.

As a final measure, the sexes were separated for a period of 6 months. The reasoning behind this action is that in Hawaii's gentle climate the males are

FIGURE 1. Female Galápagos Tortoise (*G.e. vicina*). Females frequently rest during the midday period in the mud-bottomed pool; males more often use the pool at night for sleeping.

persistent year-round breeders. The females resisted all mating attempts by the males by simply clamping down to the ground. Successful mating was not seen in a year of continuing attempts by the frustrated males prior to the separation. After the separation, the females were receptive to the males and successful mating occurred.

Probably all of these measures contributed something toward the captive propagation of the animals. In 1967, nine Galápagos tortoises were hatched and eight were successfully raised.

Since the beginning of the project, from 1967 through 1971, 191 eggs have been artificially incubated. The fertility of the 191 eggs has been 32·5 per cent. The per cent of fertile eggs to hatch has been 95·8 per cent. One factor which is not at all understood as yet is why fertility can be very high in some clutches of eggs and totally absent in others. The fertility for the viable egg clutches has been a remarkable 74·2 per cent.

An effort will be made soon to improve the physical condition of the tortoises by providing more opportunity for exercise. This might decrease the number of infertile egg clutches.

The eggs are collected as the females lay them. They are artificially incubated in cement crocks which provide a close simulation of the conditions of the nests

FIGURE 2.   Hatchlings at one month of age (September 1972). Grass hay is provided as shelter from observation, and the youngsters come out of hiding only to feed.

dug by the female. Heat and humidity can be controlled in the artificial environment, which would not be the case if the eggs were left in the ground.

The net result has been the successful rearing of 52 Galápagos tortoises in the last four years. More eggs have already been laid this year and hopes are high for obtaining still more babies.

This success has stimulated conclusion of the present Agreement with the Wild Animal Propagation Trust. The mechanics of the Agreement, in summary, are as follows:

The Honolulu Zoo will invite other zoos to place tortoises on deposit. Prior to shipment, the tortoises must undergo appropriate medical tests. Medical and shipping costs shall be borne by the zoo owning the tortoises. The Honolulu Zoo will provide, from its collection, a sufficient number of tortoises of appropriate ages and sexes to form a breeding colony. The Zoo will provide suitable care for the tortoises on deposit but not be liable for losses due to theft, vandalism or disease.

As captive propagation succeeds, the Honolulu Zoo, with advice from the Giant Tortoise Committee of the Wild Animal Propagation Trust, will release surplus tortoises in the following manner: Juvenile tortoises will be offered to depositing zoos in the order in which deposits were made. Each depositing zoo will be entitled to receive two juvenile tortoises for each adult deposited. Depositing zoos will be responsible for transportation costs.

Any further surplus may be disposed of by the Honolulu Zoo through exchange, trade, or sale. First options will be given to depositing zoos of institutions designated by the Trust.

The Honolulu Zoo will be responsible for its own maintenance costs for feeding, care, veterinarian care, and other expenditures.

It is a simple, plain document. Yet, it took the City of Honolulu many months of deliberation before the document was finally approved. The reasons for the delay are understandable. It was a very great digression from the norm for the City to acknowledge that owned property, when it is an endangered species of wildlife, must not be coveted in isolation. It is an evolutionary advance in government attitude to recognize that in the approval of the Agreement the City relinquished the ultimate right of control of valuable property to the Wild Animal Propagation Trust. In my estimation, the Mayor of Honolulu and his cabinet members are "big" people.

Captive Breeding of Crocodiles*

H. R. Bustard

Captive crocodile breeding presents something of an enigma. Some species breed very readily in captivity, even when kept in close confinement, but few people are aware of this because of the almost total failure of zoological gardens around the world to breed any of their crocodiles. So perhaps it is profitable to start by briefly outlining why zoos generally have had such a poor breeding record with crocodiles.

Most reptile house curators want to show as wide a range of animals as possible. As a result, many zoos have single individuals of a dozen or more different crocodile species which may be housed separately or in groups. Furthermore, since space is usually at a premium (and most reptile houses have to be heated for most or part of the year) they seldom house crocodiles of breeding size, concentrating rather on juveniles and sub-adults. A zoo which does decide to undertake a breeding programme of even medium-size crocodile species comes up against the problems of having to devote very considerable resources to that species unless the zoo is situated in a tropical climate.

In crocodile breeding there is a relationship between space and climate. Except in the tropics, crocodiles require heated accommodation and if this is sufficiently spacious to maintain a breeding herd it is extremely costly.

However, even the largest crocodile species do not require very large enclosures for successful breeding. For instance, I am familiar with a salt water crocodile (*Crocodylus porosus*) near Darwin, Australia, which for three successive years has built a nest and laid eggs in an enclosure measuring only 20×10 ft (the female herself measuring about 10 ft).

Nevertheless, if the eggs are to be successfully incubated under average conditions a somewhat larger enclosure will usually be required, whereas most zoo cages for crocodiles are even smaller than the small one I have just described.

It is difficult to generalize on the temperature and space requirements, due to the differing requirements of the score or more recognized species. However, an ideal breeding enclosure would include:

---

* The word "crocodile" is used in this paper to refer to any member of the order Crocodylia—crocodiles, caiman, garials and alligators.

FIGURE 1. Crocodile pen at the Bangkok Crocodile Farm, showing crocodiles almost ready for slaughter.

(1) A pool area about three times the length of the crocodile of breeding size, with a breadth at least equal to that of the crocodile's length, and a land area of similar size. The land area should incorporate secluded corners with screening vegetation or baffles behind which the female can build her nest.

(2) In the nesting season rotting vegetation or sand (here, requirements differ according to the species) must be provided for nest-building activities.

(3) For many species (and this applies to many reptiles other than crocodiles) seasonal variations in temperature and rainfall may be essential prerequisites for the initiation of breeding behaviour, since some species breed in the wet season and others in the dry. In the modern zoological garden it should be possible to provide these variations in environmental conditions.

(4) A temperature of 25–30°C should be suitable for most species other than the Chinese alligator, which may prefer a lower maximum temperature, although its requirements are actually very poorly known.

(5) Zoos often provide additives to crocodile diet in the form of vitamins, particularly for juveniles, although these should not really be necessary, given a sunlight-shade mosaic and a mixed diet. It should be noted, however, that certain fish do not provide a balanced diet, and crocodiles should certainly be fed roughage. For growing crocodiles, food which includes the skeleton is most important. Crocodiles fed on strips of meat or fish without skeletal material frequently develop calcium deficiencies.

The world's first and only large-scale crocodile farm near Bangkok in Thailand (Fig. 1) feeds its crocodiles on a range of fish species and also gives the larger crocodiles ducks which are plucked and fed whole.

(6) Nesting female crocodiles seek out conditions of maximum seclusion. This problem has been solved most skilfully at the Bangkok crocodile farm by surrounding the large breeding pools with a series of small concrete enclosures reminiscent of beach bathing huts, each about 10 × 8 ft and 8 ft high, with no roof but shaded and screened by coconut palms. A small opening in one wall is the sole means of access. When ready to nest, the female crocodile takes over and defends one of these nesting buildings. It provides her with the right degree of privacy as well as a territory to defend—from which other crocodiles can easily be excluded. In the absence of such an arrangement under crowded conditions, crocodiles may well trample incubating nests and so destroy them.

In a suitable climate the eggs can be left to incubate in the mound built by the mother. When the climate is unsuitable, crocodile eggs hatch well in chicken incubators kept at about 32°C and placed in moist sand (Fig. 2). Sand with a water content of about 8% (by weight) is ideal. (See also Bustard, 1969 and 1971.)

The baby crocodiles need to be housed by themselves and should be fed on small whole fish, frogs, crustaceans, large insects or baby mice.

(7) Size segregation is important in any breeding programme for crocodiles as larger animals will terrorize or kill smaller ones. Only crocodiles of approximately similar size should be housed together.

(8) Very little is known about veterinary problems concerning crocodiles. Prevention is better than cure and the right sort of environment and mixed diet should avoid most medical problems.

Hygiene is very important, particularly when a breeding programme is underway and the individuals may of necessity be housed quite densely. At the Thai crocodile farm all of the pens (except the breeding pools) are drained and hosed daily. All pens are constructed of concrete to facilitate adequate cleaning operations.

(9) There are no hard and fast rules on what makes a viable breeding unit for

FIGURE 2. Experimental hatching of the New Guinea fresh-water crocodile (*Crocodylus novaeguineae*) in the laboratory.

crocodiles. One pair could be enough, but the minimum recommended breeding unit would be one bull and two cows. The high fecundity of crocodiles (some species lay 40–50 eggs in one clutch) means that even such a small breeding unit could quickly improve the conservation picture for the more endangered species.

With certain species there are indications that better breeding results are obtained when a score or more of breeding individuals are housed together. Utai Yangprapakorn, who has many hundreds of breeding individuals of the saltwater crocodile (*Crocodylus porosus*), assures me he now gets much better breeding results than when he had a relatively small breeding stock.

But any zoos which can provide adequate breeding facilities for one bull and one cow crocodile of any threatened species should be encouraged to do so; they can make a valuable contribution to conservation.

In any zoo the decision whether to add more breeding units or to distribute the breeding stock to other zoos will be influenced by what facilities are available to expand the breeding programme. However, it is important not to keep the only significant breeding herd of an endangered species in one place, in case of disease, fire or the like. Every effort should be made to spread the breeding population of any endangered species among several institutes. It may well be that certain locations or institutes provide unrivalled facilities for successful breeding of a particular crocodile species, in which case every effort should be directed to building up the breeding herd at this locality, subject to the safeguard of not keeping the entire stock in one place.

It is quite impossible to lay down strict rules on the number of captive colonies required to provide a viable reservoir for ultimately restocking the wild state. Sir Peter Scott's work at Slimbridge with the Hawaiian goose offers an excellent example of this.

It is quite possible, indeed likely, that certain endangered crocodiles will be saved in the future by captive breeding activities centred on one locality or institution—although some of their specimens will have been distributed elsewhere to safeguard the gene pool.

If, as seems likely with many crocodiles, we have to maintain the captive breeding populations for some time before the right political climate for reintroductions into the wild can take place, it is, of course, essential that in the meantime the stocks do not become too inbred. For this reason studbooks should be kept from the start for any endangered species and out-breeding should be borne in mind when specimens are being exchanged between institutions.

To sum up: at least some crocodile species appear to be ideally suited for captive breeding programmes, and their high fecundity means that numbers can potentially be built up fairly rapidly in captivity.

Breeding of Endangered Wildfowl as an Aid to their Survival

J. Kear

Many essential features of successful waterfowl propagation are admirably dealt with by J. Delacour in the four volumes of *The Waterfowl of the World* (1954–64). This contribution will concentrate, therefore, on certain other factors, the importance of which has become apparent only recently. Many aspects are still inadequately investigated and recommendations are therefore somewhat speculative. Table 1 lists wildfowl species subject to propagation projects. In most cases, captive-reared birds have already been released; White-winged Wood Duck have still be to reintroduced to the wild.

In order to come into breeding condition, an individual requires the continued presence of at least one other bird, a suitable nest site, the correct diet and climate, including the correct daylength, and perhaps a certain amount of sunshine.

ACCOMMODATION

Most waterfowl require a pond, lake or similar water surface in order to copulate successfully. Some, being territorial, require a certain land area as well. But water comes first, and a number of small ponds will accommodate more of a territorial species than a single large lake of similar surface area. Waterfowl are primarily visual, so visual isolation is paramount and auditory isolation of lesser (though considerable) importance.

Three pairs of an endangered species would probably be the viable breeding unit easily dealt with in most zoos. If possible, obtain eggs from the wild and rear the young birds by hand. Not only is less harm done to the wild populations than by removing adult stock, but birds reared in captivity are more likely to breed than are those captured when mature. It is best to isolate birds in pairs to begin with and, if other forms of encouragement lead nowhere, to place two pairs in visual, but not actual contact.

Some ducks need to fly during courtship, so small species should be accommodated full-winged in flight cages. Swans and geese can safely be pinioned, since experience shows that they do well in these circumstances.

DAYLENGTH AND CLIMATE

The correct daylength has been shown to be crucial to the breeding of the majority of wildfowl. It is always best to assume that a species is strictly photo-

TABLE 1. Endangered waterfowl species that have been bred in captivity prior to re-introduction to the wild.

Aleutian Canada Goose *Branta canadensis leucopareia*	75 birds reared in Maryland were released in the Aleutian Islands in March 1971. (*Wildlife Society News* (1971) **136**: 62).
Hawaiian Goose *B. sandvicensis*	(see p. 115; WWF Project 12, The Launching of the New Ark: 67). See Fig. 4.
Marbled Teal *Marmaronetta angustirostris*	24 birds bred at Slimbridge taken to release pen in Pakistan in 1969 (Savage, 1970; WWF Project 474, Yearbook 1970–71: 109–10).
Brown Teal *Anas aucklandica chlorotis*	10 birds released on Kapiti Island, New Zealand, resulted in 45 juveniles being fledged there in 1970–71 (Reid and Roderick, 1973). See Fig. 2.
Hawaiian Duck *A. platyrhynchos wyvilliana*	Birds are being bred in Hawaii in captivity and released in the wild (Swedberg, 1967).
Mexican Duck *A. p. diazi*	The Game Mgt. Div., Dept. of Fish and Game, New Mexico, USA propagated and released 295 birds between 1963–70 (see also Huey, 1963).
New Zealand Scaup *Aythya novae-seelandiae*	10 birds released in New Plymouth, New Zealand, resulted in population in excess of 150 by 1971 (Reid and Roderick, 1973).
White-winged Wood Duck *Cairina scutulata*	Birds currently being bred for release at Slimbridge and Peakirk (Savage, 1969). See Fig. 3.
North American Wood Duck *Aix sponsa*	Between 1922–39, 2579 captive-bred birds released in New England, USA. Project is claimed to have saved the species (Ripley, 1973).

periodic until evidence to the contrary (from moults, laying dates, etc.) accumulates. Endangered species should not be moved to zoos at vastly different latitudes unless a suitable zoo does not exist at the "home" latitude. The Hawaiian goose would have done better if Slimbridge's expertise had been much further south. Conversely, Slimbridge, during the same decade, could not have saved the Light-bellied Brent, which nests much further north. A few tropical wildfowl are difficult to breed in temperate zoos perhaps because they experience the correct daylength (roughly 12 h light and 12 h dark) for too short a time in the early spring and autumn, when the temperature is too low or the sunshine insufficient. It is now widely realized that daylengths can be manipulated and, in a last-ditch stand to save a species, this technique should be used.

Solar radiation, or lack of it, may be implicated in the non-breeding in temperate zoos of some species of tropical origin. A relationship is perhaps suggested if there is a wide discrepancy between the sunshine hours available to captive birds approximately 1 month before they moult their primaries, and those typical of the natural breeding season. On the other hand, too much light will depress activity, including sexual display, in some forest-living and nocturnal species. A good deal more investigation of these points is required.

The importance of a mild climate for tropical and low temperate species, especially the smaller ones, will probably not be overlooked. Protection from strong winds and cold rain may be more helpful than a high temperature; some tropical birds breed well in Slimbridge aviaries even when they are given no extra heat. If warmth is given in winter, it must be realized that heat emitted from light bulbs will also automatically *increase the daylength*.

Lack of rainfall in tropical and low temperate zoos has also been reported to affect the breeding of captive waterfowl, but no research has been conducted into this factor.

In general, it is wise to assume that the further a waterfowl species is removed from the natural latitude, the smaller will be the proportion that actually lays, and the shorter will be the laying season. Conservationists may need reminding that some feature or features of the natural environment have been bringing the endangered animal into breeding condition for thousands of years. While it is often not advisable to place specimens in a local zoo (since there is a great deal more to waterfowl husbandry than daylength and climate), the importance of these features should not be overlooked in selecting the most suitable captive situation. In general, the most successful of the reintroduction schemes listed in Table 1 were those where both propagation and release were controlled by the same agencies in the same area.

MAKING UP BREEDING PAIRS

In general, it is important to avoid brother/sister crosses. If males are suspected of infertility, then a sample of semen can be taken and examined for sperm numbers and motility, and selection of males made on this basis. Polygamy may be worth trying if good males are scarce, but the sexes should be previously unacquainted and the females of similar age and experience. Other things being equal, the *male* is the more important partner: it is he that is most influenced by stimulatory daylengths, and it is his subsequent courtship that brings the female into breeding condition. His capacity to respond to the conditions of a particular zoo will be inherited (to some extent) and his sons are especially valuable, in their turn, at the same zoo. The female's ability to lay fertile eggs is more dependent on her having an attentive male, than on a precise daylength. So distribute the daughters to other breeders (if there is any choice offered) and keep the sons.

NEST SITES

The right nest site may be critical to success. Again, it is best initially to consider the wild situation and imitate it as closely as possible. Many wildfowl either use nests built by other species (coots, ibises, etc.) or are obligate hole-nesters. A few species (perhaps because in evolution their distribution was tied to that of woodpeckers which made the cavities they typically used) are reported to have rather rigid preferences for nest-cavity and entry-hole sizes.

When eggs are repeatedly taken for artificial incubation, plenty of new nest sites, and eventually a different pen, will be needed. Many waterfowl will not lay again in a site that has once been robbed—a sensible precaution when the predator is usually a rat, crow or snake. On the other hand, the hatching of a brood reinforces assessment of the safety of a site, and the next clutch will often be laid in the same place. With species that are not determinate layers, the use of a restricted number of dummy eggs may increase the total number of eggs laid. A brown teal laid 40 eggs in 131 days (clutches of 10, 8, 6, 7, 5 and 4) when only three dummies were left in the nest, and they and the nest were removed as soon as the bird started to incubate (Reid and Roderick, 1973).

Nesting material is best restricted to something that does not easily grow mould in warm, damp situations (wood shavings rather than hay or straw).

INCUBATION AND REARING

The need to clean egg-shells before incubation starts is sometimes overlooked. Ultra-violet radiation is reported to increase the hatching success of domestic goose eggs (Monachon, 1973).

Totally artificial incubation is still not satisfactory for waterfowl eggs. "Natural" incubation (either under the mother or a domestic hen) for the first half of the period and artificial incubation for the second half seems to work well (which perhaps suggests that a difference in turning techniques is the key). If eggs are hatched in incubators (Fig. 1), then frequent and thorough cleaning of the apparatus is necessary. The value of domestic hens as foster mothers is questionable: they may carry disease, attack their charges, eat choice items of food, and go to sleep at "night," which is incompatible with the requirements of Arctic species.

It is, as already pointed out, a good idea to allow an endangered species to hatch its own first clutch (Figs. 2 and 3), or to hatch and rear the young of some related but commoner species. This will reinforce the value of the whole set-up

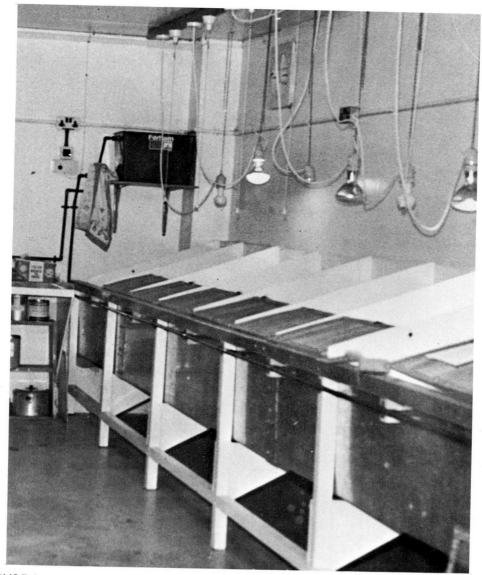

FIGURE 1. Part of the hand-rearing area at Slimbridge for young waterfowl. Important features are that: the bank of cages is at waist height; they have underfloor as well as overhead heating (and not all overhead heat is supplied by light bulbs); there is a running water supply to each cage (and a water cistern ensures constant pressure); there is a mesh-covered common drain at the front of the cages, into which water can overflow and food may be split. This drain passes through the wall at the back and out of the building; there is an extractor fan in the right-hand wall above each ten cages to ensure that airborne diseases (*Aspergillus* e.g.) are eliminated. (Photo: Philippa Scott.)

FIGURE 2. A family of the rare New Zealand brown teal rearing their first brood at the Wildfowl Trust. (Photo: Philippa Scott.)

FIGURE 3. A female and ducklings of the rare white-winged wood duck at Slimbridge. (Photo: Philippa Scott.)

for the birds, and make the laying of a clutch next season that much more likely. A strictly photoperiodic pair may not "have time" to produce a replacement clutch in a zoo at the wrong latitude in any event.

As far as possible, single individuals, expecially males, should not be reared with a foster parent or with youngsters of a different species. If this is unavoidable, the foster parents and the strange siblings must be removed early (in under 6 weeks) and the bird introduced to its correct species. Otherwise there may be difficulties at subsequent pair formation.

Factors important in successful rearing are: diet, heat (both under-floor, while the birds are very young, and overhead), the hours of darkness, the placing of any light bulb (hole-hatching species will climb towards the light almost unceasingly if it looks sufficiently like an opening in a tree-trunk and their cage resembles a dark hole), water supply (which should be constant), drainage, and cleanliness (the need to exclude disease-carrying rodents is important and sometimes not allowed for). As a practical point, cages for very young waterfowl are easier to tend if they are at waist level. The birds are, in any case, apparently less frightened by the top half of a human being (Fig. 1).

DIET

Waterfowl require a rather lower protein content in their food than is often supposed. Diets too "rich" are implicated in limb weakness, kidney damage and various degenerative diseases, and may also shorten life expectancy.

Adult Food Requirements

The representative composition figures in Table 2 give some idea of the "natural" intake.

It can be seen that a vegetarian, whether a seed, grass or root-eater, will not be taking a particularly rich diet, and most energy will come from carbohydrates. Fish-eaters obtain their energy from oil, and *total* intake may be less in these species. About 4 weeks before egg-laying, and during the moult, a relatively high protein diet is necessary, but not higher than the 16–20 per cent found in ordinary poultry layers' pellets. Greenstuff seems particularly important before breeding, at least to swans and geese.

For vegetarians such as the nene, then, a varying mixture of grain, biscuit, brown bread, poultry pellets and green food is adequate. For fish-eaters, experience has shown that eels are ideal, and sprats are a good substitute. Fish not absolutely fresh should be avoided, as well as dead fish containing thiaminase, the vitamin B_1 destroyer (or any suspect ones should be deheaded and gutted), and anything from polluted water. If fish-eaters have been reared in captivity they can be trained to take trout and poultry pellets, and do so readily. Wild taken birds are not so adaptable.

A permanent grit supply is essential, and quartz and fine gravel should be supplemented with shell grit before laying is expected.

Food Requirements of Young

Recent research has shown that growth rates vary in species originating from different latitudes. Arctic waterfowl, in general, grow faster, have a higher intake and spend more of the 24 hours feeding than temperate or tropical ones. So the treatment given should vary. Arctic birds need constant food, water and light, while tropical ones do best with roughly a 13-hour "day" and darkness at night. Temperate species need intermediate treatment. None has been shown to require a diet containing more than 20–22 per cent protein during early life. This percentage should drop progressively as feathering proceeds. Low-temperate and tropical vegetarians need little other than good grass in the later stages—cases of "slipped-wing" are more frequent when goslings are artificially fed on diets designed for turkeys. Kidney failure and leg weakness

TABLE 2. Composition of some waterfowl foods

	Protein (%)	Oil (%)	Carbohydrate (%)
Barley	9·7	1·4	54·4
Grass (close grazed)	3·1	0·6	10·3
Potato	2·1	0·1	19·7
Eels	17·0	11·0	—

also seem commoner in youngsters which are fed a high protein diet. It is likely, in any case, that a "forced" growth rate will reduce their eventual life span.

Some young waterfowl, especially of diving species, have difficulty in pecking at the dry poultry crumbs useful for the majority. They sieve their food or catch it beneath the water. Seeds, such as millet, coarsely ground grains, and live food placed in water are valuable until the young learn to feed on dry food from dishes. It is probably even more important to select a non-thiaminase containing diet for growing fish-eaters than for adults, as their vitamin B_1 requirements are so high. Trout fry, for instance, are ideal, while dead minnows by themselves may not be.

All young waterfowl tested have been shown to prefer to peck at green and yellow rather than at any other colour, at "worm" shapes rather than spots, and most prefer to peck at something that shines and moves. So sprinkling dry food with duck weed, or sieved (and therefore worm-like) egg-yolk will attract them, and most will find a wriggling green caterpillar in water irresistible.

DISEASE PROBLEMS

The water-supply to and drainage from all large ponds should be separate, since many waterfowl diseases and parasites are water-borne. Land will need to be left fallow, and water-courses empty, for 3 months from time to time to allow sunshine to disinfect them. New stock should be blood-tested, dosed with an anthelminthic agent, and perhaps vaccinated against avian tuberculosis (as should all young) before they are added to the collection.

Special disease problems can be expected with certain species from remote islands and coasts (Kelp geese), marine or Arctic situations (longtails, scoters), and mountain streams (torrent ducks, blue ducks), whose natural level of immunity is low. Only a rare individual seems able to meet the onslaught of

TABLE 3. The captive breeding requirements of the Hawaiian goose

---

Marking: Leg bands well tolerated.

Age of sexual maturity: 2 years, but 1-year-old fertile birds of both sexes are known in captivity.

Breeding group: Visual isolation for breeders in at least one-eighth acre recommended. Polygamy possible. Water area not necessary for copulation.

Breeding control: Species originates from latitude 20°N, and is non-migratory. Daylengths of minimum 8·8 h required for egg-laying at Slimbridge (52°N) but 9·5 h is more usual. Light for longer than 13·8 h causes moulting, again at Slimbridge. Low temperatures and lack of sunshine appear relatively unimportant.

Nest sites: On the ground, protected from wind. Will not usually lay a replacement clutch in a previously robbed nest.

Replacement clutches : 50% of females lay replacement clutches at Slimbridge, and 7% lay third clutches. In captivity in Hawaii, where breeding season (because of longer correct daylength) is extended, repeat clutches are more common and some females lay fourth clutches.

Incubation: 29 days. Females incubate well in warm climates, and, if allowed to hatch their own last clutch of the season, typically lay early in the same site the following year.

Rearing: Darkness at night recommended, and a temperature of 80°F at the start. Goslings should be no more than eight times hatching weight at 3 weeks of age and 85% of the adult's weight at 3 months. Fledging in Hawaii occurs at 12 weeks, and at Slimbridge at 9 weeks; perhaps associated with this is the shorter life expectancy at Slimbridge.

Diet: The gosling is adapted to a slow natural growth rate and low protein intake. Chick starter crumbs (19·5% protein, 3% oil, 4% fibre) recommended for first 3 weeks, followed by pullet growers' crumbs (16·5% protein, 3% oil, 5% fibre) until the sixth week, then mixed with barley or wheat. Access to abundant green food (water-cress and dandelion are particularly liked) is essential. Diets formulated for young turkeys (25–28% protein) appear to cause the "slipped-wing" condition.

  In the wild, the adult is a browser. Grass and herbage, grain and poultry layers' pellets (16% protein, 3% oil, 4·5% fibre) in the appropriate season seem sufficient in captivity.

Disease: Birds at banding age (3 months) have a shortish life expectancy at Slimbridge (5 years) but are not particularly prone to any single disease condition. Perhaps more individuals show degenerative conditions (e.g. hardening of the arteries) than might be expected. Females are rather prone to die of egg-binding, possibly in association with the cold weather common at the time of egg-laying at Slimbridge (and other temperate zoos.) Periodic de-worming of young and adults is of value.

Fertility: Perhaps because of inbreeding, fertility was low at Slimbridge. Selection of males on previous, or father's performance is of first importance. Males are particularly amenable to periodic semen collection.

FIGURE 4. Male Hawaiian goose at Slimbridge showing the small metal ring, bearing a number and the Wildfowl Trust's address, plus a large numbered plastic ring for individual identification at a distance. (Photo: Philippa Scott.)

pathogenic organisms that the mallard, for instance, hardly notices. Lack of crowding, and scrupulously clean water, ground and food all help. A veterinary surgeon may be able to prescribe prophylactic measures.

Lead pellets in the soil are an overlooked hazard in many waterfowl collections. If the place was once suitable for wild duck, it was probably shot over, and the lead remains. One ingested pellet can kill. So banks need protection from erosion, and concreting them is probably the best solution. Plenty of "real" grit will also help. Vegetable matter that is damp and warm is a breeding ground for aspergillosis, and all bedding for travelling and nesting boxes, and storage bins for food, should be dry, airy and mould proof. Botulism also flourishes in decaying material, and outbreaks will occur after dry spells when rotting vegetation and animal life have been exposed at the edges of ponds and streams. A changing water level, and decreasing flow should, therefore, be avoided as far as possible in hot weather.

SAMPLE REQUIREMENTS

The Hawaiian goose's requirements are outlined in Table 3. The headings serve as guidelines to the requirements of other endangered waterfowl.

RECORD KEEPING

Individuals must be banded and tagged so that they are readily distinguishable by all persons who come into contact with them (Fig. 4). Careful record keeping is essential if pairs, pens, nest sites, etc., are to be selected on the basis of previous success or lack of it. A look back through a diary of the year's events, with its references to courtship, plumage, moult, dietary preferences, etc., may indicate what is wrong, or right. Rapid publication of the results of any endeavour of this sort is to be recommended.

The Saddleback: its Status and Conservation

D. V. Merton

INTRODUCTION

One of the most successful wildlife conservation projects undertaken by the New Zealand Wildlife Service has been that involving the propagation of the saddleback (*Philesturnus carunculatus*), a starling-like passerine (Fig. 1). The saddleback, together with the rare wattled crow or kokako (*Callaeas cinerea*) and supposedly extinct huia (*Heteralocha acutirostris*), comprise the endemic New Zealand wattle-bird family Callaeatidae.

Like many other ancient elements of New Zealand's fauna, the saddleback has not fared well since European colonization began soon after 1800. Following its evolution in the absence of mammalian predators and competitors, the dramatic declines and extinctions which followed the introduction of such mammals last century are generally attributed to this cause, and in the case of the saddleback at least, the overwhelming weight of evidence points to its extinction on the main islands of New Zealand as having been induced by European man's camp followers. Furthermore, recent events have shown that the Eurasian ship rat (*Rattus rattus*) is capable of rapidly and completely exterminating saddleback, and some other indigenous fauna, from a 2250 acre (911 ha) island.

Formerly plentiful and widespread on the main islands, the saddleback had virtually vanished by the turn of the century. However, unlike other members of the New Zealand wattle-bird family, it occurred on a number of off-shore islands, some of which have remained free from vermin, and their saddleback populations have persisted: the North Island subspecies *P.c. rufusater* survived only on Hen Island (1195 acres; 484 ha) off the east coast of Northland (Fig. 2) and the South Island race *P.c. carunculatus* was, until recently, confined to Big South Cape Island (2250 acres; 911 ha) and two small adjacent islands off South West Cape, Stewart Island (Fig. 3).

Saddleback are capable of only a few yards of sustained flight and thus have not colonized other islands. Furthermore, because it is impracticable to exclude vermin from mainland habitats, it has been necessary to transfer birds to pest-free islands and to establish aviary stocks in order to expand the population, and so help ensure its survival. However, before this was possible it was necessary to learn something of the species' ecological requirements and to develop a means of catching, holding in captivity and transporting this highly active and elusive bird.

PREVIOUS ATTEMPTS TO TRANSFER SADDLEBACK

During an official Dominion Museum expedition to Hen Island in November/December 1924, the North Island saddleback was considered to be one of the most common birds present, yet the subspecies was in grave danger, being

FIGURE 1. The South Island Saddleback, photographed on Big South Cape Island. (Photo: D. V. Merton, New Zealand Wildlife Service.)

confined to a single island. Soon after, on 28 January 1925, a meeting of the Board of Science and Arts, acting on the expedition's report, resolved that steps should be taken to reintroduce saddlebacks to both Kapiti (5000 acres; 2024 ha) and Little Barrier (6960 acres; 2818 ha) Islands, in an effort to establish other populations. Permission was subsequently obtained for the removal from Hen Island of up to 12 pairs and for their release on the island sanctuaries of Kapiti and Little Barrier.

As a result, on 11 October 1925 a joint party from the Dominion Museum, the Lands and Survey Department and the New Zealand Native Bird Protection Society sailed from Whangarei to Hen Island to carry out this task. They met

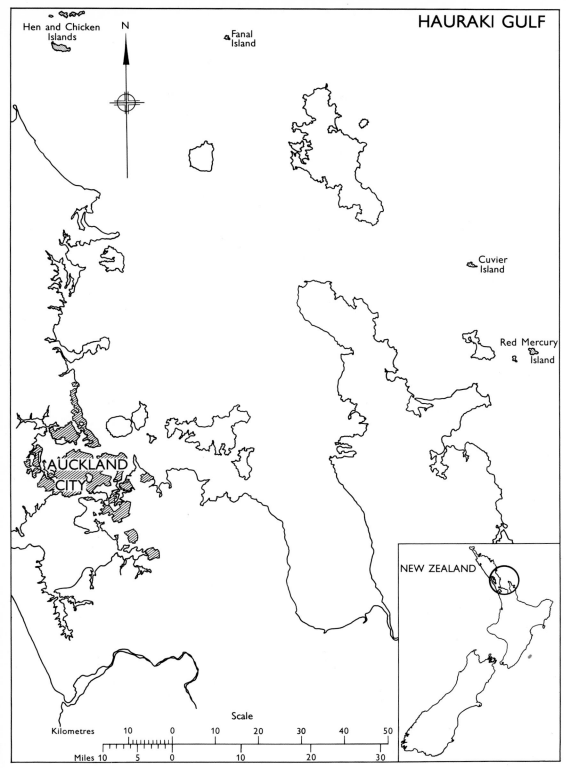

FIGURE 2. Hauraki Gulf, showing islands referred to in the text. (Map drawn by the Department of Lands and Survey, Wellington, N.Z.)

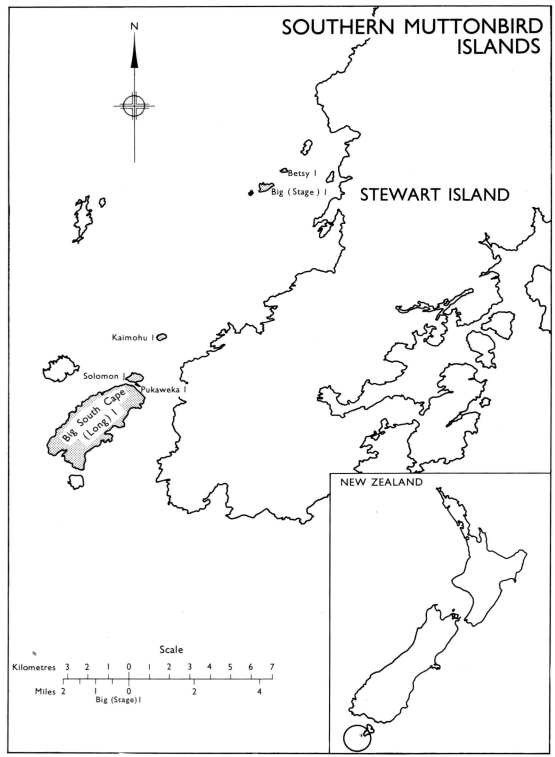

FIGURE 3. Southern Muttonbird Islands, including islands referred to in the text. (Map drawn by the Department of Lands and Survey, Wellington, N.Z.)

with success, catching the first pair of birds within minutes of leaving their camp. On 18 October, four pairs were released on Little Barrier Island but one female died soon afterwards.

By 28 October, when the party returned to Whangarei, they had obtained a further 11 saddlebacks, bringing the total caught to 19, all of which had been secured by means of bird-lime, hand-nets or drop-traps. The remaining eleven birds were transported overland by night from Whangarei to the Paraparaumu coast, from where they were taken by launch and released on Kapiti Island, 22 h after leaving Whangarei. On arrival, two birds were found to have died in transit, leaving four males and five females all of which were said to have been "a little bedraggled but perky". Successful breeding occurred at least three times during successive years, but birds were not seen after 1931 (Wilkinson, 1952). It was suggested that New Zealand falcons (*Falco novaeseelandiae*) may have been responsible for the saddleback's disappearance, but it is more likely that they, too, succumbed to the depredations of introduced rats and cats as did, it seems, Kapiti's original saddleback population. It must also be remembered that Kapiti, at that time, was over-run by introduced Australian brush-tailed possums, feral sheep and goats which had damaged the island's natural vegetation considerably. Cats, sheep and goats have since been removed.

The effect of the Little Barrier Island liberation was apparently much shorter-lived. Even under the most favourable conditions such a small liberation (three pairs and one male) could hardly have been expected to colonize an island the size of Little Barrier.

It was suggested that the saddleback were harried from the island by tui (*Prosthemadera novaeseelandiae*) on the second day after liberation and were never heard of again. This seems a most unlikely explanation for their failure to persist, as the two species live in harmony on Hen Island, and were previously found together throughout New Zealand as well as on several islands, including Little Barrier. The wild cat population of Little Barrier is the obvious culprit, as it was last century when the island's original saddleback population was quickly exterminated following the establishment of feral cats (Turbott, 1947).

After a visit to Hen Island in November/December 1933, Edgar Stead, a New Zealand naturalist, reported that saddlebacks were flourishing still and suggested that a liberation on the Chicken islands 4½ miles (7 kilometres) to the north of Hen Island would be beneficial, but it was not until 10 December 1948 that this transfer was recommended by the Rare Birds Advisory Committee.

Authority was granted to the Wildlife Branch, Department of Internal Affairs, by both the Minister of Internal affairs and the Minister of Lands, for the removal of up to 20 saddlebacks from Hen Island for release on each of the two larger Chicken islands. On 17 May 1949 a joint Wildlife Branch, Department of Lands and Survey and Auckland Museum party arrived at Hen Island to tackle the project. This attempt proved abortive, however, as by 6 June only five birds were on hand. Two of these were captured in a mist-net, two in drop-traps and the other in a hand-net. A severe storm then caused the death of two of the captured birds, so it was decided that the remainder should be set free on Hen Island again and the quest abandoned for the time being.

Another expedition was launched by the Wildlife Branch on 1 June 1950. This attempt proved more successful, as on 12 June three pairs of saddlebacks were set free on Big Chicken (Marotiri) Island (332 acres; 134 ha), two of these birds having been captured with bird-lime, and four by means of a hand-operated drop-trap baited with live insects. A visit to this island in December 1953 revealed that at least one pair of saddlebacks was still present, but none were seen subsequently.

RELOCATION OF THE NORTH ISLAND SADDLEBACK

In 1963 the ecology of the saddleback on Hen Island was studied in order that suitable alternative habitats might be selected for the establishment of further populations. Visits were made during each of the four seasons of the year and detailed observations were made (Atkinson, 1964, 1966a, b; Atkinson and Campbell, 1966; Blackburn, 1964, 1966, 1967; Kendrick, 1964; Merton, 1966a, b). The saddleback was found to be primarily insectivorous, taking its food from a very wide range of feeding stations within the forest. One of the most important of these feeding stations was the ground, where birds spent up to a third of their time foraging in leaf litter and decaying wood. Fruit was also an important item of food, but nectar was rarely taken. Young mixed forest with its rapid turnover of dead wood and leaves was the preferred habitat, rather than the more mature associations with little understorey or insect-rich dead wood.

As a result of investigations, the Wildlife Branch, in consultation with the Fauna Protection Advisory Council, decided to release saddlebacks on Middle Chicken (Whatupuke) Island (240 acres; 97 ha), and to retain a breeding stock at the Mount Bruce Native Bird Reserve in the Wairarapa district. I was assigned the task of carrying out this project, in January 1964; but first an effective method of capture had to be devised.

METHOD OF CAPTURE

The method of capture which proved most successful was as follows: A portable transistorized tape-recorder was carried through the forest and a territorial call replayed at high volume at intervals. Before long, the male of a pair would answer this challenge and rush to the scene, followed by his mate. Most pairs were obviously defending territories, particularly those with dependent young. Having located a pair actively defending its territory and after studying flight paths, a suitable site was selected in which to suspend a 20 ft or 30 ft (6 m or 9 m) 3-tier, 1½ in. (38 mm) mesh mist-net, a favourite position being horizontal to a steep shady slope. In tall bush, two nets were used, one above the other, the ties being attached to an endless rope belt over a canopy branch and under a root or log on the ground. In this manner a net could be hoisted quite simply into the canopy of tall forest trees.

It was soon found that saddlebacks, because of their comparatively weak flight and quick reflexes, were difficult to catch in a mist-net by normal methods, so certain modifications had to be made. The loops of the mist-net were brought closer together so that a 3-tier, 9 ft (2·7 m) deep net, when set for saddlebacks, would be only 6 ft (1·8 m) deep. The pockets were thereby deepened considerably, thus making it more difficult for captured birds to escape. Having set the net, a mounted saddleback decoy was placed on a perch 2–3 ft (60–90 cm) from the net on the uphill side and about level with the middle of the lower net. The tape recorder's remote speaker was set up near the mounted bird and the machine itself taken some 25 ft (7·5 m) away from one end of the net. If suitable perches were not available on both sides of the centre of the net, these too had to be provided. When all was ready, the operator at the tape-recorder set the machine going. It was found that individual territorial calls replayed at high volume at intervals were adequate to bring most birds to the netting area. If this failed, a recording of saddlebacks and other birds scolding a morepork (owl) (*Ninox novaeseelandiae*) was very effective and occasionally brought pairs from neighbouring territories as well.

Once birds were attracted to the general area, the tape-recorder's volume was lowered, and as they came closer, various calls were played. Attracted saddlebacks would generally approach rapidly from above, often high in the canopy, the male invariably leading. In reply to the recordings, he would give voice to a number of bold territorial and threat calls. At a distance of about 20 ft (6 m), he would bow and display to the decoy, his mate often doing likewise. All going well, the male would soon alight on the same perch as the decoy and cover the remaining distance to it with a series of hops and much threat-display. The operator would then make a sudden movement or throw a pebble towards the bird, so causing it to retreat downhill where the net was spread in its path.

Even greater success was obtained when two remote speakers were used. These were placed either side of the middle of the net and about 15 ft (4 m) from it. By means of a selective switch at the tape-recorder, the operator was able to call birds back and forth across the net, thus increasing the chances of a catch. With the disappearance of her mate, the female would become agitated by his failure to answer her. A few pair-maintenance calls replayed at this stage usually resulted in her being caught as well.

Birds caught were banded and placed in mutton-cloth bags for carrying back to the 20 × 10 × 6 ft (6 × 3 × 2 m) aviary where they were held pending transfer. Once in the aviary, they settled down quickly and were taking honey-water and a variety of natural and artificial foods provided for them within minutes. In fact, it was quite remarkable how these active territorial birds could live harmoniously in a confined space for up to several weeks.

During January 1964, 23 saddlebacks were released on Middle Chicken Island and nine were taken to Mount Bruce Native Bird Reserve (Merton, 1965). Unfortunately, all but four of the latter birds died in transit, due to a delay. Post-liberation checks on Middle Chicken Island revealed that birds released there survived and bred successfully during the following spring. At least seven juveniles were located there a year later.

METHOD OF TRANSPORT

During this transfer it was found that birds became greatly distressed by vibration, such as occurred on the deck of the launch, or by high frequency radio sounds, such as in the cockpit of the small aircraft, and losses consequently occurred. A carrying crate was therefore designed to reduce such disturbance. A 24 × 18 × 9 in. (61 × 46 × 23 cm) carrying crate partitioned into two was lined internally with acoustic tiles to deaden noise, and the entire exterior was sheathed with $\frac{1}{2}$ in. (12 mm) foam-rubber to absorb vibration and shock. Ventilation was by means of 18 half-inch (12 mm) holes drilled around the top of the box at such an angle that the interior remained relatively dark, for birds were least active in darkened crates. Access was via a mutton-cloth sleeve attached to the centre of the top of each compartment and up to four birds were accommodated on each side. Several hundred saddlebacks and other rare species have since been transported, often hundreds of miles/kilometres, in such crates with very few losses. Where possible birds were transported by night so as to avoid the loss of valuable feeding time. We also found it inadvisable to attempt to transfer freshly caught wild birds long distances or keep them confined in boxes for more than two or three hours. We considered it essential that they be placed in an aviary and given time to recover from the shock of being captured and to become conditioned to confinement before undergoing long periods in carrying cages. This period in the aviary also enabled birds to become accustomed to taking artificial foods. Where lengthy transfers were planned, it was necessary to rest the birds for several days at a midway point.

With any transfer operation the welfare of the birds is of course paramount and there is no doubt that the period immediately following capture is by far the most critical. Detailed arrangements for enclosures, food, carrying crates and transport must therefore be made well in advance.

Since 1964 the Wildlife Service has successfully transferred North Island saddlebacks to four other islands in the outer Hauraki Gulf. Each of these liberations has resulted in the establishment of a saddleback population on the island concerned and, with a captive stock at Mount Bruce, no further transfers are deemed necessary at present: 29 from Hen Island were released on Red Mercury Island on 30 January 1966 (Figs. 4 & 5) and a further 3 were sent to Mount Bruce; 29 from Hen Island were released on Cuvier Island* on 25 January 1968 and 1 was sent to Mount Bruce; 25 from Hen Island were released on Fanal Island on 5 February 1968; and 21 from Middle Chicken Island were released on neighbouring Big Chicken (Marotiri) Island in March 1971.

---

* Cuvier's original saddleback population disappeared soon after the introduction of cats late last century, but cats were exterminated by the Wildlife Service before saddlebacks were reintroduced (Merton, 1970).

FIGURE 4. The author (right), and Mr. Archie Blackburn, taking saddlebacks ashore in carrying boxes on Red Mercury Island, 30th January 1966. (Photo: New Zealand Wildlife Service.)

FIGURE 5. The author, and Archie Blackburn, releasing saddlebacks on Red Mercury Island in 1966. (Photo: New Zealand Wildlife Service.)

The 8 birds sent to Mount Bruce settled down remarkably well and have since bred, but not multiplied. Although nesting has occurred each year, mortality of eggs and young due to rejection by the parents, rat predation and other factors has been very high, and few have survived to maturity. However, at the time of writing (November 1973), the 4 saddlebacks held at Mount Bruce are all captive-bred birds.

RELOCATION OF THE SOUTH ISLAND SADDLEBACK

Like its more northerly counterpart, the southern subspecies also declined and disappeared from its entire mainland range at an early date. In fact, during the present century, but for several unconfirmed reports from remote areas, it was known only from three small islands off the south western tip of Stewart Island —Big South Cape, Solomon and Pukaweka Islands (Fig. 3).

In 1961 I was fortunate enough to visit these islands and found that although traditionally inhabited by several hundred muttonbirders for over two months each year, no mammal had been introduced. But for this seasonal cropping of the muttonbirds the ecology had been little disturbed and birdlife was virtually in its primaeval state. Saddleback and other species which had long vanished from the main islands were abundant. Unfortunately, this unique ecosystem was soon to be lost.

During the muttonbirding season (March/May) of 1964 a rumour reached the Wildlife Service that rats were now present and that birdlife was being affected. Knowing what this could mean, the Wildlife Service immediately sent a field party to investigate. This party found that ship rats (*Rattus rattus*) were in plague numbers at the northern end of Big South Cape Island and on Solomon and Pukaweka. Apparently they had gained access along the lines of boats moored in the various sheltered coves on these islands. Muttonbirders' dwellings and stores were being damaged and birdlife had been seriously depleted. Few rats had reached the southern end, and birdlife was as yet little affected there.

It was indeed fortuitous that we had in the previous months perfected a method of catching saddlebacks and so the expedition which visited these islands in order to salvage rare species during the following August/September was at a considerable advantage. We were entirely dependent upon the Royal New Zealand Navy for transport, but late winter was the only time when suitable vessels were available. Winter in that region is not to be taken lightly. Daylight hours are barely eight in number and the weather is cold and stormy with virtually continuous gales. Hardly the weather to be operating intricate mist-nets, or landing on the exposed rocky coasts of small islands.

By this time, however, the rat plague had swept south and was affecting the remaining birdlife, so it was imperative that our efforts should continue. We divided our small team into two, and while one party surveyed nearby islands in order to find suitable islands to which releases might be made, the others built a large rat-proof aviary and commenced trapping saddleback, Stead's bush wren (*Xenicus longipes variabilis*) and Stewart Island snipe (*Coenocorypha aucklandica iredalei*), all of which were confined in range to those three islands. However, with the extreme weather conditions and scarcity of the latter two species, satisfactory numbers of saddleback alone were obtained, and by the end of a month, 36 had been transferred; 15 to Kaimohu Island (20 acres; 8 ha) and 21 to Big Stage Island (45 acres; 18 ha). Only 6 wrens were released on Kaimohu Island, and we were completely unsuccessful in our attempts at moving snipe. Two were caught, but due to bad weather and resulting transport delays, they died. Fortunately, the saddlebacks took to captivity extraordinarily well. They fed readily and occasionally even alighted on my hand to obtain grubs. The tiny wrens, however, were kept alive by force-feeding with glucose solution and small insect larvae.

During the subsequent July, naval transport was again available and a further attempt was made to transfer the threatened species to rat-free islands. Unfortunately however, the rats had by now built up to plague proportions in the south and no snipe or wrens could be found. Small numbers of saddleback remained in some more remote southwestern parts of the island and with the greatest difficulty 36 were captured, but 5 of these died during severe storms. Breeding had of course ceased when rats first invaded the island, and the sex ratio had been upset such that males outnumbered females by 3 to 1. Apparently the rats had preyed upon the females while they incubated (male saddleback play no part in incubation). It was therefore with the greatest of difficulty that we were able to obtain sufficient females to make up the latter transfer. These birds were destined for Inner Chetwode Island (600 acres; 240 ha) in the Marlborough Sounds, 500 miles (800 kilometres) north of Stewart Island, and it was during this transfer that the soundproof carrying crates were to prove their worth. The first leg of the journey was a 10-mile (16 kilometre) launch trip to a sheltered harbour on Stewart Island, from where an amphibian aircraft conveyed the birds to Invercargill, the southernmost city in the South Island. Here, after 5 h in the crates, the only other loss occurred. One bird died from shock soon after its arrival. The remainder (30) were rested for a week in a large aviary before a Royal New Zealand Air Force "Devon" flew them by night to Blenheim at the northern end of the South Island. A light aircraft then took them on to a top-dressing airstrip in the outer Marlborough Sounds, and the last leg of the journey was again by launch. After leaving Invercargill at 3 a.m. on 14 July 1965, the birds were released at 9 a.m., all having fared exceedingly well.

By 1967, only 7 lone male saddlebacks could be located on Big South Cape, Solomon and Pukaweka Islands. Odd birds are said to have persisted there until the early 1970s, but no snipe or wrens have been seen since 1964.

The rat plague of Big South Cape has now passed, leaving in its wake a lower, more stable, rat population and a much altered ecosystem. Six species of birds disappeared from these islands; 3 of them (including the saddleback) were found nowhere else. Several other native birds are in greatly reduced numbers and the vacant niches are now occupied by mainly European species which are well able to live with rats. A rare species of bat, abundant on all three islands prior to 1964, is no longer found there, and according to Kuschel (1971) rats on Big South Cape are almost certainly responsible for the great reduction, if not extinction of a large and previously very common weevil. In fact, probably the greatest changes have been in the invertebrate fauna: conspicuous litter-inhabiting forms which were formerly abundant have been most severely depleted.

Fortunately, two of the saddleback transfers were successful. On both Kaimohu and Stage Islands birds soon bred up to saturation point and liberations have since been made from those islands. In March 1969, 16 from Stage were released on nearby Betsy Island (10 acres; 4 ha); on 2 August 1970 a boost liberation of 17 birds was made to Inner Chetwode Island and one pair retained for breeding purposes at Invercargill; and on 5 March 1972, 39 from Stage, Kaimohu and Betsy were released without loss on two islands (19 on North and 20 on Woman's Island) off the north-eastern coast of Stewart Island, and a further 6 were taken into captivity. Although the southern race has been released on 6 small islands, it has colonized only 5 of these. The two attempts to establish a population on Inner Chetwode have failed—possibly as a result of the high weka (*Gallirallus australis*) population of that island. (The indigenous weka, a predator of small birds and eggs, has been introduced from the New Zealand mainland to many off-shore islands, often with disastrous effects upon the ecology of those islands.) On Big South Cape, wekas are cropped severely each year by muttonbirders, who eat them. However, the Chetwode Islands are reserves and are not visited by muttonbirders, so that their weka populations are able to build up to a high density. Wekas there are now being controlled by the Wildlife Service.

There is no doubt that had we not taken the initiative of promptly transferring saddlebacks from Big South Cape when the rat invasion occurred, the southern saddleback, one of New Zealand's most fascinating birds, would have been extinct today. Perhaps the most unexpected result is the fact that the tiny liberation of 6 wrens on Kaimohu Island in 1964 appears to have been a success! Two wrens were seen there in 1967 and in February 1972 sightings were made which could only have been of this species, so that it, too, may have been saved from extinction. Furthermore, in February 1972 it was found that at least 25 per cent of the (banded) saddlebacks released on Kaimohu and Stage Islands in 1964 were still alive and holding territories.

Unlike the northern saddleback, which now numbers almost 1000 individuals, the southern race numbers only about 200. However, the Wildlife Service intends to continue to crop birds from the southern islands every two years and to propagate them to still further islands until they are well established in at least three island groups within their geographical range.

In the selection of these islands, care is taken to avoid those to which small craft may tie up, as these are regarded as potential rat islands. Of the many hundreds of islands off the New Zealand coast, surprisingly few have escaped modification and are suitable for the rehabilitation of saddlebacks (or other endangered species). Most have been greatly modified by clearing, farming, fire or the introduction of one or more introduced mammal species. Furthermore, it is our policy to restrict liberations to those islands where saddlebacks were once present and where the factor(s) considered to have been responsible for their former disappearance has been remedied, or to islands within the saddleback's geographical range which have suffered modification, but through chance or management are suitable for this species. Because of the impact such an introduction may have upon the unique and virtually unmodified ecosystems of some islands, saddlebacks have not been liberated on islands such as those in the Poor Knights or Alderman Groups.

In addition, the saddleback takes to captivity readily, and, when captive-propagation problems have been overcome, the Wildlife Service intends to build up aviary stocks through breeding and to allow selected aviculturists to retain these birds. Such a policy will not only help to ensure the species' survival, but will allow the public to see a rare native bird which is otherwise seen only by scientists and others fortunate enough to gain access to one of a few rather remote and inaccessible islands off the New Zealand coast.

ACKNOWLEDGMENTS

The very valuable assistance afforded Wildlife Service field expeditions, by volunteers from the Ornithological Society of New Zealand and the King's College Bird Club, in the relocation of the North Island saddleback, is gratefully acknowledged. The Service is most grateful to the RNZN for provision of launch transport in both the North and South Island saddleback projects, and to the RNZAF for, on two occasions, airlifting birds for release on Inner Chetwode Island.

My thanks are due to Drs. I. A. E. Atkinson and G. R. Williams and Mr. B. D. Bell for criticism of an earlier draft of this paper.

Breeding the Congo Peacock at the Royal Zoological Society of Antwerp

W. Van den bergh

INTRODUCTION

In various publications (Verheyen *et al.*, 1962; Verheyen, 1965; Van den bergh, 1966) the Zoological Society of Antwerp considered it a duty to make an important financial effort to acclimatize and study the Congo Peacock (Fig. 1), with a view to distributing the species in breeding pairs all over the world, after having acquired sufficient knowledge of their pathology and their biological and physiological needs. We have also described, prior to 1964, the difficulties and disappointments experienced in trying to carry out this programme. This present article provides a review of the breeding results obtained since that time.

In 1964 there was only one bird left of the original stock (the female 4, ring 705). One of the birds bred in 1965 was presented to the Zoological Gardens of Dallas (USA); the others were immediately included in our breeding experiments. In 1964 we had four hatchings and in 1965 six hatchings. In 1966 the results were even better and from four breeding pairs we obtained 9 clutches, 32 eggs and 24 young, 10 of which grew up in excellent health. In that same year, we lost 14 young, 4 of which died from aspergillosis and 5 from inflammation of the kidneys; the other 5 chicks which died were all extremely weak from the very beginning.

ACCOMMODATION

At the outset, the birds were housed in a special aviary 9 m long by 4·5 m wide. It was fitted with central heating and partly planted with ground vegetation. In addition tree-stumps and branches were supplied for the birds to rest in. The ground was partly covered with a thick layer of humus and the remaining area was covered with a layer of dry sand. One side of the aviary could be removed completely, so that the birds could move out into an open pen 4·5 m long by 3 m wide.

The temperature maintained in wintertime was 20°C, whilst the humidity was generally kept at 90 per cent.

Since we had many infections of *Capillaria* in this aviary, we decided to transform the housing into two series of inside aviaries, the floor of which was covered with a layer of dry sand. No plants were used. Nest-boxes were placed at a height of 80 cm from the floor.

FIGURE 1. Male Congo peacock (*Afropavo congensis* Chapin) at Antwerp Zoo. (Photo: Antwerp Zoo.)

DISEASE

Post-mortem findings indicated the following major agents of disease:
(1) In adult birds: aspergillosis (*Aspergillus fumigatus*); *Capillaria* parasites (*Capillaria obsignata*); coccidiosis and atherosclerosis.
(2) In young birds: *Capillaria* parasites, aspergillosis; coccidiosis and nephritis.

Other infections identified were tape worm (*Hymenolepis*); *Ascaris* sp. in the small intestine; *Heterakis gallinae* and *Pseudoaspidodera* sp. in the caeca; Trematode worms (*Euamphimerus* sp.) in the pancreas; *Candida* sp. in beak and crop and septicaemia caused by *Escherichia coli*.

CAPTIVE BREEDING

In Table 1, the Curator of birds at Antwerp Zoo (R. Van Bocxstaele) has summarized the breeding results since 1964, indicating for each year the number of breeding pairs, the total number of clutches and the numbers of eggs, hatched

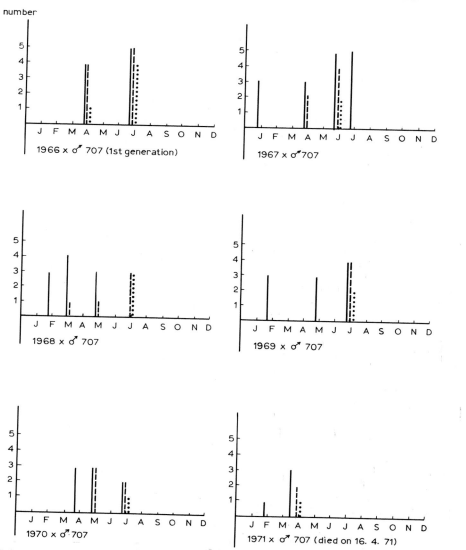

FIGURE 2. Synopsis of egg-laying, hatching and rearing for female Congo peacock 705 (imported 1962). Key: —— = egg-laying; – – – = hatching; ..... = rearing.

young and reared young. The table also expresses, in percentages, the progress of egg-laying and hatching over the 10 years of experiments. As a reference base (taken as 100 per cent) it has been assumed that there is a normal average of two clutches (= 100 per cent in column 4 of Table 1) and seven eggs per pair per year (= 100 per cent in column 6 of Table 1) under natural conditions. In order to increase the accuracy of these percentages, only the number of hens which stayed together with a fertile mate during the whole year have been taken into account for the years 1967 and 1968. Figure 2 gives an example of the

TABLE 1. Congo peacock breeding records, 1964–73.

Year	No. of pairs	No. of clutches	%	No. of eggs	%	No. of hatched young	%	No. of reared young	%
1964	2	5	125	17	121	8	47	4	50
1965	3	9	150	28	133	13	46·4	6	46
1966	4	9	112·5	32	114	24	75	10	41·7
1967	8	17	140	59	143	19	38	8	42
	−3	−3		−9					
1968	13	28	150	85	137	22	20·8	8	43·8
	−5	−4		−8		−6		−1	
1969	13	34	130·8	108	119	24	22·2	9	37·5
1970	12	33	137·5	103	122·6	21	20·4	3	14·3
1971	11	21	95·5	63	81·8	12	19	4	33·3
1972	7	11	78·6	29	59·2	4	13·8	1	25
1973	8	12	75[a]	30	53·6[b]	12	40	9	75

Specimen % calculation: [a] 8 pairs should on average produce 16 clutches, but only 12 (i.e. 75% of the expected figure) were produced. [b] 8 pairs should on average produce 56 eggs, but only 30 (i.e. 53·6% of the expected figure) were produced.

TABLE 2. Congo peacock diet

A. Basic Diet

Adult birds: universal food-mixture (home-made—see B)
a few ant-eggs and dried flies
6 mealworms per individual (morning)
grain and seed mixture
minced carrots
chopped green (salad, cress)
broken oyster-shells.

Young birds: after 24 hours, first 5 weeks:
mixture for young chickens
(Hens 0123) + chopped green;
6th week: normal food + mixture for young chickens;
after 2 months: normal food

B. Composition of the universal food-mixture

(a) VITAMINS AND MINERALS

(i) Dohyfral 13/6 50 g:

Vit. A	5,000 I.U./g	Folic acid	0·5 mg/g
D_3	625 I.U./g	Choline	100 mg/g
E	10 mg/g	Vit. C	12·5 mg/g
K_3	2·5 mg/g	Fe	1·25%
B_1	2·5 mg/g	Mn	1·50%
B_2	5·0 mg/g	Cu	0·125%
B_3	20·0 mg/g	Co	0·050%
B_6	1·2 mg/g	I	0·050%
B_{12}	0·01 mg/g	Zn	1%
PP	37·5 mg/g		

(ii) Pecutrine 100 g:

Bicalcium phosphate	40%	Oligo-elements 0·1% comprising:	
Disodium phosphate	30%	Mn	0·036%
Calcium carbonate	20%	Fe	0·007%
Sodium chloride	6%	Cu	0·00127%
Magnesium oxide	2%	Zn	0·0008%
		I	0·00038%
		Co	0·00043%

(iii) Minovit 40 g:

Vit. A	1,650 000 I.U.	Vit B_{12}	5 mg/kg
D_3	650,000 I.U.	Vit. K	1,500 mg/kg
E	2,500 mg/kg	Mn	1·010%
B_1	1,000 mg/kg	I	0·024%
B_2	2,750 mg/kg	Co	0·006%
PP	12,500 mg/kg	Zn	1·000%
D-Calcii pantho-		Cu	0·100%
thenas	5,000 mg/kg	Fe	0·630%
Choline chloride	60,000 mg/kg	Milocorn ad.	1,000 g/kg

(iv) Manganese sulphate 10 g

(v) Murnil 50 g: Hepat. Extract. in aqua insolubil.

(Min. 2 mcg biotin. natur. pro G. pulv. desicc.)

(vi) Iodised salt 250 g: NaCl 1,000 g   Kl 1 g

(b) ADDITIONAL CONSTITUENTS

(i) Wheat germ oil	100 g	(ii) Hemp seed	5 kg
		breadcrumbs	12 kg
		skimmed milk powder	5 kg
		pellets for young chicken	10 kg
		alfalfa-meal	2·5 kg
		granulated dried meat	5 kg
		dried brewery yeast	500 g
		algal-meal	2·5 kg
		honey	500 g
		cod liver oil	250 g
		fat	7·5 kg

breeding record of a single female, whilst Figs. 3, 4 and 5 illustrate some aspects of the breeding colony.

SUMMARY OF CAPTIVE MAINTENANCE*

(1) After eight generations we have noticed an increase in the number of unfertilized eggs, a decrease in hatching and a marked decrease in the number of reared young. Most of the young which were lost died of nephritis, possibly due to dietary factors (see Table 2).

FIGURE 3. Female Congo peacock on the nest. (Photo: W. Verheyen.)

(2) Mortality caused by parasitic diseases (e.g. *Capillaria*) was reduced practically to zero, thanks to the dry soil and a periodical examination of the droppings (to avoid general infection). A minor drawback to this dry atmosphere, although we tried hard to provide sufficient humidity, is the fact that the feathers never seemed sufficiently brilliant.

(3) Unfortunately we lost a few birds by accident. At least five Congo peacock died after they had been startled by cats jumping upon the roof of the aviary. Peacocks are extremely shy. Even a plastic sheet, loosely fixed at about 15 cm below the roof, did not sufficiently lessen the impact of a scared bird taking off in panic.

(4) The marked increase in the number of eggs, especially unfertilized eggs, resulted from the fact that several pairs had too many clutches in one year—we

* Prepared by Mr. R. Van Bocxstaele.

sometimes noted five and even six clutches. We believe that the lack of marked differences between dry and humid seasons could provoke this kind of negative development. A cold and hot season system might have compensated for this lack. But we have not been able to achieve the necessary conditions, as our

FIGURE 4. Male Congo peacock showing defence of the chicks. (Photo: V. Six)

heating installation did not permit exact regulation. We are now changing the coal heating system into an oil heating system with more possibilities for regulation. Although it is impossible to draw any firm conclusions, the figures shown in Table 1 for 1973 show a remarkable improvement in both hatching and rearing. The new oil heating system was put into operation in May 1972, with the result that winter temperatures in the aviaries have been reduced to 15°C.

Subsequently, there was a decrease in the number of clutches and eggs and an increase in fertilization rate. However, at the same time we also received a single male Import Cordier 1962 from Copenhagen Zoo, and this bird appeared to be a good breeder.

TABLE 3. Body weights of Congo peacock

A. Average Weight of Adult Birds
Male: 1677 g±27g
Min.: 1470 g±5 g
Max.: 1740 g±5 g
Female: 1316 g±50 g
Min.: 1140 g±5 g
Max.: 1515 g±5 g

B. Weights of Young Birds
(Based on young birds which died after a few days, weeks or months)

Age	Weight (g)
1 day	31
	35
	30
2 days	40
	40
3 days	50
	45
	55
1 month	230
	220
	230
3 months	680
6 months	830 (Male)
9 months	1250 (Male)
	1050 (Female)
	1000 (Female)

(5) The female becomes fertile at the age of 1 year, the male only at $1\frac{1}{2}$ years (see Table 3 for body weights).

(6) There is an individual characteristic of males: The white crown on the top of the head varies from less than 1 cm to 10 cm in height (see Fig. 1).

(7) The cock can live together with two hens without any sign of aggressivity, but he is only interested in a single female. He ignores the other one. In rare cases the selected female becomes aggressive towards the second one.

(8) The family bond and the breeding behaviour are not generally disturbed by the presence of grown-up young, even when these latter are already fertile.

FIGURE 5. Two young Congo peacocks (at eight days of age), photographed alongside two domestic chicks. (Photo: V. Six)

(9) We noted a remarkable development in the ratio between the sexes of the reared young, starting with 100 per cent males in 1965 and reaching 100 per cent females in 1970. We found that newly hatched males are weaker than newly hatched females at the moment of hatching.

Year	% males	% females
1965	100	0
1966	50	50
1967	33	67
1968	29	71
1969	40	60
1970	0	100
1971	0	100
1972	0	100
1973	50	50

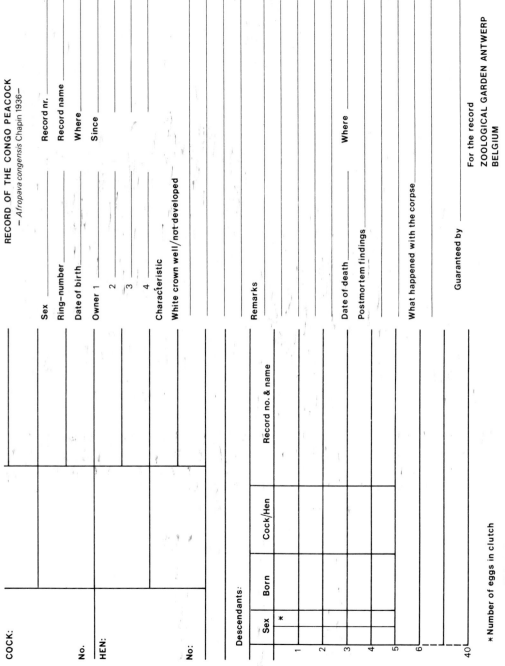

FIGURE 6. Specimen record forms for the captive stock of Congo peacock distributed in various zoos.

(10) To avoid general spread of fatal diseases and consequent great losses, we separated the peacocks into several groups; they are now distributed among three separated aviaries in Antwerp Zoo, two groups consisting of several breeding pairs and the third one containing a single pair. There is a fourth group in Planckendael, about 30 km from Antwerp.

(11) Following a decision of the Board of Trustees of the Antwerp Zoo, several other zoos have been entrusted with two breeding pairs each for the same reason. All zoos involved have signed a cooperative agreement (see appendix).

Two zoos are not yet in possession of the birds, as each is building a new house for them. The five Zoological Gardens selected for the initial programme are: Le Parc Zoologique de Cleres—in France; the Zoological Society of London—in Great Britain; the Jersey Zoological Park, Jersey (C.I.); the National Zoological Gardens of South Africa, Pretoria; and the Philadelphia Zoological Gardens, Philadelphia, USA. Dallas Zoological Gardens are next on the list.

(12) To facilitate cooperation between the Royal Zoological Society of Antwerp and the other zoos now in possession of Congo Peacocks, we worked out a record-system comparable to the studbook system used for certain mammals. We use differently coloured forms, according to the sex, namely rose-coloured for cocks and yellow for hens (see Fig. 6).

CONCLUSIONS

As mentioned above, over the last few years we have been confronted with new problems, some of which are really alarming, such as the changes in egg-laying and hatching and in the ratio of the sexes in reared chicks. There is also a lasting threat of epidemic diseases in pheasants, which could vastly reduce our breeding stock in the space of a few weeks.

All this might make one think that Nature has made up its mind and has decided that the Congo peacock has to disappear in spite of human intervention. This is a challenge which we have to meet, and we hope that the new measures taken, such as changing the acclimatizing conditions, distributing some pairs to other zoos, etc. will help to achieve our aim of maintaining viable breeding stocks of this rare species in captivity.

But this should not prevent us from facing reality. It is a fact that certain species which are fought by man with all the means at his disposal, such as rats and foxes for instance, maintain themselves, while others even succeed in extending their habitat in a spectacular way, such as the collared turtle dove, the starling, the gull.

Should we not then ask ourselves whether some species, which have now become rare, and for the conservation of which cultural and scientific zoological gardens are making the greatest sacrifices with little marked success, are not doomed to disappear and whether man's interference in these cases is fully justified?

APPENDIX

The Cooperative Agreement Signed by Zoos supplied with Pairs of Congo Peacocks

BETWEEN: Mr. Walter Van den bergh, Royal Zoological Society of Antwerp, Koningin Astridplein 26, Antwerp, Belgium.

AND: Mr.   ....

on two pairs of Congo peacocks (*Afropavo congensis* Chapin) for experimental breeding and scientific purposes. Mr. ...., Director of .... will furnish to Mr. W. Van den bergh, Director of the Royal Zoological Society of Antwerp, on or before the 1st November of each year, a report on the welfare of the Congo peacocks as well as notes on egg-laying and the number of their progeny.

Title of these pairs of Congo peacocks and their progeny shall remain with the Royal Zoological Society of Antwerp in case it is necessary to establish the species elsewhere or to replace pairs or single individuals in Antwerp Zoo.

Disposal of the progeny shall only be undertaken with the written agreement of the Royal Zoological Society of Antwerp.

The Royal Zoological Society of Antwerp will have priority in respect of all publications concerning these Congo peacocks and the right to decide whether any papers will be published in the Acta Zoologica et Pathologica Antverpiensia, or any other scientific review.

Mr. ....   Walter Van den bergh,
                                                                                  Director
Director of ....   Royal Zoological Society of Ant-
                                                                                  werp
Date: ....   Date: ....

Breeding Endangered Pheasant Species in Captivity as a Means of Ensuring their Survival

P. Wayre

INTRODUCTION

Whereas all conservationists are agreed that first priority should be given to maintaining viable breeding stocks of any species in the wild, unfortunately this is not always possible. The pheasants form a well-defined group of the sub-family Phasianinae, which also includes such closely related birds as snowcocks (*Tetraogallus*), francolins (*Francolinus*), spurfowls (*Galloperdix* and *Pternistis*), partridges (*Alectoris* and *Perdix*) and quail (*Coturnix*). More distantly related, but now included in the family Phasianidae are the grouse (Tetraoninae) and guineafowl (Numidinae). Pheasants are particularly vulnerable in their wild state, firstly because they are subject to predation, especially by man who has always hunted them both for their flesh and for their beautiful plumage, and secondly because many species have a very limited range. For this reason, they are particularly susceptible to changes in their habitat, especially the destruction of forests.

With one exception, the Congo peacock (*Afropavo congensis*) from Africa, all the world's pheasants, including peafowl and junglefowl, originated in Asia, and their centre of dispersion appears to have been in the region of the Hima-layas. During the last quarter of a century radical changes have taken place over much of Asia. The human population has increased at an unprecedented rate and concurrently the destruction of forest has taken place on an alarming scale. Much of Asia has recently suffered, or is suffering, political upheaval and under such conditions protective legislation for endangered species is out of the question; nor will field ornithologists have the opportunities to make prolonged and detailed studies of these species in the wild. Even where normal conditions prevail, the distances involved, coupled with the difficult terrain, often make any control or enforcement impossible.

Of the 48 recognized species of pheasant (Wayre, 1970) no fewer than 16 are at present considered to be in danger of extinction in the wild, and the actual number of endangered species may well be in excess of this figure.

Fortunately most pheasants thrive in captivity and, given suitable conditions, they are not difficult to breed in Britain, apart from some of the tropical forms. If a number of them are to be saved from extinction, large-scale propagation in captivity would appear to be the most practical measure. It was for precisely this purpose that the Pheasant Trust was founded at Great Witchingham in Norfolk in 1959. Its collection of pheasants is now the largest and the most comprehensive in the world.

The keeping of any wild animal in captivity has always been open to criticism on both humanitarian and moral grounds, but it is fully justified if captive maintenance helps to preserve wild populations by reinforcing them with captive-bred specimens, or even if it only diminishes the pressure on wild stocks created by the demand for species for zoos or private collections.

Luckily, most pheasant species are fairly easy to reintroduce into the wild, provided that a suitable habitat exists and they can be given some protection from predation. The common pheasant of the genus *Phasianus* is a classic example. Brought from its native home in the Southern Caucasus, this bird had established itself in the wild in Britain by the 16th century. The birds originally imported almost certainly derived from stocks bred in captivity, for it is known that the pheasants imported initially were bred and fattened in cages for the table, being considered too valuable to turn loose at that time.

Since that time, the pheasant as a sporting bird has been protected with obsessional zeal during the breeding season, only to be butchered with equal zeal a few months later. Despite this, there are parts of Britain where genuinely wild populations of the bird continue to flourish, sometimes in apparently unlikely habitats.

Turning to a less well-known species, the case of the Swinhoe's pheasant (*Lophura swinhoei*—Fig. 1) is perhaps almost as interesting. This species is confined to the island of Taiwan (Formosa) and is in danger of extinction in the wild. In 1958 a comprehensive survey showed that there were only 120 specimens alive in Great Britain (Wayre, 1959). The following year a pair of these birds caught in Taiwan was presented to the Pheasant Trust. As a result of this fresh blood, the Trust was able to breed more than 150 Swinhoe's pheasants in the following 6 years and in 1967 the Trust's first successful reintroduction took place. Fifteen pairs were taken back to their native island and some of them were released in part of the birds' original habitat in the central mountain range in a Reserved Forest belonging to the National Taiwan University, where their future protection could be assured. In 1968 a further six pairs were sent from the Trust to Taiwan for release in the same area. Reports since then indicate that this project has been successful in that the species has been sighted in the area from time to time despite the very dense sub-tropical jungle which forms its habitat. As a side effect of this scheme, it should perhaps be emphasized that shortly after the reintroduction the Government of Taiwan announced a new law protecting Swinhoe's pheasant and more than 30 other birds and mammals. Dr. Dien Zuh-ming of the National Taiwan Museum generously remarked that this step had been taken as a direct result of the Trust's activities. Even if it is

FIGURE 1. Swinhoe's pheasant. Great success has been achieved by the Pheasant Trust in returning numbers of this bird to its native island of Taiwan. The Taiwanese Government has cooperated with this project. (Photo: Philip Wayre, copyright.)

difficult for the authorities to enforce the new law, it is an important step in the right direction and shows an awakening interest of the Government of Taiwan in the wildlife of the island.

While reintroduction to a reserve in its native land is obviously the most desirable step for any endangered species, this may sometimes prove impossible because of total loss of its habitat, and in such instances a suitable alternative area must be considered. In the case of the Swinhoe's pheasant the Trust conducted a small experiment in 1966 in cooperation with the National Trust and

FIGURE 2. Young Mikado pheasants bred at the Pheasant Trust at Great Witchingham. The Trust is also working on a project to reintroduce this species into a reserve in Taiwan.

the Dorset Naturalists' Trust, who jointly own Brownsea Island in Poole Harbour. The island has extensive deciduous woodland with a heavy shrub layer of rhododendron as well as open glades, and it has supported a small population of the common pheasant *Colchicus* sp. which has not been interfered with by man in any way for the past 25 years. It was decided to release six pairs of Swinhoe's pheasant in order to see if the species could survive and multiply if left alone in such a habitat. Despite a few losses from avian tuberculosis brought to the island by peacocks which were introduced from another source some years previously, the Swinhoe's pheasants have not only held their own, but have increased to an estimated minimum of 24 birds, including young of all ages. This has taken place over the past 5 years without any additional feeding, and with birds leading a truly wild existence. While introductions, as opposed to reintroductions, should only be considered as a final measure to save a species, this example does show what can be done.

The Pheasant Trust is also working with the even rarer Mikado pheasant,

Syrmaticus mikado (Fig. 2), which is also confined to the central mountain range of Taiwan, though at a higher altitude than Swinhoe's pheasant (around 9,000 to 10,000 ft). As a result of receiving fresh specimens from Taiwan, the Trust bred no less than 140 young birds of this species in 1969. This was almost certainly more than the entire world captive population at that time. It is hoped that a suitable high-altitude reserve will be created in which young birds can be released to reinforce the very depleted wild population, and the Trust is cooperating with an American scientist (Sheldron R. Severinghaus) who is working in Taiwan on this project.

In November 1971, 12 pairs of the threatened Cheer pheasant, *Catreus wallichi* (Fig. 3), bred at the Trust were sent as a gift to the State Government of Himachal Pradesh, India, for release in a Reserved Forest near Simla, where this species used to be found in the wild but no longer occurs. This reintroduction was carried out in cooperation with the International Council for Bird Preservation, who generously financed the cost of sending the birds out to India by air. The suitability of the location chosen for this project had been verified during the author's visit to Simla in an advisory capacity as Hon. Director of the Pheasant Trust in 1967. A further scheme is in hand to reintroduce this pheasant to a reserve in the Margalla Hills in West Pakistan, where it also used to be found naturally.

The successful reintroduction of any species of pheasant with captive-bred specimens is not merely a matter of turning loose a number of young birds and hoping for the best. But here it is possible to draw on the experience of such organizations as the Game Research Association, who have made a study of the best methods in order to maintain stocks for sporting purposes. Briefly, it has been found in practice that the following procedure is necessary to assure success in reintroduction schemes and copies of this list will be sent to the authorities concerned whenever the Trust attempts a reintroduction project:

(1) The new habitat must contain all the requirements of the particular species concerned in the way of food, cover, water, etc. It is preferable if the release area is within the bird's original range of distribution.

(2) It is essential that the area can be effectively controlled so as to prevent any form of trapping, poaching or other disturbance. For this reason, well established wildlife reserves are usually the most satisfactory areas. It is important that the site chosen for the release should be easily reached by the reserve personnel, since the birds will require daily management, at least in the initial stages.

(3) It is often better if the local populace are informed of the project so that their cooperation can be sought.

(4) A wire-netting release pen should be constructed on a suitable site within the release area. The size of the mesh should be such as to exclude predators in

FIGURE 3. Cheer pheasant at The Pheasant Trust, Great Witchingham, Norfolk, England. Twenty-four birds of this species bred at The Pheasant Trust were presented to the Government of Himachal Pradesh and released in a reserve near Simla in 1971 to reinforce the depleted wild population. A further 24 birds were sent from the Trust for release in the same area in 1973. (Photo: Philip Wayre, copyright.)

the form of small mammals, snakes, birds of prey and so on. The size of such a pen depends upon the number and species of pheasants to be released, but for up to six pairs the minimum size should be 10 m in length, 5 m in width and 2 m in height. The pen should be equipped with troughs for water and with at least two rough shelters to give the birds protection from the sun and from storms. These shelters can be constructed from wood, corrugated iron or even thatch, branches and similar materials. Food, in the form of grain, should be liberally scattered on the ground in the release pen daily and fresh water must also be provided daily.

(5) In some species, the males become very aggressive when closely confined and may not only attack each other but also kill the hens. A sharp lookout must be kept for this, and any particularly aggressive males should be removed. In some cases it may be necessary to build a succession of small pens, confining one male to each. However, hens can usually be kept in quite large groups. Where more than six pairs of pheasants are to be released, the size of the pen must be increased proportionately.

(6) Upon arrival from the Pheasant Trust, the birds will be full-winged and will have been used to searching for food scattered on the ground. They should be moved immediately to the release pen and kept there for a minimum of 3 weeks. However, it is not wise to keep them confined to the pen for more than a month.

(7) At the end of this acclimatization period, four or five birds should be released one morning, and food and water should be placed for them immediately outside the pen. After an interval of 2 or 3 days several more birds should be released, and so on until all have been set free. During this time those outside the pen, as well as those remaining inside it, will need food and water daily.

(8) When all the birds have been released, the site must be visited daily and food and water provided for them until such time as they have become completely wild and no longer require it.

(9) If more than one batch of birds is to be released over a period of 2 or 3 years in the same locality, the original release pen can be used for each new batch of pheasants.

(10) During the time that they are in the pen, the birds must be examined carefully every day and any that show signs of damage due to bullying must be removed at once and kept separately until they have completely recovered.

(11) It is strongly recommended that only native species, and not foreign or exotic species, of pheasants are reintroduced in this manner. There is always a grave risk that the latter will upset the ecology of the habitat, to the detriment of the local wildlife.

The following is a list of the 16 species of pheasant in danger of extinction in the wild, together with their area of origin:

Western Tragopan	*Tragopan melanocephalus*	W. Himalayas
Blyth's Tragopan	*Tragopan blythi*	Assam and N. W. Burma
Cabot's Tragopan	*Tragopan caboti*	S.E. China
Sclater's Monal	*Lophophorus sclateri*	S.E. China, N.E. Burma
Chinese Monal	*Lophophorus lhuysi*	China
Imperial Pheasant	*Lophura imperialis*	Vietnam and Laos
Edwards' Pheasant	*Lophura edwardsi*	Vietnam
Swinhoe's Pheasant	*Lophura swinhoei*	Taiwan
White Eared Pheasant	*Crossoptilon crossoptilon*	China and Tibet
Brown Eared Pheasant	*Crossoptilon mantchuricum*	N. China
Cheer Pheasant	*Catreus wallichi*	W. Himalayas
Elliot's Pheasant	*Syrmaticus ellioti*	E. China
Bar-tailed Pheasant	*Syrmaticus humiae*	Burma
Mikado Pheasant	*Syrmaticus mikado*	Taiwan
Bornean Peacock Pheasant	*Polyplectron malacense schleiermacheri*	E. Borneo
Palawan Peacock Pheasant	*Polyplectron emphanum*	Island of Palawan

Eleven of the 16 species can be seen at the present time in the Pheasant Trust's collection, and eight are regularly bred there. However it will have already become apparent that a number of forms occur only in parts of the world which are at present in a politically unstable state and where reintroduction projects are unlikely to be possible for the time being.

The Trust has the only breeding group of Cabot's tragopan in captivity in the world and the only specimen of the western tragopan, which must rate as one of the rarest birds in the world. It is hoped eventually to carry out re-introductions with both of these species.

The Jersey Wildlife Preservation Trust has had outstanding breeding successes with another extremely rare and endangered species, the white eared pheasant. Up to 1966, very few individuals of this species remained in captivity in the world, and it was then that two pairs were acquired from China via Russia by Mr. Gerald Durrell and Mr. John Mallet, through Mr. H. J. van den Brink (Jabria). It is understood that these birds had been bred in Peking Zoo. The day after their arrival, the male that had been the more docile of the four was obviously sick and died later in the day. The body was immediately despatched for post-mortem examination and the findings were that the bird was suffering from a very advanced stage of aspergillosis. There was some concern for the well-being of the three remaining birds, for this particular disease nearly always proves fatal; there is as yet no known antidote against it. One of the female birds subsequently died, but in 1969, the remaining pair laid 19 eggs from which 13 chicks were successfully reared. In 1970 a further 11 chicks were bred from the same pair and 11 more were reared in 1971.

MAINTENANCE IN CAPTIVITY

At the Pheasant Trust, individual pairs of pheasants are kept for breeding purposes in large aviaries, many of them planted with berry-bearing shrubs which also provide shade and nesting cover. The pens are built on grassland and the smallest permanent aviaries measure 40 ft × 20 ft × 7 ft high and are completely covered by galvanized wire-netting of 1 in. mesh and 17 gauge. (Smaller mesh netting, such as half-inch, is even more effective in excluding predators of all kinds, but it is considerably more expensive.) Each pen is equipped with a dry, draught-proof shelter in the form of a small hut. The shelters for tropical species such as firebacks, *Lophura* spp., are heated by oil stoves or by electricity during the cold months. Over 100 such pens are in use by the Trust.

All the birds are provided with clean water daily and a constant supply of granite or oyster-shell grit. They are fed pelleted food which shows the following content on analysis:

Crude protein	19·0%
Oil	2.45%
Fibre	4·9%
Amino-acid values for lysine	0·94%
Methionine plus cystine	0·66%
Metabolizable energy	1190 cal/lb

Outside the breeding season, the pellets are fortified both with an anti-blackhead drug (acetylamino-nitrothiazole) and with a coccidiostat, and they are always fed *ad lib*. Grain is too fattening for some species such as tragopans, *Tragopan* spp., but it is fed in small amounts to others.

The eggs are collected daily and stored in a cool place before being set under broody bantams (small chickens) or in electric still-air incubators. The best results are obtained with bantams, and a system has been devised where 100 birds are accommodated in rows of setting boxes under cover, where they are fed and watered daily.

After hatching, each brood of young pheasants is removed with its foster-parent to a small movable coop on short grass which is kept well mown. In the English climate, additional heat is provided for the first 2 or 3 weeks by an electric element fixed to the lid of the coop. All coops are moved on to clean ground daily and the chicks are provided with a constant supply of clean water in a shallow dish. They are fed a proprietary brand of pheasant starter crumbs with the following content:

Crude protein	25·0%
Oil	2·6%
Fibre	4·0%
Amino-acid values for lysine	1·40%
Methionine plus cystine	0·88%
Metabolizable energy	1250 cal/lb

The crumbs also contain vitamins, mineral trace elements, antibiotics and drugs to control blackhead and coccidiosis. More delicate species are given maggots (larvae of the blow fly, *Calliphora* sp.), mealworms (larvae of the meal beetle, *Tenebrio molitor*) and grated yolk of hard-boiled egg in addition to crumbs, for the first few weeks.

At about 6 weeks of age, each brood is moved with its bantam foster-parent to a larger movable pen measuring 10 ft × 6ft × 4ft 6 in. high, fitted with a lean-to shelter. These fold units are moved on to clean ground every few days. When the young birds are fully feathered, their foster-parent is removed.

It is difficult to determine what constitutes a minimum viable breeding nucleus of any particular species of pheasant, but in the case of the more prolific egg-layers, ten pairs might be acceptable for a single collection, while for less prolific forms such as argus, peacock pheasants and tragopans, this number could well be doubled. On a world-wide basis, no species of pheasant can be said to be secure from the point of view of a captive population while the total number of pairs remains below 500.

Inbreeding has always been a problem with some of the rarer pheasants, but the consequences are not necessarily as damaging as might be expected. Edwards' pheasant provides a good example in that all existing specimens in captivity in the world today have been bred from a single wild-caught pair imported to Cleres, France, by Jean Delacour in 1924 (Delacour, 1951). It is true that a few more wild-caught birds were brought in in the late 1920s, which provided a change of blood, but none has been imported from the wild since then. Despite such intense inbreeding for nearly 50 years, there were at least 188 specimens in captivity in the world at the last census in 1968 and today there are probably well over 200. As this very rare species is confined to Vietnam, there is the possibility that it may now be extinct in the wild.

Since its formation, the Pheasant Trust has bred a total of 882 specimens of eight of the 16 species on the IUCN/ICBP Red Book list, and this shows what can be achieved in captivity. Furthermore, this number is being improved upon annually both in the number of species bred and in the total number of young birds. In the case of certain endangered species, including Swinhoe's, Cheer, Elliot's, Hume's, bar-tailed and Mikado pheasants, it has become necessary to limit the number of young produced each year on account of the lack of demand at home and abroad.

In conclusion, it must be stated that, given the necessary funds and the necessary encouragement by such international conservation bodies as the IUCN and the governments of the countries concerned, the Pheasant Trust could, within a very few years, breed such large numbers of at least seven of the endangered species of pheasant that their names would no longer need to be included in the Red Book. A longer period would be required to achieve the same success with some of the rare and less prolific species, such as the tragopans. Unfortunately with the exception of the projects mentioned in this paper, neither the funds, nor the cooperation from governments have been forthcoming.

Captive Breeding of Whooping Cranes at the Patuxent Wildlife Research Center

R. C. Erickson*

INTRODUCTION

In 1966 the Endangered Wildlife Research Programme was established at the Patuxent Wildlife Research Center near Laurel, Maryland, for the scientific study of threatened wildlife species in the United States. Five years of preliminary work with the relatively common sandhill crane (*Grus canadensis*) had already been completed on a limited scale in southern Colorado before the new permanent site for this programme was selected. The responsibilities assigned to us will ensure that the threatened species of wildlife in the United States, and the factors affecting their status, will receive continuing attention. They will also allow the assembling (in one place) of breeding stocks, providing opportunities for scientific study and giving insurance against extinction in the event of severe decimation or disappearance of wild populations (Erickson, 1968).

ORGANIZATION

The Endangered Wildlife Research Programme is under the immediate supervision of the Assistant Director for Endangered Wildlife Research of the Patuxent Center. It is functionally divided into three sections, namely Ecology, Laboratory Science, and Propagation. Seven biologists comprise the Section of Ecology, which is the field arm of this programme, at present operating in five states and Puerto Rico. These scientists study endangered animals within their natural ranges, giving particular attention at this time to about 20 species of Hawaiian birds and to the California condor (*Gymnogyps californianus*), masked bobwhite (*Colinus virginianus ridgwayi*), Yuma clapper rail (*Rallus longirostris yumanensis*), dusky seaside sparrow (*Ammospiza maritima nigrescens*), Cape sable sparrow (*A.m. mirabilis*), southern bald eagle (*Haliaeetus l. leucocephalus*), Puerto Rican parrot (*Amazona v. vittata,*) Puerto Rican plain pigeon (*Columba inornata wetmorei*), Puerto Rican whip-poor-will (*Caprimulgus noctitherus*), and the black-footed ferret (*Mustela nigripes*). The Bureau of Sport Fisheries and Wildlife's

---

* Assistant Director in charge of Endangered Wildlife Research, Patuxent Wildlife Research Center.

"Redbook" of Rare and Endangered Fish and Wildlife of the United States (1968) has been the basic reference source for establishing species research priorities.

The Section of Laboratory Science, when fully staffed, is expected to include about 16 scientists and laboratory assistants in the field of nutrition, physiology, veterinary medicine, pathology, behaviour, genetics, and related disciplines. Currently, only the first three fields are represented on our staff. This Section is primarily engaged in applied research into the biology and general requirements of endangered species and in providing consultative services to the other two Sections; however, it also pursues research of less immediate application.

The Section of Propagation is responsible for assembling captive breeding stock and developing effective methods of producing quality animals with which to restore wild populations. This part of the programme is no substitute for habitat preservation and management, nor for the enforcement of protective regulations, but it is directed mainly at species which have not responded sufficiently to conventional measures taken to assure their survival. This Section attempts to apply or test the most successful known maintenance procedures, subject to innovations resulting from practical experience with little known types of wildlife and to input from experimentation conducted by the Section of Laboratory Science. Wherever possible, preliminary studies are carried out with closely related, but more common, wildlife species before the findings are applied with endangered forms. About 20 species are now on hand, a dozen of which are threatened with extinction; the rest are rare or "stand-in" study species.

THE LAUNCHING OF SANDHILL CRANE STUDIES

The genesis of the Endangered Wildlife Research Programme dates back to 1956, when the director of the Bureau of Sport Fisheries and Wildlife called a conference of eminent conservation officials of the United States to discuss the plight of the whooping crane (*Grus americana*—Fig. 1). From a low point of 15 whoopers in 1941, the migratory population had risen to only 24 in 1956—a gain of only nine birds in 15 years. Whooping crane population growth seemed too slow to offset potential attrition by genetic drift, disproportionate sex ratios, senility, and other factors which may have been depressing productivity. The conference was, in fact, characterized by a clear polarity of opinion, with one faction advocating continuation and, if possible, intensification of existing management efforts in the natural state, and the other favouring the immediate capture of wild whooping cranes for captive management.

Although the meeting ended in a stalemate, the director selected an advisory group from the interested organizations to consider proposals for action. Several years later, recommendations to take sandhill cranes (Fig. 2) into captivity as a pilot colony for scientific study and for the development of effective propagation procedures were found acceptable to both factions and were overwhelmingly approved by the advisory group. The first sandhills were obtained in 1961, with subsequent acquisitions of birds or eggs taking place every year since. This has permitted establishment of a colony acting as a model for eventual management of the much rarer whooping crane (Figs. 3 and 4).

FIGURE 1. Pair of whooping cranes in enclosure at the Patuxent Center. (Photo: Glen Smart.)

EGG PROCUREMENT

Despite the fact that most whooping cranes lay clutches of two eggs, only about one-tenth of the families returning from the breeding grounds have contained more than one chick. It appeared advisable, therefore, to remove late

FIGURE 2. The greater sandhill crane has served as a surrogate or "stand-in" for studies and the development of propagation techniques for application with whooping cranes. All cranes are individually and permanently identified with laminated, plastic, numerically inscribed bands or rings located just above the hock where they are visible above most vegetation. (Photo: Glen Smart.)

in incubation only one egg from each clutch of two sandhill crane eggs to test, experimentally, whether natural productivity in this species would be substan-

FIGURE 3. Sass River marshes of Wood Buffalo National Park nesting grounds of the whooping crane. Biologist at top right is returning with egg from whooping crane nest and is approaching the helicopter. (Photo: Luther Goldman.)

tially impaired through egg loss or nest abandonment. The study in fact showed that overall production by the sandhill cranes was lessened little, if at all, by the egg removals.

The procedure has been to transport the sandhill crane eggs to the Patuxent

Wildlife Research Center in fibreboard suitcases, which are insulated with foam rubber against impact, shock and temperature change, and which are heated

FIGURE 4. One of 30 whooping cranes which have been hatched at the Patuxent Center from 34 eggs obtained in Wood Buffalo National Park, Northwest Territories, Canada. This chick, about 20 cm tall, is 3 days old. (Photo: Luther Goldman.)

with hot water bottles. Temperatures at mid-egg level are monitored by a thermometer thrust through a small aperture in the suitcase. The suitcases measure $50 \times 35 \times 25$ cm, a convenient size for carry-on luggage with most airlines and small enough for under-seat storage, though when in use they are normally carried on the courier's lap. A small saturated sponge in the suitcases provides humidification, and temperatures are maintained, in so far as possible, at 34·5°–36·7°C., with particular care taken to avoid higher values. Various portable mechanical incubators, and unattended insulated commercial styrofoam shipping containers, have been tested and found to be less reliable, yielding extremely variable rates of hatching success. With the suitcase incubators, hatching figures average about 75 per cent of all sandhill crane eggs obtained after about three weeks of natural incubation.

ARTIFICIAL INCUBATION

The crane eggs are disinfected by dipping into a 998 p.p.m. quaternary ammonia solution, and placed in a Petersime Model 4 forced draft incubator*, set at 37·6°C. This incubator turns the eggs by 90 degrees at two-hour intervals. Each egg is checked twice daily and when audible peeping is detected the egg is moved into the hatcher, which is maintained at 37·9°C. Because the standard $\frac{1}{4}$-in. (6·35 mm) mesh hardware cloth floor of hatcher compartments seems to provide inadequate footing for newly hatched chicks, $\frac{1}{2}$-in. (12·7 mm) mesh inserts have been substituted and appear to have solved the problem.

The embryo usually begins pipping about 12–18 h after the first peeping is heard, and hatching usually occurs about 24–36 h later.

The chick's down soon dries, and 24 h after hatching, the hatchling is placed in a 3 × 6 ft (about 0·9 × 2 m) elliptically-shaped pen constructed of two sheets of 2 × 8 ft (0·6 × 2·4 m) hardened masonite joined by butting the ends into two "sandwich-like" plywood couplers. A 5 cm layer of sterilized, crushed sugar cane, or bagasse, provides a satisfactorily absorbent litter. Water is available in gallon-sized (3·8 litre) poultry founts, and feed is initially placed in shallow dishes. The floor of the brooder room is concrete, and radiant heat maintains a room temperature of 26·7°C. The pens contain two 250-W infra-red lamps suspended at a level required to provide a temperature of 34·4°C immediately beneath the lamps at the level of the chicks' backs (i.e. about 12 cm above the floor). This temperature is reduced at the rate of about 2·8°C each week by raising the lamps, which are finally removed when room temperatures are reached.

AGGRESSION

The newly-hatched sandhill crane chicks may become pugnacious soon after being placed in the rearing pen during their second day of life. If only two or three are held in a pen, one or two soon establish dominance and continue attacking. Unless a technician intervenes, serious or even fatal injuries may result. This is less likely to happen if eight or ten cranes can be hatched simultaneously, so that the attacks are directed at more victims. It was soon learned that the simultaneous introduction of 10 or 12 day-old domestic turkey poults provided

---

* Use of brand names does not represent endorsement of products.

more targets for the most aggressive cranes, and although chasing continued, this activity yielded much exercise but little injury. Other methods of decreasing aggression have been the reduction of light intensity (including the sole use of infra-red bulbs as a source of illumination) and the provision of leaf lettuce, which seemed to help satisfy their pecking habit. The attacks gradually lessen and become inconsequential within 3 months, when the juvenile contour feather plumage has replaced most of the down.

CAPTIVE CRANE MANAGEMENT

After the period of most rapid growth and development, crane chicks are moved outdoors to the juvenile quarters, where the young birds experience their first contact with the soil and the pathogens it contains. These pens are managed on a 3-year rotation system, allowing natural agents to cleanse the pens during their two fallow years. The crane chicks remain in these pens for about 3 months, or until early December, when they are moved to the sub-adult or "hardening" enclosure. Here they stay for at least 18 months until they become strong enough to cope with the older cranes in the community enclosure.

Both sub-adult and community enclosures are spacious, with a density of no more than ten birds to the hectare. Each has one open-fronted shelter measuring 6 × 9 m that contains a constantly flowing watering device and two hanging-type, gravity flow, turkey feeders. The shelters are floored with a deep layer of pebbles to reduce accumulation of faeces and moisture. During especially severe weather, the sub-adult cranes may be held in the shelter overnight, although they are actually very hardy. The pens are located on well-drained soil protected from prevailing winter winds by the form of the terrain and by dense tree growth. The turkey feeders can hold about 15 kg of food pellets, and need be serviced only weekly, although both feeders and water founts are checked daily for proper functioning.

The founts receive continuous delivery of water through galvanized pipes located within larger drain pipes. The water, its flow rate controlled by a valve, moves up into a stainless steel funnel and drains through holes located at the desired level, then back down within the pipe, which serves as a sewer for the waste water. These founts have functioned in the severest weather and, since the water supply is partly protected by the drain pipe from outside temperatures, a flow of only about 250 ml per minute at $-18°C$ suffices to prevent freezing. With these watering devices, our water source of 200 l/min. can supply hundreds of founts, and the risk of plugged drains is almost non-existent.

The cranes remain in the community pens until they select and continually associate with a specific mate and show hostility at the approach of other cranes. This is a particularly dangerous period because aggression may be spontaneous and is frequently manifested shortly after dawn. Obvious sexual pairs are moved into 6 × 24 m breeding compartments. Besides feeding and watering devices, visual isolation, and provision for shade, the breeding compartments are also provided with electric clock-controlled incandescent illumination by means of which the laying season can be regulated, nearly doubling the relatively brief period of 6 weeks which is typical of greater sandhill crane breeding in the wild.

REPRODUCTIVE STIMULATION

Our sandhill cranes, though laying well for several years, initially produced no fertile eggs; but when our staff physiologist resorted to artificial illumination, egg fertility rose to 20 per cent. Later, by adding artificial insemination, fertility was increased to 60 per cent, and last year, with added staff experience and conditioning of the cranes, more than 80 per cent fertility was attained. Our present practice is to provide at least 16 foot-candles of artificial light starting at the end of Feburary; the photoperiod is increased progressively from 16–20 h, at the rate of 3 per cent per week, and the supplementary illumination is ended on June 30. Semen collection follows procedure adapted from those commonly used with turkeys. We can expect an average of about six eggs per experimental crane per season, although one individual laid a record total of 17 eggs in a single year.

Despite the good production of eggs and the ultimately favourable rate of fertility, hatchability has remained low (30 per cent) with sandhill crane eggs produced in captivity at the Patuxent Center. This rate is far below the 75 per cent average that we have experienced with sandhill crane eggs obtained from the wild and only slightly more than one-third of that found with eggs of whooping cranes. In order to increase the rate of hatchability of sandhill crane eggs, we have (a) modified egg-handling procedures, incubator temperature, humidity regimes, and disinfection procedures; (b) used highly artificial environments for better control of nutrient intake, and incubation by the natural parent; (c) dipped the eggs in water at regular intervals, varied the period of storage, and tried other procedures. However, hatchability of captive-laid eggs has improved little. Our facilities do not yet permit the degree of environmental control necessary for pursuing other intriguing research leads, though we plan this year to try to obtain semen from sandhill cranes in the wild for comparison with the quality of that obtained from our captive stock. It is of interest that the only known sexually mature whooping crane at Patuxent has yielded sperm of apparently good quality during his sixth and seventh year of life. All other whoopers at Patuxent range from 1 to 5 years old and have not yet paired. Last year, two 3-year-old birds were observed attempting to copulate; attempts to obtain semen from the male and to inseminate the female were unsuccessful.

CRANE DIETS

The staff nutritionist has developed four crane diets (Tables 1–4) as modifications of basic turkey rations. The initial starter diet is provided *ad lib.* as a pellet to newly hatched chicks. At one month, this diet is replaced by a pelleted grower ration which they receive until they are about 4 months old; at that time they are given a pelleted feeder and maintainer ration which is relieved only by a breeder ration fed to potential breeders from February through June each year.

TABLE 1. Crane starter diet

A. *Ingredients*

Yellow corn meal	Zinc oxide
Wheat standard middlings	Manganous sulphate
Dehulled soybean oil meal	Ferrous sulphate
Menhaden fish meal	Cupric sulphate
Meat and bone scrap	Sodium molybdate
Brewers dried yeast	Sodium selenite
Corn distillers solubles	Cobalt chloride
Dried whey	Stabilized vitamin A
Soybean oil	Deactivated animal sterol
Alfalfa meal	Vitamin E supplement
Dicalcium phosphate	Menadione sodium bisulphite
Ground limestone	Vitamin B_{12}
Salt	Calcium pantotothenate
Methionine	Folic acid
Ethoxyquin	Niacin
Zinc bacitracin	Riboflavin
Amprolium	Biotin
p-Aminobenzoic acid	Choline chloride
L Ascorbic acid	Inositol

B. *Calculated analysis*

Protein, %	31·4	Riboflavin, mg/lb	3·4
Fat, %	6·3	Niacin, mg/lb	48·0
Fibre, %	3·2	Pantothenic acid, mg/lb	10·9
Calcium, %	1·56	Choline, mg/lb	10,000·0
Phosphorus, %	0·87	Vitamin B_{12}, mg/lb	0·007
Metabolizable energy, Cal/lb	1294	Vitamin A, IU/lb	7507
ME/P	41	Vitamin D_3, ICU/lb	750
Methionine + Cystine, %	1·11	Vitamin E, IU/lb	11·5
Lysine, %	1·81	Vitamin K, mg/lb	1·0
Linoleic acid, %	2·54	Folic acid, mg/lb	2·9
Xanthophylls, mg/lb	6·93	Pyridoxine, mg/lb	2·9
Ethoxyquin, mg/lb	56·5	Biotin, mg/lb	0·1

DISEASE, PARASITE AND FLIGHT CONTROL

In addition to the use of a progressive shifting of immature birds through four different holding pen situations for gradual exposure to pathogens and for other purposes, the staff veterinarian has instituted other management procedures for health protection. At least once a year, all stock are tested for the major poultry

TABLE 2. Crane grower diet

A. Ingredients

Yellow corn meal	Zinc oxide
Wheat standard middlings	Manganous sulphate
Dehulled soybean oil meal	Ferrous sulphate
Menhaden fish meal	Cupric sulphate
Meat and bone scrap	Sodium molybdate
Brewers dried yeast	Sodium selenite
Corn distillers solubles	Colbalt chloride
Dried whey	Stabilized vitamin A
Soybean oil	Deactivated animal sterol
Alfalfa meal	Vitamin E supplement
Dicalcium phosphate	Menadione sodium bisulphite
Ground limestone	Vitamin B_{12}
Salt	Calcium pantothenate
Methionine	Folic acid
Ethoxyquin	Niacin
Zinc bacitracin	Riboflavin
Amprolium	Biotin
p-Aminobenzoic acid	Choline chloride
L Ascorbic acid	Inositol

B. Calculated analysis

Protein, %	28.0	Riboflavin, mg/lb	3·4
Fat, %	6·3	Niacin, mg/lb	48·0
Fibre,	3·2	Pantothenic acid, mg/lb	10·9
Calcium, %	1·56	Choline, mg/lb	1000·0
Phosphorus, %	0·87	Vitamin B_{12}, mg/lb	0·007
Metabolizable energy, Cal/lb	1294	Vitamin A, IU/lb	7507
ME/P	41	Vitamin D_3, ICU/lb	750
Methionine + Cystine, %	1·11	Vitamin E, IU/lb	11·5
Lysine, %	1·81	Vitamin K, mg/lb	1·0
Linoleic acid, %	2·54	Folic acid, mg/lb	2·9
Xanthophylls, mg/lb.	6·93	Pyridoxine, mg/lb	2·9
Ethoxyquin, mg/lb.	56·5	Biotin, mg/lb	0·1

diseases, including salmonellosis, mycoplasmosis, Newcastle and avian tuberculosis; individuals animals are inspected at more frequent intervals. Personnel attending to the incubation of eggs and the hatching and rearing of chicks avoid contact with stock more than 3 months old. When travel between functional areas is necessary, passage through antiseptic solutions with protective footgear is required of both attendants and visitors. Incubators are fumigated regularly

TABLE 3. Crane maintainer diet

A *Ingredients*

Yellow corn meal	Stabilized vitamin A
Ground oats	Deactivated animal sterol
Wheat standard middlings	Vitamin E supplement
Dehulled soybean oil meal	Menadione sodium bisulphite
Menhaden fish meal	Vitamin B_{12}
Meat and bone scrap	Calcium pantothenate
Brewers dried yeast	Folic acid
Corn distillers solubles	Niacin
Dried whey	Riboflavin
Alfalfa meal	Manganous oxide
Dicalcium phosphate	Iron carbonate
Ground limestone	Calcium iodate
Salt	Copper oxide
Methionine	Zinc oxide
Ethoxyquin	Cobalt carbonate

B *Calculated analysis*

Protein, %	19·7	Riboflavin, mg/lb	3·0
Fat, %	3·9	Niacin, mg/lb	29·0
Fibre, %	4·3	Pantothenic acid, mg/lb	9·0
Calcium, %	0·94	Choline, mg/lb	1283
Phosphorus, %	0·62	Vitamin B_{12}, mg/lb	0·004
Metabolizable energy, Cal/lb	1248	Vitamin A, IU/lb	3000·0
ME/P	63	Vitamin D_3, ICU/lb	600·0
Methionine + Cystine, %	0·71	Vitamin K, mg/lb	1·0
Lysine, %	0·99	Vitamin E, IU/lb	21·0
Linoleic acid, %	1·4	Folic acid, mg/lb	1·0
Xanthophylls, mg/lb	5·3	Pyridoxine, mg/lb	1·0
Ethoxyquin, mg/lb	56·5	Biotin, mg/lb	0·1

and, as previously discussed, eggs are dipped in disinfectant. Birds being moved to outdoor pens may be given coccidiostats, and individual medication with antibiotics has been necessary at times for the control of infections.

Some breeding stock birds, including cranes and other rare or endangered species, have been rendered flightless by tenectomy and tenotomy procedures which reach 95 per cent effectiveness, the remaining patients being successfully treated by a second operation. These surgical methods are described in a manuscript recently submitted for publication (Miller, in press). All incoming stock is carefully inspected and quarantined for at least 1 month.

TABLE 4. Crane breeder diet

A Ingredients

Yellow corn meal	Stabilized vitamin A
Ground oats	Deactivated animal sterol
Wheat standard middlings	Vitamin E supplement
Dehulled soybean oil meal	Menadione sodium bisulphite
Menhaden fish meal	Vitamin B_{12}
Meat and bone scrap	Calcium pantothenate
Brewers dried yeast	Folic acid
Corn distillers solubles	Niacin
Dried whey	Riboflavin
Alfalfa meal	Biotin
Dicalcium phosphate	Thiamine HC1
Ground limestone	Manganous oxide
Salt	Iron carbonate
Methionine	Calcium iodate
Ethoxyquin	Zinc oxide
Choline chloride	Copper oxide
Inositol (meso)	Cobalt carbonate
p-Aminobenzoic acid	

B Calculated analysis

Protein, %	22·2	Niacin, mg/lb	48·6
Fat, %	5·1	Pantothenic acid, mg/lb	13·0
Fibre, %	3·9	Choline, mg/lb	730·0
Calcium, %	3·1	Vitamin B_{12}, mg/lb	0·008
Phosphorus, %	0·73	Vitamin A, IU/lb	3006
Metabolizable energy, Cal/lb	1230	Vitamin D_3 ICU/lb	750
ME/P	55·5	Vitamin K, mg/lb	1·5
Methionine + Cystine, %	0·79	Vitamin E, IU/lb	26·0
Lysine, %	1·19	Folic acid, mg/lb	1·6
Linoleic acid, %	1·98	Pyridoxine, mg/lb	2·8
Xanthophylls, mg/lb	8·5	Biotin, mg/lb	0·1
Ethoxyquin, mg/lb	56·5	p-Aminobenzoic acid, mg/lb	10·0
Thiamine, mg/lb	5·0	Inositol, mg/lb	62·5
Riboflavin, mg/lb	3·6		

Experimentation has begun with the use of shelters which assure partial environmental control, particularly the regulation of light and protection against strong wind, rain, snow, or consumption of incidental food which may be encountered in outdoor enclosures, and which may supplant the prepared diets set out for the captive stock. The regulation of environmental factors may range from that provided by unheated pole barn type structures, with or without exterior walls, to closed buildings achieving varying degrees of heat and humidity control. In addition to the benefits to the animal, environmental control increases the efficiency and effectiveness of staff activity, lowering the overall cost, reducing the dangers of stress, accidents, disease, and also eliminating many emergency-type problems resulting from weather extremes, predators, or other hazards of outdoor situations. Such control may also enhance reproductive performance and reduce feed wastage.

NUMBER OF CAPTIVE BREEDERS

Our propagation goal is the production of maximum quantities of viable eggs. Considerable artificiality of the environment in which they are laid is essential for management efficiency, but is not expected to affect the quality of stock that is produced for the reintroduction effort. On the other hand, the survival prospects of released stock may be profoundly affected by the amount and type of conditioning received early in life in the captive environment. We would prefer to assemble this captive whooping crane flock over a period of a decade or more, so as to avoid any substantial adverse impact on the wild populations from egg-taking during any given period of time. It is also important to obtain and preserve as complete a genetic representation of the wild flock as possible in the captive breeding pairs. On the breeding grounds, nests within a territory are repeatedly located at or within a few metres of the previous years' site. To avoid inbreeding, this apparent territorial fidelity of pairs can be considered in the selection of captive mates.

On the basis of the apparent rate of attrition in wild pairs, it would seem that the average longevity of whooping cranes has been between 15 and 20 years, with a trend approaching the latter figure in the past decade. In captivity, the longevity should be much greater, and a maximum productive life of 30 years or more, with an average annual yield of six eggs for each mature female, should be a realistic goal. Judging from current and anticipated results, a breeding unit of 20 pairs of whooping cranes should produce 140 eggs with 80 per cent fertility and 60 per cent hatchability, and with 80 per cent surviving, thus yielding more than 60 offspring per year, based on current and projected progress.

For the purposes of our programme at Patuxent, 20 whooping crane pairs, plus a replacement unit of ten additional birds, would appear to suffice as a viable breeding nucleus. This number of birds should be separated into three or four separate sub-units at that location to reduce the risk of loss of the entire stock in the event of an acute disease outbreak or other annihilation of the entire flock. I would consider a total of 30 whooping cranes of breeding age in three separate units at one location to be the minimum number necessary to provide reasonable assurance of security of the species in captivity, inasmuch as the wild population has shown a substantial rate of increase in the last decade over that of the previous 30 years. However, if one also takes into consideration the favourable growth rate of the wild whooping crane population during the 4 years that eggs have been taken from nests on the breeding grounds, it would appear that these removals could continue as long as the responsible federal agencies deem it advisable to do so and as long as there is no undesirable impact upon this species.

SOME TRANSPLANTING PLANS

A subcommittee of the Whooping Crane Advisory Group has been appointed to consider locations where captive-produced stock could be released to the wild with the greatest prospects of success. The prevailing recommendation seems to favour the establishment of new breeding and wintering locations within the historic range of the species, but considerably to the southeast of Wood Buffalo National Park and to the east of the Arkansas National Wildlife Refuge, since it is preferable to keep the two populations separate, if possible, in order to ensure greater security of the species.

Among the release methods being considered, three seem most worthy of mention. First, eggs produced by captive whoopers could be placed in nests of wild greater sandhill cranes, with the expectation that the chicks would remain with the foster parents until "weaning" just before the next breeding season. The families would be expected to remain intact on the trip to the wintering grounds and back, with the chicks gaining migrating experience and protection comparable to that of other crane families in the wild. Perhaps the principal unknown factor in this proposal is the possibility of imprinting on the foster parents and subsequent hybridization of whoopers with sandhills at maturity. Tests of this possibility will be made as soon as whooping crane production begins at the Patuxent Center. Second, captive-reared whooping cranes could be held in one or more enclosures near the eastern edge of their former range in Canada for a year or two as they approach sexual maturity. Some of them would be rendered permanently flightless as a decoy flock, and others would be allowed to regrow flight feathers just before their first breeding season; it is hoped that they would develop an attachment for the locality and would remain to breed. Trumpeter swans transplanted in this manner have become successfully established in several national wildlife refuges in the United States, some of them making limited annual migrations from the breeding areas. Whether whooping crane populations established in this way would be likely to locate safe wintering grounds is difficult to predict; however, comparable releases will first be tested with conspicuously marked sandhill cranes in order to detect likely flaws in this method. Third, direct releases to the wild of whooping crane stock, reared in isolation at the Patuxent Center and held until at least the second or third year, could be made on the breeding and wintering grounds at an appropriate season of the year, with the hope that instinctive migratory traits would direct them northward or southward. Because parental training may be important in the establishment of successful migratory habits, direct releases may hold less promise than the other two methods.

Dayton O. Hyde, author of "Sandy" (1968), a story of his experiences in propagating greater sandhill cranes, described to me how he reared them behind V-shaped baffles, shielded from the sight of humans. The chicks departed from the compound as soon as they could fly and shunned association with humans as much as did their wild-reared counterparts. Conversely, cranes reared in captivity with no special effort to prevent contact with those who tended them have shown little inclination to revert to the wild following their release, but instead have returned to areas of human activity.

Judging from our experience and that of Mr. Hyde, programmes designed to release cranes to establish independent populations may have to provide ample rearing space and specialized pens to prevent visual contact with keepers. The more than 800 acres of land occupied by the Endangered Wildlife Research Programme would seem to be adequate for the rearing and pre-release conditioning of a captive-reared stock of cranes and of other types of endangered wildlife.

It should be emphasized that the above discussion of future measures for taking of wild whooping cranes or their eggs into captivity, and of the methods to be employed in returning the captive-produced stock to the wild, are my personal opinions. Actual decisions regarding these activities, as well as distribution of birds to non-federal parties will, as in the past, rest with the directors of the Canadian Wildlife Service and the Bureau of Sport Fisheries and Wildlife, in consultation with other wildlife conservation interests.

Returning the Hawaiian Goose to the Wild

J. Kear

The Hawaiian goose, *Branta sandvicensis*, is one of three species of the Family Anatidae restricted to the Hawaiian archipelago. All three are currently listed in the IUCN *Red Data Book* as being rare and endangered. Two are ducks that have features peculiar to remote island forms but are obviously still dabbling waterfowl. The goose, on the other hand, has become highly modified by its life in open, sparsely-vegetated, volcanic areas, where it finds standing water only in temporary rain pools.

HISTORY OF DECLINE

In the 18th century, the Hawaiian goose, commonly called the nene, was widespread below 9000 ft on the tropical island of Hawaii between latitudes 19°N and 21°N. In 150 years its numbers dropped from 25,000 to under 50 and only an estimated 35 wild individuals remained in 1949. A variety of man-made factors contributed to that dramatic decline. Like many island creatures, the bird is tame and after the introduction of fire-arms, was easily killed. In addition, its breeding season begins as the hours of daylight grow less, an unusual feature presumably based on the period at which the best food supply is available for the goslings. In Hawaii, the first eggs are laid in September and breeding lasts into March. One reason for the species' decline was a $4\frac{1}{2}$-month hunting season, with a bag limit of six birds, which coincided with nesting activities. The white man shot during autumn and winter in his temperate home, and saw no reason why tropical game birds should not fit the pattern to which he was accustomed. Thousands were killed and salted to provision Pacific whaling ships. The lowland breeding areas were also drastically altered by the encroachment of sugarcane plantations and the grazing of sheep and goats. Pairs nesting in the high lava fields suffered from the introduction of predators such as mongoose, rat, wild pig, cat and dog.

THE RESTORATION PROJECT

The history of nene conservation has come to be something of a classic case. A combination of good fortune, the farsightedness of certain Hawaiian agencies and the fact that the species will breed readily in captivity has contributed to the success of the conservation programme. As long ago as 1902, H. W. Henshaw pointed out the foolishness of the winter shooting season and the need for planning to save the nene from extinction. Hunting ceased in 1911, but it was not until 40 years later that an official survey was sponsored by the Hawaiian Board of Agriculture and Forestry. The objectives were to study the biology of the wild population, to prepare management recommendations, and to assess the efforts being made by the Board in Hawaii and the Wildfowl Trust in England to rear nene in captivity. The Board began breeding in 1949 with two pairs of geese, and a third pair was added in the following year. The Wildfowl Trust birds, two females and a male, produced nine goslings for the first time in 1952. All geese were lent by Herbert Shipman, a Hawaiian ranch owner who, realizing the perilous state of the species, had maintained a small flock on his property since 1918.

Initially, the production of goslings in captivity was rather disappointing. At both breeding centres, the first and second clutches of eggs were removed and hatched by foster mothers (hens or muscovy ducks). Some geese then laid replacement clutches, up to two in England, and occasionally three repeat clutches a season in Hawaii. Despite the high fecundity of the females, a large number of the eggs laid in the 1950s failed to hatch, mainly because they were infertile, but also because of poor incubation techniques. However, by 1955 there were probably more birds in captivity than in the wild, and nearly one-third of the world's population was in England.

It seemed likely that the problem of low fertility had arisen from inbreeding, since all the captive stock in the world stemmed from a few original pairs in Shipman's flock. It was felt that an introduction of new stock was essential, and a pair of wild nene and one young bird were captured in March 1960 for breeding purposes, and taken to the Pohakuloa headquarters of the restoration project. Goslings obtained were later paired with captive geese both in Hawaii and England. This out-breeding had considerable success and fertility levels rose at both centres.

Improved incubation procedures, sound nutrition and vigorous selective breeding also helped. Males known to be fertile, or males with particularly fertile fathers, were paired with females known to lay a large number of eggs each season, or with their daughters. Ganders with poor fertility records were shown to produce relatively few sperm. These and other unsuccessful nesters and their offspring were eliminated from the breeding programme. As a result, the fertility of eggs laid at the Wildfowl Trust rose from 40 per cent to over 80 per cent in 4 years. One hundred goslings were produced in Britain in 1970 (Figs. 1, 2 and 3), and 114 at Pohakuloa in the same year (Fig. 4).

RELEASE INTO THE WILD

March 17, 1960 saw the first release of 20 Pohakuloa-reared geese to augment the 50 or so birds in the wild flock. An area of one acre had been acquired near the known breeding ground and surrounded by a predator-proof fence. Birds selected for release were colour-banded and put into the open-topped pen with plucked primaries, so that they could become conditioned to natural foods while also receiving their routine diet. After the growth of new feathers, they gradually flew farther and farther from the release pen, at first returning to feed and rest at night. Finally, they joined the wild birds during their normal flocking season. Two more nene sanctuaries and release areas were acquired, and the project seemed to be working out ideally.

FIGURE 1. Hawaiian goose, or nene, nesting at Slimbridge. Adult female with a newly hatched gosling. (Photo: K. W. Holder.)

The first release of 30 English-bred nene was made on 26 July 1962, not on the island of Hawaii, but in the 20 square miles of the Haleakala crater on Maui (Fig. 5), where the species had become extinct during the 19th century. This was done to ensure that the remaining wild birds would not be contaminated by any undesirable features acquired by the English stock. The geese were, of course, as disease-free as careful treatment and a 21-day quarantine at Clinton, New Jersey, could make them; but precautions were taken to exclude the remotest chance of trouble. Ten of the 30 birds were 4 months old, seven just over 1 year old, ten 2 years old, two 3 years old and one 4 years old. Five Pohakuloa-reared birds were released with them.

The trip to Haleakala was made by truck. Here the birds, in cardboard boxes, were loaded on to packs and a group of volunteer Boy Scouts carried them the 8½ miles down into the crater and across to the release pen on the other side.

It had been decided to locate the release pen near the Paliku ranger cabin within the Haleakala National Park because: (a) the area was excellent nene habitat and contained year-round feed; (b) its remoteness would insure minimum disturbance and (c) accommodation was available at the Park Service cabin for personnel caring for the birds.

FIGURE 2. A pair of Hawaiian geese with 5-week-old goslings at Slimbridge. Note that both parents have moulted their flight feathers and are also losing body plumage. There is a female Hawaiian duck in the background. (Photo: Philippa Scott.)

The following quotation (from the Report on the Nene Restoration Programme (1972), State of Hawaii, Division of Fish and Game) provides a good description of the release pen:

> The pen is situated at the edge of an ancient "aa" lava flow It encompasses about an acre of good grass cover, mostly mesquite grass (*Holcus lanatus*) and mountain pili (*Panicum tenuifolium*), plus sheep sorrel (*Rumex acetocella*) and gosmore (*Hypochaeris radicata*). There are also small amounts of kukaenene (*Coprosma ernodeoides*) and pukiawe (*Styphelia tameimeiae*) within the pen. All of these plants are good nene foods and are very abundant in the general vicinity.

The pen was constructed of one-inch poultry wire, six feet high supported by steel posts. An additional three-foot piece of one-inch wire was clipped to the bottom, buried one foot and turned out for a foot or more and covered with earth. All of the materials were hauled some 12 miles on mules furnished by the National Park Service.

Prior to placing the nene in the pen, the perimeter and immediate vicinity were heavily baited with poisoned meat. This was done to eliminate any mongooses, feral cats or dogs which might be in the area.

FIGURE 3. A flock of Hawaiian geese reared at Slimbridge. The adults can be distinguished by their pale necks; the juveniles (mainly in the centre) have darker necks and a more spotted appearance of the plumage. (Photo: Philippa Scott.)

As the birds were removed from the boxes, each was examined and the clipped primaries pulled. This was done so that new feathers would start growing immediately. They were supplied with native berries and scratch feed daily, and soon settled down and appeared to get on well. While in the pen, they were treated for coccidiosis and caecal worms, since an examination of droppings indicated that these parasites were present.

The birds began flying within the pen during early September and the first flights out occurred on the 12th. By the end of the month, 27 of the 35 nene were flying. It became apparent that four birds had damaged primaries, probably incurred when the replacing quills brushed against the wire of the pen. These primaries were pulled again, and the birds were able to fly by January 1963.

In December, two females were found dead in the pen and sharp puncture wounds indicated that mongoose were the probable cause of death.

An extensive search was made for nests during 1963; however, none was found. No broods were seen and it is assumed that since no unbanded nene were reported, breeding did not occur during the first year. Birds were seen as far as 15 miles away, and a number did not return to the release pen for some months.

FIGURE 4. The captive-rearing centre for Hawaiian geese at Pohakuloa, Hawaii. Over 1000 birds have been reared here since 1949. (Photo: Russ Kinne.)

On 30 July 1963 a second release was made of 19 nene from England, five from Dillon Ripley in Connecticut, and five from Pohakuloa. The operation followed a similar successful pattern. Only two of the 1962 birds were seen in the release area; the rest had been tempted out, apparently by the lush growth of vegetation. The new birds began to feed immediately on the mesquite grass (seeds and leaves) and the gosmore (leaves, stems and flower heads). The Hawaiian and English birds, though remaining in rather distinct flocks while in the pen, mixed well outside, and pecking and chasing was non-existent.

Releases have continued, and by July 1973, 391 birds had been placed on Maui (Table 1), and a total of 1195 on both islands.

RESULTS

In terms of breeding success, birds that are able to join a wild flock appear to be at an advantage, probably because traditional feeding patterns, flight lines and nesting areas are readily acquired. During the 1966–67 season in Hawaii, a record number of 15 nests and broods were recorded with a total production of 22 young, and wild and banded (released) nenes have together produced goslings in at least two places.

There are 600 square miles of suitable habitat on the "big island" as compared with 20 on Maui. Nests have been found on Maui (seven in the 1967–68 season, for instance), but goslings seldom survived beyond a week or two. Bad

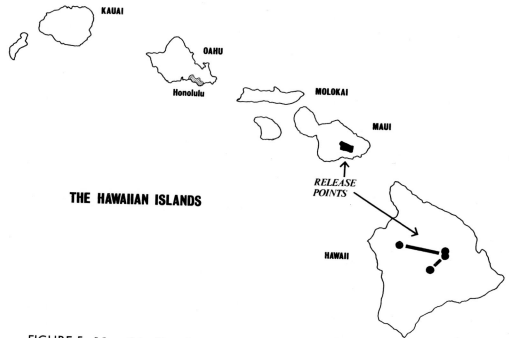

FIGURE 5. Map of the Hawaiian Islands, showing the release points (see also Table 1).

weather at hatching, rainstorms and hail seem to have been principally responsible. However, in July 1971, an adult banded pair was seen with (for the first time) three fully fledged goslings. The goose was a Hawaiian-reared bird released in 1968, and the gander came from England in 1969. The birds seemed to have nested within a mile-and-a-half of the release site, and the successful brood was probably the result of re-nesting. One conservationist on the spot feels that all first clutches on Maui should be removed for artificial rearing (and release), thus forcing birds to lay again at a time when the climate is more favourable.

Certainly the later releases on Maui seem to have been more successful than the first. Perhaps this is because there are more birds to join, but it probably also reflects the younger age of later releases, in which no birds have been older than 4 months. They are almost certainly more adaptable than geese that have spent at least 1 year in captivity.

In March 1972, three pairs of pinioned birds were brought from Pohakuloa to pens at the headquarters of the Haleakala National Park on Maui. The plan, conceived by Jerome J. Pratt of the park staff, is that the birds will give visitors a chance to view an endangered species at close range. The birds' breeding can be supervised, and their offspring allowed to go free, perhaps to join the geese already released some 8 miles away across the park, or to nest nearby. If the scheme is successful, it will be far less costly than shipping birds from England.

TABLE 1. Nene releases on Hawaii and Maui, 1960–1972 (May)

| Year | Numbers reared at Pohakuloa and released on Hawaii | Numbers released on Maui: | | | Total | Grand Total |
		From Britain	From Pohakuloa	From Connecticut		
1960	20	—	—	—	—	20
1961	31	—	—	—	—	31
1962	35	30	5	—	35	70
1963	42	19	5	5	29	71
1964	—	19	8	—	27	27
1965	49	24	8	2	34	83
1966	—	—	25	—	25	25
1967	75	—	—	—	—	75
1968	85	—	20	—	20	105
1969	155	50	22	—	72	227
1970	110	55	—	—	55	165
1971	110	—	—	—	—	110
1972	45	—	44	—	44	89
1973	47	—	50	—	50	97
Totals to date	804	197[a]	187	7	391	1195

[a] 200 were actually sent, but three died before release.

In 1969 and 1970 an assessment was made of the cost of returning 100 nenes to the wild, from breeding to release.

Apart from the £12 per bird for international air freightage from London to New York, payments amounting to £1400 for housing, feeding, veterinary care, quarantining, local transport, agents' expenses, cables, etc. were made. The larger part of this was met by the Wildfowl Trust, but contributions also came from J. Rank Ltd (Foodstuffs), Wildfowl Foundation Inc., the US Fish and Wildlife Service, and various Hawaiian agencies, including Honolulu Zoo, the National Park Service, Hui Ahinahina, Hawaii Audubon, Hui Manu (Bird Club), the Conservation Council, Fong Construction Co, and the Maui Electric Co.

A grant from the World Wildlife Fund had generously been made to cover the shipment costs of earlier releases. The Fund's financial position was such that no grant could be made in 1969 and 1970. So the £1534 freightage charges were also met by the Wildfowl Trust, though in July 1972 the World Wildlife Fund was able to make a donation of £500 towards this.

For the 200 nenes returned since 1962, total costs were probably in the region of £25 per bird (or £5000 in total).

Whatever the future holds, it seems that a real achievement has been made in the augmentation of a vanishing wild species from captive sources. The nene has been saved from extinction; the world population is probably now over 1000 birds, of which at least 600 are thought to be in the wild, and the current annual production of goslings in captivity is far in excess of adult mortality. Nearly 900 goslings have been produced in Britain and 1200 in captivity in Hawaii since 1952. A direct result has been the arousal of tremendous public interest in the nene and, thereby, an increased awareness of the value and possibilities of other conservation programmes. To that end, pairs of geese have been distributed to 39 zoological gardens and wildlife collections in Europe and North America. As well as making attractive and educational exhibits, the dispersal of birds helps to ensure that no single disaster overtakes the population in future.

PREDATOR CONTROL

Even today, when the nene is rigidly protected—since 1957 it has been Hawaii's state bird—exotic predators are a serious threat to its survival. From February until May, some young and adults are likely to be flightless, and fall easy prey. The mongoose, for one, will probably never be eliminated, and without strict and constant control of predators at the nesting sites, the wild goose population remains at risk.

FUTURE RESEARCH

Of course, problems still exist in the captive rearing programme, and further research is being undertaken into the fertility and hatchability of eggs, and into the control of breeding condition and good health in the adult birds. The captive flock at Slimbridge has provided considerable data over the years. At 3 months of age, the sex ratio was found to be equal, but birds dying at hatching or before they were 3 months old were more likely to be female. The average expectation of life at 3 months is only 5·1 years, and most deaths have occurred before the birds were 9 years old. Those living longer have usually been male. Ganders die at all times of the year, while female mortality is greatest between February and April (which includes the laying season). Mean clutch size has been 4·3, with a mode of 5 and a range of three to six eggs. Four- and five-year-old females lay the largest number of eggs. Females of this same age also lay most of the repeat clutches. Egg weight is similarly greatest at 4 and 5 years, and the heavier eggs are more likely to hatch. Male performance has matched that of the females, the percentage of eggs fertilized first increasing and then decreasing with age.

However, no captive-bred adults should be released by this method, owing to their inability to adapt suddenly to life in the wild.

3. A mated pair of owls is kept in a suitable cage for some weeks in the release area. The male is then set free, followed by the female 2 or 3 weeks later. This method has met with success on several occasions in the Black Forest.

4. The release of a captive-bred female in a territory known to be inhabited by a lone wild male, as in Sweden.

Only a few cases have been confirmed in Germany in which birds originally bred in captivity have been known to breed successfully in the wild. Herrlinger states: "If one wants to sum up the results one must say that there has been no real success of the reintroduction project till now. . . . Nevertheless there might be a chance of success after all, if people continue setting free 20–30 specimens each year". He also states that "the fact that the experiments as a whole have had no convincing success up to date, is not due to false methods of setting the birds free, but to the dangers which threaten the lives of the birds, e.g. traffic and high-voltage lines".

During the period 1969–71, 24 barn owls, *Tyto a. alba*, and 19 little owls, *Athene noctua vidalii*, have been bred at the Norfolk Wildlife Park, and of these seven barn owls and nine little owls have been released locally, following the Swedish procedure. Young owls of both species have been observed to return to their parents' aviaries for food and for up to 6 weeks after their release and both species are seen regularly in the release area, although they were rarely observed prior to the reintroductions. At the time of writing, a pair of little owls (almost certainly released birds) have taken up their territory in a hedgerow only 50 yards from the breeding aviaries.

While owls are generally much easier to breed in captivity than diurnal birds of prey, the same reintroduction procedure can be carried out successfully with both hawks, *Accipiter* spp., and falcons, Falconinae. In this instance, the writer's personal experience is confined to the kestrel, *Falco tinnunculus*, of which seven specimens bred in the Norfolk Wildlife Park, have been released between 1969 and 1971. The behaviour was the same each year, the young birds returning to the immediate vicinity of their parents' aviary daily for food for up to a month before wandering off.

To summarize: the most important point in the re-establishment of any bird of prey (diurnal or nocturnal) under the above system is that, if young birds are to be used, they must have been bred in the area of release and they must be fed in the immediate vicinity of their parents' aviary until they have completely reverted to the wild and have learned to kill regularly. This does not apply to the translocation of wild adult birds, but there is no method known whereby such adults can be induced to settle within a given area.

The birds of prey and owls in the Norfolk Wildlife Park are all kept in individual aviaries, the size of which depends upon the requirements of each particular species. Owls are much less demanding than diurnal birds of prey because they are not only less active, but by nature they are far steadier. Indeed, the larger species often show no fear of people and may even attack intruders during the breeding season. On the other hand, nearly all diurnal birds of prey are liable to take fright and to dash themselves against the wire-netting of their aviary if disturbed.

The minimum size of aviary used for small owls such as the little owl or tengmalm's owl, *Aegolius funereus*, is 5 m in length by 3 m in width and 3 m in height. The framework is made of timber creosoted under pressure and covered with galvanized 13 mm mesh wire-netting. All the aviaries are planted with natural vegetation, usually coniferous trees, and are provided with nest-boxes or hollow logs. The floor is of natural turf, with patches of sand where contamination by droppings is concentrated beneath favoured roosting perches. Similar but rather larger aviaries are used for medium-sized owls such as barn owls or long-eared owls, *Asio otus*; but for eagle and snowy owls, *Nyctea scandiaca*, the measurements are increased to a minimum of $10 \times 4 \times 3$ m in height. Furthermore, these large owls are also provided with a wooden shelter at one end of the aviary, measuring $3 \times 2 \times 2 \cdot 5$ m in height and equipped with open nesting boxes 60 cm square by 20 cm in depth, lined with earth and pine needles. For snowy owls, the nesting boxes are situated on the ground; but for eagle owls they are raised to about $1 \cdot 5$ m. These shelters ensure that the owls have sufficient privacy to breed satisfactorily. Netting of 38 mm mesh is used for the larger species.

Similar aviaries can be used for the diurnal birds of prey, the smaller species such as kestrels needing about the same amount of space as the medium-sized owls, while the larger hawks and falcons (e.g. goshawks, *Accipiter gentilis*, and peregrines, *Falco peregrinus*) require considerably more room than the largest owls. Furthermore, they are all highly susceptible to disturbance by human beings and for this reason their aviaries are better situated in a secluded position. Even then, it is usually necessary to erect a solid screen right round each aviary to ensure maximum privacy for the occupants.

Owing to the disparity in size between the sexes in all birds of prey and owls, the arbitrary pairing of individuals may often lead to fighting, sometimes with fatal results. This is especially the case with the larger owls and hawks such as goshawks. For this reason, it is advisable to divide the aviary into two sections and to keep the sexes separate until they have become accustomed to one another. Even then, a close watch must be kept on them when they are first put together.

Nearly all the smaller owls and hawks will thrive on a diet of day-old chicks, which are often readily available from poultry hatcheries. This is the basic diet of all the owls in the Norfolk Wildlife Park and no other food appears to be necessary, even when the birds are rearing young. However, it is important to remember that the quantity fed must be increased progressively from the time the chicks hatch so that there is always a surplus of food while the young are growing. Failure to do this may result in the younger, and therefore weaker, nestlings starving, or even being eaten by their parents or larger siblings. The diet of the diurnal birds of prey is varied by the addition of rabbits, *Oryctolagus cuniculus*, hares, *Lepus europaeus*, and adult domestic chickens, all being fed whole or merely cut into large pieces.

There appears to be so much variability in the breeding potential in captivity of the various species of raptorial birds that it is difficult to determine what number constitutes a viable breeding unit, or how many such units a collection should establish before distributing some of the breeding stock to other zoological institutes. In the case of most owl species, four or five breeding pairs might be considered a minimum viable unit for one collection. With the diurnal birds of prey, the position becomes more complex since it may be necessary to keep a comparatively large number of pairs to ensure a reasonable level of reproduction, as some birds may not breed at all. This is probably due to the temperament of individuals or to incompatability in arbitrarily paired couples.

A large-scale experiment conducted from 1965 to 1968 with the American kestrel, *Falco sparvinus*, at the Patuxent Wildlife Research Centre showed that it was possible to establish a breeding colony whose reproductive performance was comparable to that of a wild population. In 1967, 16 pairs of these hawks laid clutches averaging 4·9 eggs, hatched 85 per cent of their eggs and fledged 88 per cent of their young, while in 1968 nine yearling pairs, hatched in captivity, laid clutches averaging 5·1 eggs, hatched 87 per cent and fledged all their young.

To sum up, the breeding of owls and birds of prey in captivity and the subsequent release of young birds is still in its infancy. Much more will have to be learned, particularly with regard to the regular breeding of diurnal birds of prey and also of release procedures. However, the foregoing experiments give reasonable hope that for some species captive breeding will eventually prove to be a more widely applicable tool for the conservationist.

Breeding Peregrine and Prairie Falcons in Captivity

R. Fyfe

This report is intended as a preliminary outline of experience in North America with respect to the conservation and the development of management techniques for peregrine and prairie falcons. It should be pointed out initially that, as a member of the Canadian Wildlife Service, the author does not represent private interests of any kind nor any zoological garden but rather is a representative of a Canadian Federal Government Agency.

The primary developments leading to the recent concern for the birds of prey in North America began at the Madison Peregrine Symposium in 1965. At that time, there was a sudden awareness of the magnitude of the problem of population decline in birds of prey generally, and particularly of the population decline of the peregrine falcon in Europe and in continental North America. Following this 1965 symposium there were four main developments in relation to the birds of prey:

1. Beginning in 1966 and continuing to the present time, there was an increased involvement by naturalists and biologists in the monitoring of populations of birds of prey, and similar species at the ends of food chains.

2. There has been increased monitoring of chemical residue levels in the environment. Concurrently studies have been undertaken of the effects of these chemicals on various species, using birds at the ends of food chains as possible indicator species.

3. Regulations relative to the taking of birds of prey from the wild were tightened and more rigidly enforced. This meant that falconers, zoological gardens and other people were no longer able to obtain wild birds of prey so readily in North America.

4. The Raptor Research Foundation was formed. This is a voluntary non-profit organization composed of interested people, both professional and non-professional. As with the Hawk Trust in Great Britain, the primary dedication was to furthering the survival of the birds of prey and the dissemination of information about them.

In Canada the Conference was followed by the implementation of surveys of several species of birds. Initially, these surveys showed that the populations of

FIGURE 1. Wild adult female prairie falcon incubating.

three species of raptors had declined in Canada: the prairie falcon (Fig. 1), the Richardson's merlin (a subspecies of the merlin) and, most severely, the peregrine falcon. The first two species had not suffered to the same extent as the peregrine, but had clearly experienced population declines. Of the three peregrine races in North America the eastern or anatum race (which may be described as the interior continental race), had decreased in numbers almost to extinction. Surveys further showed that in our sample areas, the tundra race (*Falco peregrinus tundrius*, a highly migratory race breeding in the Arctic) had declined by about 60 per cent. Information on the third race, the west coast Peale's peregrine, indicated that this group had apparently been able to maintain its numbers. Consequently our initial response and concern was centred on the anatum or eastern race (Fig. 2), and on the tundra birds.

Concurrent population data and field studies on chemical residues suggested that the primary cause of the decline of the peregrine was the presence of residues in tissues of the birds. In North America these chemicals include DDE, dieldrin, heptachlor and mercury. I am happy to say that since then we have had some success in changing the patterns of use of some of those chemicals.

In 1970 a special North American peregrine survey was conducted. Dr. Tom Cade and I were in charge of the coordination of this survey, and the results confirmed that the eastern race was indeed very close to extinction. Canadian Federal and Provincial Government Wildlife Agencies, and the various scientific organizations, were faced with the choice between leaving the birds to their fate in the wild (knowing that some residues would persist in food chains for a minimum of 10 years), or taking young peregrines into captivity in order to establish a captive flock from which birds could be released eventually. It was decided that the latter course was the more promising, so birds were taken into captivity for captive breeding experiments. In all instances however, the adults were left in the wild, as were some of the young birds. After the Canadian Government embarked upon this programme (Fig. 3), I was placed in charge of this particular aspect; hence my involvement with endangered species.

In the United States, Cornell University, under the direction of Dr Tom Cade, set up a large project and constructed a new building for raptor breeding in 1971. The U.S. Fish and Wildlife Service Research Laboratory at Patuxent also procured peregrines to add to studies which they were already conducting on other birds of prey. In addition, as a result of the tightening of capturing regulations, many private individuals began attempts at breeding falcons in captivity. It was here that the Raptor Research Foundation first came into its own through the coordination of these projects and in the publishing of procedures and results.

The breeding programme to date can be briefly summarized as follows: In North America there have been at least three successes with prairie falcons, two achieved by falconers and one by research workers. We raised prairie falcons in captivity successfully in 1971 and 1972, with the adults on both occasions breeding and raising four young in captivity (Fig. 4). As is well known, the first captive breeding of peregrine falcons was achieved years ago in Germany, and I

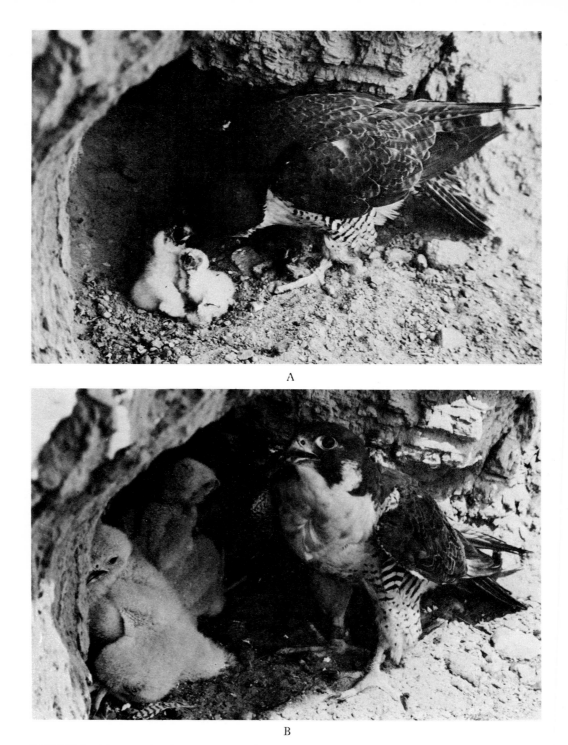

A

B

FIGURE 2. (a) Adult female anatum peregrine feeding newly-hatched young at one of the last known active nest sites of this race in North America, east of the Rocky Mountains and south of the Taiga. (b) Adult female anatum peregrine with 2-week-old nestlings.

understand that there was at least one success in 1971 in Europe. I am aware of three well-documented successes in North America.* Other species including kestrels, Harris hawks and red-tailed hawks have also been bred successfully in captivity.

Recently artificial insemination has been used in captive breeding attempts with a number of species. One of our colleagues (Robert Berry) had imprinted

FIGURE 3. Construction of a breeding pen for falcons at the Endangered Species Facility in Alberta.

goshawks which would accept him as a mate but no birds of their own species. Consequently he tried artificial insemination and succeeded in fertilizing the female. In 1971, at Cornell, red-tailed hawks were artificially inseminated successfully, and this year we are carrying out a similar programme with peregrine and prairie falcons†. Cornell has also successfully inseminated golden eagles, and I understand that they have nine fertile golden eagle eggs at the

---

* In 1973, notable success was achieved in breeding peregrines in North America and in Europe, the most significant being the production of a large number of fertile eggs, successful rearing of all three North American races of the peregrine, and the production and rearing of no less than 20 peregrines at the Cornell Facility.

† Two peregrine eggs were fertilized, but the chicks died at hatching.

present time. The obvious suggestion here is that this may be a very useful technique in working with rare birds like the monkey-eating eagles. If such birds could be imprinted on human beings, there is little doubt that this technique could also be used with them. Problems of imprinting could be overcome to a large extent by having the inseminated parent raising the young. This is what was done with the goshawks and what will be done with the golden eagles.

FIGURE 4a. Captive breeding pair of prairie falcons. The female is incubating four fertile eggs early in May of 1972.

There are problems, of course; in particular the problems of stress that were discussed with other species at the conference. Stress responses vary between species and within species. One breeder has tamed prairie falcons so well that he can lift the female off her eggs to look at them and put her down again. His birds have bred successfully. In contrast, our pairs of captive prairie falcons are so wild that screening has to be provided so that they cannot see people; otherwise all activity ceases. One must be able to read the signs of stress, as has been pointed out so beautifully in some of the papers in this volume. Stress is a major element in captivity, and you have to know your animals very well in order to compensate for its effects. Stress may be a factor in parental breakdown where parents do not feed their young ones. In cases like this the offspring can only be given to another pair of birds. There are also photoperiod problems with tundra peregrines because they are trans-equatorial. Dr. Cade may have overcome the difficulties this year through photoperiod manipulation; he now has tundra peregrines sitting on eggs and they have been observed breeding.

FIGURE 4b. Captive breeding pair of prairie falcons feeding captive bred young in June of 1972.

One of our chief concerns is the reintroduction of captive birds into the wild. Here we are fortunate in that for birds of prey the old falconry technique of hacking seems a most useful tool (Fig. 5). Because falconers have pretty well perfected this, there has been a suggestion that we use conscientious falconers to help hack birds back into the wild. It may even be possible to use a natural hack, i.e. releasing the young from a hack house, or a method we use, allowing captive parents to feed young birds through the mesh of an adjacent enclosure from which the fledglings are free to escape. Such techniques could be carried out on cliffs and similar places and various possibilities are being examined with the intention of trying this with prairie falcons in autumn 1972.

Another method, of course, is to increase the number of eggs under wild birds, as was done with prairie falcons in summer 1972. Our birds laid more eggs than were required and because we had no use for another ten captive prairie falcons, the fertile eggs were put under wild birds nesting under natural conditions. However, to more fully understand the outcome in the future field behaviour observations will be conducted from hides. It is also intended to conduct experimental movements of family groups, and to establish actual cliff nest breeding pens to explore the feasibility of releasing the young from them. Obviously, there are many potential techniques, but the one we have tried with

FIGURE 5. Immature male prairie falcon raised in captivity and being "hacked back" to the wild early in August 1972.

reasonable success is the use of foster parents. Twice the infertile eggs have been taken from a captive peregrine falcon and replaced with eggs from a red-tailed hawk or Swainson's hawk, and she has raised the offspring as if they were her own. We have also successfully tried using captive prairie falcons as foster parents for other species. This year (1972) we are holding prairie falcons that have been raised by another species and will keep them to look for any behavioural changes. The potential of this technique of releasing birds back into the wild state is excellent; but these and other techniques must be examined and tested, since the primary concern in saving a species is reintroducing individuals into the natural habitat.

We are not yet close to achieving the sophistication of some of the beautiful achievements with waterfowl we have heard about, but we are very encouraged to know that we can breed falcons in captivity. Research activities between government agencies, private facilities and private individuals are to a large part coordinated through the Raptor Research Foundation news reports and meetings. To date, cooperation has been excellent as the concern for the species provides a common basis for everyone to work together, and I am convinced we will succeed.

General Principles for Breeding Small Mammals in Captivity*

R. D. Martin

INTRODUCTION

The approach of this paper differs considerably from that of most of the other contributions to this volume. The attempt will be made to examine *general* sources of problems which arise whenever the attempt is made to breed wild-trapped mammals in captivity. This is a matter of concern for various institutions, but zoo staff are probably faced with such problems in their most acute form, since they must cope with a wide range of species which are often maintained only in small numbers and which in many cases are imported directly from the wild. One of the main aims of the Jersey conference was, I believe, the provision of a central information source to serve as a guide for many people concerned with breeding wild animals. However, most of the guidelines provided in individual papers are in the form of "recipes" for maintenance of individual species; yet it is equally necessary to analyse some of the generalized sources of difficulty encountered in the husbandry of *any* exotic animal species in captivity. In fact, zoos and other institutions often face the problem of attempting to maintain and breed a species which is totally new in captivity, or which has never been bred successfully under artificial conditions, and in many cases only a few extremely valuable specimens are available. As a preliminary move in this direction, it may be useful to suggest some of the steps which might be taken in an economical search for ideal captive breeding conditions for any small mammal species, and perhaps for other animals as well.

Before proceeding to this central issue, however, it is worth discussing briefly the reasons for attempting to breed *endangered* species in captivity. The main reason assumed at the Jersey conference was that such breeding efforts could potentially provide pools of captive-bred animals for subsequent reinforcement of dwindling populations in the wild. There has been some criticism of this proposal, notably by Miss Moira Warland (see pp. 373–377), and in view of this it would perhaps be valuable to carry out an experimental project involving reintroduction of a well-established and carefully documented captive stock to the wild under controlled conditions, following the initial steps taken with the

* This work has been supported by grants from the Medical Research Council and the Science Research Council.

Hawaiian goose (p. 115), various raptorial birds (p. 125) and the white rhino. It would be highly instructive to take a given well-studied, non-endangered animal species which can be easily monitored in the wild, and to observe in detail the consequences of a period of captive breeding followed by re-introduction. The questions of genetic variability and long-term viability of the reintroduced stock would be of special concern. Only with such a pilot study can one realistically assess the potential contribution of captive breeding to the conservation effort (see also p. 383).

It should be noted, in passing, that current evolutionary theory (e.g. see Simpson, 1940 and 1952) is heavily dependent upon the concept of small numbers of individuals ("founder populations") effecting chance passage across a prominent geographical barrier and colonizing new areas. It is generally accepted among biologists that all evolution has depended upon a combination of this colonization process and the parallel process of chance subdivision of previously continuous species populations through the formation of new geographical barriers (mountain-chains, glaciers, rivers, arms of the sea, etc). With respect to genetics, any observations made following introduction of captive-bred animals to an area with appropriate environmental conditions would thus be equally interesting for conservation programmes and for evolutionary theory in general. Even in cases where natural reserves are established in the wild, it is vital to know the minimal population required for long-term survival of any species, particularly in view of the fact that naturally-occurring climatic and other changes could reduce the effective area of any of our present reserves in the years to come.

A second major consideration is that data obtained from breeding of captive animals can be of value for programmes aimed at conservation of the same species in the wild state. Knowledge of the potential life-span, the age of attainment of sexual maturity, seasonality of breeding, the period of development of the embryo, the clutch or litter size, the annual frequency of breeding and so on can provide a preliminary basis for assessing the extent of a threat to the survival of a wild population.

Thirdly, studies of *behaviour* in captivity (as well as in the field) can provide a significant source of information which is useful in terms of effective conservation as well as in extending our general knowledge of the species involved. We are, thankfully, now slowly emerging from the era where zoos were usually regarded as museums for live animals, and with every year that passes more and more zoos are accepting the idea that they have a duty to find out as much as possible about the habits of the animals in their care, and that particular emphasis must be placed on successful breeding in captivity. There is also a clear trend for zoos to recognize that they have an important part to play in furthering the conservation effort. Although it may be said that zoos work against conservation in that they might encourage further depletion of decreasing wild stocks of rare species (e.g. see paper of Perry et al., p. 362), this relatively small effect can be more than offset by the immediate educational advantages of well-organized zoos and by the scientific contribution that can be made in those zoos where every effort is made to ensure that the captive animals are adequately maintained and observed.

Finally, if we consider special cases where given species are threatened by commercial exploitation (e.g. various primate species, which are trapped in incredibly large numbers for medical research), it is particularly vital to try to breed these species effectively in captivity. Ultimately, not only the zoos but also those who are interested in commercial exploitation should be able to establish captive breeding colonies and thus significantly diminish the pressures on wild populations. For various reasons, this trend towards captive breeding is already evident among those who utilize primate species for medical research, and part of the battle has been won already (see Beveridge, 1972).

If we now return to the general problems involved in breeding animals in captivity, at least three main factors emerge: first and foremost there is an overall requirement for *systematic information*. There can be no doubt that it would be widely beneficial if one could develop a set of basic principles as guidelines for the maintenance and rearing of all wild animals in captivity. Secondly, there is a close-knit relationship between studies conducted in the field and observations carried out on wild animals in captivity. There are some studies which can only be accomplished in the field, notably where ecological relationships are to be established, and others which can only be conducted under artificial conditions (e.g. where manipulation of some kind is involved); but it is the sum of information from these two sources which is really important. Effective conservation will only be possible in the long term if it is supported by a sound basis of detailed biological data relating to the species involved. It is therefore of primary importance that rare species should be maintained in captivity wherever possible in order to obtain knowledge required for their effective protection. This leads on to the third point. Those who keep endangered species in captivity now have an *obligation*, as yet recognized only by a minority, to ensure that their charges are studied as fully as possible under optimal conditions. All three factors are closely associated in that those who do have rare specimens in captivity (i.e. primarily the zoos) must be informed about the wider issues involved and must be prepared to communicate fully with the special community concerned in the conservation and study of wild animals. It is in this spirit that this paper had been framed.

THE SPECIES STUDIED

The viewpoints outlined in this paper have been developed in the course of laboratory work extending over the last 8 years, in which the main emphasis has been placed on effective breeding of small animals in captivity. This emphasis on breeding has been maintained in a systematic attempt to determine optimal conditions for the maintenance of exotic mammal species for a wide variety of purposes (e.g. observations of general behaviour). As a general rule, it can be assumed that animals which will breed reliably in captivity are subject to better conditions than others of the same species which fail to breed in confinement. In fact, it is often overlooked that the behaviour of wild animals can be distorted by conditions of captivity, and no study of the behaviour of a captive animal can be regarded as complete until at least some attempt has been made to discover how far that behaviour has been modified by artificial living conditions, in particular by constant close contact with human beings. As will be shown below, breeding in captivity is one of the most sensitive indicators of behavioural distortion. Thus, it is necessary to pay attention to effective breeding in discussing behaviour under captive conditions, whilst at the same time it is necessary to pay due attention to behaviour in captivity in order to develop a reliable breeding programme in the first place. This concern with the animal as a whole and with its reproduction goes hand-in-hand with an interest in the natural conditions under which the evolution of the species has taken place. It is only in terms of the *natural environment* that the inherent, species-typical behavioural features of an animal species can really be understood, and a search for natural correlations can often be of assistance in developing programmes for captive maintenance and breeding. In sum, a broad biological approach to each animal species can pay great dividends with respect to husbandry in captivity, and observations conducted in captivity (when related to this overall naturalistic approach) can deepen our understanding of survival mechanisms operating in the wild.

This underlying rationale was first applied by the author to a laboratory colony of the common tree-shrew (*Tupaia belangeri*, Fig. 1). Initial observations were conducted in Seewiesen (Germany) from 1964 to 1966 with a colony established by I. Eibl-Eibesfeldt with animals imported from Thailand, and a daughter colony was later established (in 1966) at the Department of Zoology in Oxford. Subsequently (1967–69), further experience was gained with a colony of various lemur species, established by J.-J. Petter in Brunoy (France). After some preliminary observations, the lesser mouse lemur (*Microcebus murinus*, Fig. 2) was selected for detailed study, partly because it appeared to present a number of unexplained difficulties in laboratory maintenance and breeding. This species was also studied in the field in Madagascar in the course of two field-visits conducted in July–December 1968 (Martin, 1972*b*) and July–September 1970 (Martin, 1973), and a laboratory colony has been maintained in London since 1969 (see Martin, 1972*a*).

Neither the tree-shrew nor the mouse lemur can be regarded as severely threatened under natural conditions. The common tree-shrew still seems to occur over a wide geographical range in South-East Asia, and the lesser mouse lemur is the least threatened of all the surviving lemur species on Madagascar. It is nevertheless useful to refer to these two species because they illustrate particular problems which can arise with captive colonies, and because the solutions which were found in these two cases may have a general application to cases where small mammals (and possibly other animals) are imported directly from the wild and established in laboratory colonies. The tree-shrew, for example, provides a classic case of sources of difficulty arising with a species which was at one time considered "difficult" to breed in captivity (see Sprankel, 1959, 1961; Martin, 1966, 1968). Experience with this species laid the basis for a certain number of general principles, and the mouse lemur was subsequently selected for further work since it seemed surprising and intriguing that this tiny lemur species should breed much less readily in captivity than some of the larger lemurs (e.g. see Petter's contribution, pp. 187–202). Investigation of the reasons for the poor breeding record of the mouse lemur in captivity is still in progress; but some preliminary results have been obtained (Martin, 1972a) which

FIGURE 1. Hand-reared male common tree-shrew (*Tupaia belangeri*), photographed when almost adult. This animal was exceptionally tame and can here be seen "marking" a technician's hand with his sternal gland ("chinning behaviour"). This male, together with a hand-reared female, provided the initial basis for the successful breeding colony at Jersey Zoo.

indicate that the measures already taken are beginning to have an effect. The latest results (as yet unpublished) are extremely encouraging, and it seems likely that this research will establish a number of further principles of general applicability.

GENERAL PRINCIPLES

The first concern with animal colonies is, of course, the mundane question of routine, day-to-day maintenance. Whenever a species is imported from the wild to establish a captive breeding stock, immediate problems arise with straightforward questions of housing and feeding. At the outset, one must

decide upon a suitable enclosure size, which will in most cases be close to the
permissible minimum. With the mouse lemur, for example, it is possible to
maintain single animals in cages of 1 cubic metre capacity, or perhaps somewhat
less (Martin, 1972*a*) without markedly distorting behaviour or completely

FIGURE 2. Young, hand-reared male mouse lemur (*Microcebus murinus*) photographed at approximately 1 month of age. Like many other small mammals, the mouse lemur is nocturnal in habits. This
animal is now the "stud male" for the author's mouse lemur colony in London.

suppressing reproductive activity. Yet from data obtained in the field (Martin,
1972*b*, 1973) it is known that the average home range of any individual mouse
lemur is at least 30,000 times greater in volume. This provides just one indication of the vast disparity between those field conditions under which natural
breeding takes place and the conditions which are usually provided for general
activity and reproduction in captivity. Whatever steps may be taken in captivity,

one can never provide a living-space comparable in dimensions to that available in the wild. This is the central problem of all captive situations, and every time an animal is taken from the field to be enclosed in a cage (however luxurious), it is immediately subjected to potentially pathological conditions. This is, for instance, well illustrated by Maynes' observation (see p. 167) that female parma wallabies became anoestrous when kept at a density of one per 30 sq. ft of floor space, but that breeding occurred when the available space was increased to 50 sq. ft per animal. With artificial provision of food and other amenities, one can of course replicate some of the natural *availability levels*, and many wild-trapped species will actually breed in the relatively tiny enclosures customarily provided. However, as a general rule, it is probably best to provide rather large enclosures initially and then to reduce the enclosure size progressively until the permissible minimum is reached. This procedure has been successfully followed by the author with both tree-shrews and mouse lemurs in captivity.

As soon as the enclosure size has been decided, there are many specific features of maintenance which need attention. Nesting and resting facilities and other cage fittings are vitally important. It is, for example, a matter for astonishment that many people have only recently grasped the importance of providing branches (or artificial equivalents) in cages containing arboreal mammals (cf. Fig. 2). Appropriate cage-furniture is one of the prerequisites for ensuring the general well-being of captive animals. In the first place, their natural behaviour is adapted for a particular environment; secondly, the provision of branches and similar fittings can effectively increase the living-space within a cage. With nest-living forms, another especially important feature, for which a striking illustration will be provided with the tree-shrew (see below), is the location and the *number* of nesting facilities. Even species which do not habitually use nests may require special structures for resting in a small enclosure. Within the home range under natural conditions, most mammals will be confronted with a wide range of available retreats of varying shapes and sizes. Presumably, each individual selects one (or perhaps more) maximally suited to its behaviour. In the cage environment, it is customary to provide only one retreat of standardized form; but it is a useful device to provide a range of retreats of different kinds, so that the animal can select one best suited to its needs. Provision of only a single nest-box in various institutions was, in fact, one of the main factors which initially rendered tree-shrews difficult to breed (see Martin, 1966). With tree-shrews, because of their bizarre maternal behaviour, a breeding pair must always be provided with at least two nest-boxes of suitable dimensions. Over and above this, it is advisable to provide each pair with a small raised platform in the cage, since they will select this for resting at midday, rather than returning to the nest. With mouse lemurs, it is a good idea to provide at least one more nest-box than the number of adults in each cage and a relatively thick tangle of fine branches amongst which the animals may hide and rest without returning to the nest.

There is also the central problem of diet in captivity, though this really deserves a volume in its own right. Most people who are concerned with animal maintenance in zoos and other institutions are well aware of the basic problems involved in feeding a suitable diet; but there does not yet seem to be an established code of practice for developing a diet for a novel species, nor for dealing with the various specific problems which arise. A handbook on this subject would doubtless be invaluable to all concerned. It is, of course, generally recommended that one should provide any captive animal with a diet which is suitably varied, and hence is also well balanced, and it must be appropriate to the animal's natural requirements. Due attention must be given to an adequate supply of vitamins and of essential mineral components such as calcium, and there are many commercial products which may be used as dietary additives for this purpose. In the maintenance of tree-shrews and mouse lemurs, for example, the food has always been dusted daily with a powder supplement (e.g. *Vionate*, from E. R. Squibb & Sons), and a solution of vitamins (e.g. *Abidec*, from Parke Davis & Co.) is added to the drinking-water and to a cereal paste (*Cérélac*, from Nestlé Co.) from time to time*. Like many small mammals, tree-shrews and mouse lemurs are "omnivorous" and can be fed upon chopped fresh fruit (apples, oranges, bananas, pears, apricots, avocado pears, etc.) and various insects (mealworms, crickets, locusts, etc.). Both species will eat baby mice, and tree-shrews will eat meat of various kinds (e.g. minced meat, chopped heart, chopped liver). It is customary to give mealworms as insect food to captive animals, but it is not often appreciated that commercially supplied mealworms do not seem to be suitably fed themselves. In order to control the diet of the insects as well, the author has set up breeding colonies of mealworms, crickets and locusts, all of which are given (in addition to greenstuff, in the case of crickets and locusts) a basic diet of coarse flour, bran, *Vionate* and *Yeastmin*. Tests conducted with captive mouse lemurs indicate that they prefer laboratory-reared mealworms to those available commercially.

However, the development of a suitable diet for any given species in captivity does seem to depend too heavily on trial-and-error, and it is a pity that there is as yet no standard reference work available to provide guidelines for establishing appropriate diets for novel exotic species in captivity. This is one particular area where knowledge of the natural habits of an animal species can provide essential information for maintenance in captivity (for example, for the maintenance of extremely specialized herbivores such as the sportive lemur; see p. 197). Provision of a balanced and adequate diet is certainly of particular importance for reproduction in captivity, and with mammals various specific problems can arise with both gestation and lactation if the diet is imbalanced. Overall, it is usually possible to determine from the external appearance of an animal whether it is in good general health, and a mammal with a poor pelage and aberrant body posture will often prove to be suffering from straightforward dietary imbalance of some kind. With zoos and similar institutions, there is now a widespread tendency to use mass-produced food-pellets, since this simplifies feeding and provides a simple way of ensuring that important dietary components are readily available.

---

* But see addendum on possible dangers of vitamin overdose (p. 166).

However, each pellet type is usually suitable only for a restricted range of animals (e.g. carnivores or rodents) and it is unfortunate that provision of food in pellet form removes the animal even further from natural conditions. Where pellets are given alone, it is essential to ensure that this procedure does not itself have a deleterious effect. It is also necessary to bear in mind the fact that under natural conditions animals usually obtain their food by *foraging*, and that presentation of a large batch of food at one spot at a particular time of the day is far removed from the natural situation. One possible approach to this problem, using a combination of food-pellets and other foodstuff, is illustrated in Brambell's paper on orang-utans (p. 238).

In terms of its relation to breeding stocks for subsequent return to the wild, the diet in captivity could prove to be a highly significant feature, in that long-term artificial selection of animals for a diet in captivity (operating through differential mortality) could lead to physiological difficulties when a stock is released back into the wild and abruptly faced with the problem of adjustment to natural foraging. A careful check should be kept on this with any captive colony maintained with the objective of subsequent replenishment of declining natural populations.

With respect to diet, one must also consider the *social environment* of any captive animals kept in groups, since additional problems can arise from competition for food under conditions of forced proximity. In order to ensure that *all* animals in a group enclosure receive a balanced diet, it is advisable to provide several feeding and watering points, so that several animals can feed or drink separately. The number of times that the animals are fed a day, which is also an important aspect in its own right, can have an influence here. The more often that fresh food is offered in the course of the day, the greater is the likelihood that weaker members of the cage group will be able to select food in sufficient variety and quantity. For this and several other reasons, food should usually be provided in excess, since the caged animals (particularly subordinates within a group) might otherwise be compelled to eat inappropriate food. However, excessive food-intake can also give rise to problems.

General climatic features such as temperature and humidity also play a part. Once again, there is a need for information on the natural habitat of the animals concerned, indicating whether they come from dry or humid areas with high or low temperatures and showing whether there are any pronounced seasonal fluctuations. When working with Malagasy lemurs, for instance, one is confronted with an entire range from classical tropical rain-forest to semi-arid bush, associated with marked variations in maximum, minimum and average daily temperatures (Martin, 1972c). Now this would seem to be an obvious point which is automatically taken into account when exotic animals are taken into captivity. However, it is possible that the general approach to the question of climatic conditions is too simple in many cases. For instance, there is a general tendency to believe that tropical animals must be provided with high temperatures throughout the day. In the first place, it should be remembered that temperatures may vary widely over the course of the year, even in tropical areas. In the case of the mouse lemur and other nocturnal tropical forms, one must also note the marked variation in temperature which occurs over each 24-h period. In some areas of Madagascar, there can be a daily difference of 20°C between the temperature at midday (e.g. 35°C) and that at midnight (e.g. 15°C). In fact, the mouse lemur, being nocturnal (like many other small mammals) is naturally active at times when the surrounding air is much colder than the constant daily temperature normally maintained in the laboratory or in tropical mammal houses. For this reason, it was suggested (Martin, 1972*a*) that provision of a daily cycle of ambient temperatures might encourage mouse lemurs to breed more reliably in captivity. Since mouse lemurs are active at relatively low temperatures (approximately 15°C) in the wild, it is possible that maintenance of a constant ambient temperature of 25°C or above in captivity might have an adverse influence on fertility, particularly through overheating of the testes of the males. With the author's laboratory colony of mouse lemurs, a daily cycle of temperature has now been established, and this may have been one of the factors leading to the fair breeding successes so far achieved (12 offspring conceived, born and reared in captivity). The temperature is at present cycling daily between 28° and 20°C.

In a similar way, it may not be appropriate to maintain constant humidity levels in animal enclosures. Humidity varies over daily and annual cycles, and in some cases it may be necessary to consider this along with the fact that actual rainfall may be sporadic. Watering of cages at selected times with a sprinkler system could in some cases replicate natural conditions which may be associated with breeding. In some seasonally-breeding mammals, such as the lemurs, the time of the breeding season is closely associated with the occurrence of the annual rainy season, usually such that the offspring are weaned during the period of maximum rainfall and food availability (Martin, 1972*c*).

Maintenance of a constant temperature day and night usually goes hand-in-hand with maintenance of a constant schedule of light and darkness (constant daylength) in captivity. Again, it is often forgotten that there are natural cyclical patterns of variation under natural conditions. In particular, there is usually an annual cycle of increase and decrease in daylength, the magnitude of which increases with the distance from the equator. Animals from equatorial areas frequently do not depend upon the annual cycle of daylength in the regulation of their activities, but in most other areas of the world there is sufficient difference between the daylengths in summer and winter for this to be utilized by various animals as an indicator of the time of the year. As has already been noted, the Malagasy lemurs are all seasonal in their breeding activities, and in the case of the mouse lemur it has been experimentally demonstrated that it is the phase of increasing daylength which triggers reproductive activity (see Martin, 1972*a* for references). Thus, in order to ensure that a colony of mouse lemurs regularly enters into reproductive activity, it is necessary to introduce an annual fluctuation in daylength into the light schedule. In fact, many animals which have annual cycles of this kind will continue to exhibit them in the absence of the natural triggers; that is to say, the cycle becomes "free-running". One may therefore see some breeding activity and obtain breeding successes even in the absence of proper regulation of the light-cycle in captivity; but the danger is that the animals will become *desynchronized* because of differences in individual "free-running" rhythms. The natural daylength cycle can easily be replicated in captivity, and synchronized breeding can be obtained with species such as the mouse lemur (Martin, 1972*a*). In fact, with the mouse lemur, the natural 12-month cycle of daylength variation can be accelerated so that the animals come into breeding condition at intervals of 10 months, 9 months or 8 months. In this way, it is possible to increase breeding potential by increasing the number of breeding seasons over a number of years. This has been carried out with some success with mouse lemurs. With tree-shrews, on the other hand, breeding does not seem to be strictly seasonal under natural conditions or in the laboratory (Martin, 1968), though there may be fluctuation in the number of litters born each month. Here, it is not necessary to maintain an artificial annual cycle of daylength, and the animals will breed quite freely when "free-running" with respect to their annual rhythms. Thus the significance of the annual daylength cycle varies from species to species, though subtropical and temperate animals may be expected to be more dependent upon such cycles generally than are tropical animals (especially those from definitely equatorial localities).

One final, generalized feature of enclosures in captivity is that of the cleaning arrangements. It is, of course, necessary to clean cages from time to time in the interest of hygiene. This is particularly necessary with small, indoor enclosures, since close confinement (particularly of animals kept in groups) increases disease hazards. It must not be forgotten, however, that cage-cleaning represents a major intrusion into an animal's living-space, and that it has no equivalent under natural conditions. In the case of small mammals, there is the added effect that they usually spend long periods of time marking their surroundings with various body secretions (see Fig. 1). Under conditions of close confinement, such marking behaviour is inevitably concentrated far more than in the wild, and this means that the enclosure rapidly becomes "dirty". Yet it is highly likely, at least with some species, that in the wild such marking behaviour may serve an extremely important function in "reassuring" the home-range owner that it is on familiar (and hence relatively safe) ground. Over-enthusiastic cleaning of cages, particularly when combined with strong-smelling disinfectants, can temporarily abolish this reassurance effect in captivity, and the outcome may be almost as drastic as placing an animal in a totally unfamiliar cage. Although thorough cleaning is necessary from time to time, it is probably best to keep this to a minimum and to rely extensively on good aeration to remove "offensive" odours. It is probably advisable to reduce the general level of marking gland odours, without touching the marked areas themselves, since there is some experimental evidence with certain rodent species that high levels of species-specific odours may reduce fertility in captivity (see Bruce, 1963*a*, *b*). Further, regular careful watering of a cage could easily be used as a dual-purpose device for removing superficial dirt and for replicating the effect of natural rainfall.

As has already been implied above, removal of an animal to a different cage in captivity can be particularly traumatic. Quite apart from removing the animal from all existing scent-marks and their accompanying "reassurance" influence, the animal is subsequently placed in a situation where it may be totally disoriented, both visually and physically, for some time. In many cases, the result is that the animal's behaviour is distorted for some time, and the likelihood of reproductive success is greatly reduced. With both tree-shrews and mouse lemurs, transfer of an untamed animal to a new cage effectively eliminates it from the breeding pool for at least 3 months, largely because of the psychological effects of the transfer. With animals imported fresh from the wild, this phenomenon may be even longer-lasting.

All of these aspects of familiarity with a given cage are related to the general level of well-being of the captive animal, and the effects are likely to be most pronounced with animals brought directly from the wild and maintained under conditions which are not entirely appropriate. On the other hand, the effects of adverse conditions in captivity are generally reduced with animals born and reared in captivity. In some cases, one can take advantage of this by hand-rearing animals, so that they become completely accustomed to the proximity of human beings and to human handling (see Figs. 1 and 2). However, hand-rearing must be used with caution, since it may lead to imprinting (or some other form of attachment) to human beings, with consequent reproductive problems when maturity is reached. In addition, there are strong possibilities of artificial selection in the favouring of animals which adapt well to captivity and in the usual loss of some animals which do not respond to hand-rearing. Hand-rearing has, in fact, worked quite well with tree-shrews (Martin 1968; see also Fig. 3) and with mouse lemurs (Martin, 1972a); but with some mammal species, such as the great apes, and with various bird species it is apparently unfavourable for later reproductive potential. With small mammals generally, imprinting effects during hand-rearing seem to be lacking or unimportant, and with tree-shrews and mouse lemurs hand-reared animals have proved to be very suitable for breeding colonies.

STRESS IN CAPTIVITY

Many of the adverse effects on the general well-being and breeding of animals in captivity can be traced to the "stress syndrome" defined by Selye (1950). Basically, the harmful effects of certain aspects of captivity on caged mammals can be viewed as due to long-term activation of a physiological mechanism adapted for short-term response to emergency situations. Many of the pathological symptoms of caged mammals can be ultimately attributed to stressful features of their surroundings (stressors)—either the physical environment or cage companions of the same species—and even the question of disease in captivity may depend heavily on stress, in that stressed animals are probably far more likely to

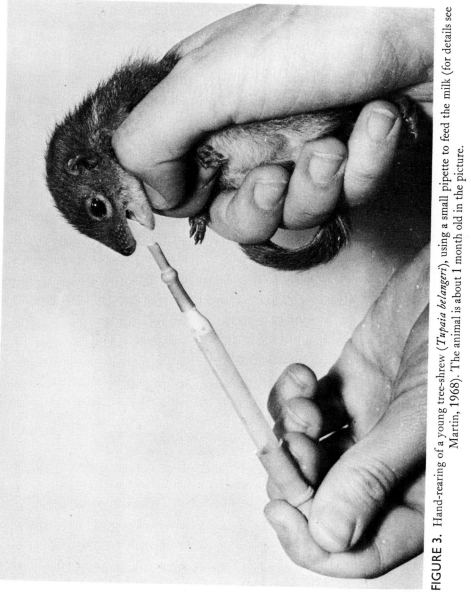

FIGURE 3. Hand-rearing of a young tree-shrew (*Tupaia belangeri*), using a small pipette to feed the milk (for details see Martin, 1968). The animal is about 1 month old in the picture.

succumb to pathogenic agents which are often present more or less continuously in the captive environment. Both the mouse lemur and the tree-shrew can exhibit pronounced stress responses under certain conditions in captivity, and various illustrations of these will now be provided in order to show the wide range of disruptive effects which can operate in captivity.

THE VISITOR EFFECT

One aspect which is rarely considered in the maintenance and breeding of captive animals is the effect exerted when unfamiliar people are permitted to approach or even enter an enclosure. As a general rule, it can be assumed that any change in an animal's surroundings is potentially harmful, and the sudden appearance of a strange human being (particularly within the animal's normal living-space) represents a particularly drastic intrusion. It is apparent that "familiarity breeds contempt", to the extent that most captive animals—given time—will usually cease to over-react to familiar human beings. Thus, a keeper or animal technician, if regular in their activities, will gradually be accepted as a "regular" feature of the captive animal's environment. With small mammals, such recognition of individual human beings is probably based heavily on smell, and it is important to bear this in mind (e.g. in selecting suitable clothing). This dependence on recognition by smell may explain why many mammals generally take some time to *generalize* their responses from a known individual to all human beings. Significantly, hand-reared mammals seem to generalize much more readily from the rearer to other humans, and greater use of hand-rearing might provide a useful device in attaining breeding successes with mammals on continuous display to the public (provided that the species concerned do not show imprinting effects). Basically, this is a question of familiarity and unfamiliarity, and the essential point is that animals will normally become accustomed to regular features of the captive environment, and will almost invariably over-react to any change in the environmental pattern. Such changes can be represented by human visitors or by physical changes, such as sudden noises (e.g. arising from repair to installations near a cage) or modifications of the visual environment (see later).

Again, this may seem an obvious point to many who are concerned with the husbandry of captive animals. However, it is not generally recognized that a brief visit by a strange veterinarian, or by an electrician to repair a cage-fitting, however discreet, can wreak havoc with a breeding programme. If a stranger enters a cage, even for a short time, the effects can be pronounced; if that strange person touches or handles an animal, the effects can be disastrous. It is for this reason that with the author's colonies of tree-shrews and mouse lemurs every effort has been made to exclude *any* intervention by unfamiliar human beings, at least when animals are breeding. Visitors are generally excluded from the animal houses, and repairs are carried out as far as possible without recourse to outside personnel. Where animals *must* be handled, this is done on a regular basis, so that the animals eventually become partially adapted to this initially traumatic experience. Finally, great care is exercised whenever there is a change in the technical staff, so that the animals can become adapted *gradually* to the presence of a strange human being. It is only with hand-reared tree-shrews and mouse lemurs that abrupt exposure to unfamiliar human beings has failed to exert a pronounced effect on breeding.

Some of the effects of unfamiliar visitors can be seen in mild form when the stranger does not actually enter the animal's enclosure. For example, one case was observed where regular nest-building activity by a male tree-shrew was arrested every time one or more visitors came to work in the laboratory containing the

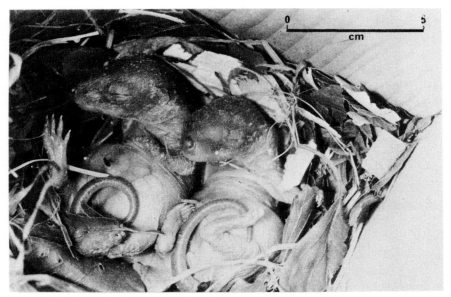

FIGURE 4. Two baby tree-shrews (*Tupaia belangeri*) photographed just after birth. The stomachs are bulging with milk, since the babies are visited for suckling by the mother only once every 48 h. This nest-box was not used by the mother (or father) for sleeping or resting during the period that the young were totally dependent (approximately 1 month).

animal's (large) cage. Here, the disruptive effect was roughly proportional to the magnitude and duration of the unusual activity of the visitors in the laboratory area. In other cases, the effects can be far more serious, leading to disruption of mating behaviour or maternal care. The tree-shrew provides a particularly striking illustration of this, because the maternal behaviour of this species is so unusual that any disturbance is very clear. The central feature of the maternal behaviour of the common tree-shrew (*Tupaia belangeri*) is that the babies are reared in a nest separate from that occupied by the mother (and father, if present in the cage) for resting and sleeping, and they are visited by the mother only briefly every 48 h for suckling (Martin, 1966; see also Fig. 4). This phenomenon was not reported by several previous workers (e.g. Sprankel, 1961; Conaway and Sorenson, 1965; Kuhn and Starck, 1966), and the absence of this clear-cut pattern of maternal behaviour in their studies was associated with only poor to medium breeding successes. In fact, it would appear that this pattern of maternal behaviour, which would seem to be natural, is extremely fragile in captivity, and it is only under very favourable conditions that one can observe this behaviour and obtain really reliable breeding and rearing.

However, it is in itself a highly successful measure merely to provide *an extra nest-box* in the cage of a tree-shrew pair in order to cater for this peculiarity of maternal care. In cages with only one nest-box, the parents are *forced* to sleep and

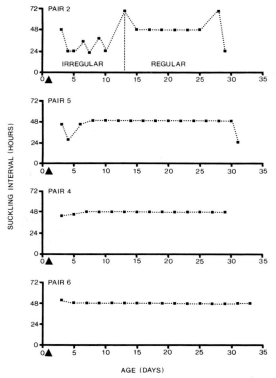

FIGURE 5. Suckling records for four litters of tree-shrews reared by four different pairs. Each point on each graph indicates both the day on which suckling occurred (Birth = Day 1) and the interval elapsed since the previous suckling visit (adapted from Martin, 1968).

rest in the same nest-box as the young, and the result is often suppression of lactation and even "cannibalism" by the parents. Both London Zoo and Jersey Zoo have reared tree-shrews in captivity with considerable success following advice from the author to provide at least two nest-boxes and a fairly large cage for each pair. At London Zoo, one female (with two successive males) successfully reared to emergence from the nest 25 offspring in the period February 1970–May 1972, which is close to the possible maximum (M. R. Brambell, pers. comm.). Jersey Zoo received a hand-reared pair from the author's stock which eventually produced 20 first generation litters and 25 second generation litters in the period 1967–72 (J. C. Mallinson. pers. comm.). With the Jersey tree-shrews, 30 of the total of 45 litters were successfully reared, again a relatively good yield.

In the light of this knowledge, it is possible to trace one source of disruption of tree-shrew maternal behaviour to the "visitor effect". Figure 5 illustrates the overall regular 48-h rhythm of suckling with four separate litters where the babies eventually survived to adulthood. However, in the case of the litter born to Pair 2 (top of Fig. 5) there was an initial irregularity in the suckling rhythm, which was associated with the arrival of a new laboratory technician to feed the animals. After about 2 weeks, the tree-shrew mother settled down, and the suckling rhythm returned to a regular 48-h pattern. In this instance, the disruptive effect was relatively mild in its ultimate effect, but with a marginal increase in disruption of the suckling rhythm the two infants could easily have died. In other cases, disruption certainly is more severe, and the mother may cease suckling altogether or even eat her own babies ("cannibalism").

Disruption of reproductive/parental behaviour in captivity is by no means uncommon in mammals. For example, Hick (see p. 228) has reported that her douc langur mothers did not sever the umbilical cord to free the placenta with their initial births in captivity. This abnormality later disappeared, presumably as the two females concerned became better adapted to conditions of confinement in captivity.

SOCIAL STRESS

The presence of other members of the same species in a restricted space can, under certain conditions, exert the same harmful effects upon an animal as disruptive features of the physical environment. In both cases, the response of the animal affected can be interpreted in the same way in terms of Selye's stress concept (Selye, 1950). Put simply, any alarming feature of the environment, physical or social, evokes a state of readiness for fight or flight. Under natural circumstances, such alarms are presumably normally short-lived, and the physiological response to alarming stimuli ("stressors") is thus only transitory. The state of stress only becomes harmful when the stressful conditions are persistent, such that the continued physiological state of readiness begins to damage the organism. In captivity, there are many ways in which unsuitable choice of cage design and cage companions can give rise to such persistent stress, and great care must be taken at every stage of selection. In fact, most animals will usually become accustomed to strange or inappropriate physical conditions over time (provided that those conditions are maintained constant); but responses to forced proximity to other members of the species do not seem to decline in this way. Unsuitable choice of cage companions, at least with certain species such as the tree-shrew, can lead to chronic stress which will usually inhibit breeding by the individuals affected and may even lead to death.

In fact, there is some suggestion (e.g. see Christian, 1950, 1963) that stress responses to conspecifics are part of a natural mechanism for regulation of

FIGURE 6. Illustrations (from photographs) of an adult female tree-shrew (*Tupaia belangeri*) showing the tail with the hair flattened (A) and with the hair ruffled (B). The amount of tail-ruffling over the day is a good indicator of stress in the tree-shrews (after von Holst, 1974).

population numbers, at least in some species such as various rodents. This suggestion is still controversial, but it has certainly been established that even under natural conditions interactions between members of a given species (not necessarily physical interactions) may give rise to adverse physiological effects. In captivity, in view of the tremendous reduction in living-space, it is particularly important to be aware of the existence and possible disastrous consequences of such interactions between conspecifics leading to physiological disturbances.

The common tree-shrew (*Tupaia belangeri*) has actually been the subject of an intensive and highly informative series of studies concerned with social stress in captivity (von Holst, 1969, 1972a, 1972b, 1974). These studies have quite definitely shown that tree-shrews can, under captive conditions, affect one another in the manner suggested by Christian; persistent social stress does give rise to physiological disturbances. *Tupaia belangeri* is an especially suitable species for such study, because the hairs on the tail remain ruffled whenever any individual is under stress (see Fig. 6). Long-term tail-ruffling is correlated with all of the classical physiological measures of stress (increase in blood leucocyte count, loss in body weight or retardation of growth-rate, increase in weight and activity of the adrenal glands), and this easily observed external feature can be used as a simple indicator of stress *without handling* the animals under observation. On this basis, von Holst has developed a "tail-ruffling index" (TRI), defined as the percentage of time during each 12-h activity period that an animal's tail is in the ruffled state. Given constant environmental conditions, the TRI-value is constant over long periods of time. Through a large number of observations and experiments, von Holst has been able to establish the following relationships between TRI-values and aspects of reproduction in captivity:

(1) At TRI-values of between 20 and 40 per cent, females were seen to exhibit male copulatory behaviour.

(2) At TRI-values of 50 per cent and above, females become sterile. Readiness for copulation disappears almost entirely and the ovary exhibits clear signs of degeneration (follicular atresia; ovarian cyst formation).

(3) In males, at TRI-values of 50 to 70 per cent, the testes—which are fully descended in normal, unstressed adult males—become labile in position, and at TRI-values in excess of 70 per cent the testes are definitively retracted into the abdomen, with the result that spermatogenesis is arrested.

(4) With young tree-shrews growing up in captivity under stressful conditions, there is a decrease in the rate of growth and an increase in the time taken to attain sexual maturity (e.g. full descent of the testes). These effects become more pronounced as TRI-values increase.

(5) If a TRI-value of more than 90 per cent is maintained by any individual tree-shrew for 8 days or more, death always follows.

(6) Perhaps the most surprising finding is that even at relatively low TRI-values (below 20 per cent) there are disturbances in the maternal suckling rhythm. That is, at levels of stress which leave other aspects of reproduction unaffected, there is still some disruption of maternal behaviour. In response to

brief or persistent mild disturbance, female tree-shrews exhibit irregularities in the suckling rhythm, often visiting their offspring *more often* than once every 48 h. However, despite the increased frequency of the mother's visits, the total amount of milk given is less than with a regular 48-h suckling rhythm, and the offspring exhibit a reduced rate of growth. Long-term stress at TRI-values of more than 20 per cent and less than 50 per cent is associated with gradual reduction in the lactation capacity of the female, through reduced mammary gland development, and in any case most offspring born to a female exhibiting TRI-values greater than 20 per cent are promptly devoured by the mother or some other adult in the cage. Such "cannibalism" is associated with the activity of the female's sternal marking gland, which develops in late pregnancy and is used to mark the offspring in the nest (von Holst, 1969). If the TRI-value exceeds 20 per cent, this sternal gland development fails to occur in the pregnant female, and the offspring are no longer marked with the secretion. Normally, the presence of the secretion on the babies acts as an "anonymous" signal inducing any visiting, lactating female to suckle and repelling any other adult tree-shrews from attacking the offspring.

All of the above effects, with the exception of growth-rate retardation in young animals growing up in stressful conditions, are reversible; thus, provision of more suitable conditions can lead to effective reproduction even with adults which have perviously exhibited stress symptoms. Various experiments conducted by von Holst have shown that these stress effects can be brought about by manipulating the relationships between adult tree-shrews in the cage situation. For example, increasing the number of females in a cage will bring about stress responses in all or most of the female occupants, whilst increasing the number of males will affect only the male occupants. If an original pair produces and rears offspring in a series of litters which are left in the original cage with the parents, the original male and female will gradually come to exhibit stress symptoms (and thus impairment of reproduction) as the numbers of male and female offspring increase. When the breeding female's TRI-value exceeds 20 per cent, no further litters will be reared until measures are taken (e.g. removal of the female offspring) to reduce the level of social stress.

Parallel experiments have yet to be conducted on other mammal species, such as the mouse lemur. However, certain preliminary observations indicate that in the mouse lemur, too, interactions between animals in the same cage or even in the same laboratory may be operative in reducing reproductive output. For example, with the two species at present maintained in the author's laboratory (*Microcebus murinus*; *Microcebus rufus*) only one male of each species has proved to be fertile at any one time to date (i.e. over a period of 4 years), though all males are in separate, individual cages. With females, on the other hand, there is evidence that inclusion of too many females in one cage may suppress successful breeding, despite the fact that all females come into oestrus normally. Suppression of reproduction seems to occur through a reduced conception rate, resorption of embryos in females judged to be pregnant at some point through palpation, premature birth, cannibalism of infants at birth and failure of lactation. For example, two female *Microcebus murinus* were originally kept in a large cage together (approx. 3 cubic metres capacity) and they each successfully produced and reared litters (one of two and one of three offspring). Three female offspring from the two litters were left in the cage with the two mothers to give a total group of five adult females for the next breeding season. When the breeding season arrived, all five females came into oestrus normally and were mated with the same "stud male". All five seemed to mate effectively, and increases in body-weight and palpation indicated that all five commenced gestation. Yet only one female went to term and continued to begin to rear her two offspring, both of which were eaten within a week of birth. Two other females apparently went to term and gave birth (as indicated by dramatic overnight weight-loss and patches of blood around the open vulva); but no trace of the offspring was found. The remaining two females appeared to have undergone resorption, since palpation in early pregnancy indicated that gestation had commenced, yet no births ensued.

Finally, stress may exert an effect in mouse lemurs in a context where it is apparently lacking in tree-shrews. Tree-shrews (*Tupaia belangeri*) can be maintained as breeding pairs with no difficulty at all, provided that at least two nest-boxes are provided within the cage. With mouse lemurs, on the other hand, it does not seem to be possible to keep a male in a cage together with even a single female, and breeding in small cages (of 1 cubic metre capacity) is only effective when the male and female are kept separately, except for introductions of 3–7 days' duration when the female is in oestrus. In fact, the only successful matings to date have occurred when the female has been placed in the male's cage for copulation, rather than *vice versa*. Both of these observations indicate that males are easily dominated by females and will only mate successfully in "secure" surroundings (i.e. in an exclusive home cage). This corresponds well with observations in the field in Madagascar (Martin, 1972b, 1973), which indicate that female mouse lemurs live in loosely organized, communally nesting groups of about four, whilst males tend to occur singly and do not nest or range with the females except during the mating season.

It is therefore obvious—at least with tree-shrews and mouse lemurs—that great care must be exercised in selecting cage groups and in arranging for mating to take place. Lactating females with infants would appear to be particularly vulnerable to stress, responding adversely under conditions which seem to be acceptable in other respects. An awareness of the likely causes of stress and knowledge of the natural habits of the species concerned represent two powerful tools for planning a successful breeding programme and for overcoming many of the problems which arise in practice.

ENVIRONMENTAL STRESS

As has already been suggested above, even quite minor variations in the physical environment surrounding a captive animal may give rise to stress responses. For instance, von Holst (1968) has noted that loud noises may temporarily disrupt the normal 48-h suckling rhythm of a female tree-shrew whilst more radical disturbance (in the form of reconstruction of the holding cage) produced persistent disruption of the suckling rhythm and pronounced retardation of the growth-rate of the offspring. In the author's laboratory, a quite accidental phenomenon provided a very clear demonstration of this effect. Following the birth of a litter of two *Tupaia belangeri*, the mother had initially settled down to a regular 48-h suckling rhythm and was giving 13–16 g of milk to the offspring at each suckling visit (see Fig. 7). At about the half-way point of the nest-phase of

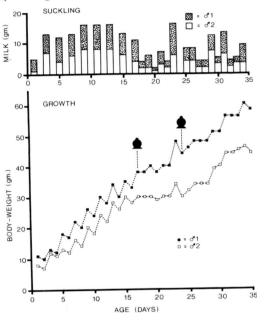

FIGURE 7. Diagram illustrating disruption of suckling in a litter of two male tree-shrews (*Tupaia belangeri*) reared by their mother under laboratory conditions. Suckling began normally, with suckling visits every 48 h providing the offspring with large quantities of milk (upper diagram) and giving rise to the typical zig-zag growth-curve (lower diagram). Two fire-bell tests (indicated by bells) accelerated the suckling rhythm, but reduced the overall quantity of milk given and retarded the rate of growth. If the disruption had not occurred, the two offspring would normally have attained body-weights of about 75 g by Day 35. (*N.B.* It is easy to tell the time of suckling and the amount of milk given by examining the offspring at appropriate intervals and by weighing them just before and just after suckling.) See also D'Souza and Martin, 1974.

this particular litter, on Day 17, a fire-alarm bell outside the laboratory was tested by continuous ringing for 30 seconds. The test occurred a few hours after the mother had suckled the infants, and she returned to feed her offspring the next day. There followed a period of acceleration of the feeding rhythm (i.e. with intervals less than 48 h), but the quantity of milk given over each 48-h period was reduced to 9–10 g (a reduction of about 33 per cent). A week after the test, the 48-h suckling rhythm was just reappearing when the fire-alarm was tested again, this time just over 24 h after a suckling visit. Once more, there was an acceleration of the suckling rhythm and a reduction of the quantity of milk given over 48 h. This is, of course, a relatively mild effect, since the offspring nonetheless survived to adulthood; but the time of opening of the eyes and the age at emergence from the nest were delayed, and on emergence the offspring weighed about 20 g (30 per cent) less than they would have done if suckling had proceeded according to a normal 48-h rhythm. All the same, this effect is somewhat surprising in that the mother had, on both occasions, almost 24 h in which to recover from the 30-second burst of noise prior to her subsequent suckling visit.

Even more drastic effects were found with breeding colonies of rodents (rats and mice) in adjacent laboratories, where the mothers were present with any young offspring at the time of testing of the bell. With the rats, the percentage mortality of young born during the 2 weeks of the fire-bell tests increased from the usual level of about 10 per cent to about 50 per cent, whilst with the mice there was an increase from about 5 per cent to almost 45 per cent. In fact, most of the offspring lost died during the 2 days following each test. Rats and mice which were in late pregnancy, rather than rearing young offspring, at the time of the tests continued to term and produced the usual numbers of offspring with the customary relatively low level of mortality in the week following the tests. However, in the 3 weeks thereafter there were less young born and once again a higher level of mortality (about 40 per cent) among those that were born. Since the minimum gestation period is about 21 days for both rats and mice, this indicates not only that there was a lower incidence of fertile matings during the 2 weeks when the fire-alarm bell was tested, but also that those infants whose embryonic development commenced at that time were for some reason less likely to survive in the days immediately following birth. Since all of these adverse effects were produced with two long-domesticated species by two 30-second bursts of bell-ringing at an interval of 1 week, the magnitude of the problem of environmental stress in captivity needs no further emphasis.

CONCLUSIONS

There is still much work to be done before one can establish a set of general principles for breeding wild mammals in captivity. However, it is apparent that a knowledge of an animal's natural behaviour (which can to some extent be determined through careful observations in captivity) is a great asset. In addition, the animal keeper must be aware of the problems of social and environmental stress and pay constant attention to any symptoms which indicate that some feature of the captive environment is stressful. With each individual species, a certain amount of trial-and-error will be involved in the search for optimal conditions of captive maintenance, but the approach outlined in this paper will hopefully provide some basis for an initial choice of strategy. Certainly, the author's own prior experience with tree-shrews has greatly facilitated the task of searching for suitable conditions for captive maintenance of mouse lemurs, and it would be more than worthwhile if this account were to similarly assist other people to economize in their search for ideal breeding conditions for other species.

ADDENDUM

Since this paper went to press, evidence has come to light that excess of vitamin A may be a relatively common cause of ill health and even death in captive colonies of mammals. Typical symptoms of extreme vitamin A poisoning seem to be: internal haemorrhaging, yellow discoloration of fat deposits and of the liver, weight-loss, deformation of embryos and neonates, and fractures of long bones in growing animals (F. D'Souza and J. P. W. Rivers, pers. comm.) An additional side-effect of excess vitamin A is induced deficiency of vitamin K and hence an increased prothrombin time. This latter symptom can be specifically treated as for simple vitamin K deficiency, but the basic problem of vitamin A excess will remain.

In fact, all fat-soluble vitamins (A, D, E and K) are deleterious when given in excess in the diet. Accordingly, great care must be exercised in adding vitamin supplements to diets. On balance, it is probably safer to keep vitamin additives to a minimum in mammal diets and to take compensatory action if any symptoms of *deficiency* are recognized, particularly since more seems to be known about the effects of vitamin deficiency, as opposed to *excess*.

Breeding the Parma Wallaby in Captivity

G. M. Maynes

INTRODUCTION

The parma wallaby (*Macropus parma*) is yet another example of an "extinct" species of marsupial which has been rediscovered in recent years. Prior to their rediscovery on Kawau Island, New Zealand (Wodzicki and Flux, 1967) only three specimens had been collected in this century. In 1921 one was taken at Point Lookout Gorge (30°30'S; 152°24'E), while the other two were taken at Cascade (30°16'S; 152°47'18"E) in 1932. Several workers since that date had considered the species to be extinct. Following the report of their rediscovery in New Zealand a female with a male pouch young was obtained near Gosford, New South Wales. I have recently discovered a population near Cascade and believe I have seen a parma wallaby in the area from which Darlington most probably obtained his two specimens in 1932 (Maynes, 1974).

Following the rediscovery of the parma wallaby on Kawau Island, there was a flurry of activity as various conservation groups attempted to establish breeding colonies. In December 1967, 31 wild-caught parma wallabies were imported into Victoria by the Sporting Shooters Association of Victoria. Twelve of these were sent to the Melbourne Zoological Gardens, three were subsequently sent to the Healesville Sanctuary and the remainder were kept at Monash University.

The first parma wallaby born and bred in Australia from the Kawau Island stock was born at Monash University on 10 March 1968.

MAINTENANCE IN CAPTIVITY

Animals in my breeding stock are fed a basic diet consisting of hay and a proprietary compressed stock food. Occasional carrots, cabbages, and green feed are also supplied. All animals have maintained excellent physical condition on this diet.

The animals at Monash were initially held for 3 months in a quarter-acre of semi-natural bush in the Jock Marshall Memorial Reserve before being transferred to small holding pens. Both the quarter-acre enclosure and the holding pens were constructed from 3 ft 6 in. high chicken mesh wire on a simple wire fence (Fig. 1). The fences were not covered and although some animals initially ran into them they quickly learned to avoid them. Two animals jumped out of the holding pens back into the quarter-acre enclosure shortly after being introduced to the pens. However, none escaped from the quarter-acre enclosure into the rest of the reserve.

Initially, animals were kept at a density of about one animal per 30 sq. ft of floor space in the holding pens. This, however, resulted in all female animals going into anoestrus. Subsequently, reasonable breeding success was obtained by keeping the wallabies at a density of about one animal per 50 sq. ft. At this

FIGURE 1. Wild-caught parma wallaby in a holding pen in the Jock Marshall Memorial Reserve.

density, regular oestrous cycles and matings were obtained and about 50 per cent of matings resulted in a young in the pouch.

CAPTIVE BREEDING

The normal penning arrangement was to keep one pair together or a male with two to four females. Males can be kept together as bachelor groups, provided that they are either kept away from breeding females or else kept in a large enclosure to reduce the frequency of interaction. Males appear to establish some form of social order or hierarchy after some initial fighting. Females, however, do not normally fight although on occasions short periods of mild antagonism have been observed.

Under these conditions, parmas breed moderately well. Table 1 summarizes the basic reproductive data for the parma wallaby. Post-partum oestrus and mating, which occurs in the majority of macropodid species that have been studied in detail, have only occurred in a small proportion of the parma wallabies that have been studied. The post-partum oestrus occurs at the same time after birth as a normal return to oestrus when the young fails to reach a teat. However, most parma wallabies do mate at some time during pouch life although a few females have been observed to carry the pouch young through a complete pouch life without returning to oestrus. If a female returns to reproductive condition following permanent pouch exit of the young wallaby, she may give birth 6–11 days after pouch exit, if carrying a quiescent corpus luteum and associated diapausing embryo, or she may return to oestrus and mate 12–24 days after pouch exit.

The situation regarding a breeding season is rather confused, but various information suggests a decrease in breeding potential during the last half of the year (July-December). The species as a whole can be said to breed throughout

TABLE 1. Reproductive data for the parma wallaby (*Macropus parma*).

Stage	Detail	No. observed	Mean (days)	Range (days)
Oestrous cycle	Interval between successive matings or oestrous periods in females without pouch young	51	40·4	48–36
Gestation period	Mating to birth	28	34·5	36–33
Post-partum oestrus	From birth to mating	6 of 34	9·5	13–4
[a]Return to oestrus	Following removal or loss of pouch young	12	9·5	15–4
[a]Delayed gestation period	From removal of pouch young to birth	6	31·3	32–30·5
Pouch life	From birth to permanent pouch exit	10	211·9	218–207

[a] These are mutually exclusive. An animal only returns to oestrus at this time if not carrying a quiescent corpus luteum.

the year, but there is considerable individual variation with some females being anoestrous for periods up to 6 months, others having irregular oestrous cycles, and yet others totally unaffected and breeding throughout the year.

Young spend 7 months in the pouch before permanent exit (Table 1) and continue to suckle from outside the pouch for a further $2\frac{1}{2}$—$3\frac{1}{2}$ months. During this period, they are permanently attached to the teat for the first 70–80 days. The first observation of a young with its head out of the pouch was at 146 days of age. They first start to leave the pouch for short intervals at 160 days and most, if not all, have been out of the pouch by 175 days of age. The young begin to develop the ability to regulate their body temperature at about 130 days. By 195 days they can maintain a constant body temperature. Permanent exchange of pouch young of about the same age between mothers has been detected in three cases, all at about the time when they are first leaving the pouch for short intervals. It is possible that some form of "imprinting" is involved in the recognition of mothers by their young and vice-versa.

In a few cases naked, blind young have been found in the pouch free of the teat but suckling either the tail or one of their feet. When found they have had the foot or tail removed by gentle traction and have been returned to the teat they were originally suckling. It is possible that the pouch young would have returned to the teat of its own volition after some time, but it is also possible that it may have been lost if action had not been taken.

Females reach sexual maturity at 12–16 months of age while males do not mature until aged 20–25 months. One female is now breeding at 6 years of age while another was still breeding at an estimated age of 8 years. Much more data are required before the actual length of the reproductive life of this species can be delineated. The position of teeth in the holotype male (see Ride 1957) suggests that the maximum longevity for the species may be considerably more than eight years.

Since the Conference, four more extensive papers on the parma wallaby have been published, providing further information on this rare species (see Maynes, 1972; 1973; 1974; Wallis and Maynes, 1973).

Status and Husbandry of Australian Monotremes and Marsupials

R. Strahan

INTRODUCTION

Just as the status of a species in the wild may change dramatically in a year or two, so may that of a species in captivity. At the time of the Jersey conference, *Burramys parvus* had not been held in any zoo: it is now breeding in Taronga Zoo's large nocturnal house. *Planigale ingrami* is now breeding in the second captive generation.

The birth of an orang-utan in Taronga Zoo is now so routine that it arouses little local interest: the hatching and rearing of an echidna would probably evoke even less public enthusiasm, despite its zoological significance. The motivation of zoo directors to provide space, facilities, and staff effectively to encourage the propagation of rare and endangered species seems often to be determined by cost-benefit considerations in which novelty and visitor-appeal rank highly—a postulate which is again referred to in the last section of this paper.

Any consideration of the breeding of rare or endangered Australian mammals is hampered by lack of information as to what species fit into these categories. First, we have not settled the taxonomy of all of our species at the generic level, and there is often disagreement between authorities as to whether a given population is to be regarded as a species, a subspecies, or part of a continuous cline. Such disagreement among specialists could be regarded as irrelevant but, in fact, has serious implications for conservationists: from the point of view of a "lumper", the status of a species will always appear more satisfactory than from that of a "splitter".

Secondly, we have detailed knowledge of the distribution and abundance of only a few species. Some species such as the large kangaroos, common wombat, brush-tailed and ring-tailed possums have been so well surveyed that they can be

---

Note: Subsequent to submission of this paper, Collins (1973) has published a comprehensive compilation of available data on the captive husbandry of monotremes and marsupials. It is a paper of such value and depth that my contribution should be regarded as a local supplement to it, dwelling more on status than husbandry.

declared unequivocally to be common. Evidence of the status of others may rest on infrequent systematic trapping carried out as part of post-graduate research programmes, on the rate at which dead animals are sent to museums, or upon the opinions of diligent naturalists. No systematic survey of the mammals of Australia has yet been carried out.

Thirdly, there has been a great deal of misdirected effort on the part of amateur conservationists who have mounted an extensive emotional campaign against the economic exploitation of the larger kangaroos. Public response to this pressure has been so great that the Select Committee on Wildlife Conservation of the Australian House of Representatives found it necessary in 1971 to bring out an interim report specifically devoted to kangaroos (see: House of Representatives Committee on Wildlife Conservation, 1971). Although this report demonstrates that the larger kangaroos exist in pest proportions in many parts of the country, it has failed to convince the campaigners—who prefer to whip up enthusiasm against the culling of excess large kangaroos rather than for the conservation of smaller, less familiar marsupials that are undoubtedly endangered.

THE AUSTRALIAN MAMMAL FAUNA

The native terrestrial mammals of Australia (see Marlow, 1968; Ride 1970) fall into five groups:

(1) *The monotremes*, including the purely Australian platypus and the echidnas which are better represented in New Guinea than in Australia.

(2) *The marsupials*, all of which are markedly different from those of the Americas but which have many links with the New Guinean marsupial fauna.

(3) *The rodents*, which show many relationships with those of New Guinea and Eurasia.

(4) *The bats*, which are similarly related to the fauna of New Guinea and Eurasia.

(5) *The dingo*, probably introduced by human beings about three thousand years ago.

The account which follows is restricted to the monotremes and marsupials of Australia, first, because of the greater intrinsic interest of these groups; secondly because little is known of the status or husbandry of native rodents and bats. The dingo, *Canis familiaris*, may be treated as any other feral member of the species.

STATUS OF AUSTRALIAN MONOTREMES AND MARSUPIALS

The survival of a population is endangered when its death-rate consistently exceeds the rate of recruitment of new members of the species. Many factors may contribute to such a decline, including:

(*a*) Long-term climatic changes in rainfall or temperature.

(*b*) Long-term biotic changes involving improved efficiency of endemic predators or competitors, or a decline in numbers of endemic food species.

(c) More rapid biotic changes arising from the invasion or introduction of non-endemic, non-human predators or competitors.

(d) Indirect human intervention involving the destruction of natural environments by agriculture, forestry, dams, irrigation, soil erosion, pollution, etc.

(e) Direct human predation in the form of hunting and "pest" control.

As in the other continents of the world, all of these factors have operated to reduce the numbers of many species of Australian mammals. Although the palaeoclimatic record is incomplete, it is clear that there was an overall increase in aridity during the Pleistocene era and that, as recently as fifty thousand years ago, the Australian deserts were far smaller. In general, however, the species that inhabit the plains of Australia are well adapted to aridity, and animals of the deserts and fringing areas of Australia are probably the most ecologically secure of all the Australian fauna. Nevertheless, an overall reduction in rainfall and glaciation has led to the isolation of some populations in relic forest or alpine habitats.

Examples of relic fauna in relic habitats are not hard to enumerate. The Tasmanian wolf (*Thylacinus*) became restricted to the island of Tasmania before the advent of man to the Australian landmass. The quokka (*Setonix brachyurus*) and the boodie (*Bettongia lesueuri*) are now essentially restricted to islands off the western coast of Australia; the musk rat-kangaroo (*Hypsiprymnodon moschatus*) is restricted to a small area of rain-forest in northern Queensland. *Burramys parvus*, the mountain pygmy possum, is so rare that it was known only as a fossil until 1966, when a live specimen was found in the Victorian alps.

Human activities often affect wildlife adversely, but it must be recognized that, even in a state of nature, some species decline and fall: the process of evolution is inseparable from the process of extinction. Some Australian mammal species may well have been on the way to extinction before Europeans set foot on Australian soil and, although we may have hastened the demise of some of these, we cannot be held directly responsible for their fate. It may even be that zoos will save a few species which would have disappeared in the absence of human intervention.

The basic philosophy of the conservation authorities of Australian state and federal governments is that faunal conservation depends upon habitat conservation. In general, each authority aims at setting aside, as faunal reserves or National Parks, reasonably large samples of every major ecosystem in Australia. To a considerable extent, this has been achieved and it may therefore be expected that a halt will be called to the decline of many species. Admittedly, many will be restricted to areas far smaller than their original distribution and may be vulnerable to epizootics, random population fluctuations, inbreeding, and the many other hazards of "island" communities.

The question arises: how is one to designate the status of a species which once was widespread but is now abundant and protected in a restricted area such as an offshore island? The temptation to attach the label, "endangered", should be resisted unless there is evidence that the death-rate is consistently in excess of the rate of recruitment.

The catalogue below is based largely upon the compilations of Calaby (1971), Marlow (1968) and Ride (1970) but remains somewhat subjective and represents the opinion of the author. (Note: The symbol (R) after the name of a species indicates that it is given a white page in the *Red Data Book*.)

A. ORDER MONOTREMATA (= PROTOTHERIA)

(i) Family Tachyglossidae
Echidna:
Tachyglossus aculeatus is widespread and common.
(ii) Family Ornithorhynchidae
Platypus:
Ornithorhynchus anatinus is widely distributed in Eastern coastal rivers and is not uncommon.

B. ORDER MARSUPIALA (= METATHERIA)

(i) Family Macropodidae
Kangaroos:
Macropus giganteus, M. fuliginosus, M. robustus, M. antilopinus, M. bernadus, Megaleia rufa. Currently abundant, none of these is endangered—even by present commercial exploitation.
Large Wallabies:
Macropus agilis, M. rufogrisea, M. dorsalis, M. parryi, Wallabia bicolor. Common. *Macropus irma* is either extinct or extremely rare (not having been recorded since 1924).
Small Wallabies and Pademelons:
Macropus eugenii, M. parma (R), *Thyogale billardierii, T. thetis, T. stigmatica, Setonix brachyurus.* None of these is rare or endangered, although all have suffered considerable reduction in range since the advent of Europeans. *Setonix* is essentially restricted to Rottnest Island where, however, it is very common. *M. parma* is extremely rare in Australia, but is common on Kawau Is., New Zealand, where it was introduced in the 19th century. It is now breeding well in many zoos.
Nail-tailed Wallabies:
Onychogalea unguifera is common in many areas of northern Australia. *O. lunata* (R) has declined in range and numbers and is endangered. *O. fraenata* (R) is either extinct or extremely rare.
Hare-Wallabies:
Lagorchestes conspicillatus is common in northern Australia, *Lagostrophus fasciatus* (R) has declined in range and numbers, but is abundant upon Bernier and Dorré Islands. *Lagorchestes hirsutus* (R) is extremely rare. *L. leporides* and *L. asomatus* are probably extinct.
Rock-Wallabies:
Petrogale penicillata, P. rothschildi, P. purpureicollis, P. brachyotis and *Peradorcas concinna* are reasonably common in appropriate habitats. *P. xanthopus* (R) has declined in range and numbers; although protected, it may be endangered (see Figure 1).

Tree-Kangaroos:

Dendrolagus lumholtzi and *D. bennettianus* are decreasing in range and numbers due to removal of rain-forest habitats. These species are not currently endangered, but may become so.

Rat-Kangaroos:

Hypsiprymnodon moschatus (R) is seldom seen, but Calaby (1971) regards it as existing in satisfactory numbers. *Caloprymnus campestris* (R) is rare and possibly endangered. *Aepyprymnus rufescens*, *Bettongia penicillata* (R), *B. lesueuri* (R) and *B. gaimardi* have declined in range and numbers, but are common in appropriate habitats,

FIGURE 1. The Yellow-footed Rock-wallaby (*Petrogale xanthopus*) has adapted poorly to captivity in most places, but a colony exists in the Adelaide Zoo, South Australia. (Photo: Harry Millen.)

the latter two species now being restricted essentially to islands. *B. tropica* is either extinct or extremely rare.

Potorous tridactylus (R) has declined in range and numbers, but appears not to be endangered. *P. platyops* is probably extinct.

(ii) Family Phalangeridae

Brush-tailed Possums:

Trichosurus vulpecula and *T. caninus* are abundant.

Scaly-tailed Possums:

Wyulda squamicaudata (R), recently rediscovered, is rare but may not be endangered.

Cuscuses:

Phalanger maculatus is not common in Australia, but is so in New Guinea. *P. orientalis* (R), is restricted and rare.

(iii) Family Petauridae

Ring-tailed Possums:

Pseudocheirus peregrinus, represented by many subspecies, is common and widespread. *Hemibelideus lemuroides* and *Petropseudes dahli* each have restricted ranges, but are not uncommon.

Gliding Possums:

Petaurus breviceps and *P. norfolcensis* are widespread and common, *P. australis* somewhat less so. *Schoinobates volans* is diminishing in range and numbers, but is not rare. *Dactylopsila trivirgata* is uncommon in Australia, but common in New Guinea.

FIGURE 2. The mountain pygmy possum (*Burramys parvus*) was known only as a late Pleistocene fossil until 1966 when one was caught in a ski hut in the Australian alps. The first captive breeding of the species occurred in 1972 in a large air-conditioned enclosure in Taronga Zoo's nocturnal house. (Photo: Harry Millen.)

Leadbeater's Possum:

Gymnobelideus leadbeateri (R), rediscovered in 1961, is rare. Until more is known of it, the species should be regarded as endangered.

(iv) Family Burramyidae

Pygmy Glider and Pygmy Possums:

Acrobates pygmaeus, Cercatetus concinnus, C. nanus, and *C. lepidus* are cryptic, but not uncommon. *Burramys parvus* (see Figure 2) rediscovered in 1966, appears to be rare and should tentatively be regarded as endangered.

(v) Family Tarsipedidae

Honey Possum:

Tarsipes spencerae is seldom seen, but is not uncommon.

(vi) Family Phascolarctidae
Koala:

Phascolarctos cinereus has diminished in distribution and numbers since European settlement, but appears now to exist in satisfactory numbers in many areas.

(vii) Family Vombatidae
Wombats:

Vombatus ursinus is common. Lasiorhinus latifrons is diminishing in range, but is common in appropriate habitats. L. barnardi is rare and endangered. L. gillespiei is probably extinct.

(viii) Family Peramelidae
Short-nosed Bandicoots:

Isoodon obesulus, I. macrourus and I. auratus are relatively common.

Long-nosed Bandicoots:

Perameles nasuta is abundant. P. gunni and P. bougainvillei (R) have declined and exist only as island populations. P. eremiana is either extinct or extremely rare. Echymipera rufescens is rare in Australia, but not in New Guinea.

Pig-footed Bandicoot:

Chaeropus ecaudatus (R) is probably extinct.

Rabbit-eared Bandicoots:

Macrotis lagotis (R) is diminishing in range and numbers and is probably becoming rare. M. leucura is probably extinct.

(ix) Family Dasyuridae
Dasyures:

Dasyurus (= Satanellus) hallucatus is widely distributed and common. D. maculatus and D. viverrinus (R) have declined in range and numbers and are now common only in Tasmania. D. geoffroyi (R) has declined in range and numbers and is probably endangered.

Tasmanian Devil:

Sarcophilus harrisii is common in Tasmania.

Phascogales:

Phascogale tapoatafa is seldom seen, but is common over most of its range. P. calura (R) is endangered.

Kowari:

Dasyuroides byrnei is uncommon, but not endangered.

Mulgara:

Dasycercus cristicauda fluctuates in numbers, but is not rare.

Antechinuses:

Antechinus flavipes, A. stuartii and A. swainsonii are common; A. bellus and A. macdonanellensis reasonably so; A. godmani and A. apicalis are uncommon; A. minimus is rare.

Pygmy Antechinuses:

Antechinus maculatus is widely distributed and not uncommon; Planigale ingrami is uncommon (see Figure 3); P. subtilissima (R) and P. tenuirostris (R) are rare and probably endangered.

Narrow-footed Marsupial Mice:

Sminthopsis murina, S. crassicaudata, S. leucopus, and S. macroura are common; S. granulipes and S. hirtipes are rare; S. longicaudata (R) and S. psammophila may be extinct. The status of S. rufigenis, S. nitela and S. froggatti is unknown.

Long-legged Marsupial Mice:
  Antechinomys spenceri is relatively common. *A. laniger* (R) is uncommon.
Numbat:
  Myrmecobius fasciatus (R) has diminished seriously in range and numbers and is endangered (see Figure 4).
(x) Family Thylacinidae
Tasmanian Wolf:
  Thylacinus cynocephalus (R) is almost certainly extinct.
(xi) Family Notoryctidae
Marsupial Mole:
  Notoryctes typhlops is cryptic and seldom seen, but may not be rare.

FIGURE 3. Ingram's planigale (*Planigale ingrami*) is probably not endangered, but is very little known. It is breeding beyond the second captive generation in the nocturnal house of Taronga Zoo, Sydney. (Photo: Harry Millen.)

Before dealing specifically with husbandry in captivity, it will be useful to list the conclusions that may be drawn from the above data.

(1) No Australian monotreme is either rare or endangered. The echidna is widespread and common and the platypus is well established on the eastern coast of Australia and Tasmania. Both species are apical carnivores and could be ultimate accumulators of DDT but there is, as yet, no evidence that their populations are so affected. Present husbandry methods have led to great longevities of captive echidnas but only a few hatchings, and no rearing of young beyond a few days. The platypus has bred once in captivity.

Lack of success in these areas is a matter of concern to zoologists but is not strictly pertinent to the problems of husbandry of rare or endangered species.

(2) The large grazing macropods have not been adversely affected by the advent of industrial-agrarian man: on the contrary, the conversion of sclerophyll forest and savannah into grasslands has increased the range and populations of the big kangaroos.

(3) The larger wallabies, which have always occupied more specialized habitats than the big kangaroos, are now much more restricted. Nevertheless, within smaller areas they may still increase to pest proportions.

(4) Many of the smaller wallabies are under extreme and cumulative human pressure, but some species have found island refuges where they are currently protected.

FIGURE 4. Until 1968, the greatest longevity of a captive Numbat (*Myrmecobius fasciatus*) was less than 2 months. Since then, a male Numbat has survived in Taronga Zoo for 5 years and its mate is still living after 6 years, this success being attributed to an exclusive diet of live termites. Numbats have bred twice in Taronga Zoo, but the young have not survived longer than 9 weeks.

(5) The rat-kangaroos and their allies tend to be specialized in habitat needs and to include a proportion of animal food in their diets. As quasi-carnivores, they are more vulnerable than herbivores to disturbance of an ecological balance. It is no coincidence that viable populations of most of these species are now found mainly on offshore islands or, as in the case of the musk rat-kangaroo, to a relic rain-forest area.

(6) The arboreal phalangers include generalized omnivores and specialized

herbivores. The former, exemplified by the brush-tailed and ring-tailed possums, are in no danger; the latter include some endangered species.

(7) The bandicoots are essentially insectivorous, although some are omnivores. Not surprisingly, the omnivores have fared better and at least one species is a garden "pest".

(8) The carnivorous dasyurids, occupying the apices of food-pyramids, are extremely vulnerable to disturbance at lower trophic levels. Most of the larger coastal forms are in present or future danger. As previously indicated, the desert dasyurids probably have a more secure future.

(9) The numbat is a specialized dasyurid which feeds exclusively on termites. Without appropriate fallen trees to provide termite habitations, the numbat cannot obtain its food. Clearing of land for agriculture or forestry has reduced the distribution of the numbat to the point of imminent extinction.

(10) The marsupial mole is insectivorous. It may or may not be rare. As a desert animal, it could be expected to be widespread and therefore relatively secure.

HUSBANDRY OF RARE MARSUPIALS

The following notes demonstrate, by their poverty, the paucity of available information on the successful husbandry of indubitably rare or endangered marsupials. With few exceptions, recommendations are based on knowledge of the requirements of the more common members of the genera rather than the particularly endangered species.

(i) *Onychogalea* spp. These may be fed in the same way as any of the large wallabies. They appear to have no unusual habitat requirements.

(ii) *Lagorchestes* and *Lagostrophus* spp. There is little information on the captive husbandry of these species, but they appear to be typical herbivorous macropods. They are easily frightened and may injure themselves in panic. Being gregarious, they are best kept as groups.

(iii) *Petrogale* spp. These thrive on a normal macropod diet but should be given rather drier food than that of the coastal kangaroos. They are prone to panic and subsequent damage against enclosure walls. Their climbing ability is uncanny and care must be given to the design of their enclosures to prevent escape.

(iv) *Dendrolagus* spp. These survive on a normal macropod diet, but should be given a supplement of fresh fruit and vegetables such as oranges, apples, carrots, etc. Males may be very aggressive and should be separated, each with three to five females. Tree kangaroos adjust well to captivity.

(v) *Hypsiprymnodon*. Unknown in captivity. From what little is known of its biology, an appropriate diet would include grass, fresh leaves, soft oily nuts, soft or hard dog-food, and insects.

(vi) *Caloprymus*. Unknown.

(vii) *Bettongia* spp. Can be fed on a basic macropod diet supplemented by fruit, dog-food, insects and fresh fish. Solitary, burrowing animals, they should be given sufficient area to establish separate territories and sufficient depth of soil to make burrows.

(viii) *Potorous* spp. Can be fed a basic macropod diet. Solitary and shy, they require large areas with good ground cover and an opportunity to dig burrows.

(ix) *Wyulda*. Feeds on blossoms, fruits, nuts. Requires warmth and shelter.

(x) *Phalanger* spp. Feed on soft fruits. Vitamins (especially B and D group) may be administered in honey solution from a drinking bottle. They require warmth and security and readily succumb to shock when surroundings are suddenly altered.

(xi) *Dactylopsila*. Eats soft fruits and small quantities of meat, and requires supplementary insect food.

(xii) *Gymnobelideus*. Eats blossoms, fresh eucalypt leaf-tips, honey, soft fruits; requires secure shelters.

(xiii) *Burramys*. Thrives on a basic diet of oily seeds, supplemented by meal-worms: accepts honey and peanut butter.

(xiv) *Lasiorhinus*. Thrives on a general herbivore (macropod or ungulate) diet. Requires secure burrow and ability to avoid other individuals.

(xv) *Perameles*, *Echymipera* and *Macrotis* spp. Eat fresh minced meat, dog-food, freshly-killed mice, insects, and fruit. Solitary and aggressive. Require large area and secure refuges.

(xvi) *Dasyurus* and *Phascogale* spp. Eat fresh minced meat, mice, chicks. Solitary and aggressive. Require secure refuges.

(xvii) *Dasyuroides* and *Dasycercus*. Eat fresh minced meat, young mice, chicks, insects. Require opportunity to burrow. Reasonably social, but males are aggressive in breeding seasons.

(xviii) *Antechinus* spp. Eat small mice and insects. Solitary and aggressive. Require secure refuges.

(xix) *Planigale*, *Sminthopsis* and *Antechinomys* spp. Eat small mice and insects. Solitary and aggressive. Require secure refuges.

(xx) *Myrmecobius*. Survive only on diet of living termites in freshly-broken termitaria. Although solitary, may be held as pairs. Require safe refuges. Numbats have bred twice in Taronga Zoo but young have not yet survived beyond the age of nine weeks.

(xxi) *Notoryctes*. Eats live insects. Requires warmth and ability to burrow.

CONCLUSIONS

There can be no satisfactory summary of this unsatisfactory catalogue, unless it be that most of the rare and/or endangered species of Australian marsupials tend to share the following characteristics: They are small in size; nocturnally active; require insects as part of their diet; are solitary, aggressive and not particularly beautiful.

None of these characteristics is such as to endear an animal to an undiscerning public. I believe that it is for this reason that far more attention has been given, for example, to the bongo, okapi, and Sumatran rhinoceros than to the nail-tailed wallaby, musk rat-kangaroo and spiny bandicoot. With the exception of the numbat (a beautiful, diurnal, and non-aggressive species), there seem to be no insuperable difficulties in the captive husbandry of rare Australian marsupials, yet only one other species, the yellow-footed rock wallaby, is consistently bred in captivity. It is perhaps no coincidence that this is large, diurnal, herbivorous, social, and very beautiful.

APPENDIX

Macropod Diet

The following formula, developed by Prof. A. R. Main of the University of Western Australia has proved satisfactory for a wide variety of grazing macropods.

Composition and Preparation of Ration Mix

INGREDIENTS	kg	*Minerals %	%	†Trace Elements	g
Wheat Chaff	50	Sodium chloride	40	Ferric citrate	150
Starch	15·2	Calcium carbonate	17	Copper sulphate	
Sugar (sucrose)a	6·2	Calcium phosphate	20	pentahydrate	60
Molasses	6·0	Magnesium sulphate		Manganese sulphate	9
Casein	7·2	heptahydrate	12	Potassium iodide	1·5
Minerals*	3·6	Potassium chloride	8	Cobalt chloride	
Rovimix E.25b	0·15	Trace elements†	3	septahydrate	0·6
				Zinc carbonate	15
				Sodium sulphate	
				(anhydrous)	1008·5

a Winter use 12·4 kg.

b Rovimix E.25 Roche Products Pty. Ltd.; Stabilized Vitamin E powder. Manufacturer: F. Hoffman, La Roche and Cie, S. A., Basle, Switzerland. Potency per gram 250 I.U. Vi. E (250 mg. dl. alpha to—copherol acetate).

PREPARATION

(1) Dissolve flour and casein in about 15 l of water with about 10 g sodium A.R./kg of casein. (2) Dissolve Rovimix E and sugar in 22 l of water and add molasses and minerals. Mix well. (3) When all components except chaff are in solution, add to the chaff in mixer while mixing slowly. (4) Mix for 5–10 min and then dry in forced draught oven at about 60°C. Supplements: greens, stale bread.

Note on the Breeding of the Eastern Native Cat at Melbourne Zoo

E. Weber

The Eastern native cat (*Dasyurus viverrinus*) is a small carnivorous marsupial. Its distribution ranges through eastern New South Wales, Victoria, South Australia (probably extinct) and Tasmania (Troughton, 1965). In the late thirties and early forties, Eastern native cats were quite common in Victoria. The last specimen collected in Victoria was in 1955 (pers. comm. Robert Warneke, Senior Research Officer, Fisheries and Wildlife Division). The present status in Victoria is very rare, possibly extinct. Circumstantial evidence points towards an epidemic disease as being responsible for the animals' rapid disappearance from most of the mainland at the turn of the century (pers. comm. R. Warneke). In Tasmania the Eastern native cat is still plentiful and reports indicate that their range is extending. In the wild they are very shy and secretive, hunting over large areas during the early hours of the morning and night. Food consists of any animal prey that can be caught, from insects to birds, mammals and reptiles.

We were extremely pleased when we received a pair of these interesting nocturnal marsupials from the then "Animal and Bird Protection Board of Tasmania" now incorporated into the "National Parks Wildlife Service". The animals arrived at the Melbourne Zoo in good physical condition in April 1969. They were placed in a small weldmesh cage, 50 cm wide by 100 cm deep by 50 cm high. An empty bag was placed in the cage to enable the animals to take refuge when disturbed. The cage was placed in the garage of my residence in the Zoo for a period of ten days while a large enclosure was constructed in my backyard. I felt that by keeping the animals under close surveillance I would be able to observe their matings and, at the appropriate time, separate the pair to allow the female to give birth without the male's interference. The first mating was observed approximately 3 days after their arrival in 1969 and continued, with only short pauses, for 4 days. Three days after the last mating was observed, the female was removed and placed in the large enclosure measuring 7 m wide by 3 m deep by 2 m high; but she escaped the same day through a narrow gap under the fence. When she was recaptured approximately 2 weeks later a check of the pouch revealed five embryos fastened to five of the six teats. As the female was very distressed and struggled desperately, I did not endeavour to measure the embryos, though they appeared to be approximately 8 mm long. I did not think it wise to interfere too much as my main aim was to breed and raise these animals successfully. The sexing of the young revealed one male and four females, all of which were raised by the female without difficulty.

The following year (1970) I intended to keep a more accurate record of the growth and development of the young. Matings, which took place in June as compared to late April the previous year, occurred late at night and in the very early hours of the morning. For this reason, direct observations were very difficult. I checked the pouches of the mated females daily, but no young were found even though the pouches were cleaned frequently by the females and were well developed. I wondered if this extent of interference may have caused the female to become too nervous during birth and to kill the young.

In November 1970, the original pair and one of their female offspring were placed together in a large enclosure. Mating commenced late in June 1971. Although no matings were actually observed, they were evident from the fact that both females showed signs of saliva and ruffled fur on their necks. (From previous observations, it was noticed that the male grasps the neck of the female in his mouth when mating). The male remained with the females for another 4 days and was then removed to his bachelor quarters. The two females were separated and each provided with a wooden nesting box which measured 37 cm wide by 20 cm deep by 20 cm high, with a narrow opening on one side. After separation the pouches were not checked for 24 days to allow the female sufficient time to give birth before disturbance. The check at the end of that period revealed five embryos in the pouch of the old female and three embryos in the pouch of the young female. The old female lost one young in the first month but raised the other four without problems. They were later found to be all males. The young female raised one male and two females. When discovered on 10 July 1971 the old female's embryos measured approximately 8 mm long. The embryos of the younger females were slightly smaller (see Table 1 and Fig. 1).

The diet should be varied as often as it is possible. Our animals are fed mainly on whole prey animals, including skin and intestines. Four to five good meals per week seems to be sufficient to keep them in good condition. If the animals leave a large portion of their food, they are not fed the next day. However, once the female is suspected of being pregnant and the male has been removed from her enclosure she is given as much food as she can eat. This is a safety precaution to make sure that she is not hungry when giving birth; otherwise she may eat her young.

The size and design of the enclosure might be of importance too, if breeding is the aim. 3×2 m should probably be the minimum. The enclosure should be furnished with rocks and some branches to facilitate climbing. Even though in the wild the native cat does very little tree climbing, the furnishings would stimulate exercise and would make it more interesting for the animals. They do a

TABLE 1. Development of the young female's litter in 1971.

Date	Average size (cm)	Average weight (g)	Appearance
July 16	$1\frac{1}{2}$	—	Naked (eyes closed)
July 23	$2\frac{1}{2}$	—	Naked (eyes closed)
Aug. 8	5^a	—	Fine spots appeared
Aug. 28	6	—	Sparse hair growth Spots more apparent Eyelashes appeared
Sept. 9	$8\frac{3}{4}$	—	Spots very pronounced Fully covered with fine hair
Sept. 17	11 (body) $5\frac{1}{2}$ (tail)	57	Fully haired, eyes open
Sept. 29	$15\frac{1}{2}$ (body) $9\frac{1}{4}$ (tail)	130	Teeth well established
Oct. 12	$18\frac{3}{4}$ (body) $11\frac{1}{2}$ (tail)	222	Observed running around by themselves, coat well developed

^{a} Young very difficult to measure.

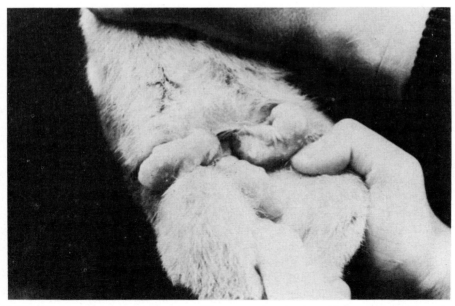

FIGURE 1. Three native cat pouch-young (*Dasyurus viverrinus*) at 46 days of age. Note the white spots on the dorsal surfaces. (Photo: Christian Schmidt.)

fair amount of digging, especially along the perimeter and under rocks and other objects in their enclosure. This is probably a good thing, as it provides additional activity and might keep them from pacing up and down along the walls of the enclosure. Even though they are shy animals by nature, if hand-fed they will become quite tame, accepting food from their keeper's hand. However, they struggle desperately if handled for pouch checking. One way of reducing the struggle is to prevent them from entering their usual sleeping box and to place an empty bag inside the enclosure. After a short while the animals will either enter the bag or crawl under it. The animals can then be restrained much more easily and by exposing the hind quarters only the pouch can be inspected relatively easily. Once the young are born, and have fastened securely to the teats there is little chance of them being dislodged during routine inspection, if care is taken to ensure that examination is carried out swiftly and without too much struggling.

After two successful litters had been born and raised in 1971, following the initial litter in 1969, all our males (which were kept in a separate enclosure) were unfortunately stolen and we have so far been unable to obtain another male. We are hopeful that we will have a male for the 1974 breeding season, so that expansion of our stock can continue.

Breeding of Malagasy Lemurs in Captivity

Over a period of several decades attempts to breed various species of Malagasy lemurs have been made in zoological gardens in different parts of the world, and there is now a great deal of relevant literature, though this is primarily devoted to the maintenance and reproduction of species of the genus *Lemur*. However, it is evident that for many species we still lack adequate experience and that there is a vital need for detailed studies of the natural habits of these species within their respective biotopes.

Positive results from attempts to breed animals in captivity are often regarded, quite justifiably, as a good test of the success of the techniques of maintenance. On the other hand, lack of reproductive success is not necessarily a sign of poor health, and it is important to recognize that animals which are in very good physical condition may fail to breed for a variety of reasons. One of the principal reasons is quite certainly related to the rhythm of illumination in captivity. The island of Madagascar is located between 12° and 26° latitude south and possesses a tropical climate with a daylength rhythm the reverse of that in the northern hemisphere. The endemic lemurs are seasonally polyoestrous, that is, they exhibit a small number of oestrous cycles within a restricted breeding season each year. They also show accompanying marked seasonal physiological cycles which are reversed when the animals are transported to the northern hemisphere.

Recent experiments carried out on the mouse lemur, *Microcebus murinus*, (Petter-Rousseaux 1970, 1972) have demonstrated that the physiological cycles of these animals are modified extremely rapidly after the shift from one hemisphere to another, and that their reproduction is greatly influenced by the variation in the circadian (day/night) rhythm. Similar effects have been observed with several other lemur species, and it would seem that they are common to the entire group of lemurs. It is therefore hardly surprising that these animals are difficult to breed if one pays too little attention to the light cycle. This is the case, for example, with ringtail lemurs, *Lemur catta*, maintained in some modern European zoological gardens, where the cages are provided with regular electrical illumination during the day to meet the needs of visitors and of the keepers. In this way, the natural illumination rhythm is disrupted (sometimes to the extent of complete suppression of variation in daylength), the physiological rhythms of the animals are modified, and they fail to breed.

The light factor is certainly not the only one within the group which we may refer to as *climatic factors*, and it is likely, although we have as yet very little information on this subject, that variations in cycles of ambient temperature or humidity may also exert an influence on physiological rhythms.

On another tack, it is equally important to take into account various *behavioural factors*, but since these vary from species to species it is necessary to discuss them separately in the account which follows. On the basis of our own experience since 1954 with laboratory colonies of lemurs and in the light of information provided by our colleagues for colonies maintained in Madagascar, Europe or America, it is possible to provide for each lemur species a tentative list of the main technical requirements for effective maintenance and eventual breeding in captivity.

1. THE LESSER MOUSE LEMUR (*Microcebus murinus*)

As already stated above, the influence of the light rhythm has already been clearly demonstrated for this nocturnal species, which is the smallest of the lemurs and little bigger than a mouse. The light rhythm is particularly concerned in the cycle of fat deposition and loss, and in the annual onset and arrest of oestrus (Petter-Rousseaux, 1972). Mouse lemurs which are subjected to that part of the illumination cycle where the days are increasing in length exhibit increase in activity and corresponding loss in body-weight. If the experimental exposure to increasing daylength is prolonged, the animals may lose weight to a dangerous extent and they may accordingly be driven to a critical state which can only be remedied by inversion of the light rhythm.

It is possible that a cycle of variation in temperature and humidity may also play a part in influencing physiological cycles in this species, though the influence exerted may differ according to the subspecies concerned. The subspecies *Microcebus murinus murinus* (grey mouse lemur), which normally lives in areas where the climate is very dry for at least part of the year, in the north-west, west and south of Madagascar, adapts better to conditions in captivity (where the atmosphere is generally drier) than does the subspecies *Microcebus murinus rufus* (brown mouse lemur), which inhabits the humid eastern coastal region of Madagascar.

In general, with a captive colony of lesser mouse lemurs, it is necessary to provide the animals with a fairly high ambient temperature of at least 25°C for a large part of the time, and it is desirable that the temperature should not fall below 18°C. Lesser mouse lemurs maintained in captivity in London (Martin, 1972*a*), where they have bred with reasonable success over the last 2 years, are subjected to a daily cyclic variation of temperature, ranging between 25°C during the night phase and 31°C during the day.

The small body size of lesser mouse lemurs permits maintenance and breeding in cages of relatively small dimensions, even as small as $50 \times 50 \times 50$ cm.

However, somewhat larger cages (e.g. $100 \times 200 \times 200$ cm) are preferable, as they permit the animals to exhibit more normal activity. It is important to equip the cages with branches and foliage. In addition, it is necessary to provide a nest-box which will permit the animals to shield themselves from the light during their day-time sleeping phase. Following the results obtained by Martin (1972*b*), who collected data on the dimensions of the nests utilized under natural conditions, the nest cavity should have a diameter of 6–14 cm.

If the cage-size permits, it seems to be preferable to group adult animals in batches composed of one male and two or three females. In some cases, births have even occurred in cages containing one male and six females. Particularly during the period immediately following introduction to the cage, the animals must be carefully observed so that any fighting is immediately noticed.

If an animal seems to be ailing for no apparent reason, it is generally preferable to isolate it for a while to allow it to regain weight, but it is usually very difficult to re-integrate such an animal with its group after recovery. It would seem, in some cases at least, that psychological factors may be responsible for loss in weight of this kind.

Under natural conditions, lesser mouse lemurs have an insectivorous/frugivorous diet; but they also eat resins, buds and leaves and will lick flowers. In captivity, one can attempt to replicate this diet as closely as possible, or completely modify it by providing mainly insects and fruit, perhaps with some milk. In any event, it is necessary to add multivitamin preparations to the diet and the diet must always contain proteins and fats which can be found in insects or in certain fruits (such as avocado pears) which are generally found to be consumed readily by mouse lemurs. Eggs and cheese are also usually accepted, but mouse lemurs are particularly interested in insects (crickets, locusts, mealworms) and new-born mice. In addition, it is usually quite easy to induce them to accept a cake made of cooked semolina and eggs, to which one can add various supplements such as vitamins and mineral salts. This technique, which is being tested at present, may eventually lead to rationalization of the diet in captivity.

It is important that the food should be broken up into small pieces which the animal can pick up with ease and, if necessary, carry to a branch in order to eat it undisturbed. The diet should be varied according to the phase of the annual physiological cycle, and it may be advantageous to modify the supply of food partly according to the demand. In some cases, probably as a result of the conditions in captivity, mouse lemurs may exhibit exaggerated fat accumulation, and here it is best to limit the food supply.

Water, provided by a dispenser or an automatic nozzle, must be available at all times.

This species has been frequently bred in captivity, but various factors have always kept the breeding rate in our colony well below that found under natural conditions. In fact, maintenance and breeding of lesser mouse lemurs would seem to be a delicate matter requiring great attention to cleanliness as well as continued surveillance of the animals. In some cases, it seems that taming of the young by manipulation from birth onwards promotes successful reproduction of the animals by rendering them less sensitive to external stress factors.

The lesser mouse lemur, despite its small size, survives for long periods in captivity. We have kept some individuals in captivity for more than 10 years, whilst rats (for example) rarely live for more than 2 years.

The main reasons for breeding failure would seem to be due in all cases to inadequate conditions of maintenance, such as inappropriate diet, the stressful influence of other mouse lemurs present nearby and frequent disturbance (for example, an animal whose cage has been moved may lose several grams in weight in the course of the next few days).

The main pathological symptoms that have been observed in our colony seem to be almost exclusively attributable to what one knows of the phenomenon of stress (Perret, 1973). In fact, one often finds pulmonary oedema, nephritis and ulceration of the stomach. Among the other pathological manifestations encountered are glucidic disorder, with more or less pronounced glycosuria, anaemia, various parasitic infestations and some cancers.

In order to avoid sources of stress, it is extremely useful to make use of information about the natural structure of populations in designing techniques in captivity, as has been recently attempted by Martin (1972a, 1972b). It must be remembered that the animals may influence one another by communication not only at the visual level, but also through olfactory means (e.g. urine-marking) and by auditory interaction (including numerous ultrasonic vocalizations). In any event, if one wishes to maintain a large number of animals in a small space, it is necessary to utilize a fan which will change the air regularly, thus removing marking odours, and whose noise will to some extent cover communication through sounds.

2. COQUEREL'S MOUSE LEMUR (*Microcebus coquereli*)

Coquerel's mouse lemur (Fig. 1) is a nocturnal species fairly close in body-size to the European squirrel. The conditions necessary for maintenance in captivity of this species, which has rarely been collected for zoological gardens, would seem to be fairly close to those necessary for the lesser mouse lemur. However, the much larger body-size requires the use of far bigger cages in which three or four animals can comfortably be installed. If they are provided with brambles and creepers along with a number of well-situated branches, they will quite rapidly construct a nest in which they will spend their day sleeping (E. Pages, pers. comm.).

The diet is similar to that for the lesser mouse lemur. They readily eat minced meat, milk, insects and dead adult mice, of which they usually eat everything but the skin.

We have maintained several of these animals in our colony for 3 years, and they have remained in excellent condition. Although there were no breeding successes initially, one infant was born in 1973. This was the first recorded birth in captivity.

FIGURE 1. The rare Coquerel's mouse lemur (*Microcebus coquereli*) photographed in captivity. A small colony of these animals has now been established at the Muséum National d'Histoire Naturelle in Brunoy.

They are lively and active animals, but seem to be relatively unaffected by disturbance. In particular, they react very little to noise near at hand, and they only rarely utter vocalizations.

3. DWARF LEMURS (*Cheirogaleus major* and *Cheirogaleus medius*)

Dwarf lemurs are nocturnal animals; the brown dwarf lemur (*Cheirogaleus major*) is similar to Coquerel's mouse lemur in size, whilst the fat-tailed dwarf lemur (*Cheirogaleus medius*) is intermediate in size between the above two types of mouse lemur. The former lives in the humid eastern coastal forest of Madagascar, whilst the latter inhabits the drier forests of the northwest, west and south of the island.

Cheirogaleus major requires a relatively humid atmosphere, whilst *Cheirogaleus medius* adapts quite well to much drier conditions. Their temperature requirements are comparable to those of the mouse lemurs.

In order to maintain the animals in good health, it is preferable to provide them with a relatively large cage. In addition, they must be supplied with a nest-box of appropriate size which will permit them to shelter from the light during their daytime resting period. It is possible to group several animals in the same cage; but—as with the mouse lemurs—it is preferable not to place two adult males together if one wishes to avoid fighting, which may sometimes become quite serious.

Under natural conditions, *Cheirogaleus* species feed primarily upon fruits, but they also eat flowers and buds and will prey upon insects.

With *Cheirogaleus medius*, we have experienced great difficulties in maintaining them in good health for any length of time. These difficulties are probably due to an inadequate diet. Their natural diet, as with their general behavioural repertoire under natural conditions, is poorly known, and it is likely that the variety of food which we can provide in captivity (or which they will accept under caged conditions) is insufficient. The animals remain quite fat for some time and the tail, in particular, is swollen with reserves, but gradually signs of paralysis appear. The first pathological sign observed is a poor condition of the pelage, which is often accompanied by loss of hair on the tail and certain parts of the body. Motor disturbance affecting the muscles of the hind limbs slowly develops, and the muscles of the fore limbs are then affected in their turn. Injections of vitamins of the B group seem to retard the development of this ailment, but it is difficult to cure the animals, despite the fact that it is possible to arrest the progress of the paralysis and even to achieve transitory improvement. The animals may survive for long periods of time with paralysis of this kind, which sometimes renders them completely infirm. This remarkable fragility is most characteristic of *Cheirogaleus medius*, but initial symptoms have also been noted with *Cheirogaleus major*.

These animals are very sensitive to noise in their surroundings, but their responses are generally relatively slow and discreet. They mark the branches along which they pass with their faeces.

Breeding successes have been obtained in captivity with tame *Cheirogaleus major* (see Petter-Rousseaux, 1962).

4. THE FORK-CROWNED LEMUR (*Phaner furcifer*)

This nocturnal species, which resembles *Microcebus coquereli* in body-size, is also very rare in captivity, despite the fact that it is fairly easy to maintain. Most of the conditions for maintenance are similar to those required for the preceding species, but it would appear that its diet does not include insects under natural conditions, contrary to what one would expect—particularly from an examination of its canine teeth and its well-developed, pointed premolars.

The fork-crowned lemur feeds naturally on sap, resins, honey, the secretions of certain parasitic homopterans, and the nectar of various flowers, which it can reach with its very fine tongue (Petter *et al.*, 1971). In captivity, this species only seems to accept insects if the remainder of its diet does not contain a sufficient proportion of proteins; it will feed on honey, pastes made with milk-based baby-foods, milk containing multivitamin preparations, and very ripe fruit.

These animals are very active and responsive to noises of all kinds. They often produce a great deal of noise themselves. The male marks his surroundings with a gland situated beneath the chin and neck.

We have maintained several specimens of this species in excellent condition in captivity for more than 3 years, but so far no breeding successes have been obtained.

5. TRUE LEMURS AND VARIEGATED LEMURS (Various species and subspecies of *Lemur*; *Varecia*)

These animals, all of which are as large as, or somewhat bigger than, a cat, are either diurnal or crepuscular in activity. In general, they are easy to maintain in captivity and some types are relatively common in various zoological gardens.

Since the various species and subspecies exhibit different degrees of adaptation to arid conditions, it is preferable to attempt to provide appropriate humidity conditions in each case.

Species of the genus *Lemur* (*Lemur catta*; various subspecies of *Lemur fulvus*) will usually support quite well much more varied temperature conditions than those tolerated by the species so far discussed. They are less sensitive to cold, and they adapt relatively well to the normal temperatures of spring and summer in a temperate climate. In our cages at Brunoy (France), they will even venture out into the external enclosure in winter, and this leads to more pronounced development of the pelage. Even under the climatic conditions of Tananarive, however, it is necessary to provide a shelter of some kind, in the form of a partially closed box of suitable size in which they can sleep during the night.

Mongoose lemurs (*Lemur mongoz*), which are adapted to the relatively dry and hot conditions of the west of Madagascar, require somewhat higher temperatures in captivity than the other *Lemur* species, and they will often remain in poor condition if they are subjected to the same conditions as the latter.

The size of the cage does not seem to represent a very important factor for the health of *Lemur* species in captivity, and breeding successes have been obtained without difficulty in cages measuring only 1 × 1 × 1 m in Tananarive. However, it is obviously preferable to provide the animals with a cage of at least 8 sq.m in surface area, supplied with branches permitting the animals to exercise themselves. In general, *Lemur* species avoid walking across the ground, and they prefer to leap from one support to another; accordingly, it is preferable to include logs or rocks in the cage as well. Under natural conditions, they do not seek out special retreats for sleeping; in fact, their body-size is too large to permit easy acquisition of suitable retreats. *Lemur macaco*, *L. fulvus*, and *L. catta*, which live naturally in troops, can be placed in groups of five to ten animals in the same cage; but it is necessary to keep a careful watch on their behaviour and to separate any individual which is regularly chased by another. Any persecuted individual of this kind has only restricted access to food, and it may die of exhaustion after a few days. In most cases, it is the females which are most intolerant and most dominant within the group.

It is possible to keep several subspecies of *Lemur fulvus* in the same cage, and even to mix them with a group of mongoose lemurs, but the latter are always inferior in the rank-order. In fact, mongoose lemurs seem to be more difficult to maintain in large groups. Intolerance is often noticed as soon as four or more animals are present in a cage. In our own colony, in which a pair produced an infant regularly every year, from the age of 3 years onwards any young females would begin to attack the mother or to fight among themselves, and it was necessary to remove them from the group. The same applies to variegated lemurs (*Varecia variegata*), which are always encountered in small groups in the wild and may in fact live as family parties.

With most *Lemur fulvus* subspecies and with *Lemur catta*, the males, even if they are very tame, may become extremely aggressive from puberty onwards, and they will often attack any strange person and on occasions even their keepers. However, in most cases such males will remain friendly towards the keeper if he is alone and is not afraid of being bitten. Bites from *Lemur* species are quite dangerous, since at about the age of 2 years the canine teeth of the males become long and pointed, and the animals are capable of launching rapid, unexpected attacks which may occur when one has one's back turned to the animals, or even when one has simply shifted one's gaze. A characteristic posture, with the head slightly lifted, betrays aggressive intentions of this kind.

The natural diet of *Lemur* and *Varecia* is very varied, consisting of numerous fruits, leaves, buds, flowers, resins and bark. It is obviously impossible to provide them with the same dietary variety in captivity, but one can nevertheless achieve good breeding successes with regular reproduction by assuring a fair variety of food and providing multivitamin additives.

Under natural conditions, most true lemur species seem to exclude insects entirely from the diet, but in captivity they may accept insects and even consume them readily if they become adapted to this diet, particularly if there is some degree of protein deficiency in the food which is otherwise given. In many cases, it is advisable to provide fresh branches, in addition to fruits (bananas, apples and any fruit in season) and various greenstuff (lettuce; grass). A regular source of protein can be provided in the form of monkey biscuits, which are frequently utilized in laboratories for feeding macaques.

In Tananarive, the basic ration fed to the true lemurs and variegated lemurs is as follows (R. Albignac, pers. comm.):

1.

Bananas	200 g
Various fruits	150 g
Bread	25 g
Cooked rice	50 g
Carrots	25 g
	total:	450 g

2. 50 ml of milk with a few drops of multivitamin supplement.

3. Grass is regularly scattered in the cages, and large mango-tree branches are renewed every 2 days.

With conditions of this kind, mortality is very low in *Lemur* colonies and breeding occurs regularly. With *Lemur* species, one can obtain one infant and sometimes two infants per year; with *Varecia*, two infants per year is the rule.

In the various colonies with which we are acquainted, the main cause of mortality is accidental death (following wounds inflicted during fights, effects of injuries during capture; etc.). Whenever the birth of an infant is expected in a cage containing a group, it is advisable to isolate the female with, at the most, the male and one other individual, since with a larger group the infant may suffer from fights or lose its mother by clinging to the belly of another adult which may injure the infant in trying to remove it, and which would in any case be incapable of caring for the baby.

In Tananarive, there were at one time many instances of pulmonary damage followed by sudden death during the humid period January-March and during the cold month of July. However, installation of a heating system in the retreats and immediate treatment with antibiotics when necessary have almost completely eliminated this cause of mortality (R. Albignac, pers. comm.).

In Tananarive, cases of toxoplasmosis and of rupture of the aorta have been recorded, and the cause has been traced to a parasitic infection by *Spirocerca* (R. Albignac, pers. comm.).

6. THE GENTLE LEMUR (*Hapalemur griseus*)

The gentle lemur is a crepuscular animal which is somewhat smaller than the true lemurs, and which is more sensitive to cold than the latter species. *Hapalemur griseus* typically occurs in extremely humid forest areas of Madagascar, and it is advisable to provide this species with a relatively high ambient humidity.

They will adapt to relatively small cages, but it is preferable to provide them with cages of several square metres surface area, and to supply various branches and other supports.

Under natural conditions, they usually sleep during the day in the middle of dense foliage of bamboo or reeds. In captivity, they prefer to remain hidden during the day and, where possible, they will try to isolate themselves in a bunch of foliage or in a nest-box (despite the fact that they never attempt to hide in hollow trees in the wild).

Gentle lemurs normally live in small groups, and in captivity it is difficult to keep more than four or five in the same cage. The females, which are far more aggressive than the males, are often intolerant, and the most dominant female may inflict serious injuries if she persistently attacks another.

Animals which are captured as adults in the wild often remain sensitive to the presence of human beings for a long time after capture. They are far more nervous and sensitive than *Lemur* species. Because of their small size, they are probably subject to heavier predation in the wild, and their vigilance and greater sensory acuity may be the result of severe selection. Animals of this kind often develop nervous tics and exhibit performance of stereotyped movements. Some adopt the habit of licking themselves very frequently and they gradually remove their own hair and that of other animals. In our own colony, a female gentle lemur which was particularly excitable removed the hair of other animals and provoked them to exhibit the same behaviour to such an extent that she had to be isolated. Subsequently, she devoted all such attention to herself and remained permanently bald from the waist downwards, and even her skin suffered from this activity. However, after she had been placed in a calm place, the animal gradually lost this habit and in the course of a few months developed a fine pelage. Yet, following accidental flooding of the cage, the behaviour abruptly reappeared, and it has been impossible to suppress it since then.

Such animals, which are continually stressed by conditions in captivity, are incapable of reproduction. The only breeding successes that we have had have been achieved with completely tame animals which were raised in semi-liberty from a very early age and had become totally accustomed to the presence of human beings.

At the time of birth, the mother may temporarily become very aggressive, and it is necessary to provide her with a nest-box in which she can deposit her offspring, since the latter is very rarely carried on her fur (Petter and Peyrieras, 1970).

Under natural conditions, gentle lemurs seem to feed exclusively on bamboo shoots or reeds (according to the subspecies). In captivity, it is apparently possible to feed them exclusively with grass, which they eat very readily. This also provides a good means of avoiding tics and stereotyped behaviour, since this kind of food forces them to engage in long periods of feeding activity. They will accept most kinds of fruit and milk containing multivitamin additives, and they have a particular liking for tomatoes and (especially) cucumbers.

Apart from stress symptoms, which must in any event be reduced to a minimum, gentle lemurs are easy to keep in captivity, and the only cause of mortality which we have so far encountered (apart from stress) is that of complications arising from wounds, usually resulting from fights, which have been inadequately tended.

7. THE BROAD-NOSED GENTLE LEMUR (*Hapalemur simus*)

The biology of this species of *Hapalemur*, whose body-size is comparable to that of *Lemur* species, was unknown until recently, when A. Peyrieras and I were able to capture a pair in 1972, in order to attempt to breed them in Tananarive (Fig. 2). The habits of this animal (which is extremely rare) are comparable to those of *Hapalemur griseus*, except that the larger broad-nosed gentle lemur is more terrestrial in its behaviour. In the cage, animals of the latter species will often remain sitting on the ground, and, in contrast to most other lemur species, *Hapalemur simus* often runs across the ground in the forest. These animals seem to be much less sensitive and fearful than *Hapalemur griseus*, and they will not hesitate to attack anybody who enters the cage. Their bite is more serious than that of a *Lemur* species since, rather than simply making a rapid attack, like the latter, *Hapalemur simus* attacks calmly and may take a strong grasp with both hands to bite vigorously, as it will do in tackling a large bamboo stem.

Its diet seems to be more varied than that of its smaller relative, and under natural conditions these animals live close to stands of large bamboo, where they eat the buds and stems as well as attacking the wood with their powerful jaws and eating the pith at the nodes.

In captivity, *Hapalemur simus* eats large quantities of bamboo, but it will also accept the diet provided for *Lemur* species. It is probably a robust animal which has a fair probability of establishing itself well in captivity, though no breeding successes have been recorded as yet.

8. THE SPORTIVE LEMUR (*Lepilemur mustelinus*)

Sportive lemurs are found in almost all of the different kinds of forest in Madagascar. They resemble *Hapalemur griseus* in body-size, but they are exclusively nocturnal. They normally spend the day sleeping in a tree-hollow, and in captivity it is necessary to provide them with a nest-box of relatively narrow dimensions in which they will be closely confined if they use it as a refuge.

It is also necessary to ensure a fairly high temperature (at least 25°C). In view of their very low metabolic turnover, a nest-box and high ambient temperature are probably essential for survival in captivity.

The size of the cage seems to be of relatively minor importance, since sportive lemurs are usually very placid and do not move around very much even if they are provided with plenty of room. Two or three may be maintained together in one cage, but larger groups result in frequent aggressive interactions. As with the other lemur species, it is necessary to try to replicate as far as possible the social conditions found under natural conditions (see Charles-Dominique and Hladik, 1971). There have been no breeding successes to date, however.

Sportive lemurs are very fragile and extremely sensitive to stress in captivity, and they must be progressively accustomed to conditions of confinement.

Lepilemur mustelinus is strictly herbivorous and possesses a large caecum containing a flora which is quite unstable if the animals are not kept under ideal

FIGURE 2. The broad-nosed gentle lemur (*Hapalemur simus*). This lemur was until recently believed to be extinct or on the verge of extinction. A recent expedition succeeded in locating a natural population, and a few animals were collected for maintenance in captivity.

conditions. In captivity, they will eat lettuce fairly readily, and they can be accustomed to eating leaves from the mango-tree, from chestnut-trees, from brambles and from willow. They will also accept apples, pears and milk. They have a particular liking for carnations, from which they eat the petals and the base of the flower, and they can also be given composite flowers and clover flowers.

By taking careful precautions, we have been able to preserve specimens of this species in captivity on several occasions, though each time there have been crises to counter. The condition of the faeces must be carefully watched; as soon as there is any sign of diarrhoea, it is necessary to give immediate treatment with orally adminstered antibiotics (Tetracycline or Typhomycine). If treatment is delayed, the animal dies with all the usual signs of toxicosis. In some cases it is necessary, whilst waiting for the equilibrium of the intestinal flora to be re-established, to rehydrate the animal with injections of physiological serum.

9. THE AVAHI (*Avahi laniger*)

The avahi is a nocturnal indriid of a size comparable to that of *Hapalemur* and *Lepilemur*. Its area of distribution in Madagascar is much more restricted than that of the two latter genera, but there are two different subspecies, one adapted to the humid conditions of the east coast rainforest and one adapted to the drier conditions of the west. However, they are not found at all in really dry areas.

They do not seek out retreats for the daytime sleeping period, but remain in small family groups of two or three individuals, rolled up in balls in clumps of foliage.

This species is even more difficult to keep alive than the sportive lemur. In the avahi, too, there is a very large caecum, and the diet is exclusively vegetarian. In captivity, they are extremely fragile animals, and once signs of toxicosis have appeared it is very difficult to treat them effectively. Conditions during transport generally contribute to their weak state, and it is important to transport them only in cotton bags; with a normal cage they will usually injure themselves against the walls, since their normal locomotion is ensured by powerful thrusts of the hind limbs.

So far, all of the attempts at maintaining them in Tananarive have been unsuccessful.

10. SIFAKAS (*Propithecus verreauxi* and *Propithecus diadema*)

Like the avahi, the sifakas (Fig. 3) are primarily folivorous, but they are diurnal and their body-size is much larger. Several attempts at maintaining them have been made in Tananarive and in diverse other centres in Europe and America. The difficulties involved in keeping them are the same as those encountered with the avahi, but the sifakas are larger and more resistant. However, various attempts to keep *Propithecus diadema*, the species from the east coast rain forest, have all met with failure.

On the other hand, maintenance of *Propithecus verreauxi* is quite practicable, and breeding successes have been obtained repeatedly since 1956 in Tananarive, thanks to special techniques for their care (see Petter-Rousseaux, 1962). Breeding has also been achieved at Duke University over the last few years (Buettner-Janusch, pers. comm.).

FIGURE 3. Close-up photograph of Verreaux's Sifaka (*Propithecus verreauxi verreauxi*). A colony of sifakas from various areas of Madagascar is maintained at the Zoological Gardens of Tsimbazaza, Madagascar.

These animals must be provided with temperature conditions somewhat better than those required for species of *Lemur*. In winter, it is impossible to leave them without supplementary heating, even in Tananarive.

They require quite large cages, and they can be very active during the hottest part of the day. Under natural conditions, they live in family-sized groups, and it is important to bear this in mind since, particularly in February and March in Madagascar, ferocious battles may take place between neighbouring groups. They may even bite each other's hands through the intervening cage-wire if care is not taken.

Their diet in captivity consists of various fruits. In Tananarive (R. Albignac, pers. comm.), they are given the same food as that given to the *Lemur* species (450 g per day; see p. 195). In addition, their cages are furnished with branches of bamboo, tamarind trees and *Eugenia* trees. It is apparently necessary that their diet should include tannin, since they are often observed eating bark under natural conditions.

The secret of success in maintaining sifakas is probably to start off with young animals, as had been the case at Tananarive and at Duke University. If they are tamed, they can become very friendly and they are no longer subject to extreme stress.

11. THE INDRI (*Indri indri*)

Maintenance of the indri, which is a slightly larger species than the sifaka and equally diurnal, poses similar problems. The only long-term success in keeping this species to date has been achieved by the Service des Eaux et Forêts at Tamatave (Madagascar), a town where the temperatures are much higher than in Tananarive. The animal, which was maintained in a large cage, was young when it was captured. It was fed every day with fresh foliage and diverse fruits, and it lived for more than a year in good condition.

12. THE AYE-AYE (*Daubentonia madagascariensis*)

The aye-aye survives quite well in captivity, and it is apparently able to adapt to a wide range of diets. One specimen lived for quite a long time at London Zoo, and another was kept at the zoological gardens in Paris. For several years now, a pair has been maintained in Tananarive, with a view to obtaining breeding successes eventually.

In captivity, this species spends the day rolled up in a ball in a large nest-box, where it will construct a nest of branches. The aye-aye is nocturnal, and it does not become active until nightfall.

It is necessary to take great precautions to provide a complete diet. In Tananarive, the aye-ayes are provided with various foodstuffs given to the *Lemur* species, and in addition they are provided each day with a dish of wood-boring larvae and a coconut. They are extremely destructive animals, and they will vigorously attack any wooden structures, including the cage if it is only lightly built. It is important to provide them with a continuous supply of wood so that they can utilize their rodent-like teeth for gnawing whenever they wish. An animal which was kept in London did, in actual fact, die of hunger as a result of exaggerated growth of the upper incisors, which it had been unable to expose to the correct kind of wear.

The aye-aye has never yet been bred in captivity.

ACKNOWLEDGMENT
This paper was translated from the French by Dr. R. D. Martin.

Breeding Marmosets in Captivity

J. J. C. Mallinson

INTRODUCTION

World zoos seldom have many species of marmosets* in their collections, and those which do rarely succeed in breeding a second generation. As far as the records show, less than half of the marmoset species have so far bred in captivity (Table 1), and only a small percentage of these are bred frequently.

TABLE 1. Checklist of species of Callitrichidae (= Hapalidae) bred in captivity.[a]

Common name	Scientific name
Common Marmoset	*Callithrix (= Hapale) jacchus*
White-eared Marmoset	*Callithrix (= Hapale) aurita*
Black-pencilled Marmoset	*Callithrix (= Hapale) penicillata*
White-fronted Marmoset	*Callithrix (= Hapale) geoffroyi*
White-shouldered Marmoset	*Callithrix (= Hapale) humeralifer*
Silvery Marmoset	*Callithrix (= Mico) argentata*
Pygmy Marmoset	*Callithrix (= Cebuella) pygmaea*
Red-handed Tamarin	*Saguinus (= Tamarinus) midas*
Saddle-back Tamarin	*Saguinus (= Tamarinus) fuscicollis*
Moustached Tamarin	*Saguinus (= Tamarinus) mystax*
Red-mantled Tamarin	*Saguinus (= Tamarinus) illigeri*
Black and red Tamarin	*Saguinus (= Tamarinus) nigricollis*
White-footed Tamarin	*Saguinus (= Marikina) leucopus*
Cotton-headed Tamarin	*Saguinus (= Oedipomidas) oedipus*
Geoffroy's Tamarin	*Saguinus (= Oedipomidas) geoffroyi*
Golden Lion Tamarin	*Leontideus rosalia*

[a] Fourteen of the sixteen species listed above are recorded in the International Zoo Year Book, vols I–XI (1959–69). The Zoological Society of London recorded the first breeding of *Saguinus (= Tamarin) midas* in 1951; and Dr. and Mrs. W. C. Osman Hill recorded the first breeding of *Callithrix (= Hapale) humeralifer* at Yerkes Primate Center in 1965.

* The word "marmoset" is used in this paper to refer to any member of the marmoset/tamarin/pinché family—Callitrichidae (= Hapalidae).

FIGURE 1. Female red-handed tamarin (*Saguinus midas*) (left) carrying twin female infants born in captivity in September 1970. The twin infants (right) were also photographed whilst temporarily moving around away from the mother. (In both photographs, the infants are 56 days old.)

In the course of the last 10 years, 15 marmoset species have been represented in the Jersey Wildlife Trust's collection, although (because of the difficulties of securing many of the rarer species), the collection has on no occasion comprised more than 25 specimens. The numbers dealt with by us are therefore small in comparison to those now being used extensively in biomedical studies. However, our success with their maintenance, and in some cases with their breeding (Figs. 1, 2 and 3), originally stemmed from our own experimentation with a variety of diets and patterns of accommodation; for it is only comparatively recently that extensive research has been carried out by primate research laboratories, which have published important papers dealing with the maintenance and breeding of marmosets in captivity.

From the conservation standpoint, the three closely related species of the golden marmoset genus, *Leontideus*, are the most endangered of the marmoset family. In 1969, it was considered that no more than 600 of the golden lion species, *L. rosalia*, remained in the wild state, and 2 years later it was estimated that this population had fallen to 400 (Coimbra-Filho, 1969). As exports from Brazil have now ceased, it has been found that the captive population has decreased from 102 specimens in 1968, to 84 specimens in 1970 (Perry, 1971). From the data amassed in the preliminary studbook for the golden lion species (Jones, 1972), it can be seen that captive breeding has so far proved to be unsatisfactory.

This paper presents data gathered from our own practical experience here in Jersey, combined with some information accumulated by a number of specialists directly involved with marmosets in primate research centres (Epple, 1970; Hampton *et al.*, 1966; Kingston, 1970; Wolfe *et al.*, 1972). It is hoped that some of these findings will contribute materially to conservation of the endangered golden marmoset in captivity.

ACCOMODATION REQUIREMENTS IN CAPTIVITY

Until comparatively recently, the majority of marmosets to be seen in European collections were confined to rather cramped inside accommodation which was rarely maintained at temperatures above 70°F (21°C). The marmosets had little opportunity to exercise properly or to benefit from the sun's ultra-violet rays.

Initially, in the absence of any established guidelines, all the marmosets in the Jersey collection were kept in indoor cages which measured 8 × 5 × 7 ft high, with the room temperature ranging from 62°–70°F. This environment proved to be unsatisfactory, although it was found that the introduction of infra-red lamps into each cage improved general conditions, and that the habitual huddling together of the specimens was consequently alleviated. The main reason for this improvement was considered to be that the marmosets were able to get into a zone of temperature up to 85°F (29°C). It has since been generally accepted that laboratories are able to maintain marmosets successfully at a room temperature of 80°–82°F (27°–28°C) (see Hampton *et al.*, 1966; Wolfe *et al.*, 1972). Each cage is furnished with a nest-box and a frequently-changed arrangement of sloping branches, for it has been found that alteration of the cage environment, by regular renewal of the branching, helps to stimulate and promote the maximum amount of exercise and scent marking by the marmosets.

As our interest in this family has not been confined solely to that of captive propagation, we realized that in order to study various aspects of behaviour, it was important to experiment by maintaining some of the animals in the collection under conditions as close as possible to those present in the wild. For, as others have experienced (Epple, 1970), marmosets confined to laboratory-type cages,

FIGURE 2. Male emperor tamarin (*Sagiunus imperator*), maintained at Jersey Zoo since July 1961. This animal is probably over 13 years old.

which can be as small as $18 \times 18 \times 21$ in. high (Wolfe *et al.*, 1972), have only a limited repertoire of social responses and vocalization.

In 1965, from mid-May to mid-September, we experimented by accommodating some of our specimens outside, with only unheated waterproofed boxes for shelter. It was found that this exposure to the elements greatly benefited their condition, and on this basis it was decided to allow a family group of marmosets to have access to a large outside aviary throughout the year, with the inside accommodation heated up to 80°F (27°C). Even when the outside temperature fell as low as freezing point, the five specimens maintained their excellent physical condition.

We have found from these experiences that in order to study the general

FIGURE 3. Male Geoffroy's tamarin (*Saguinus geoffroyi*) maintained at Jersey Zoo since July 1961. This animal is probably at least 14 years old. (The two animals shown in Figs. 2 and 3 hold longevity records in captivity.)

behaviour of marmosets, in addition to breeding them, the optimum accommodation requirements are for them to have a heated inside area with access to a large outside aviary-type enclosure throughout the year. At the same time, it is necessary to ensure that physical contact between neighbouring pairs is impossible. In agreement with the findings of others (Epple, 1970; Hampton *et al.*, 1966), outdoor housing requires large cages with sufficient space for exercise in both cold and warm weather. When this type of accommodation is not available, marmosets that are kept indoors must have the opportunity to move into a heated area with a temperature of up to 85°F (29°C).

A new marmoset complex for Jersey Zoo has been designed to take account of these various considerations (Figs. 4 and 5).

DIETARY REQUIREMENTS

Little has been published on the natural diets of marmosets, but it is generally considered that they thrive on a diet high in animal protein. Marmosets have been observed in the wild state to feed on a range of foodstuffs including sweet fruits, buds, berries, seed pods, spiders, grasshoppers, small lizards, freshly killed bats and small birds (Bates, 1864; Moynihan, 1970).

In order to prevent the animals from becoming bored by an unchanging diet in captivity, we have always attempted to vary the food as much as possible. We have found that a well-balanced diet comprised of mixed fruit, vegetable matter, a Complan/Vitamin Plus mixture, omnivorous nuts (mineral, vitamin and vegetable protein supplement) and animal protein (mealworms, crickets, locusts and pink mice) has sustained the marmoset collection well. However, like others (Kingston, 1970), we had to find out the importance of vitamin D_3 supplementation the hard way: osteomalacia frequently occurred with the adult specimens at intervals of 11–12 months, and with infants the condition developed during the first 3–5 months of life.

The first successful remedy used by us to combat this condition was the injection of vitamin D_3 intramuscularly, giving 62,500 i.u. per adult at intervals of 10 months, and 20,000 i.u. to the young at approximately 4 months of age. However, it has since been found preferable to administer vitamin D_3 orally and, as advised by Hampton *et al.* (1966), the supplementation was first given at a level of 1000 i.u. per specimen daily for a period of 11 weeks, subsequently dropping to 700 i.u., and then to a maintenance level of 500 i.u. daily. Since this oral administration of vitamin D_3, our marmoset collection has shown no further signs of what is commonly referred to as "cage paralysis". (The vitamin product used is Rovimix D_3 400, manufactured by Roche Products Ltd., Switzerland.)

GENERAL HUSBANDRY

1. Breeding Conditions

From our findings, and from those of others (Hampton *et al.*, 1966; Kingston, 1970; Wolfe *et al.*, 1972), we consider that in order to obtain satisfactory breeding results it is more advantageous to keep breeding pairs by themselves, as opposed to keeping marmosets in large family groups. More often than not, adult females will inhibit the young and prevent them from breeding, and unnecessary fighting amongst the family generally develops after the young have

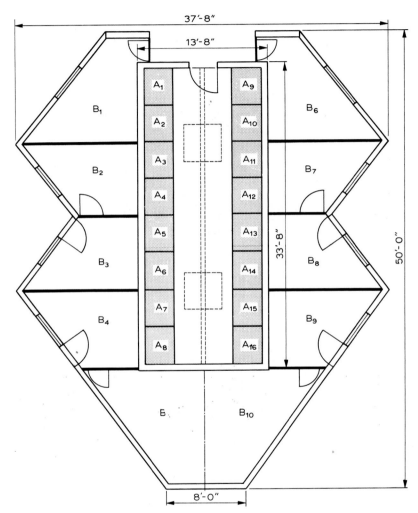

FIGURE 4. Ground plan of the projected marmoset complex, showing the layout of the 16 indoor cage-units (A) and the 10 connecting outdoor cages (B), which will be richly furnished with vegetation. The inside area containing the cage-units will not be accessible to the public and the animals will only be on view when in the outdoor enclosures. The outdoor cages will be constructed of hollow steel section, 7 ft in height, and the cage-fronts will consist of alternating panels of Twill-weld and glass. Partitions between cages will be made of opaque corrugated Perspex.

reached sexual maturity. The keeping of unrelated adult pairs together is seldom if ever successful, for fighting among animals of the same sex invariably occurs.

Having a collection of marmosets on direct view to the public, we have found them to be timorous animals that do not enjoy such close proximity to strangers unless they are able to retire to a "sanctuary" part of their cage environment, which can only be approached or entered by the attendant in charge of them. Some specialists consider that the main secret for the welfare of marmosets is for them to have a full sense of security, with respect to both territory and personnel (Kingston, 1970; Wolfe, 1972).

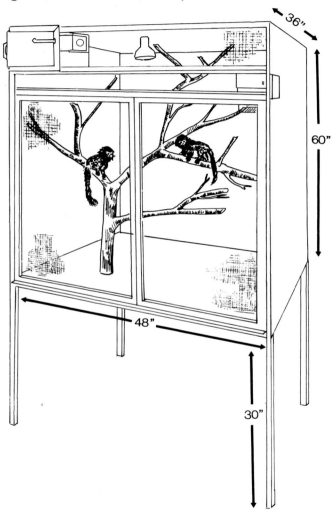

FIGURE 5. Artist's impression of one of the 16 indoor cage-units of the marmoset complex, within the area closed to the public. The frame consists of hollow steel section, whilst the sides, floor centre partition and feeding shelf are made of opaque self-extinguishing ICI Dorvic PVC. The floor is inclined towards the front to facilitate cleaning. A single, removable nest-box is attached to the top left-hand corner of the cage, and food is provided on a shelf reached through sliding partitions in the upper part of the cage. The remaining area of the cage-front consists of 4 in. gauge Twill-weld. Each unit has an infra-red lamp to act as a heat spot.

Breeding conditions in laboratories are perhaps more easily established, and less costly to maintain, than when marmosets have to be on view to the public, where more space is required in order to minimize the stress experienced by marmosets in contact with strangers, and to allow for any behavioural studies which are to be carried out.

Care must be taken in both zoo and laboratory environments to avoid physical contact between marmosets caged separately. It is recommended that, between the sides of the cages in outside accommodation, vegetation should be grown to create a visual barrier between the pairs, and for indoor accommodation a solid partition is advocated. This will prevent fighting between the pairs, and also eliminate any redirected aggression.

We have had occasions when infants have been lost after falling from the backs of the parents to the floor of the cage. We therefore consider it important to either restrict the height of the inside area, or to pad the floor with hay or straw to prevent the infants from being damaged should such a fall take place.

2. Reproductive Data

Marmosets have an approximate gestation period of 135–145 days, and will breed throughout the year. Some of the specimens in the Jersey collection have bred twice a year, and there have been cases of laboratory specimens breeding three times within 12 months. It is considered by some authorities that in order to minimize the interbirth interval and so produce the maximum amount of progeny, the infants should be removed at birth and hand-reared, for the technique of hand-rearing marmosets now appears to have been perfected (Wolfe *et al.*, 1972).

We have found that the interval between one birth followed by normal lactation and the next birth was, in three cases, 144, 155 and 159 days respectively. It is therefore our practice to leave the young with the parents until they are approximately 12 months old. For if the parents do produce further young within this time, the first generation offspring can assist in the post-natal handling of the new infants, and also benefit from the various other family interactions. With the absence of newly-imported stock from the wild state, this early social contact with the parents could prove to be an important factor in the long-term breeding of marmosets in captivity.

As far as development is concerned, infants have been observed to climb about independently and eat soft fruit at 21 days old, eat pink mice at 25 days. Twin marmosets which had lost their mother at 35 days old successfully reared themselves on the rations provided, without further human intervention. Although the father plays an important part in carrying the young, passing them back to the mother during feeding periods, we have had one case with twin marmosets which lost their father at 3 days old and were successfully reared by the mother alone.

Marmosets become sexually mature at approximately 12 months. Epple (1970) has recorded a female giving birth to twins at the age of $16\frac{1}{2}$ months.

That these animals are monogamous by preference, has not been supported by some of our observations, for when separation of breeding pairs has taken place and one partner has been given access to another animal of the opposite sex, copulation has been observed on a number of occasions.

Out of 25 litters born to four different species, including one hybrid cross in Jersey, three singletons, 21 sets of twins, and one set of triplets have been recorded. A set of quadruplets has been recorded by Kingston (1970). In a recent paper (Mallinson, 1972), analysis of more than 200 parturitions selected from five different collections, including the Jersey one, showed that 70 per cent of the recorded births involved twins.

CONCLUSIONS

From our experience, and from those of others, we find that many of the problems of care, maintenance and husbandry with marmosets are now more fully understood, and the optimum conditions for establishing viable breeding groups can be more easily estimated. A number of places, including Jersey Zoo, have recorded second generation—F_2 births, and recently some third generation —F_3 births have been achieved (Wolfe et al., in press).

Marmosets can breed within the second year of life, can reproduce regularly at least twice a year, and have a breeding life expectancy from 8 to 10 years. As multiple births are the general rule, marmosets may have a reproduction potential of some 30–40 young during their lifetime.

The survival of many non-human primates in South America seems to depend on how much of their natural habitat will remain inaccessible (Harrisson, 1971). It is therefore of the utmost importance for zoos and primate research centres to combine in their efforts to breed various species of marmosets, for it is considered that if sufficient numbers of different species can be brought together, and careful attention is paid to both dietary and environmental requirements, the survival of these species could be ensured.

The Breeding of Endangered Species of Marmosets and Tamarins

W. R. Kingston

INTRODUCTION

An editorial note in the current "Oryx" magazine (January 1972) states that wild populations of the three *Leontideus* species have almost reached the point of no return, and that efforts are now being made to establish a reserve and meanwhile to attempt captive breeding. In this present contribution, a few suggestions are made on the basis of our considerable experience in the breeding of marmosets and tamarins (Callitrichidae) under captive conditions.

For the past 7 years we have maintained at Fison's Pharmaceutical Division a breeding colony of six species of this family, during which time we have reared some 250 young from an average of 24 breeding pairs. Some of the original pairs are still producing four young annually, and one pair of *Callithrix jacchus* have successfully reared nine sets of twins. We have not, of course, had *Leontideus* in our colony; but our experience with *Saguinus oedipus*, *S. nigricollis*, *S. illigerii*, *Callithrix jacchus*, *C. argentatus* and *Cebuella pygmaea*, and published information about *L. rosalia*, coupled with the ecological and morphological similarities shared by all members of the family, would seem to indicate that *Leontideus* would thrive equally well under our conditions. A previous paper (Kingston, 1969), sets out our experience with marmosets and tamarins, but after a further 3 years of experience I would consider the following points to be of greatest significance.

CAGING

The very poor overall record of zoos in maintaining and breeding these animals, and similar experience in the primate centres in the USA, is largely due to a failure to appreciate the importance of territorial security, which is certainly essential for breeding success. Large glass and wire pens do not provide this security and a smaller, more enclosed, structure is far better. Once established neither the animals nor the position of the cage should be changed and when the latter is changed for cleaning purposes at least some part, such as the nest-box or perches, should be left unchanged at the time. The habit of "sanitizing" everything in sight with gallons of highly scented disinfectants is for the same reason undesirable. These animals go through an elaborate scent marking routine which is obviously an important feature of their behaviour. Even when these rules are strictly followed, breeding will not occur for at least 6 months; but every single

FIGURE 1. Unit of four standard marmoset cages, each including a removable nest-box and a sliding droppings tray. The stand raises the lower cage by 9 in. above floor level, and the overall height of the unit is 75 in.

randomly mated pair of all the species we have had has produced young within 12 months. The cages used here are $36 \times 20 \times 20$ in. the largest dimension being the height (see Fig. 1). They are constructed from light-gauge galvanized metal and are fitted with a 9 in. cube nest-box (also in metal) which hangs on the outside of the cage. The fronts are in $1 \times \frac{1}{2}$ in. weld mesh and the rest solid sheet metal. They are in my opinion rather small, but the fact remains that the nine sets of twins mentioned earlier have been born to a pair of *C. jacchus* which have lived under these conditions for 7 years and remain to this day in perfect health and completely free from any sign of stereotyped behaviour patterns (see Fig. 2).

FIGURE 2. Battery of marmoset breeding cages at Fison's Pharmaceutical Division. The photograph shows four units of the kind shown in Fig. 1, but equipped with nest-boxes of modified design.

DIET

Whilst these animals certainly eat a lot of fruit under natural conditions, they also have an intake of something over 20 per cent of animal protein in the form of arthropods, birds' eggs and young arboreal lizards. In captivity, we feed a synthetic diet suggested by Levy and Artecona (pers. comm.) which we auto-clave and then seal in cans; analysis indicates a content of about 22 per cent available protein. It is perhaps better to feed locusts, which can easily be bred for the purpose, or mealworms (*Tenebrio* larvae) together with fruit; but the snag is that these insects can act as the intermediate host for a very troublesome helminth parasite, *Prosthenorchis elegans*, with which many animals are infested when imported and which is extremely difficult to eradicate without killing the host as well! Young mice, fresh liver, fish (of which they are, oddly enough, very fond), or a canned dog food can all be used and the animals will also eat brown bread very freely. We are in the process of changing to a less troublesome regime consisting of a standard pelleted primate diet (Cooper Nutritional Products Ltd.) and a freely available malt loaf (Soreen) which appears to be a satisfactory substitute for the specially prepared diet of Levy and Artecona, though one must of course provide the fruits as well. An important point is to cut the fruit into pieces small enough for the marmosets to pick up, because they will not bite pieces out of whole bananas or the like. When they first arrive in captivity they often refuse to eat and at this time they should be given anything they will eat to get them going. Dehydration often occurs at a serious level and plain water is often refused, especially if presented in a bowl or dish. Diluted sweetened condensed milk or, better still, the paediatric B.12 syrup "Cytacon" (Glaxo), presented in a bottle with a drinking spout placed well up towards the top of the cage, is usually accepted.

Another point frequently overlooked is the fact that these animals are strictly diurnal and very nervous until settled down. If housed in rooms with no natural lighting, with human activity or other forms of disturbance occurring all day, and the lights turned out when personnel leave, the marmosets will starve to death, as recently happened in the premises of a London dealer.

DISEASE

Normally very healthy animals, once over the trauma of importation, require relatively enormous amounts of pre-formed vitamin D_3. This is best given orally in arachis or cotton seed oil at 5000 i.u./ml, given at 1 ml fortnightly. For bacterial infections and malaise of unknown aetiology, Chloramphenicol as "Intramycetin" given intramuscularly at 0·25 ml once daily for 3 days has proved to be the most effective treatment, but all antibiotics seem to be well tolerated. Heat is a very good therapeutic agent, and many apparently moribund animals will make uneventful complete recoveries if put in an incubator or hospital cage and kept at 30°C for 24 h with the temperature gradually falling to normal housing levels over the next few days.

BREEDING

Parturition usually takes place overnight and there is very rarely any trouble. Primiparous females often fail to nurse the first litter. If young are found on the floor, they will starve unless hand-reared. Hand-rearing is quite simple using SMA baby food prepared as for human infants, which is best fed with a 1 ml syringe. The syringe itself should not be put in the mouth of the infant. A bubble should be formed at the tip of the syringe, and the meniscus applied to the lips, when it will nearly always be taken into the mouth.

This very much reduces the chances of inhalation of diet, which is the principle cause of losses in hand-rearing. Four-hour feeding intervals are quite often enough, with feeding finishing around midnight and starting again at 0800 h. The infants begin to take solids at about 6 weeks and can be weaned from the parents safely at 4 months. Post-partum oestrus results in birth intervals of less than 6 months, despite the 20-week gestation period. Ninety per cent of births are twins (dizygotic), but occasional triplets occur. Third young are never reared, but they can be saved by hand rearing. A nesting/sleeping box should always be provided (a cube of about $9 \times 9 \times 9$ in.), but the entrance hole should not be too small or too near the top of the box. Otherwise, the young, which are normally carried on the back of the male, will be knocked off or receive skull fractures if the parent makes a hurried retreat to the box when frightened. It is essential that the young should be given vitamin D₃ from the age of 6 weeks onwards in order to avoid rickets. The infants can be handled perfectly safely from birth onwards and returned to the parents after handling; we have never had a rejection. In *Callithrix jacchus* the babies weigh about 30 g at birth and gain 5–10 g weekly and reach 100 g at 10 weeks of age. Fig. 3 illustrates the growth of *C. jacchus* based on 67 young weighed at weekly intervals. Fig. 4 extends the curve to 21 months, from which it will be seen that adult weights

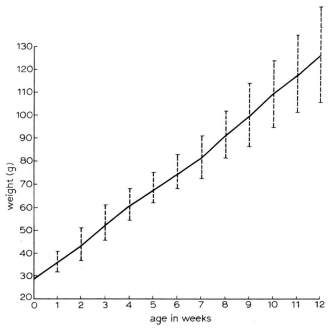

FIGURE 3. Growth curve for captive-bred *Callithrix jacchus* from birth to 12 weeks of age, prepared from data on 67 infants. The solid line passes through the mean weights at intervals of 1 week, whilst the dotted vertical lines indicate the standard deviations for each set of readings.

are reached at around 15 months (at which time overt sexuality is demonstrated by both sexes). Fig. 5 gives growth curves for the three other species which we have bred in reasonable numbers. The adult weight (150 g to 450 g, according to the species) is attained at about 15 months. Cage-bred young are normally finer and heavier animals than wild-caught parents. They reach puberty at around 15 months; but we have had some difficulty with the second generation, due, we believe, to behavioural rather than physical factors.

This failure to achieve second generation breeding has been a source of great disappointment to us, particularly since our cage-bred animals appear to be physically superior to their wild-caught parents We have had numerous examples of successful breeding using a wild-caught animal of either sex with an opposite sex cage-bred specimen; but in spite of the occurrence of sexual display by both sexes when both adults were cage-bred, it proved impossible to produce full second generation young in our colony. Recently, however, another laboratory has reported that if the weaned young are allowed to grow up in community cages of mixed sexes, and any pairs displaying mutual sexual interest are subsequently removed and caged separately, successful breeding occurs without difficulty with the isolated pairs. They have now been able to obtain third generation breeding using this technique. This occurs without the presence of adults and would therefore seem to indicate that it is a question of

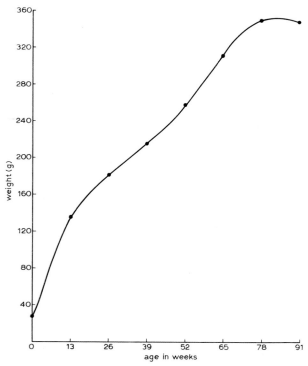

FIGURE 4. Growth curve for captive-bred *Callithrix jacchus* from birth to 91 weeks of age, showing the means for an initial sample of 42 animals declining to 11 at the end of the graph.

mate-selection; but since no randomly-mated pair of wild-caught animals have ever failed to breed in captivity it is rather difficult to explain on this basis. Incidentally, attempts to keep families together have not proved successful in our experience, for two reasons: firstly, the 6-month-old young interfere with the newly born siblings (in the case of some *S. oedipus*, this resulted in the death of the new infants); secondly, the adult female has been seen to attack her daughters when they have reached puberty. With regard to the actual breeding performance of the breeding colony, the results to date are set out in Table 1, which gives the total young born to each pair during the time they have been in the unit. By and large, *C. jacchus* have proved the most reliable breeders under our conditions and once established will produce young regularly at 22-week intervals. There is therefore obviously immediate post-partum oestrus. The tamarins breed less regularly and are more likely to abort, but individual pairs have produced records almost as good as those obtained with *C. jacchus*.

Table 2 sets out the litter sizes and indicates very clearly the high incidence of twins. The numbers of male and female infants are almost exactly equal and the ratio of heterosexual to unisexual twins is such that there can be no doubt that the vast majority of them are of dizygotic rather than monozygotic origin.

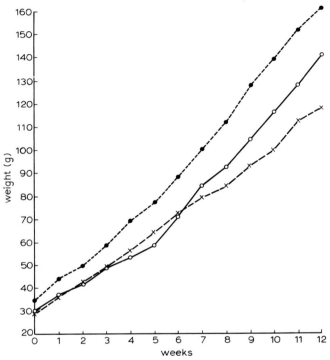

FIGURE 5. Growth curve for three species of captive-bred marmosets from birth to 12 weeks of age, based on mean weights at weekly intervals. ●----● = *Saguinus oedipus* (N = 18); ×---× = *Saguinus nigricollis* (N = 11); ○——○ = *Callithrix argentatus* (N = 7).

The demonstrable chimerism in many tissues and the immune tolerance proved by skin grafting in marmoset twins must therefore arise from shared placental circulation. The absence of freemartinism in heterosexual twins, which would normally be expected to occur with such placental sharing, is therefore also of great scientific interest and makes the embryology of these animals unique. Another fact which emerges from our experience with these animals is the relatively long breeding life. Pair No. 1 of *C. jacchus* and pair no. 1 of *C. argentatus* were imported as adults in 1965/6 and pair No. 4 of *S. oedipus* in 1967. They are still (November 1973) in apparently perfect health and breeding regularly. We have had obviously senescent animals which showed all the

TABLE 1. Breeding performance of individual pairs.

Species	Pair no.	Time in colony	No. of young born	Abortions
Callithrix				
jacchus	1	1966 to date	22	—
	2	1966 to 1970	10	—
	3	1966 to 1968	3	1
	4	1966 to 1971	18	—
	5	1966 to 1970	13	1
	6	1966 to 1967	6	—
	7	1967 to 1971	12	—
	8	1967 to 1970	12	—
	9	1968 to date	19	—
	10	1969 to date	14	1
	11	1970 to date	9	—
	12	1970 to date	8	—
	13	1970 to date	8	—
	14	1970 to 1971	4	1
	15	1970 to date	7	—
	16	1970 to date	7	—
	17	1970 to date	9	—
	18	1970 to date	6	—
	19	1970 to 1971	2	—
	20	1971 to date	4	—
	21	1971 to date	7	—
	22	1971 to date	3	1
	23	1971 to date	3	—
	24	1970 to date	6	—
	25	1970 to date	5	—
	26	1971 to date	9	—
	27	1971 to date	5	—
		Total	231	5
Callithrix				
argentatus	1	1966 to date	10	1
	2	1968 to date	4	1
		Total	14	2
Saguinus				
oedipus	1	1967 to 1970	2	1
	2	1967 to 1968	2	—
	3	1967 to 1971	6	1
	4	1967 to date	13	2
		Total	23	4

TABLE 1.—*continued*

Saguinus				
nigricollis	1	1968 to date	4	1
	2	1968 to date	11	2
	3	1968 to date	4	1
	4	1970 to date	6	—
		Total	25	4
Cebuella				
pygmaea	1	1967 to 1968	2	—
		Total	2	—

TABLE 2. Litter-sizes.

Species	No. of litters	Single-tons	Twins	Triplets	Quads	Total young
Callithrix jacchus	115	12	86	16	1	233
Callithrix argentatus	7	—	7	—	—	14
Saguinus oedipus	12	1	11	—	—	23
Saguinus nigricollis	13	3	11	—	—	25
Cebuella pygmaea	1	—	1	—	—	2
Total	148	16	116	16	1	297

symptoms familiar in our own species, i.e. loss of teeth and hair, failing eyesight, slow movement; but the above animals (which cannot be less than 9–10 years old) show none of these signs as yet. A total life expectation of something in the region of 15 years would therefore seem likely—a remarkably long life for such a small animal.

CONCLUSION

From our experience, it seems to me that captive breeding of Callithricidae presents one of the few cases where an endangered species could undoubtedly be saved at very moderate expense by such intervention, and although survival in a suitable reserve is undoubtedly the optimum solution, colonies could easily be kept by any reasonably competent zoo.

On the general conservation issue, it is suggested that a specific zoo should be provided with funds in order to construct an installation with optimum breeding conditions, not on show to the public.

Animals thus bred could then be sent to other suitable collections to ensure a good spread of breeding nuclei. It is also advocated that various companies which have embarked on primate research programmes should make a gesture of retribution by contributing to such a conservation breeding programme.

It is hoped that some of the information provided in this paper may be helpful to whoever will eventually undertake such captive breeding.

Breeding and Maintenance of Douc Langurs at Cologne Zoo

U. Hick

INTRODUCTION

It was not until 1970 that, by using modern feeding methods and taking special care, we succeeded in keeping the sensitive douc langurs (*Pygathrix nemaeus nemaeus*) alive in captivity. Even today they are still the greatest treasures of our zoo.

The douc langurs belong to the group of Asiatic langurs, and they are particularly difficult to keep because of their highly specialized nutritional requirements. In the literature there is hardly anything written about these monkeys, and very little is known about their general behaviour in the wild. Fiedler and Wendt (1967) give a short description and then say: "Up to now it has been impossible to acclimatize them to zoological gardens, the longevity record is four months at the London Zoo, the stock may be endangered by the Viet Nam War".

There is no doubt that the existence of the douc langurs under natural conditions is endangered by the wars which are raging in their home countries and destroying large areas of their habitat. For this reason, the breeding and maintenance of these animals in zoos is of particular importance.

There are two subspecies: the southern one (*Pygathrix nemaeus nemaeus*), with a yellow face; and the northern one (*Pygathrix nemaeus nigripes*), with a black face. The group at the Cologne Zoo belongs to the southern subspecies (Fig. 1). They are distributed in the tropical rain-forests of Laos, Viet Nam and the Isle of Hainan. They have a rather unusual appearance, with their inclined, gentle eyes imparting an almost Asiatic expression to their naked faces. Their name was chosen because of the varied colouring of their short-haired, shiny fur, which shows a richness of colours hardly ever found in other mammals. Their heads are grey, their faces a deep yellow. Their necks are decorated with two rings, one white and the other chestnut. Their bodies and their upper arms are grey, while thighs, hands and feet are black. White forearms and reddish-brown shanks increase the colour contrasts, while a white tail (of approximately the same length as the body) and a white saddle-spot on their backs add further variety. The hair on their heads is directed backwards without forming a tuft. Their faces are embellished by beautiful white side-whiskers. An orange-

FIGURE 1. Two douc langur mothers with their infants. (Photo: Rolf Schlosser.) Note the pale face typical of the southern subspecies *Pygathrix nemaeus nemaeus*.

coloured stripe is drawn across the forehead and round to the ears (see Table 1 for body dimensions).

The Cologne Zoo started keeping douc langurs in 1968. On 8 June 1968 the first animals (1 male and 2 females)—imported direct from a Bangkok dealer—arrived and were housed in the Lemur Division of the zoo.

When the animals were collected from the airport they appeared to be in satisfactory condition. They were active and seemed to have a good appetite, for on their way to the zoo they continually searched the bottom of their transport box for something to eat. As soon as they arrived at the zoo, they greedily threw themselves on the food offered to them. At that time they were extremely gentle and it was quite possible to touch them. All three langurs were rather thin and some of their body-hair was missing.

On the afternoon of the following day they completely collapsed, due to the stress of transport and the change of diet. They were lying outstretched on the shelves and did not show any interest in the food they were offered. The following morning, the situation had become even worse, for they were suffering from disturbances of balance. They could no longer hold themselves on the shelves,

TABLE 1. Measurements of an adult male douc langur.

	Length (approx.)
Head and body (tip of nose to tail-root)	60 cm (24 in.)
Tail (from tail-root to tail tip)	65 cm (26 in.)
Arm	39 cm (15 in.)
Leg	39 cm (15 in.)
Foot (from heel to tip of the longest toe)	17·5 cm (7 in.)
Hand	15 cm (6 in.)

but fell to the ground, where they remained prostrate. They did not eat anything and did not defaecate. No response was shown either to noises or to the approach of people. I spent the next 3 days in their cage, trying again and again to draw them out of their lethargy by offering them food. With gentle massage, I continually tried to reactivate their circulation. The second day, I gave each an enema, and repeating this treatment led to defaecation.

The next morning, the situation had improved a little. The langurs remained lying on the shelves, but as soon as they tried to run they again fell into the straw beneath. But they began to drink some water, and some hours later they ate grapes and cherries for the first time since the beginning of their illness. The following day, their condition had further improved, and 2 days later it seemed that they had passed the crisis. During the period which immediately followed these events, the Botanical Garden was kind enough to provide us with the leaves of some *Acacia* species, which the douc langurs ate greedily. The animals became acclimatized quite well; their fur became shiny, the bare spots on their bodies disappeared, and by the spring of 1969 they were in excellent condition. However, on 2 June 1969 one of the females died following a miscarriage. This

miscarriage was apparently caused by the extreme excitation the animals experienced when the male had to be caught and removed from the cage to be
examined and treated for a severe cutaneous disease.

On 24 September 1969, two more female douc langurs arrived from Laos.
We had no difficulties with them at all. Following a 6-week quarantine they
were moved into the cage with the other two langurs. All the langurs were very
trusting at the beginning, but became considerably shyer during the ensuing
weeks. Most of all, they disliked being caught in the summer for transport to the
outdoor cages. From this time onwards, the female animals became very shy
and impossible to touch. However, they again became trusting following the
birth of their offspring. During the summer, Boris (the male) had always freely
followed the females into the outdoor cage, but on one occasion he had to be
caught and taken out of the cage to be examined. It then took some time before
he again lost his shyness towards me.

We subsequently decided not to treat his skin disease outside the cage, which
meant having to catch him. I therefore treated him inside the cage for several
weeks, cleaning the inflamed spots with camomile tea and powdering him several
times a day.

HOUSING

The douc langur group is housed within the Lemur Division, in a cage measur-
ing $6 \times 2 \times 2$ m ($19\frac{1}{2} \times 6\frac{1}{2} \times 6\frac{1}{2}$ ft). This cage is subdivided by a partition wall,
so that the animals can be moved into one part while the other is being cleaned.
During the summer months of 1968 and 1969, langurs were taken to an outdoor cage, where our lemurs also spend the warm months of the year. In 1970
we did not risk catching and transporting the group, for it was obvious that one
of the females was gestating and the other one had had a baby in May; so they
remained in their winter quarters throughout the year. In 1971 we put them
outside, although the youngest baby (a male) born on 14 May 1971, was only
about 4 weeks old.

The Lemur Division, a provisional installation, is not accessible to the public.
The room is heated by gas and has a steadily maintained temperature of
20°–25°C (68°–77°F). The langur cage is equipped with two perches running
around the walls and a rope hanging down from the ceiling. As a hiding place,
the animals have a little hut where they can shelter whenever they want.

NUTRITION

Our langurs are given as much dietary variety as possible. It seems to me to be
of particular importance that food is offered to them in small amounts and often.
Since their arrival more than 3 years ago, the langurs have been fed only by me.
They are given all kinds of fruit and vegetable, with nuts and leaves included as
often as possible. For drinking purposes they are given black tea in the morning
and boiled water in the evening. Our animals do not eat meat.

BREEDING

On 19 August 1968 copulation was observed for the first time between Boris and Tanja, the stronger of the female animals. Copulation then recurred approximately every 3 weeks, and always took place over a period of 2 or 3 days.

At the beginning of 1969 Tanja seemed to be pregnant. Her girth had increased and her sexual skin had reddened (it was white in the other female animals). Formerly, this reddening had only occurred when the females were in oestrus, but it now remained throughout pregnancy. In fact, a readiness for copulation was also apparent throughout pregnancy.

On 10 March 1969, the male langur began to suffer from an evil-smelling, bloody and purulent eczema covering the whole of his forequarters. On 17

TABLE 2. Main measurements of the premature foetus born to Tanja.

Length of the umbilical cord	15 cm (6 in.)
Weight of the placenta	50 g (1¾ oz)
Weight of the foetus	80 g (2⅘ oz)
Length of tail	16 cm (6·4 in.)
Length of body and head	23·2 cm (9.3 in.)
Length of foot	3·8 cm (1·5 in.)
Length of arm	6·3 cm (2·5 in.)
Length of hand	3·5 cm (1·4 in.)
Length of thumb	0·3 cm (0·125 in.)
Circumference of head	10·6 cm (4·25 in.)
Length of ear auricle	1·6 cm (0·6 in.)

March, he had to be caught and taken out of the cage to be examined and treated by the veterinary officer. All the animals became terribly excited by this event, and the pregnant female (Tanja) developed violent diarrhoea and refused to accept any kind of food. Two days later, on 19 March, at 1300 h, she went into labour. First, the tail and legs of the young animal became visible. Contraction continued at shorter intervals and the mother touched the foetus with her hand, but did not pull at it. By 1400 h, only the head of the foetus was still within the mother's body. The other animals were not interested in what was happening, only now and then glancing at the foetus hanging from the mother. After another contraction at about 1430 h, the foetus and placenta were expelled and fell to the ground. Tanja immediately jumped after the foetus, seized it with her hands, but then left it and returned to her place. The foetus had no hair, but its hands, fingers, nails, feet and toes were fully formed. It was not possible to determine its sex. Some measurements of the premature foetus are given in Table 2.

From the following day until her death Tanja could no longer move normally, but only fidget bit by bit along the shelves. She exhibited haemorrhage and suffered from severe diarrhoea until her death.

THE BEHAVIOUR OF PREGNANT FEMALES

On 4 October 1968, copulation was first observed between Boris and Lara, later the mother of the first surviving offspring. It was always the female who invited copulation. She first looked at the male intently, then ran away, turning round to see whether he was following her. If he did follow, she would lie down. If the male accepted the invitation, they copulated; after copulation the animals separated at once. Very often, play preceded copulation.

By the end of January 1970, it was obvious that Lara was pregnant. Her abdomen was swollen, and the sexual skin was redder during her pregnancy than when she was merely on heat. During pregnancy, she exhibited a desire to copulate and did so. I observed copulation for the last time on 6 April. For this reason I am unable to give the exact duration of pregnancy.

The pregnant female gradually became considerably quieter and by the end of January she frequently withdrew into the little hut when the other animals played too wildly. She became much more trustful towards me and did not hesitate to take fruit from my hand. Her behaviour towards her companions, however, was more aggressive than before. Her increased appetite for green food was striking; indeed, she preferred lettuce to any other food. During the ensuing period, I occasionally observed Lara trying to climb on the other females or attempting to climb on the male when he was mating with another female.

By the middle of March, we believed that Sonja was also pregnant. She became quieter, and no longer participated in play, although she was somewhat more lively during her pregnancy than Lara and did not move so lethargically. Even on the day of giving birth Sonja still jumped to the floor to look for food, a thing which Lara had not done for a long time prior to giving birth. Towards the end of the pregnancy, a dilation of the vagina could be observed in both females. Several days before parturition, Sonja seemed to feel something in her vaginal area, for she repeatedly touched it with her hand.

PARTURITION AND THE NEW-BORN YOUNG

On 26 May, Lara behaved normally throughout the day; but when I brought them their food at approximately 1900 h and all the other langurs rushed towards it, Lara remained sitting on her shelf and then lay down. When I looked at her again at 2000 h, she was obviously in pain. She changed her perch several times, lay down on her shelf for several moments and made groaning noises.

In order not to disturb her any further, I left the hall. The next morning, at 0700 h, I found the baby already clinging to its mother, who was sitting among the other animals holding the young one tightly. The blood stains on the shelves indicated that Lara had not even withdrawn to the little hut for the birth. The umbilical cord was still attached to the infant and to the placenta. When Lara moved she walked on her hind legs, pressing her offspring to her breast with her arms. However, the placenta was heavy and the baby was pulled downwards, so that Lara could not hold it properly and became very nervous.

By about 1500 h Lara had not eaten the placenta nor chewed at the umbilical cord, and she did not behave as though she intended to do so. I succeeded in cutting the cord a short while later without the animals noticing it. The long umbilical cord attached to the baby subsequently dried, and fell off 2 days later.

The two other females showed interest in the baby from the very beginning. Both tried several times to take it from its mother. When they succeeded in doing so and the young one cried, Lara immediately took it back. In order not to disturb her too much the first day, I removed the other females and left her alone with the male. Lara ate with her normal appetite, but the birth had tired her and she slept a good deal.

Sonja similarly did not show any special signs on the day before the birth, and she ate her food as usual. On 2 August 1970 she was also found holding her baby in her arms when I entered the hall in the morning. This young animal was similarly still connected to the placenta by the umbilical cord, but as Sonja was much more trustful towards me than Lara, I was able to cut the cord quite easily while I was caressing her. The placenta weighted 90 g ($3\frac{1}{2}$ oz). The infant suckled for the first time at 1200 h.

Of the two mothers, Sonja was the less anxious, and she was well able to assert herself against the other females. We therefore decided to leave her with the group and no isolation proved to be necessary.

The new-born douc langur has its eyes wide open. The face is black, with the exception of two light stripes beneath the eyes. The top of the head is reddish-black. A black line runs along the back, which is otherwise a light chestnut colour. The arms and legs are a chestnut-reddish-brown, and this is somewhat brighter on the legs than on the arms. The hands and feet are black, the tail is whitish and has a grey tip. The neck and tail-root are chestnut and the ventral surface is the same colour, although a little paler.

After the second birth Boris behaved very aggressively, as he had done after the birth of the first baby, and tried to attack passers-by through the bars. He repeatedly placed himself so that the mother and infant were protected behind his broad back. When cleaning the cage I had to be careful, for at the slightest noise from the mother Boris adopted a warning position and hit out towards me with his arms.

BEHAVIOUR OF THE YOUNG

On the day of its birth, Lara's baby crawled actively over her mother and turned her head to look at me. She was interested in the two female langurs sitting in the next cage. At the age of 5 days, she grasped the bars and her father several times. The infant frequently changed her position on the mother and climbed about on her body whilst making chirping noises. One day later, the baby reached for the leaves its mother was eating. When the baby became too excited during these early days, Lara withdrew with her, holding the infant closely and hiding her in her arms.

The activity of the young animal increased steadily. When she was 9 days old, she had become so strong that she was continuously moving her arms and trying to crawl away from her mother, although Lara did not allow this. The young langur watched everything that happened in her surroundings with increasing interest. At 10 days of age, the baby tried to move a little towards her father. However, when the father tried to touch the infant's head, Lara immediately pulled the little one back and pressed her closely to her body.

The young langur left her mother for the first time when she was 13 days old, but only for a short time. At the age of 14 days, she sat next to her mother on the board, and at 17 days old the infant was very busy with her hands, trying to hit her mother, to scratch her own tail and so on. At this age, she walked along the running board for short distances, but in apparently dangerous situations (e.g. with unusual noises, quarrels, or when the young one was crying) the mother immediately came to take the baby back.

While the infant was still uncertain when running on all fours, she was considerably more skilful in climbing and jumping. When she was 19 days old, she almost fell off the shelf, but her parents caught her in time. The floor of the cage was therefore covered with a thick layer of hay, which proved to be very useful for both little animals in the future.

At 4 weeks of age, the youngster was allowed to move away from her parents over longer distances. Her walking and running along the shelves had become more certain, and the young langur was also able to hang from the roof of the cage holding on with one hand. When I tried to stroke Boris on 30 June, he became angered. I had not noticed that he was carrying the young animal, and, while he is usually very trustful, when he is carrying one of his daughters he does not allow anyone to touch him.

By 42 days of age, the youngster tried to get hold of all kinds of bits of food and even ate small quantities of peach and plum. Ten days later, she often jumped into the leaves offered as food; but in the middle of such play she went from time to time to find her mother to suckle. We did not notice that the youngster had any preference for a particular nipple, but sometimes it changed from one to the other.

At the age of 66 days—shortly before the birth of the second infant—the young langur showed interest in rose leaves and turnip-cabbage and tried to eat them. We also watched her playing with sticks at that time, trying to jump over them and turn around with them.

Sonja's female infant developed as satisfactorily as Lara's. On 5 August, at 3 days of age, this second little langur tried to crawl away from her mother for the first time, but was held back. When sleeping, she was always held upright by her mother, and very often had a nipple in her mouth. By 6 days of age, the young one was grasping for the bars and for leaves with her hands. Two days later, she released her hold on her mother with the hands, although she held on with the legs. She first left her mother completely at the age of 2 weeks. Further development followed the same course as that of Lara's infant. It was not considered possible to take the young from their mothers in order to measure and weigh them, for fear of the distress it would have caused. At the age of 3 months

FIGURE 2. Baby douc langur (born on 2.8.70) at the age of 24 days. (Photo: Rolf Schlosser.)

the young animals climbed off the boards and followed their mothers over the ground to the neighbouring cage. At this time, they no longer took the larger pieces of food from the plates with their mouths, but held them in their hands.

Their skill had greatly increased, and we frequently saw them walking along in an upright position for short distances. However, even now, at the age of 4 and 7 months respectively, they run back to their mothers when they feel disturbed or uncertain, and are still regularly suckled.

THE RESPONSES OF THE ADULTS TO THE YOUNG

Immediately after the birth, Lara and her baby were the focus of the little caged community. The females, especially, were very interested in the new-born baby, and repeatedly tried to get hold of it. When separated from the mother and young both the females sat where they were able to see them and closely watched any movement the baby made. Initially, the father's role consisted mainly of protecting the mother and child against both their cage companions and human beings. He was prepared to attack as soon as either the mother or the young animal uttered a cry of fear.

When Lara's baby was 3 days old, I left the group together while cleaning the cage. Sonja immediately took hold of the infant and started to clean it. She did so much more thoroughly than the infant's own mother had done and repeatedly licked its navel, which I had never seen its mother do. I also observed the father grooming the infant when she was 5 days old, and he was carrying her by the time she was 4 weeks old.

The reunification of the group did not cause any difficulties, since the youngster was sufficiently well developed to be able to jump away from the female carrying her at any time. Neither of the other females retained the infant. It was very striking that about 17 days before the birth of her own child, Sonja's interest in the young animal not only disappeared, but actually gave way to a certain aggressiveness towards her. However, after she gave birth to her own infant, she was kind towards the youngster as before.

When Sonja's infant was born, it, in its turn, immediately became the focus of attention, and all the members of the group were extremely interested. Since there had not been any difficulties with the first baby within the group, we left Sonja and her baby in the common cage. As before, all of the members of the group participated in carrying the young one, and sometimes Lara could be seen with both young animals in her arms. However, I did not see either infant suckling from the wrong mother. During the following weeks, it became very obvious how tolerant all members of the group were towards the two youngsters, who were permitted to do anything they liked. They climbed and jumped about on the adults, hung and swung on their tails and hit their faces with their hands; but none of the adults ever became angry.

I frequently observed that Lara's baby, a particularly lively infant, wanted to be carried by Sonja, who for some reason or other refused to do so and pushed the young one away. I do not think it is asserting too much to say that the youngster then had a real fit of rage, screaming loudly and stamping with its feet. Sonja did not want to give in, but the father immediately hurried over and took the baby into his arms: the baby calmed down at once. I observed that the father/infant relationship became more pronounced as the juveniles became older.

By the middle of September, games of pursuit began, and all members of the group, including the two young ones, took part. In the course of these the langurs grasp one another's heads and roll about the floor, with their arms wrapped tightly around one another and with their eyes closed. It very often happened that the two young ones were in the midst and, fortunately, although these games appear dangerous, they are in fact always harmless.

APPENDIX

On 14 May 1971, the third female douc langur (Tanja) gave birth to a male youngster.

On 19 November 1971, the female Sonja, who had lost her previous baby when it was about 8 months old, gave birth to a male infant. Subsequently, on the 20 and 25 January 1973, the two females Tanja and Sonja each gave birth to a female infant. Our douc langur group then consisted of the original adults and five surviving young animals born at Cologne Zoo. It is worth noting that with the latest two births (20 and 25 January 1973) the placenta was separated normally by the mothers.

On 18 November 1973, the breeding group of douc langurs was moved to a newly constructed monkey house with much more space than was available in their provisional installation.

On 17 and 24 August 1974 Tanja and Sonja each gave birth to an infant. Our douc langur group now consists of the adults and a total of seven young animals born at Cologne Zoo.

From births recorded to date the gestation period would seem to be about 165 days.

Breeding Orang-Utans

M. R. Brambell

INTRODUCTION

This is not the place for me to comment on why orang-utans are an endangered species. This state of affairs has arisen as a result of several local and some global factors and it is up to the ecologists and politicians to prevent the situation from getting worse.

Conservation of a species has two major aspects which may clash, but which must not be confused.

1. Conserving the species by conserving the wild ecosystem, which is the fundamental problem.

2. Conserving the species, as a unique vehicle of its chromosomal genotype, to pass on to our descendants irrespective of whether we are also successful in saving the ecosystem.

I believe that there comes a point in the battle against premature extinction when one has to decide that there is not enough hope in saving the ecosystem to leave all our eggs in that basket, and that a viable breeding nucleus should be removed to a place of greater protection.

This happened by accident in the case of Père David's deer, and the world is grateful to the 11th Duke of Bedford for his action. It happened by design in the case of the Arabian oryx, and our thanks in this instance are very much due to the Fauna Preservation Society, and to the other bodies which cooperated in that venture.

In the case of the orang-utan, I believe that there are now enough orang-utans in zoological collections for us to halt imports from the wild. There are now about 500 orang-utans in captivity, of which about one quarter were born in captivity. Indeed, the time may not be more than 5 or 10 years away when orang-utans may be available from such zoological collections for return to their native habitat, assuming that the natural habitat is not already overcrowded. However, even this would not mean that the zoological collection would cease to have a function in conserving the species. What is meant by "conserving the species" is that we do what we can to ensure that there are still orang-utans around in a thousand years and in ten thousand years. Humane management within collections may prove to be the only way to bridge the ravages that the overpopulated world of the 21st century will wreak on the natural environment.

A most important requirement is that any manager of a breeding collection should know the history of his stock. Here we have the help of the studbook. But studbooks are backward-looking. We also need some way of disciplining the future. We need to ensure that the genotype of the species is altered as little as possible by ill-judged selection. We do not want connoisseurs of the external morphology of orang-utans to tell us that a particular specimen is a good example and that another one should not be used for breeding, for such is the way of poodle breeding. We need to get together and work out how to recognize and eliminate genetic traits that would be lethal in the wild, and then to work out how to allow the remaining genetic pool to mix in captivity much as it might in the wild. This means that there must be careful planning on a zoological basis and not with an eye to prestige and the gate receipts. Once a species is endangered, its individuals should have no cash value. Animals should be placed where they are most needed to keep the genetic pool viable.

So much for the strategy of the conservation of this species. The manager has to deal with individuals, which are not abstract ideas like species but are real living things that can suffer pain and discomfort if they are not cared for.

CAPTIVE ENVIRONMENT

The planning of captive environments must be based on a knowledge of the animal in the wild. For orang-utans, we are very fortunate to be able to draw on the work of many well-known investigators, in particular the recent report of John MacKinnon, who has spent nearly 16 months observing these animals in Borneo (MacKinnon, 1971). On the basis of such reports, one can estimate the minimum conditions necessary for successful maintenance of orang-utans in captivity.

Orangs live in trees and do not as a rule move around on the ground. They brachiate and they are heavy. In my opinion, it is wrong to keep these animals in situations where they cannot move around horizontally off the ground. I would also add that, because of the danger of drowning, it is unsafe to keep these animals where they may risk falling into water.

It is hard to say what is the minimum set of requirements, but we have designed for London Zoo a complex of cages covering an area of about 300 sq. m in which we expect to keep six to ten orang-utans (Fig. 1).

Adult male orang-utans fight with one another and cannot normally be kept together. Females with babies may be threatened and may need temporary removal. However, it is our experience that orangs are slightly more social in captivity that would be expected from observations in the wild.

Orang-utans are immensely strong, very observant and highly intelligent. If they can work out how a particular structure comes apart, they may well

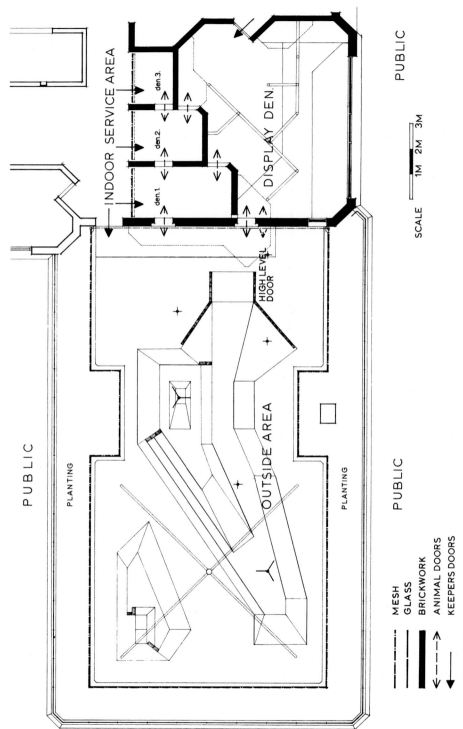

FIGURE 1. Ground plan of the indoor quarters (dens) and outdoor enclosure for the orang-utans at London Zoo, Regent's Park.

start to dismantle it. People who have no experience of these animals just will not believe how strong they are (Fig. 2). Engineers patronizingly but disbelievingly grin when told that orangs can undo a nut tightened with a wrench, but all those who have kept these animals must have had many experiences which show this to be true.

Humidities of less than 60 per cent are probably irritating. Temperatures of 10°C or less can be tolerated for short periods. The animals must have shelter from wind and rain, unless the temperatures are in the neighbourhood of 25°C. If one remembers that orangs once lived in Southern Asia at colder times than now, it would seem probable that with careful acclimatization they can happily tolerate quite severe conditions.

As a general rule, I think it best to provide them with warm, sheltered spots and leave them to choose how much they expose themselves to the prevailing conditions, as long as it is a real choice and is not influenced by a bullying cage companion (Fig. 3).

DIETARY REQUIREMENTS

Orang-utans are adapted to digest plant foods. They have large abdominal cavities; in the caecum and large intestine they harbour bacteria capable of digesting cellulose. The wild diet is probably made up of bark, shoots, nuts, berries and fruits as well as of insects and bees nests, and probably birds eggs, young birds and young mammals as well.

In captivity they thrive on a daily diet of about 450 g of expanded monkey pellets with a couple of oranges, a quarter of a cabbage, four bananas, a lettuce and a Haliborange tablet. Variety can be given in the vegetables; the essential nutrients are in the pellets. Some people become rather emotional about never varying the pellets. But if the pellets are regarded as if they were bread and the plant foods as if they were the jam, then I think most people would agree that the diet is satisfactory. Vary the jam and the bread will remain wholesome and appetizing.

In the wild, animals generally tend to spend most of their time eating or searching for food. In captivity, they tend to get through their food quickly. To fill the time left over it is good practice to sprinkle low-energy but tasty titbits, such as sunflower seeds, about the enclosure to encourage the animals to spend the rest of their waking hours doing what they would be doing in the wild—looking for food.

Clean water on tap is the best. We use Lixit drinkers, modified to overcome the orang-utans' destructive ways.

GENERAL HUSBANDRY

Know your animals and have them know you, but keep them among their own kind. If an animal has to be removed from a group, keep it in vocal and tactile contact with the rest. It is essential to have quiet, but not silent surroundings and plenty for the animals to do and to look at. Orang-utans, like gorillas,

FIGURE 2. Adult female orang-utan using the space frame for horizontal movement above the ground in the outside area of the new orang building. Note the sturdy construction of the cage, reflecting our experience of the strength of these animals.

FIGURE 3. Orang-utans using playground climbing posts to reach the space frame. Note the doors with plastic flaps allowing free access to the indoor dens, whilst conserving heat.

appreciate a room with a view. Orangs are very manipulative and like to have things to use their hands on. Twigs and wood wool are excellent, so are cardboard boxes, old plastic dustbins and such like.

MATING, PREGNANCY AND LACTATION

Unlike chimpanzees, orang-utans are not dependent on learning by example in order to mate in captivity. They just get on with the business as soon as they are old enough. Nor does the male restrict his attentions to the times when the female is at the fertile stage of her cycle. Copulation may go on right up to the time when the female gives birth. Thus, the start of a pregnancy cannot be judged by any change in copulatory behaviour.

Menstruation is not usually apparent in orang-utans, so it is not possible to estimate pregnancy on the basis of arrested menstruation. As a result, it is quite possible to make an error of 4 months in judging the expected time of birth, unless the two sexes were left together only for a short period (a procedure which reduces the likelihood of conception).

The only hope of obtaining an accurate prediction of the end of pregnancy is to use information on some foetal parameter which changes as pregnancy proceeds. The simplest of these is size, but there is so much else in the mother's abdomen that the finer aspects of foetal size are lost.

My veterinary colleague, Malcolm Hime, has been looking into the changes in foetal heart rates. We have listened to too few foetuses to draw any firm conclusions, but using an ultrasonic blood-flow detector (a conventional stethoscope is useless for this purpose), he has gained the impression that birth occurs at about the time when the foetal heart rate slows to below 120 beats per min.

Unlike mating behaviour, maternal behaviour does not come as easily to orang-utans. This may well be because the over-zealous manager tries to protect the baby by isolating the mother. This isolation may well be a cause of stress. It is relevant in this context to mention that London's first wholly successful mothering without any keeper help has been with a baby whose father was present at the birth.

If hand-rearing has to be done, the foster-parents have to face looking after the baby for about a year. What is so difficult to achieve during this period is frequent mixing with other orangs. Anybody who has reared a great ape baby must have realized that, charming though the experience is for the foster-parents, it is a disaster for the baby, and the sooner it can be returned to its own kind the better.

PREVENTIVE MEDICINE

Nutritional diseases are the greatest danger under conditions of artificial management. If the means of recognizing the early changes of rickets and other nutritional diseases are available (i.e. especially X-ray equipment), early remedial action can be taken. However, these diseases can of course be avoided by a well-managed dietary regime.

Orang-utans suffer from the common cold, but not to the same extent as chimpanzees. Nevertheless, keepers with colds should keep away from the animals.

Tuberculosis is a hazard in some countries. The greatest danger is from people or from infected milk.

Inactivity can give rise to lethargy which may eventually lead to the animal's death. Heavy males will cease to climb if they distrust the strength of the structure on which they climb, or if the hand-holds are so sharp as to hurt.

POPULATION CONTROL

There are two well-established geographically isolated subspecies of orang-utan: the Bornean and the Sumatran forms. I am not satisfied that the varieties within Borneo represent more than clannish traits. It is reasonable therefore, to treat all Bornean orang-utans as Bornean and all Sumatrans as Sumatran, but not to mix the two. Hybrids should not be allowed to contribute to the breeding pool.

RESTOCKING THE WILD

Return of orangs to the natural habitat depends on: (1) whether the techniques are available for ensuring that an animal will thrive and reproduce once again in the wild, and (2) whether there is enough of the wild habitat left to support the animals.

VIABLE BREEDING UNITS

Two males and four females provide a good basis for captive groups, though of course the males have to be kept apart. The more of these groups that are available for the interchange of members the better. At London, we are in the process of establishing two such groups, and I foresee the establishment of a third, based on animals bred at London Zoo to be located at Whipsnade. If there were three or four more such groups in England, I would be confident about the future prospects for captive orang-utans in England.

ESTABLISHMENT OF GROUPS IN OTHER COLLECTIONS

As long as the recipient collections are able to manage these animals properly, surplus captive groups should be moved from centre to centre in order to reduce the risk of disaster affecting a large number of animals. However, orangs have been kept too often in under-sized groups and it is better to wait until a group has been built up to about six animals and well established before it is moved. The great problem seems to me to be in having a practical control over the movements of orang-utans. At present such movements seem to be a matter for individual initiative.

I would like to see established a group of pragmatic people experienced in the management and zoology of orang-utans who are not afraid to say where an animal should go and to rule out places which are not able to manage the animals properly. Such a group should be in charge of the movements of these animals. I would add that I would be horrified if any fanciers were to obtain a foothold. Preserving a genotype will prove to be a very difficult and disciplined task, and there will be no room for those who have not taken the trouble to understand the zoology of orang-utans.

The Maintenance and Breeding of Pygmy Chimpanzees

F. Jantschke

INTRODUCTION

The history of captive maintenance of pygmy chimpanzees or bonobos (*Pan paniscus*) has been a long but not very successful one. According to the files of Marvin Jones, the earliest record of a bonobo is of one kept at Berlin Zoo as early as 1884. Amsterdam Zoo kept a bonobo from 1911 to 1916, while Antwerp had what was probably its first specimen in 1926, and a second in 1946. Paris had a male bonobo in 1940.

The first *pair* of bonobos to be kept in any zoo was one in Munich from 1936 to 1938. After the female died, the zoo received two more in the same year and kept them until 1944. At the time when the three animals died in an air raid, one female was reported to be pregnant. Since then, only three zoos outside the Congo have potentially been able to breed bonobos (apart from three doubtful records in the *International Zoo Yearbook*: in 1962, Barcelona reported possession of 2, 2; and Mexico City reported 1, 3; in 1963, Abidjan reported possession of 5, 2.).

Antwerp has for a long time kept bonobos, though most have been females. In 1968, the zoo received a male, which according to Marvin Jones did not survive for long. San Diego received a male in 1960 and a female in 1962. This pair is still alive, having bred in 1966, 1967, 1969 and probably at least once more in the meantime. All the offspring have been hand-reared.

Frankfurt received the first bonobo, a male, in 1955 and females were obtained in 1958 and 1959. One female has since given birth four times. After the first unsuccessful rearing attempt, the other three animals were raised by the mother and are still living in the group. So far, no other zoo seems to have bred bonobos, and most other zoos seem to have kept only single specimens (e.g. Paris, 1, 0, 1940; Rotterdam, 1, 1962; Lisbon, 1, 1958; Duisburg, 1, 0, 1962; Adelaide, 1, 0, 1962; Fort Wayne, 1, 0 from 1967 until 1971, when it received our surplus, non-breeding female).

BONOBO MAINTENANCE AND BREEDING AT FRANKFURT

Our male came from Leopoldville Zoo in April 1955, weighing 8·7 kg and aged approximately $3\frac{1}{2}$ years. More than 3 years later, the fully mature female Camilla arrived. She immediately established dominance over the male, Camillo, when she was introduced to him 6 months later. She maintained this dominant relationship until she was given away to Fort Wayne in 1971. In November, 1959, we were able to acquire a second female, Margrit, estimated to be 7–8 years old at that time. She, too, became dominant over the male when she was introduced to the pair. A third female which had come with her unfortunately died of enterocolitis and subileus 2 years later.

With Camilla it soon became apparent that she never ceased to exhibit a genital swelling. In spite of frequent matings with the male, she apparently never conceived. Margrit, however, did not exhibit such continued swelling; she ultimately proved to be fertile and gave birth to a male infant on 22 January 1962. This parturition was observed and it is described in detail by Kirchshofer (1962a, b). The mother took good care of the infant, which unfortunately developed acute bronchial pneumonia at the age of 2 months. It was taken away from the mother, but died 4 days later.

One year and eleven months later (on 22 December 1963) Margrit again gave birth to a male, called Mato. This baby was raised successfully by the mother. Mato is still living in the group and is now mature. After the female raised her infant, a long time elapsed before she became receptive again. Furthermore, the dominant, non-breeding female Camilla was interfering with mating attempts. Four and a half years after the birth of Mato, his sister Daniela was born (on 17 June 1968). She was also raised by her mother. Both Mato and Daniela subsequently developed very well and on 2 May 1973 Margrit gave birth to her fourth baby (a female, Salonga), which she is still nursing (see Fig. 1). Mato, at the age of 8 years and 3 months, weighed 27 kg, and he has now attained an adult weight of about 40 kg. (Camillo weighed 31 kg at the estimated age of $8\frac{1}{2}$ years.) Daniela (see Fig. 2) weighed 12·5 kg at the age of 3 years and 9 months. Camillo attained his full weight at about 14 years of age and is now oscillating in weight between 42 and 46 kg. Margrit weighs between 27 and 34 kg (taking the weight before births).

While the bonobo group at San Diego has always consisted only of one pair, in Frankfurt we have had two females with the male at all times. As it was found that the dominant female was interfering with copulation, she was taken out during the periods of receptivity of the second female. We were able to acquire a young female at the end of 1970, and when she was successfully introduced into the group with Camilla, we decided to give the latter, non-breeding female away. Our group now consists of one male and one female (each probably aged more than 20 years), the male born here at the end of 1963, one female of about 7 years of age, the young female born in June, 1968, and the infant born in May 1973. After the female with the apparent hormone disturbance had been taken out, the atmosphere in the group became much more relaxed and there is now less nervousness than before. The introduction of the new, young female went off very smoothly and without the least sign of aggressiveness, although the two males mated with her frequently during the first few days. The rich social life

FIGURE 1. The fourth bonobo infant born at Frankfurt Zoological Garden, resting on its mother's belly. The infant (Salonga) is about 3 months old in the photograph, but it already shows the long limbs typical for the smaller species of the chimpanzee genus (*Pan*). (Photo: E. Müller.)

FIGURE 2. The mother bonobo, Margrit, with her two daughters—Salonga (approximately 3 months old) and Daniela (5 years old). When infants were naturally reared by the mother, the interval between births was always more than $4\frac{1}{2}$ years. (Photo: E. Müller.)

of the group has been studied and described in comparison to common chimpanzee social behaviour by Hübsch (1970).

The animals are housed in an inside cage of 5·5 × 5·1 m (about 17 × 15·5 ft) and a height of 3·8 m (about 12 ft). The outside enclosure is 5·5 × 6·5 m (about 17 × 20 ft) with a height of 3·5 to 4·2 m (about 11 of 13 ft). The material and equipment used in these cages is described in detail by Scherpner (1967). The cages are richly furnished with stainless steel bars, *Eternit* plates, rubber ropes and plastic chains, and they offer a variety of niches for sub-dominant animals along with playing and entertainment possibilities for all. During clement

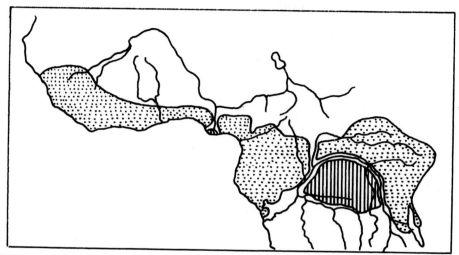

FIGURE 3. Distribution map (after Deblock, 1973) showing the former geographical ranges of common chimpanzees (*Pan troglodytes*—stippled area) and pygmy chimpanzees (*Pan paniscus*—vertical hatching). The dividing line between the two chimpanzee species is the River Congo and its tributary the Lualaba.

weather, even in winter, the animals can freely choose to spend their time in the inside or outside enclosure.

For all of our anthropoid apes we prepare a main diet high in animal proteins containing: 4·5 kg cottage cheese, 2·5 kg boiled minced meat, 0·5 kg skimmed milk powder, 30 eggs and about 1 kg of our standard mixture for omnivores. This consists of the following: 15 per cent maize, 20 per cent wheat, 30 per cent oats, 5 per cent barley, 10 per cent soybeans (all ground), 3 per cent lucerne flour, 10 per cent skimmed milk powder, 5 per cent dry yeast, 2 per cent mineral salts and 4 g Rovimix vitamin mixture. The mature bonobos receive about one pound of this food, which is semi-liquid and is fed by spoon. The young animals are given about half this amount. In addition, a variety of fruit and vegetables are fed in the afternoon (especially apples, a few bananas and oranges and one or two onions and lemons and fruits of the season). In the morning, the animals are given an eight-litre bucket full of carrots, lettuce, cale, germinated barley (6 or 7 days old), biscuits, peanuts, dried fruits and sunflower seeds—more for entertainment than for nutrition. Also, in the morning, the animals are provided with tea containing vitamin C and grape-sugar, and in the afternoon they are given a Nesquick drink containing 20 per cent chocolate, 20 per cent grape sugar and 60 per cent crystal sugar. This drink is very popular and can be used for administering medicine etc.

Since we started feeding the standard food mixture high in animal proteins, we have had excellent results in breeding all four species of anthropoid apes.

The only preventive medical treatment which has been used with our apes is BCG vaccination against tuberculosis. Since such vaccination was introduced about 15 years ago for all the apes, no case of tuberculosis has been recorded. The only two special problems we have encountered with our bonobos were: The one case of hormone deficiency in the female, which was treated for years by specialists in human medicine, without the desired results. When even a treatment with contraceptive pills and other procedures did not alter the situation and the animal was apparently disturbing normal social interactions in the group, we took the decision to give Camilla away. The other problem was amoebic dysentery, which for some time affected the whole ape house. It was successfully cured with Clont (Bayer-Leverkusen). Since then, we have not had any more trouble (Klöppel, 1971).

BREEDING POTENTIAL OF BONOBOS IN CAPTIVITY

As can be seen at San Diego, successful breeding can be achieved with only a pair of bonobos. However, we definitely believe in keeping the young animals with their mothers if possible, not only for nutritional but also for social, psychological reasons. We feel that the chances that the zoo-born animals will eventually breed and raise young themselves are much greater than with artificially reared apes. Therefore we have tried to build up a family group (as with all of our apes), which seems to us more natural and which has been working perfectly. The young male is often seen mating with our new female without any interference by the father. Accordingly, we believe that this breeding unit of two males and three females is not only safe at the moment but will also increase the chances that the young animals will breed at the earliest possible date. We think that our number and grouping of animals is the minimum requirement for any one zoo before it can start giving away any animals. We would even prefer to increase the size of the group by one or two animals, if possible.

To my present knowledge, there are only two captive breeding groups of bonobos and there will probably be only a few more in the years to come, given the present rates of breeding and importing of this species. Therefore, at the moment I can see no likelihood that there will be enough animals available for any attempted reintroduction into the wild. The interest in this species is apparently so limited that there is unlikely to be a large enough stock in zoos for them to be returned to the wild. At present, I know of no attempt to observe these animals in the wild, and there seems to be no estimate of the numbers of bonobos in the natural habitat. Thus, we have only a very limited knowledge of this species, and I am afraid that the situation will continue in this state for several years to come. Bonobos have unfortunately been neglected by scientists and zoos alike, and only a fundamental change in attitudes can improve the prospects for their conservation.

Progress in Breeding European Bison in Captivity

J. Raczyński

INTRODUCTION

The history of the rescue of the European bison from extinction as an endangered species dates from 1932, when the first census of these animals was made, including all pure-bred animals living in captivity at that time, together with those of their progeny which it proved possible to register (van den Groeben, 1932). This material formed the beginning of the currently continued *European Bison Pedigree Book* (Żabiński, 1966, 1971), in which a continuous record is kept of all European bison bred in the world, together with their exact genealogy.

As soon as the first steps had been taken towards saving the European bison as a species, these animals became the object of a wide-scale restitution action aimed at maintaining strict standards to ensure that bison born were pure-bred (in view of the ease with which fertile hybrids are obtained from cross-breeding with American bison), and also at achieving intensive reproduction in order to reach numbers which would guarantee perpetuation of the species (Żabiński, 1957; Krysiak, 1963).

The cataclysm of the Second World War brought with it a most serious threat to the developing action for protection of the European bison, and it was not until after the war that international cooperation began to produce any visible signs of success. The effect of this cooperation has been rapid growth, especially in recent years, of the number of these animals and the formation of an increasingly large number of breeding centres. The turning-point in the work of restitution was the initiation in 1952 of a free-living herd of bison in Poland (in the Bialowieża Primaeval Forest). Organization of free-living herds was continued successfully in successive years in both Poland and the Soviet Union.

The present paper is based on material accumulated by the Editors of the *European Bison Pedigree Book*, and its purpose is to assess the effectiveness of reproduction among European bison in both enclosed breeding centres and under free-living conditions, as a basic factor in the restitution of the species and in increasing its numbers. The analysis made covers a 20-year period of breeding these animals on a world scale (viz. from 1950 to 1969), which would appear to be a sufficiently representative period for considering breeding tendencies

FIGURE 1. Bison mother with calf, photographed 18 May 1974 at Puszcza Bialowieża. (Photo: J. Raczyński.)

and results of reproduction by European bison, both under conditions when their numbers were small and also during the phase of intensive growth in the world herd of these animals. Reproductive potential will shortly permit attainment of a total number of 2000 animals, which constitutes a threshold level below which a species may be considered as endangered.

DIFFERENT SYSTEMS OF BREEDING EUROPEAN BISON AND TRENDS IN THEIR DEVELOPMENT

At the present time the two main systems of breeding European bison are in enclosures and in free-ranging herds, the chief feature of the former being that the animals are kept in enclosed areas, which permits far-reaching control over and care of the given herds. The breeder decides upon the composition and numbers of the herd he keeps and also selects individuals for purposes of reproduction. The size of the enclosure may vary greatly: from the small enclosures found in some zoological gardens to those of 50–80 ha in extent in the large breeding centres. Centres of this type can be classified as follows:

1. For exhibition purposes—the function of such areas is limited to exhibiting single individuals. These are usually zoological gardens or parks open to visitors, possessing single males or groups of bull bison, and exceptionally pairs of old or barren animals. Centres of this kind are not concerned with the aim of breeding bison.

2. For reproductive purposes—possessing breeding pairs or herds and concentrating on intensive reproduction of bison. These are usually municipal, state or private zoos and parks and also breeding centres belonging to states, associations or limited companies (etc.).

3. Quarantine stations and enclosures belonging to firms dealing with the sale of wild animals. European bison are usually kept in such stations for a short period only, and births of these animals under such conditions occur only sporadically.

Centres in which the herds live in freedom are characterized by the fact that the animals live in a natural habitat—in large stretches of wooded land where the bison are assured, at least during the summer period, of natural living conditions. The breeder's interference with this state of affairs is limited to constituting the initial breeding herd and (later) to providing, in case of need, supplementary food during critical periods, and to regulating numbers. After herds have lived in freedom for a fairly long time natural populations are gradually formed, in which biological/ecological mechanisms play an important part.

When viewed from the aspect of reproductive intensity and growth in the numbers of the breeding herds, both systems of breeding—in enclosures and in free-ranging herds—fulfil similar functions. Consequently, it would appear to be pointless to exclude free-ranging herds when considering the problems of the European bison's reproductive dynamics and the increase in the "world herd" of pure-bred European bison. It must also be emphasized that the present phase of development of free-ranging herds is marked by the absence of factors limiting reproduction, and the numbers so far reached make it possible to trace the processes defining the numbers of these herds.

REPRODUCTION AMONG EUROPEAN BISON IN ENCLOSED CENTRES

When evaluating different centres it is justifiable to consider those which are concentrating on increasing the number of European bison quite separately from all other centres. Consideration of suitable utilization of the European bison's reproductive potential must take into account the realities of the present breeding situation on a world-wide scale. The restitution of this species is taking place in a very specific situation, in which breeding centres have been fragmented and transformed to small-scale arrangements, and where the number of breeders (not all of whom have identical aims in view) has become very considerable. It is therefore essential to treat the entire "world breeding herd" as a unit, primarily on account of the specific composition of breeding herds, which are usually composed of a certain number of cows together with their growing progeny and one or two males, the reproducers. The excess of males which is thus created (especially of adult bulls, which have to be kept separately in enclosures) is dealt with either by centres intended for exhibition purposes, or by special reserves for males (e.g. the reserve for bull bison at Smardzewice in Poland), or by transferring bulls to reserves concerned with breeding hybrids with American bison in the Soviet Union. These males, "superfluous" from the breeding point of view but valuable on account of their potential contribution to the gene pool, form an integral part of the world European bison herd, however, and their exclusion from analysis would cause over-estimation of indices.

THE SEASONAL CHARACTER OF REPRODUCTION

The mating season has been determined from the times at which calvings are known to have taken place, taking 264 days as the average gestation period in these bison (Krasiński and Raczyński, 1967) and omitting all instances of births of dead calves in order to eliminate abortions and premature births, as this might distort the final picture obtained. It emerged, however, that abortions took place in every month of the year and therefore one cannot exclude cases of mating outside the main mating season (Fig. 2).

The main calving season covers the three summer months, May, June and July (Fig. 2), during which period 63 per cent of the world herd of female European bison calve. The studies made by Krasiński and Raczyński (1967) of calving times in Polish breeding centres for the period 1954–65 showed that 71 per cent of all calvings occurred during this period. In view of the fact that the various Polish centres are characterized by considerable differences in conditions and that they are situated within the bison's natural range, the results given for world breeding therefore point to a great degree of regularity of reproductive processes in the world herd of European bison. A characteristic feature of the reproductive season among captive bison is the occurrence of calving during the autumn months up to an including December. This phenomenon is caused by prolongation of the rutting time beyond the main period, lasting from August to October and including part of November (Fig. 2). The extension in time of the rutting season (and consequently of the calving season) can be regarded as a manifestation of domestication caused by the constant character of breeding conditions over the full yearly cycle.

During the first 9 years of development of the free-ranging herds of bison in the Bialowieża Primaeval Forest it was observed that 80 per cent of the calvings took place during the period from May to July, and calvings in November and December were only sporadic, while no calving was observed during the period from January to April, which corresponds to the absence of oestrus in female

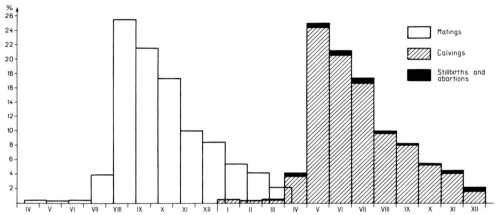

FIGURE 2. Annual distribution of matings and calvings of female European bison in world breeding centres in the period 1950–69. Mating dates were calculated from normal calving dates, taking the average gestation period as 264 days. Total number of matings (excluding those leading to stillbirth or abortion) = 1488; total number of calvings = 1558. The months of the year are indicated by Roman numerals.

bison during the period from April to June (Krasiński and Raczyński, 1967). It must, however, be emphasized that under natural conditions ecological factors, and particularly behavioural factors, play a significant role in the course taken by the rut in bison herds. From the late autumn onwards there is a tendency for the bull bison to separate from the herds of cows with their progeny, and for the sexes to rejoin only at the start of the mating season. A situation of this sort cannot occur under the conditions prevailing in breeding enclosures, where breeding pairs often remain together all the time. Disturbances in the fertilization of cow bison (ineffective mounting by bulls) cause recurrence of oestrus in cows, and this can lead to calving at atypical times. It must be assumed that, during the period when natural herds of European bison were still in existence, the reproductive season was certainly shorter, because natural selection acted as a natural factor in its stabilization, eliminating calves which were born late. Tendencies of this kind can also be observed in the free-ranging herd in the Bialowieża Primaeval Forest (Krasiński, pers. comm.).

In general, it can be said that breeding in enclosures has not as yet caused any great disturbances in the natural rhythm of the European bison's reproductive processes, proof of which is the sudden onset of the rut in August and of calving in May. A certain number of calvings at atypical times can also be explained as due to international breeding operations undertaken by different breeders.

REPRODUCTIVE DYNAMICS

The fecundity of the world bison herd concentrated in enclosed breeding centres is shaped by the sex and age structure of the herd, and depends on the calving index of female bison. The sex structure of the world herd exhibits constant predominance of females. The average value for the sex ratio for the 20-year period considered is 0·85, with annual fluctuations from 0·74 to 0·91. Average frequency of female bison in the world herd is 53·9 per cent. This situation is due both to the naturally greater longevity of females (female bison

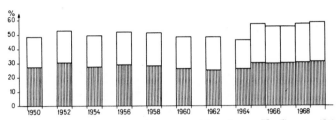

FIGURE 3. Proportion of female European bison capable of reproduction in relation (*a*) to total number of females, and (*b*) to world herd numbers (enclosed breeding centres). (*a*) = vertical columns; (*b*) = striped sections of vertical columns.

predominate in the higher age classes), and to the greater care breeders take of females. Some adult males are eliminated from centres on account of their aggressiveness, infertility, etc., and also because of the necessity for limiting the number of bison in overcrowded centres.

Shifts in sex ratio also take place naturally in the early period of individual development—during embryonic development and also during the period of rearing the young animals. The sex ratio of stillborn and aborted calves pointed to a predominance of males (41 : 26), but this difference proved to be statistically non-significant when checked with the Chi-square test. The same applies to calves dying during the rearing period, before the end of the first year of life (95 : 71). However, if these two groups are treated together it can be seen that total mortality of males during the embryonic and juvenile periods is significantly higher than that of females ($x^2 = 6·53$, $0·01 < P < 0·05$).

The percentage of females capable of reproduction in breeding enclosures is shown in Fig. 3. Females up to the age of 4 years have been included in this group. Under breeding conditions in Polish enclosures some of the young females calve as early as the third year of life (Krasiński and Raczyński, 1967) and the combined percentage of calvings for both these age-classes is almost 100 per cent. The percentage of cows with reduced reproductive capacity due to age or barrenness after reaching the 20th year of life is small, and has been omitted from the calculation.

On average, about half of the total number of females (52·3 per cent) are included in the reproducing group and this index has exhibited considerable constancy over the 20-year study period (Fig. 3). In recent years, there has even been a tendency towards increase in this reproductive group of female bison. This situation is probably transitory in character and is due to exclusion of young animals from breeding enclosures in connection with intensive formation of new free-ranging bison herds in the Soviet Union during this period.

In relation to the total number of sexually active females, calving cows con-

TABLE 1. Fertility of European bison bred in enclosures.

Year	World herd Nos.	Total No. females	No. females capable of reproduction	No. of calvings	Calvings in relation to No. of adult females[a] (%)	Calvings in relation to world herd Nos. (%)
1950	142	80	39	28	71·8	19·7
1952	177	102	54	35	64·8	19·8
1954	200	111	55	35	63·6	17·5
1956	265	146	76	52	64·8	19·6
1958	320	173	89	67	75·3	20·9
1960	403	217	105	66	62·8	16·4
1962	497	260	124	101	81·4	20·3
1964	518	290	134	111	82·8	21·4
1965	562	300	171	107	62·6	19·0
1966	605	325	180	108	60·0	17·8
1967	593	319	177	116	65·6	19·6
1968	623	334	191	120	62·8	19·1
1969	711	375	219	137	62·6	19·3

[a] Alternatively: percentage of calvings in relation to number of females capable of reproducing.

stitute on average 68 per cent; the highest index, 82·8 per cent, was observed in 1964 (Table 1). It would appear that the calculated indices represent the real reproductive potential of the bison herd bred on a world scale, despite scattering among a large number of centres, and show the high degree to which the existing herds are used for reproduction of the species. Although this index was higher in Polish breeding centres, since the average value was 76·8 per cent, with fluctuations from 63 to 91 per cent annually (Krasiński and Raczyński, 1967), it must be borne in mind that these data referred solely to centres already established, in which large herds of these animals were concentrated and had for many years been directed at attaining maximum production of young, whereas average conditions in world centres differed from this state of affairs.

Reduction of the fecundity of European bison may under such conditions be caused by factors such as breeders lacking experience, difficulties in ensuring optimum living conditions for the bison, temporary difficulties in making up the complete breeding herd, inappropriate qualitative and quantitative composition of these herds, constant exchange of animals between centres, and intentional limitation of production on reaching the maximum herd of animals for a given centre. This last factor cannot have played a decisive part in the current situation, in view of the opportunities available for sale and exchange of bison with other breeding centres.

The direct cause of decrease in fecundity or occurrence of infertility in female bison is to be found in such factors as late calving, death of progeny during the period of intensive lactation and genetically conditioned infertility, or reduced fecundity of certain animals (Krasiński and Raczyński, 1967). Some influence towards reduction in fecundity of females is also exercised by the considerable degree to which many European herds are inbred, since their herds originate

TABLE 2. Increase in the world herd of European bison and the percentage represented by free-ranging animals.

Year	World herd Nos.	Free-ranging animals	
		No.	%
1965	780	218	27·2
1966	859	254	29·6
1967	942	349	37·0
1968	1019	391	38·4
1969	1145	434	37·9

from one pair of bison. In addition, some centres fail to carry out selection of breeding material for fertility and healthiness of progeny. While intentional elimination takes place to a limited degree in relation to males (although even in this case it is not always governed by findings with respect to fertility), it is almost never applied to females, and consequently there is an increase in the percentage of cows calving rarely and irregularly, exhibiting disturbances in the course of oestrus, producing weak progeny or feeding their young badly. At least some of these characters must in due course be manifested in their surviving progeny. This phenomenon, combined with inbreeding in various centres, must inevitably lead to degeneration of the breeding herd and constitutes a serious threat to the quality of the breeding material present in the world herd of bison kept in enclosed breeding centres.

It is therefore necessary, as a matter of urgency, to implement measures to counteract the harmful effects of breeding in enclosures in its present form, and in this way to initiate a qualitatively new stage in the restitution of this species.

REPRODUCTION AND INCREASE IN THE WORLD HERD OF EUROPEAN BISON

In recent years development of free-ranging herds has had an increasingly important influence on effective increase in the world herd of these animals

(Table 2). Free-ranging breeding centres are of importance not only from the point of view of quantity, but also with respect to quality. Free mating of animals under conditions closer to the natural situation and reconstruction of the form of herd life proper to this species eliminate a large number of unfavourable phenomena which occur in centres of the enclosed type. A typical example of development of free-ranging breeding of European bison is the formation of a bison herd in the Polish part of the Białowieża Primaeval Forest, which has been the object of detailed observations (Krasiński, 1967; Krasiński and Raczyński,

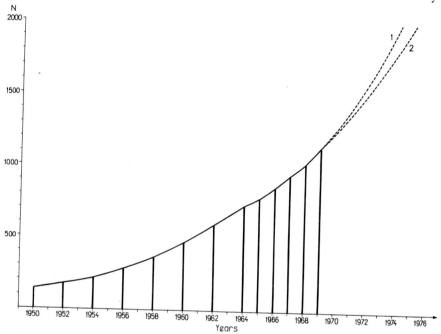

FIGURE 4. Increase in world herd of European bison since 1950. Dotted lines indicate forecast for the next few years, assuming absence of factors limiting population growth. (1) assuming average annual increase of 11·2 per cent; (2) assuming average annual increase of 9·5 per cent.

1967). The process of reproduction in the herd is characterized by a tendency to regeneration of the natural seasonal rhythm. During the initial phase of a herd's development, when it contains a predominant proportion of young animals, there is a high intensity of reproduction. The calving index of females is on average 71 per cent, with increase in the herd representing an average 19 per cent annually. All the currently existing free-ranging herds are still relatively new and have not yet attained either the full range of age structure or numbers at which the capacity of the habitat could act as a factor limiting the population. The fact must, however, be taken into account that such phenomena are inevitable in the future, and it has already proved necessary, for economic reasons, to control the numbers of the free-living herd in the Białowieża Primaeval Forest.

When the situation of this species is considered on a world scale it is obvious that the results so far obtained by breeding European bison provide genuine possibilities for its reproduction above the threshold number of 2000 animals in the not-too-distant future. The curve of European bison numbers (Fig. 4) is at present in the phase of logarithmic increase. Average annual increase for the 20-year period on a world scale is 11·2 per cent, and for the last 5 years it has been 9·5 per cent.

The fact that the European bison is officially recognized as a protected animal and is included in the *Red Data Book* of IUCN constitutes a guarantee that, at least in the range demarcated as a zone in which the species is endangered, progress in world breeding of these animals will not be arrested. The results so far brought about by protection support this conclusion, which is further borne out by the constant proliferation of breeding material from overcrowded centres to newly created centres, and by the successful development of free-ranging herds both in Poland and in the Soviet Union. This justifies hypothetical extension of the logarithmic curve over the next few years. On this basis, assuming that the index of increase continues at the level typical of recent years, one can forecast that the number of 2000 animals will be reached by 1976.

Breeding of Przewalski Wild Horses

J. Volf

The Zoological Garden of Prague owns a group of Przewalski horses which has bred for the longest time without interruption in captivity.

The original stock for the Prague breeding colony can be traced to a shipment which was sent from Central Asia to Hamburg for C. Hagenbeck in October 1901. Most of the 28 foals were sent to England, some of them to the USA, one stallion to Paris, and several foals to different places in Germany. The High School of Agriculture in Halle/S. became an important breeding centre in Germany, because the pair they had obtained gave birth to 13 foals. The High School of Agriculture in Prague bought from Halle the stallion Ali in 1921 and the mare Mika in 1923. In 1933 Ali died and was replaced by the stallion Horymir, imported from Washington. Those three original horses provided the basis for the Prague breeding stock.

At the late date of 1965 a new stallion, Bars, of strikingly typical appearance, was imported to refresh the blood of the Prague stock. He was born in 1963 in the Soviet Acclimatization Station of Askania Nova in Ukraine; his father was a stallion of Munich breeding, his mother, Orlica III, is the only Przewalski horse from the wild still living today in captivity. Bars (Fig. 1) transmits his characteristics to his offspring very expressively, and this stallion is thought to exert a strong influence not only on the characteristics of the Prague breeding herd but also on the entire world breeding stock of wild horses. As a matter of fact, the Prague herd of wild horses has been the biggest in the world for many years and an outstanding one in terms of its extraordinary reproductive capacity. More than a third of the wild horses living today in captivity have originated directly from Prague, and surplus animals continue to be exported every year.

In the Zoological Garden of Prague, the Przewalski wild horses are kept isolated from other kinds of animals. They have a separate brick pavilion consisting of three open stables and several closed stables for separating the horses. While the closed stables have only small concrete courtyards (50 sq. m each), every open stable is directly connected with its own paddock (Fig. 2). The size of each of the three paddocks is 2000–2500 sq. m. The surface of the paddocks consists of a hardened sand alluvium deposited on a tertiary bed. The paddocks are situated about 230 m above sea level on the middle terrace of the river Vltava, whose level lies some 55 m lower.

The paddocks have an inclination of 10–15°, they are oriented mostly towards the north and exposed to prevailing north-west winds blowing from the valley of the river Vltava. The average annual temperature in this area observed over the years 1931–60 is 9·1°C, and the average annual precipitation during the same

FIGURE 1. Photograph of the stallion Bars (Archiv Zoo Praha), the leading stud horse of the Prague herd. He is the offspring of the only wild-caught mare still surviving in captivity today.

period is 498 mm. The distributions of temperature and precipitation for individual months can be seen from Table 1.

It is evident that the microclimate of this area is close to the continental type, even if it does not actually attain the values observed in the area of distribution of Przewalski horses living in the wild state. Their natural habitat is 700–1800 m above sea level, the average annual temperature is +2° to −4°C; the average temperature in January is −15° to −16°C and in July +20° to +25°C; the annual precipitation amounts to about 100 mm, most of which falls in summer.

The dietary requirements of Przewalski horses kept in captivity are very limited. The daily feeding ration of an adult individual in the Zoological Garden of Prague averages out at: 5–6 kg coarse hay; 3 kg carrot or beetroot; 1·8 kg crushed oats; 0·20 kg wheat bran; 0·03 kg mineral substances; 0·02 kg salt (rock salt is always available).

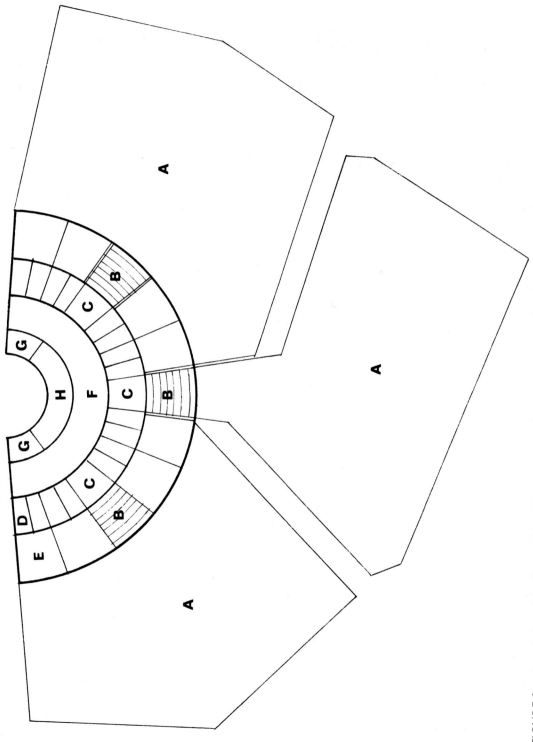

FIGURE 2. Ground plan of the Przewalski wild horse compound at the Prague Zoological Garden. A, paddock (outside enclosure); B, passage; C, open stable; D, closed stable; E, separate concrete courtyard; F, main passage between stables; G, food preparation room; H, store room.

In the summer season, hay is replaced by fresh green fodder obtained by foraging and the ration of corn fodder is reduced accordingly. The daily feeding ration is offered in two parts, one in the morning and one in the evening.

Preventive veterinary measures are limited to faecal examinations and to occasional doses of antihelminthic preparations. As for diseases, only *Coryza contagiosa equorum* has appeared—so far amounting to three cases which all occurred at one and the same time. It is not necessary to clip the hooves of our horses, as the surface of the paddocks suitably takes care of this requirement.

From the total number of 20 horses in the present stock in Prague, about half are placed in the breeding herd; a second herd is formed by foals 1–2 years old, and the third consists of over-age horses. The breeding herd is composed of a

TABLE 1. Average monthly temperature and precipitation for the years 1931–60.

	Temperature (°C)	Rainfall (mm)
January	−0·7	23
February	0·3	22
March	4·2	25
April	8·8	35
May	14·3	56
June	17·3	64
July	19·2	78
August	18·0	67
September	14·2	37
October	8·8	40
November	4·1	25
December	0·7	26
Averages	9·1°C	498 mm

Snow cover 33 days.

stallion, some mares and suckling foals. When they reach 3 years of age, the captive-born horses are again released into the breeding herd, although they actually achieve sexual maturity earlier than this.

The manner in which a new horse is introduced into the breeding herd depends entirely on the character of the breeding stallion. For example, although the stallion Uran was very aggressive towards people, he was always ready to accept a new mare in his herd. On the contrary, the stallion Bars tolerates any human beings in his paddock, but a new mare can be released into his herd only when she is on heat. He even drives older, barren mares away from his herd.

The stallion lives together with his herd throughout the year. Pregnant mares are separated shortly before parturition; they are then returned to the herd with foals 1 week old so that they can be mounted in the following rut. The foals remain with their mothers for 5 to 6 months. We originally tried to keep young mares permanently in the herd with their mothers until they reached sexual maturity, but the stallion Bars started to pursue the young mares when they were about 1 year old and we had to transfer them to the herd composed of other weaned foals.

In my opinion, the Przewalski wild horse, as a herd animal, should not, under any circumstances, be kept alone. Such treatment conflicts both with its behavioural needs (mutual defence of individuals, play behaviour, etc.) and with its physical needs (sexual drive, care of pelage, etc.). One pair of horses must be considered as the minimal group of animals to be kept in captivity.

I believe that the stock of 206 Przewalski wild horses living in captivity on 1 January 1973 would already provide possibilities for releasing a certain number back into the natural habitat. However, problems of financial, political, and technical nature will perhaps present obstacles. I think that it is out of the question to release wild horses in the area of their last refuge at the southwestern Mongolian frontier (in the mountain ranges of Bajtag Bogd and Tachiin Schara Nuruu). The best place for release of the horses would be an isolated, easily controllable reserve area fulfilling the requirements with respect to the security of the animals as well as to their climatic, soil and dietary requirements. As a practical example one can take the release of Tourkmenian wild asses (*Equus hemionus kulan*) in the island reservation of Barsa Kelmes in the Aral Sea. In that case, however, it was a question of transfer of animals within the territory of one state. Many problems which must be taken into consideration for release of Przewalski wild horses thus fell away in the programme for release of the wild asses.

The Przewalski horses now kept at the Zoological Garden of Prague belong to the fifth to eighth generation born in captivity. Comparative skeletal material conclusively indicated some time ago that the process of domestication in these hoofed animals very rapidly led to change in some somatic characteristics, particularly in the cranium (Volf, 1967) and in the long bones (Andreyeva, 1939). However, processing of data from individual Przewalski horses kept in captivity demonstrates that some pronounced changes have also occurred in fundamental physiological characteristics, especially in reproductive biology.

The original Przewalski horses brought from the wild between the years 1899 and 1903 (Mohr, 1959) did not attain sexual maturity before 4 years of age. This finding, of course, is sharply distinct from that established for wild horses kept in captivity later on. Among the Prague breeding stock there are already four stallions known to have mated successfully before reaching the age of 4, and five mares have become pregnant at an age of less than $2\frac{1}{2}$ years!

It is noteworthy that such extremely early sexual maturity occurs in the Prague breeding stock in wild horses born in the fifth to eighth captive generation. One can assume that this early attainment of sexual maturity depends directly on the degree of domestication of these animals (see Table 2).

Early sexual maturity in animals kept in captivity has been found relatively frequently, especially in bison (Hilzheimer, 1926), goats, elephants, and a number of other mammals. In hogs (Suidae), two rutting-seasons and births in a

TABLE 2. Summary of extreme early sexual maturity of Przewalski wild horses in the Prague breeding stock.

Studbook number	Studbook name	House name	Date of birth	Generation in captivity	Age in months at first successful mounting	Age in days at birth of first foal	1st foal	Date of birth
					MALES			
85	Praha 18	Ivan	18.vi.1953	5	31	1273	219. Blijdorp 1	11.xii.1956
81	Praha 14	Divoch	15.iv.1952	5	38	1497	184. London 8	19.v.1956
303	Praha 57	Václav	28.ix.1963	6	39	1517	385. Habana 1	23.xi.1967
245	Praha 37	Martin	6.v.1960	6	43½	1654	325. Praha 68	6.v.1960
287	Praha 52	Vilém	26.v.1963	7	49½	1845	398. Köln 1	12.vi.1968
					FEMALES			
286	Praha 51	Luisa	24.v.1963	5	24	1064	349. London 11	21.iv.1966
372	Praha 82	Myra	17.v.1967	6	24½	1080	466. Paris 8	30.iv.1970
283	Praha 50	Hosana	26.iv.1963	6	25	1099	352. Askania 8	3.v.1966
86	Praha 19	Vesna	17.v.1954	5	26	1126	93. Praha 26	15.vi.1957
290	Praha 54	Vlára	5.vi.1963	5	29	1221	363. Praha 80	7.x.1966

single year, as a product of domestication, have frequently been observed (Hediger, 1942).

The hypersexuality of captive animals is influenced by several factors. Zuckerman (1932) holds that it is one of the ways of dispensing energy accumulated from the calorie-rich food which captive animals obtain without adequate effort. However, it would seem certain that not only physiological but also psychological burdens of captive individuals (e.g. in their mutual social relationships and their general daily rhythms) play a significant part.

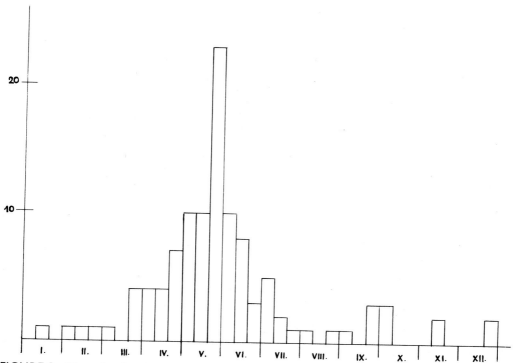

FIGURE 3. Chart showing the annual distribution of births of Przewalski horses of the Prague stock for the period 1933–73. Each column represents the total for 10 days.

The data given in Table 2 for the stallion Ivan and the mares Luisa, Myra and Hosana are extreme values not only for the Prague Zoo but also for world-wide breeding of Przewalski horses (Volf, 1970). Although the horses of the Prague herd are kept under extraordinarily favourable sociological, climatic, soil and nutritional conditions, it is necessary to underline the fact that they are descended from the Halle pair, which showed the earliest sexual maturity among all the original wild horses. One may therefore assume that the extremely early sexual maturation of some Przewalski horses is dependent upon genetic factors.

Both our own direct observations and other reports (Noack, 1902; Schirneker, 1921) lead us to believe that Przewalski horses give birth to their foals in the wild during a relatively limited period of the year, probably from the end of April to the middle of June. The situation is different, however, with captive animals.

By 1 January 1973, a total of 113 Przewalski horses had been born at the Zoological Garden of Prague, the exact dates of birth being known for 109 of these. In most cases, the times of birth correspond with the breeding pack of this species under natural conditions. By far the largest proportion of births (21 per cent) have occurred during the last 10 days of May. Sixty-two per cent of all foals in Prague have been born between the 20th of April and the 20th of June. The other births are scattered over the whole year with a slight peak at the end of September and the beginning of October (Fig. 3).

The foals born outside the main breeding season would obviously have had no chance of survival in the wild, partly because of climatic conditions (in cases of births in winter or early spring) and partly because of unfavourable nutritional conditions (in cases of births at the end of summer or in autumn). We have no reports on whether such premature or belated births of foals occur in the wild at all. They would, in any case, represent rare exceptions. In captive breeding of stocks throughout the world more than one-third of Przewalski horse foals have been born outside the main season, as a consequence of the process of domestication of the species.

breeding unit should not be contemplated if there is evidence to suggest that the species will not breed under captive conditions".

One aim should be to bring about a change in Article 3 of the Peruvian-Bolivian agreement, so that a small number of reproductive vicuña could be exported. This point was originally included to preserve the vicuña wool monopoly for the South American countries. However, this could easily be

FIGURE 2. Female Southern vicuña Argentina 22 in alert mood with tail erect. (Photo: R. Schmidt.)

guaranteed if zoos were to undertake not to sell any vicuña wool. So far only two collections have sheared their vicuña, on rare occasions.

THE VICUÑA STUDBOOK

Late in 1969, I started the Vicuña Studbook, which was authorized by IUCN and IUDZG. It covers all pure-bred vicuña living outside the four native countries since 1945. 208 vicuña were included by the end of 1971. At present, 34 males and 25 females are still living in 19 collections. Two-thirds of the total of 208 (139 specimens) were captive-bred, 22 were imported from Argentina, five from Peru and one from Bolivia. The origin of the remaining 41 vicuña is unknown. They were probably also imported, as most of them were sold by dealers. Obviously, cross-bred specimens and their progeny have been excluded from the Studbook as well as from the above numbers. Figure 3 shows the number of vicuña kept in captivity since 1945 and the annual importations.

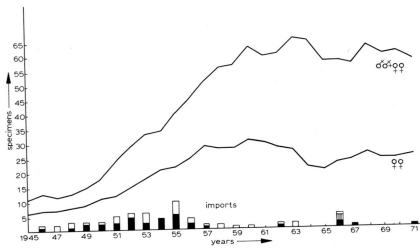

FIGURE 3. Total number of vicuña (upper curve) and number of female vicuña (lower curve) kept in captivity between 1945 and 1971. Blocks show the minimum number of vicuña imported from South America (white = males; black = females; hatched = unsexed specimens).

HUSBANDRY

Heavy losses occur after capture. Females with babies are usually caught with bolas by campesinos. The females are killed and the babies are raised as pets. Of five vicuña caught during 1966 in Argentina, one died before reaching Buenos Aires and the other four arrived dead in Europe. Mortality of freshly imported specimens after reaching good zoos is relatively low, at about 10 per cent (7 out of 69 within the first 6 months).

It is quite astonishing that the vicuña, a typical species of the high Andes, also thrives excellently in subtropical and coastal zoos. San Diego Zoo used to have a breeding group and Antwerp Zoo has had the best successes, with 35 births so far. At Zürich Zoo, with an altitude of 650 m, we have recorded 25 births.

The size of the enclosure does not seem to play an important role either; the extremes are 50 sq. m (Antwerp Zoo) and 10,000 sq. m (private collection in Brasschaat), both with fine breeding records. The height of the fence for large enclosures need be only 1·25 m (Cologne Zoo), whereas small enclosures need a fence of 2–3·5 m (Amsterdam Zoo and Antwerp Zoo). As male vicuña often make stereotyped movements along the fence, especially if other llamoids are present nearby, it is very important that the fence should be of good quality without wire ends sticking out. Otherwise, males often injure their eyes. Sometimes a tree-trunk placed on the spot where stereotyped behaviour patterns occur will keep the animals away from the fence. Vicuña hardly ever rush blindly into a fence, even after having been shifted to a new enclosure. Two zoos have dry moats (1·5 m wide at San Diego Zoo, 3 m wide at Cologne Zoo) and two have water moats (at Tierpark Berlin and Frankfurt Zoo, 2·6 and 3 m wide, 0·5–1·25 m deep). A wide variety of flooring is used in the different zoos, ranging from

FIGURE 4. Enclosure formerly used for vicuña at Zürich Zoo. Only one-third of the area at the rear and was used by a pair with offspring, whereas lush vegetation is seen growing in the other areas. (Photo: R. Schmidt.)

concrete through sand and gravel to grass. Two zoos with gravel flooring are sometimes obliged to trim the hooves (London Zoo, Pretoria Zoo), and one zoo with grass and sand has to trim the hooves twice yearly (Tierpark Berlin). However, all the specimens concerned are old and therefore probably rather inactive. In Zürich, we are very satisfied with our enclosures floored with grass, gravel and sand (see Fig. 4). Reinfection with parasites in grassy pens is no problem because vicuña use one or more central defaecation spots. Vicuña very much enjoy wallowing in the sand. They scratch their fleece on the fence or on pine trees. Koford (1957) reports that some vicuña bathe daily in shallow water, whereas others never do so. Our vicuña have no opportunity to bathe. However, they seem to like rain, as they rarely retreat to the shelter during rainfall. Stalls are very seldom used voluntarily. Even during winter, females prefer to give birth out in the snow. Naturally, an open shelter is necessary. Most single males and some group-leaders become very aggressive towards the keepers. Therefore, separation stalls or pens are desirable.

A strange feature reported by three zoos with medium-sized enclosures (400–500 sq. m) is that vicuña do not always make use of the whole range available. Grass, trees and other vegetation start to grow in those parts which are left untouched (see Fig. 4). At Zürich Zoo, only one-third of the area at the rear end of one enclosure was used by a pair with offspring. Vicuña in zoos are as territorial as they are in the wild. The door of one enclosure stood open for 3 hours, but the vicuña did not leave their artificial territory.

In some zoos vicuña are kept together with other species, such as rhea, African ostrich, waterfowl, marmots, Patagonian cavies, llamoids, camel, deer, antelopes, zebu, domestic sheep and goats. The combination with ostriches, waterfowl, deer and antelopes should be avoided because fatal accidents have occurred. Other llamoids should be separated to prevent interbreeding. The best American breeding group was spoiled because the breeding female was probably cross-bred with a guanaco in a communal enclosure. Darwin's rheas and Andean geese are best suited for association, because they live in the same natural habitat.

FEEDING

Food for vicuña poses no problem as they feed mostly on short grass in the wild. One zoo offers ruminant pellets exclusively. Most zoos add hay or alfalfa, branches, oats, barley, maize bran, potatoes, carrots, salad, bread, ground carob, wheat germs and a mineral mixture. In Zürich, we use *Vionate* (vitamin/ mineral powder, made by E. R. Squibb & Sons, Inc, New York). Captive vicuña like to lick salt stones. The daily intake of a male at Cologne Zoo was 100 g food pellets, 100 g oats and 1 kg carrots, in addition to hay. Our vicuña mainly graze during autumn and spring.

As is well known, the incisors in this species have open roots and grow continuously throughout life. Three zoos have to correct the incisors yearly, or every other year, obviously because the food provided is too soft. However, there may be individual variation in teeth growth, as one zoo had to correct the incisors of one specimen only. We have never had this problem at Zürich Zoo— surely because the animals can perform natural grazing and feeding on branches.

On cold, rainy days vicuña drink very little, but in the summer they drink daily in captivity.

GROUP COMPOSITION

Two different social units occur in the wild (Koford, 1957): (1) *All-male-troops* are open and non-territorial; the size of these troops varies between seven and 75 members. (2) The composition of the average *family band* is one male, five females, one yearling and two juveniles. They occupy territories of 8–40 ha.

In captivity, there is at present a large surplus of male vicuña. As a result, six zoos keep single males, most of which are very aggressive towards the keepers. Seven more zoos are keeping pairs, of which only two have bred during the last few years (at Alberta Game Farm, Edmonton and at Munich Zoo). The latter zoo exhibits an additional male vicuña and guanacos in adjoining pens. With three other pairs, the male has not shown any sexual interest in the female. The reason why the other pairs fail to breed is unknown. However, it might well be that a social group or the stimulus of an odd male prompts successful breeding. This stimulus may perhaps be substituted by neighbouring llamoids. Eleven out of the 17 females in the five larger collections (Amsterdam, Antwerp, Brasschaat, Paris, Zürich) breed regularly. Four of the remaining females are too young to breed, one was recently imported and only one has totally failed to breed without obvious reasons.

Most males which are kept singly for some time become highly aggressive towards females. In two cases, they are known to have killed freshly introduced females. Males of pairs may become aggressive at times. I know instances where leaders of groups have even chased certain females. Generally, this is not harmful as it is difficult for a male to persist in chasing the same female. Therefore, we keep the male together with the females and young ones all the year round. This is the normal association in the wild, and this procedure is followed by several other zoos too. Some zoos separate the female before, or just after, giving birth. Very few zoos leave the pair together only for mating. Crandall (1964) reports the procedure with a dangerous male at San Antonio Zoo, where the director restrained and muzzled the male before giving him brief access to the females. I am fairly sure that this male had been kept in isolation over a long period. In one private collection, the males are reported to become aggressive towards the young ones when they reach an age of 3–4 months.

MARKING

In a larger group of animals there is always the problem of individual identification of specimens. One zoo tattoos the vicuña (San Diego Zoo) and another zoo uses ear-tags (Frankfurt Zoo). Both methods have the disadvantage that one has to catch the specimens for individual recognition. In any case, ear-tags are not appealing to visitors and they may be torn out. In Zürich, I have initiated a marking system using small ear-slits (see Fig. 5). One can individually mark 99 specimens with no more than four slits per animal. These markings look natural and are not obvious to visitors, but the zoo-staff can recognize specimens from a distance with the use of binoculars. This enables us to keep an accurate studbook.

REPRODUCTION

Vicuña in Peru and Bolivia exhibit seasonal reproduction (Koford, 1957). The main mating period is in April, and March is the birth season. Gestation accordingly lasts 11 months. We have recorded gestation periods of 346 and 356

(a)

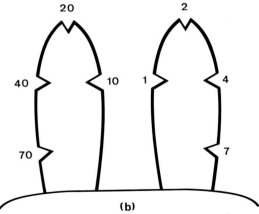

(b)

FIGURE 5.—(*a*) Group of Southern vicuña at Zürich Zoo. The front right specimen is male "Antwerp 28" and the front left specimen female "Zürich 19". The latter shows on its right ear a marking slit. (Photo: R. Schmidt.) (*b*) Ear-marking system used for vicuña and other mammals at Zürich Zoo. More than 99 specimens can be marked with up to four slits. The slits—some 7 mm in length—can be made with ordinary scissors or with special ear-notching pliers.

days, respectively, for two males born in captivity. Mating is performed in a lying position and lasts 10–30 min. In Northern zoos (Amsterdam, Antwerp, Barcelona, Basel, Brasschaat, Frankfurt, London, Munich, Bronx, Paris and Zürich), 68 per cent of all births are concentrated from July to October, with a peak in September (see Fig. 6). The birth peak is shifted by 6 months and the scatter of birth dates is more extended in comparison with the wild. A small peak

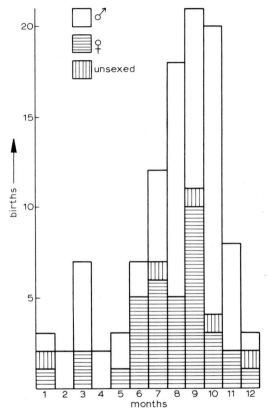

FIGURE 6. Distribution of vicuña births in 11 Northern zoos, showing a birth season in the period July–October.

in March is due to only two females living in Antwerp Zoo. The distribution of births in the two Southern zoos (Johannesburg, San Diego) shows the main peak in March (see Fig. 7).

Three males and two females at Zürich Zoo were born between 09·28 h and 11·55 h. They were able to stand after about 24 min, and suckled for the first time after about 38 min. The placenta was expelled some 42 min after birth and was never eaten by the female. Mean birth weight for four males was 6·5 kg (range: 5·9–7·8 kg) and for six females 6·2 kg (range: 5·0–7·9 kg). Figure 8 shows the growth rates for two males and one female at Zürich Zoo. Mean weight for six adult males was 51 kg (range: 40·5–61·0 kg) and two adult females weighed 35 and 50 kg respectively.

Fourteen of the 139 babies recorded since 1945 were stillborn. Sixteen further babies died within the first 2 weeks, mainly due to weakness, starving and accidents. Sixty-two per cent of the offspring survived the first year, which compares favourably with the 50 per cent survival rate in wild infants (Koford, 1957). Some of the females produce insufficient quantities of milk. At Zürich Zoo we give mothers Galactogene-tablets (Intervetra, Geneva) to stimulate the production of milk. However, one female has never had enough milk to raise her babies. Her babies have been fed with the bottle in addition to natural suckling. They were given first two-thirds of pasteurized milk and one-third of lime-blossom tea. Later the tea was replaced by baby-food (Galactina from Dr. Wander, Berne). One female baby drank about one-tenth of its body weight daily until it started feeding at an age of 17 days. We totally rejected artificial

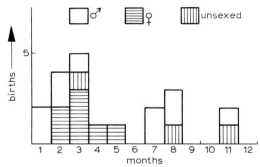

FIGURE 7. Distribution of vicuña births in two Southern zoos, showing a birth peak in March.

rearing to avoid imprinting on human beings. Juveniles suckled for more than half a year.

The sex ratio at birth is about 3:2 (76 males, 52 females and 11 unsexed). Juvenile mortality in females (36 per cent) is higher than in males (20 per cent). These two factors contribute to produce a large surplus of males in captivity. However, females reach a more advanced age than males. The longevity record in captivity is held by the female Bronx II at 24 years and 9 months. The average lifespan for animals older than 1 year is only slightly in excess of 8 years (imported animals are considered to be 1 year old on arrival).

Males start successful breeding when they are from 2 years to 4 years and 7 months old (the mean for eight males is 3 years and 3 months). Females give birth to the first infant at from 2 years to 4 years and 3 months of age (the mean for nine females is 3 years). On average, females give birth every 18 months (calculated for all eight females which have given birth to six or more young ones). The most prolific females are Argentina J, which gave birth to 11 babies in 15 years, and Zürich 4, which gave birth to seven babies in 8 years. Some females in Zürich are still breeding at an age of 19 years.

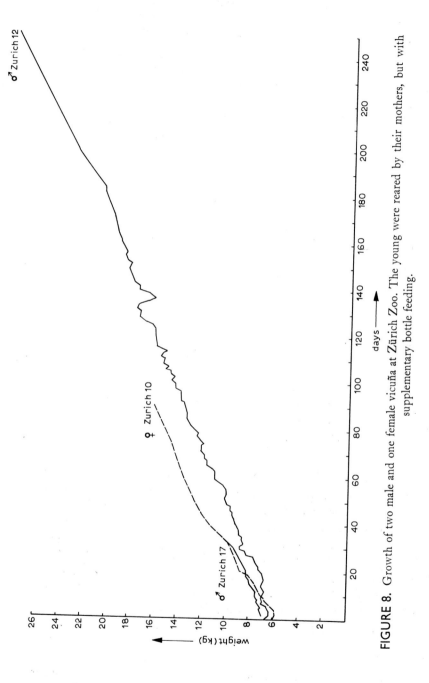

FIGURE 8. Growth of two male and one female vicuña at Zürich Zoo. The young were reared by their mothers, but with supplementary bottle feeding.

PATHOLOGY

A total of 139 vicuña have died and ten specimens have disappeared since 1945. A summary of the 99 known post-mortem findings is given in Table 1.

The high percentage of accidents in this list is very sad, as they could so easily have been avoided. I would like to cite some cases:

1. The head of a female baby was fatally struck by the wings of a black swan.
2. Another female baby drowned in the mud of an emptied pool.
3. Several adults and young ones were killed by deer, antelopes, male vicuña and by an African ostrich.
4. A male attacked a keeper, who threw him to the ground and choked him, producing pulmonary congestion. A similar case occurred in a second zoo.

TABLE 1. Causes of death in captivity, recorded for 99 cases.

Causes	%	Specimens
Accidents	28	17·9 +1
Infections	15	5·9 +1
Stillbirths	14	4·4 +6
Gastrointestinal	13	5·8
Weakness, starving (young)	6	4·2
Cardiovascular	5	1·4
Expiratory	5	2·3
Parasites	4	4·0
Senility	4	3·1
Blindness	3	3·0
Arthritis	1	1·0
Metabolism	1	0·1
Miscarriage	1	0·1

Six cases of tuberculosis are the most serious among the infections. Therefore, Tbc-tests should be performed and positively reacting animals should be destroyed. Blindness occurred in three old males, partly due to injuries from fences, and partly due to degeneration of visual nerves and centres. Among the parasites, three cases of mange are of interest. The most common parasites reported are *Trichostrongylus*, *Strongyloides*, *Trichuris* and *Coccidia*.

Mangili and Baschieri-Salvadori (1970) have successfully tranquillized a male vicuña (60 kg) with 115 mg Perphenazin (Trilafon) given intramuscularly. P. Weilenmann (pers. comm.) tranquillized another male with 1 mg/kg Sernylan intramuscularly, though the animal was still able to stand shakily.

SUBSPECIES

We probably need to distinguish two subspecies, *Lama v. mensalis* Thomas, 1917, from Peru and Bolivia and *Lama v. vicugna* (Molina, 1782), from Argentina and perhaps from Chile. All captive specimens, except two females (at Antwerp Zoo and Frankfurt Zoo), belong to the latter subspecies. It would therefore be a much welcomed move to import a small band of the Northern subspecies, so that—with the help of the two females already in captivity—this subspecies could be kept pure bred.

CONCLUSIONS

I do not believe that the wild population of vicuña is decreasing so much that we need captive specimens for restocking of natural areas. News from Pampa Galeras National Park in Peru is encouraging. The population has increased from 800 to 5000 specimens over the last 18 years (Jungius, pers. comm.). Vicuña reserves were recently created in Bolivia (Ulla-ulla; Jungius, 1972) and in Chile (Lauca Valley, 300,000 ha; J. Rottmann, pers. comm.). Therefore the future of wild vicuña looks better than the future of captive specimens! We will not be in a position to release any vicuña for many years, because the captive population is hardly holding its own without new importations. Indeed, we must admit that the existing management of captive vicuña is a total failure in comparison with that of the Przewalski horse, for example. The problem we now have to solve is that of saving the vicuña in captivity! We must undertake everything to reduce mortality and to increase breeding successes. I make the following proposals to achieve this aim: the seven collections where vicuña are already breeding (Alberta Game Farm, Amsterdam, Antwerp, Brasschaat, Munich, Paris, Zürich) should each build up two family bands of one male and at least two to five females. The grassy enclosures should cover a minimum area of 500 sq. m. A third enclosure of the same dimensions should be reserved for an all-male-troop. Males and pairs should no longer be sold separately. All as yet non-breeding females should be concentrated in a specially selected zoo (with a climate similar to that of the high Andes and a good management record), together with a youngish male. Single males can just as well stay in zoos where they are at the moment, because they are already spoiled and too aggressive. In my opinion, further distribution of captive vicuña should no longer depend on dealers alone, but should be arranged in agreement with an international committee. This could either be IUDZG or the SSC-Vicuña Group. Hybrid specimens should be kept totally apart from pure-bred female vicuña. I am fully aware that these are very rigorous recommendations and that the present level of international cooperation betwen zoos is still one of the weakest points (despite contrary publicity), but perhaps the future will bring the necessary changes.

ACKNOWLEDGMENTS

It is a great pleasure for me to acknowledge the kind and valuable help given by all but one collection for establishment of the Vicuña Studbook. I would like to thank Dr. P. Weilenmann and my colleagues for their advice in the preparation of this paper, and Mr. R. Schlageter for financing the visit to Jersey for the Conference.

Breeding the International Herd of Arabian Oryx at Phoenix Zoo

W. G. Homan

INTRODUCTION

I am certain that many people are already familiar with the history of the international herd of Arabian oryx located in Phoenix, Arizona, but a brief summary will perhaps help put things in perspective.

In 1962, the Fauna Preservation Society with the help of the World Wildlife Fund undertook an expedition to capture as many of these vanishing ungulates as proved to be practical. At that time, estimates of as few as 35 surviving wild specimens were being received.

The expedition, under the leadership of Ian Grimwood, succeeded in catching three adult animals (two males and one female). These were transported to Kenya for safe keeping and to form a core for a future captive-bred herd. It was soon realized that the threat of foot-and-mouth disease, endemic to that country, together with the high humidity, were not favourable for captive propagation. Mr. Grimwood then undertook a global search to locate a more suitable holding area (see Grimwood, 1963, 1967).

It was at this point that the Phoenix Zoo became involved. In January 1963, Mr. Grimwood visited Phoenix and was impressed with the general environmental similarity between the south-western United States and Arabia. We experience only 6–7 in. of rain each year in the Phoenix area as in Arabia, the soil types are quite similar and the plants of Arabia and the desert region of Arizona show evolutionary convergence because of these particular conditions.

An agreement was worked out between all parties involved and the first group of four animals arrived at Phoenix in June 1963. Three originated from the expedition, while the fourth (a female) was contributed to the operation by The Zoological Society of London. September 1963 witnessed the addition of another adult female to the herd, a gift from the ruler of Kuwait to the Fauna Preservation Society. One female, Edith, produced the first calf to the herd during October 1963. Mating between her and one of the males, Tomatum, had taken place during their quarantine in Naples, Italy. The second birth occurred in May 1964. The sire was again Tomatum, the dam was Caroline

FIGURE 1. (*above*) The barns constructed in 1963 to house the original stock of five animals. Each barn contains four separate stalls, with individual outside doors. (*below*) One of the two breeding groups at Phoenix Zoo. All but one of the animals pictured were born at Phoenix.

and the mating occurred at the Phoenix Zoo. In July 1964, two more adult pairs were received from the zoo in Riyadh, negotiations having been made through the King of Saudi Arabia by the World Wildlife Fund. This provided the final addition to the nucleus for the world herd.

ENCLOSURES AND FEEDING ARRANGEMENTS

Preparations to receive the animals in Phoenix were made in 1963, with the construction of two barns containing four adjoining pens (Fig. 1). Virgin

FIGURE 2. Breeding pen constructed in 1964 to accommodate the increase in the oryx herd. The pen contains one bull of breeding age, four to six breeding females and their offspring.

ground was selected for the site, in order to eliminate the possibility of cross-contamination from other zoo animals. Each barn contained four wood-lined stalls and each pen measured 40 × 195 ft. All pens are crossed by a natural wash, or wadi, which provides drainage and allows additional exercise by inducing the animals to climb the uneven sides. The natural terrain, strewn with small rocks, was left intact so as to offer an abrasive to wear the hooves.

The addition of the four new adults received in 1964 presented accommodation problems which were solved by two modifications to the facilities. A large herd breeding pen was developed to the east, adjoining the existing facilities (Fig. 2). This enclosure measures 220 × 440 ft. It is of rolling terrain and, for desert growth, quite heavily wooded. A second fence set 15 ft back creates a buffer zone and is used as an animal run when moving animals.

To facilitate daily close individual animal inspections in such a large area, only one feeding station was installed (Fig. 3). Each animal must come to this station in order to water and to receive its food ration. The feeding station, with its large over-hanging roof, offers the only man-made shelter for the enclosure.

FIGURE 3. The feeding station provided for the large breeding pens (inset of Fig. 2).

The only inclement weather condition which drives the oryx to seek protection is a cold drizzling rain which can develop in Phoenix during the mid-winter months.

The procedure employed with this feeding station consists of the keeper entering the public pathway through two gates and into a central alleyway. He distributes the daily ration of concentrates evenly along a trough located just below the hay racks. The keeper provides one pound of concentrate per adult animal and a graduated lesser amount for each juvenile. The mixture is now given in pellet form, as opposed to the powder tried earlier, in order to control inhalation and prevent loss by wind; the animals also show a better response to the pellet.

The formula for this ration was developed by a local feed manufacturer in order to provide the necessary nutrients not found in the hay we use. It consists of the following:

	%
Cottonseed meal	36·5
Soybean meal	20·0
Linseed meal	10·0
Dehydrated alfalfa	10·0
Dicalcium phosphate	10·0
Calcium carbonate	5·0
Plain salt	5·0
Trace minerals	2·5
Vitamin A	0·05
Cottonseed meal carrier	0·95

Immediately after distributing the concentrate, the hay racks are opened and filled. We use a strain of Bermuda hay, referred to as Coastal Bermuda, which is grown in the warmer parts of Arizona. It is a fine-stemmed hay, high in roughage and somewhat lower in protein in comparison with timothy. Other hay types have been tried and have been found to be either too rich, causing digestive disturbances (alfalfa) or (in the case of hay/straw mixes) so low in nutrients as to produce hay bellies.

Approximately three pounds of Bermuda per adult animal is given, and again lesser amounts are offered by being tossed farther out on to the ground for the juveniles and those animals of lower social rank.

The quantity offered daily is critical and depends upon many factors. Natural plant growth is used by the animals to a limited extent in the winter months, when our desert trees bloom and produce bean pods, and during spring the wild grass filarie is relished and can supply the animals' entire food requirements. A rapidly incoming weather front will strengthen the desire for food, as has been reported in studies of domestic herbivores. Conversely, food amounts are cut back in order to prevent a dominant individual from gorging.

To ensure that adequate amounts of concentrate are consumed by the younger animals, a creep-feeding arrangement was devised, using the keeper's area of the feeding station. A trough was inserted within this area, and the gate width from the station into the pen was reduced to produce a 12-in. gap. Concentrate is placed in the trough as a last procedure and, after the keeper leaves, animals of under a year in age can squeeze through and feed unmolested by adults.

A second modification to the 1963 enclosures was later carried out in the form of cross-fencing of the existing pens adjacent to the barns. The resulting enclosures are thus four pens, each measuring 30 × 15 ft and connecting with an indoor stall. The small pens are used to hold animals requiring close observation and also to hold breeding males for short periods before their use in the herd breeding area. Solid partitions along adjacent fence lines prevent fighting through the wire. Persistent challenging through wire fences by breeding age males produces major problems. Pawing at the fence base removes the covering earth and exposes the sharp ends of the wire-netting. Horns thrusting through the wire creates a pressure which causes these ends to turn up, thus presenting a hazard to the animals. An immediate solution to this problem has been that of sandwiching the bottom edge of the wire-netting between heavy planking. As a more permanent answer, all enclosures constructed in the future will be double-fenced in order to create a buffer zone between animals.

The abrasive wear on the horns resulting from through-fence challenging can become extensive in the more aggressive males. Pat, the oldest breeding male, has reduced his horns to a half of their original length. A male from the Riyadh Zoo, where masonry walls are used, arrived in Phoenix with mere stubs of the horns remaining, and the front horn surfaces were honed flat.

Preventive medicine for oryx at Phoenix Zoo runs the gamut from mundane periodic stool inspections to the complete quarantining of facilities. Keepers assigned to the oryx barns are not allowed to enter other ungulate pens during the day, tools may not be taken out of the area, and hay is stored separately from the central zoo supply, in order to prevent contamination through contact with other personnel. Personal experience combined with keen interest have been our greatest asset. One member of staff, Mr. Mohney, has been assigned to the oryx since their arrival. His acute daily observations of individual animal behaviour has developed into a monitoring device for our veterinary officer.

To date, the greatest threat to continuing growth of the world's herd in Phoenix has been the development of early "navel ill" in the new-born calves. It was suggested that our procedure of isolating expectant cows in the small pens previously occupied by other adult animals was exposing the newly dropped calves to contaminated ground. Accordingly, in 1970, construction of a maternity area was commenced on a site unoccupied by other ungulates (Fig. 4). Five outdoor pens with connecting stalls were built adjacent to the previously described buffer area. Through a series of gates and runs, animals can be moved from the original pens and either passed around the herd enclosure to the maternity pens or moved directly into these pens from the herd area. Pregnant females are transferred approximately 30 days before they are due to give birth, and they remain there until the calves are eagerly consuming solid food, usually at an age of about 30 days. Prior to joining the herd, every new calf's permanent number is tattooed on the ear. The use of metal ear clips for this purpose has been discontinued because of their failure to remain permanently attached. The maternity stalls remain under 24-h observation; calves are picked up immediately after birth and cleaned, and the umbilical stump is swabbed with iodine.

The stall areas were designed in such a way as to allow maximum circulation of air and penetration of sunlight. Impervious stall walls were used, and their bases were elevated to prevent accumulation of liquid. Chemically sealed concrete covers the stall floor area. Both indoor and outdoor areas are sanitized after animals are removed and the pen is allowed to stay vacant 30 days before re-use. Since this maternity area has been in operation nine calves have been born without a loss. [For further information, see Turkowski and Mohney, 1971; Turkowski and Tinker, 1972.]

FIGURE 4. (*above*) Maternity pens constructed during 1970 to provide isolation for pregnant females. (*below*) A 3-year-old and a yearling oryx born at Phoenix Zoo.

FUTURE DEVELOPMENTS

The Arabian oryx is a highly social animal and this is taken into consideration before distribution is made to other institutions. If we are to carry out the original intention of holding the Arabian oryx in captivity only until such time as their protection and survival in the wilds is assured, we must make sure that we release individuals bearing temperaments and behaviour patterns identical to those exhibited by the animals which we removed.

In a socially orientated animal such as the oryx, patterns of behaviour are often acquired by young through contacts with adults. The greater the number in a group, the more varied the contact will be and the less the likelihood of development of an abnormal behaviour pattern. Institutions responsible for such animals should maintain as large a herd as their facilities and finances allow. When limits are reached and further distribution is to be made, the same considerations must apply. Although there are many worthy and proven institutions today, rather than release a pair to each it would be far better to release breeding groups to only one of them.

Today's captive Arabian oryx population numbers more than 75 animals located in six collections situated on two continents. In Arabia, there are collections at Qatar, Riyadh and Abu Dhabi, whilst in America there are herds at Phoenix Zoo, Los Angeles Zoo and San Diego Zoo. The potential of such a large number of individuals should sufficiently establish this species in captivity. The primary point or vulnerability is the limited number of collections. However, we at Phoenix Zoo are rapidly approaching our maximum facility capabilities and will shortly be contacting our fellow members of the world herd with a proposal to help relieve this situation.

The Indian Rhino in Captivity

E. M. Lang

HISTORY

From earliest times, the Indian rhino (*Rhinoceros unicornis*) has been treated as a celebrity by man (see Fig. 1). The oldest record of such interest in this large mammal is a seal (Lang, 1961), depicting an Indian rhino, which dates back to the 3rd century B.C.; it was discovered in the Indus Valley near Mohenjodaro (West Pakistan). A mosaic in a Roman villa in Sicily, preserved from the 3rd century A.D., features, among other animals, an Indian rhino. I personally own a Chinese bronze dating from the Ming period (1386–1644); it obviously represents an Asiatic rhino, probably the Javan species. Of wide repute are the pen-and-ink drawing and woodcut by Albrecht Durer, both modelled in 1515 on contemporary descriptions and sketches.

In the year 1748 an Indian rhino was to be seen on tour in Europe. A coin was struck in its honour and, in Venice, it was painted by Pietro Longhi. As early as 1834, the London Zoo possessed an Indian rhino. Two specimens (a male and a female) were kept in Berlin about 1872. Further specimens lived at about that time in the zoos of Cologne, Frankfurt, Hamburg, Vienna, Amsterdam and also in various zoos in America.

In 1971 Wolfgang Ulrich (see Ulrich, 1971, p. 15) estimated the world population of the Indian rhino at only 250 specimens, distributed in national parks in Assam and Nepal. It is therefore high time for zoological gardens to recognize the task confronting them: that of preserving these rare large mammals in captivity with a view to restoring their progeny to regions where wild populations have been exterminated. I consider that it should be feasible to re-establish the Indian rhino, even after generations of captive breeding, in well guarded national parks in the natural areas of origin. The first captive-bred Indian rhino was born in Basle Zoo on 14 September 1956. Since then, 11 more calves have been produced in Basle and eight in other gardens. Our experience of breeding in captivity is thus confined to 20 cases, a modest number indeed. However, according to the 1971 edition of the *International Zoo Yearbook*, in 1970 only 24 male and 20 female Indian rhinos were kept in 25 zoos, and the limited breeding successes to date must be viewed in this light.

FIGURE 1. Indian rhino (*Rhinoceros unicornis*) mother and offspring in Basle Zoo. Note the difference in the shape of the head between adult and infant.

CAPTIVE ENVIRONMENT
1. Accommodation

Establishing the minimum accommodation requirements and defining the optimum conditions: In Basle, the Indian rhinos are kept in three stalls, each 4·5 × 5·7 m. The floors are fitted with "Stallit" stall tiles which possess a heat conducting coefficient closely corresponding to that of wood. The walls are made of concrete, but, as the rhinos frequently lean against them, they have been lined with vertical wooden boards to reduce loss of heat. Moreover, the boards reduce the tendency of the animals to rub their horns against the wall, though this habit disappears altogether when a cow has a calf. Next to the row of stalls is a

FIGURE 2. This spacious outdoor enclosure for the rhinos at Basle Zoo is regarded as the minimum area which will permit freedom of movement of the animals.

heated pool; a daily bath keeps the animals' skin supple and healthy. A reserve stall serves to accommodate a female from another zoo for mating purposes from time to time. The Hamburg female "Nepali" has already been here twice and the Stuttgart and Berlin females once each. Successful breeding results have been achieved in all four cases. A service corridor, 2–2·20 m wide, which can be divided into sections by lateral doors, runs behind the stalls, The dry moat, separating the stalls from the public area, is 1·5 m deep; it contains gravel distributed to leave a shelf on the animals' side (Lang, 1960).

The house opens out to an enclosure of some 1000 sq. m, surrounded by a ditch of only 170–180 cm wide and 170–190 cm deep. A pool, occupying the middle section, can be heated during the cooler seasons; with the onset of winter, it is drained dry and padded with straw to break the fall of any animal which should happen to charge into it. The terrain has been sharply profiled; its hilly character, as compared to a flat surface, considerably increases the scope for chasing activities (see Fig. 2). We have the impression that, with respect to overall size, the enclosure verges on the minimum to permit freedom of movement. During oestrus, various aggressive bouts occur which necessitate evasive tactics. If there is not enough space, the animals can seriously damage one another.

A small area of the enclosure has been partitioned off with wooden planks to permit separation of the animals if necessary. For instance, a cow in oestrus is confined there during the preliminary aggressive mating phases, while the bull gives full "vent to his passion" in the main enclosure. The Brookfield Zoo, Chicago, has owned a pair of Indian rhinos for many years, but has never been able to leave the two animals together because of lack of space. I am afraid that several other enclosures, constructed recently, will also prove to be too small. A short while ago Charles Schroeder, San Diego, related the following story: In San Diego Zoo a pair of white rhinos lived peacefully together in a relatively small enclosure. The time went by with no signs of oestrus or of any kind of sexual activity. In 1971, 20 white rhinos were imported to the USA from South Africa. A new pair was acquired for the San Diego Zoo and the old pair was transferred to join the new arrivals in the spacious new enclosure in San Pasqual. The old bull immediately became interested in the cows and by autumn 1971, had already mated with seven of them. Probably, sexual activity was induced by availability of adequate space.

2. Dietary requirements

Our Indian rhino diet is based on the system adopted by H. L. Ratcliffe, Philadelphia, and has been adapted to meet our special requirements by H. Wackernagel, the scientific assistant at Basle Zoo (see Wackernagel, 1966). Ratcliffe holds that all wild animals need a balanced diet, comprising protein, fat and carbohydrates in the right proportions, as well as vitamins and mineral salts. We feed good hay *ad libitum* and a concentrate in the form of pellets. In addition, the animals receive large quantities of fresh branches, bearing buds in winter and leaves in the period of green vegetation. The branches are offered more to provide occupation than extra nourishment. Fresh carrots and other vegetables are also strewn on the hay.

3. General husbandry

We keep our rhinos according to the farming system. Each animal has a stall where it feeds and rests. Otherwise, the animal's time is spent in the indoor pool and in the enclosure. The cows with their young usually pass the morning and afternoon in the main enclosure, while the bull is either in the indoor pool or in the fenced-off area. Over midday, the cows and calves rest in the stalls, whilst the bull enjoys the run of the main enclosure. All of the animals pass the night in their stalls.

The bull is only allowed to join a cow when she is in oestrus and, even then, special precautions are taken. Oestrus in the cow is heralded by expiratory, two-phased whistling; she simultaneously lifts her tail and urinates intermittently, soon impregnating her entire surroundings. The bull shows interest in the cow and reacts with "Flehmen" (lip-curl) and increased urination (Lang, 1961; Schenkel and Lang, 1969). We visit the rhinos every morning. If a cow is seen to be in oestrus she is let out into the fenced-off area. The bull enters the main enclosure. Contact is established and the bull can subsequently "let off steam" by galloping round the enclosure. If necessary, the cow is turned out into the main enclosure for a while and the bull takes her place in the smaller area. After some 5 h, the aggressive phase has usually subsided and the animals are allowed to meet each other. They stand together, or the bull lies down for a time while the cow stands near him, whistling and squirting urine. Finally, they stand side by side (see Fig. 3) and, sooner or later, copulation takes place (see Fig. 4). The intromission of the penis often involves difficulties. Erect, the penis is approximately 1 m long and curves sharply at the tip. Thus, after mounting, the bull is obliged to draw back until the actual copulatory position is achieved. Copulation lasts for roughly an hour, ejaculations occurring at the rate of almost one per minute. After separating, the animals are very tired. In rare cases we have noticed ulceration on the cow's back, resulting from friction caused by the bull's fore-feet. The following day, the animals want nothing more to do with each other. It is then necessary to wait 35–45 days to see whether oestrus sets in again or not; if oestrus does not appear the cow is probably pregnant.

PREVENTIVE MEDICINE

So far we have suffered the loss of only one animal, the adult bull "Gadadhar". The bull was attempting to mount a cow over a fence. She evaded him and he became wedged, sustaining a rib injury. His condition deteriorated after the accident, as a piece of broken rib irritated the pericardium, causing chronic inflammation. To ease the situation, a permanent straw mattress was put in the bull's stall for the whole winter. The straw contained moss mites (Oribatidae) which were carriers of cysts of a tapeworm (*Anoplocephala gigantea*). A hyperinfection with this parasite ultimately resulted in the rhino's death. This example shows us the importance of eliminating potential causes of accident on the one hand and, on the other, of preventing the ingestion of tapeworm cysts, via moss mites, by maintaining a high standard of hygiene. Permanent mattresses should not be used and the enclosure should be closely supervised to keep down moss and grass.

Following parturition, one of our Indian rhino cows suffered from slight endometritis which manifested itself through a chronic yellow discharge from the vulva. She came into oestrus again and mated, and, as no further oestrus occurred, we assumed she was pregnant. The discharge continued, however, and treatment was given. Evidently conception had not taken place for, after a series of injections of metritis vaccine, the cow again came into oestrus. She then mated and conceived normally.

We feel that Indian rhinos adapt easily to zoo life. However, the importance

FIGURE 3. In the prelude to copulation, the cow and the bull are seen to remain close to one another without aggressive interactions.

of the right nourishment, on the one hand, and of sufficient space, on the other, can hardly be emphasized enough. If the animals receive an unsuitable diet (i.e. excessive quantities of carbohydrates), they will become fat and sluggish. If the enclosure is too small, the preliminary mating ceremonies cannot take their course, or the crowding-effect blocks the mating urge from the very beginning. Sterility in captivity may be attributed to either of these deficiencies.

FIGURE 4. When copulation takes place, following the mating prelude, it usually lasts for about an hour.

TABLE 1. International Studbook for the Great Indian Rhinoceros.

Studbook-number	Sex	Studbook-name	House-name	Born	Died	Father	Mother	Location since
1	♂	Assam 1	Kasi	1941	—	—	—	Mysore 1941
2	♀	Kaziranga 1	Kamala-Rani	?	6.5.68	—	—	Brookfield 24.6.48
3	♂	Kaziranga 2	Kashi-Ram	?	13.11.70	—	—	Brookfield 24.6.48
4	♀	Kaziranga 3	—	16.5.48	16.5.48	—	Kaziranga 1	Brookfield 24.6.48
5	♂	Kaziranga 4	Gadadhar	1948	25.11.64	—	—	Basle 30.5.48
6	♂	Assam 2	Tomy	1944	—	—	—	Rome 5.9.51
7	♀	Kaziranga 5	Joymothi	1947	—	—	—	Basle 8.7.52
8	♀	Assam 3	Mohini	?	—	—	—	Whipsnade 16.7.52
9	♀	Assam 4	Kanaklota	?	—	—	—	Philadelphia 17.6.53
10	♂	Assam 5	Kanakbala	?	—	—	—	Philadelphia 14.9.55
11	♀	Assam 6	Ranni	1948	—	—	—	Mysore 1956
12	♂	Kaziranga 6	Many	?	—	—	—	Trivandrum 25.5.56
13	♂	India A	Manik	?	1962	—	—	Whipsnade ?
14	♂	Basle 1	Rudra	14.9.56	—	Kaziranga 4	Kaziranga 5	Milwaukee 20.7.59
15	♀	Whipsnade 1	Mohinija	18.7.57	—	India A	Assam 3	Milwaukee 20.7.59
16	♀	Kaziranga 7	Nepali II	1956	—	—	—	Hamburg 11.8.57
17	♀	Basle 2	Moola	17.8.57	4.1.73	Kaziranga 4	Kaziranga 5	Basle
18	♂	Kaziranga 8	Arjun	1958	—	—	—	W.-Berlin 22.9.59
19	♂	India B	Tarun	1.59	—	—	—	Washington 26.5.60
20	♂	Whipsnade 2	Manik	18.8.60	—	India A	Assam 3	Whipsnade
21	♀	India C	Lauie	?	—	—	—	Tokyo 1961
22	♂	India D	Tamao/Lupsin	?	—	—	—	Tokyo 1961
23	♂	India E	Sneha	12.3.61	—	—	India C ?	Alipore
24	♂	India F	Siraji	?	—	—	—	Gauhati ?
25	♀	India G	Padmini	?	—	—	—	Gauhati ?
26	♂	Basle 3	Lasai	31.8.62	—	Kaziranga 4	Kaziranga 5	San Diego 12.10.63
27	♂	Basle 4	Khunlai	9.3.63	—	Kaziranga 4	Basle 2	Paris 29.4.64
28	♀	Gauhati 1	Rajkumari	10.4.63	—	India F	India G	Washington 16.12.63
29	♀	Gauhati 2	Jaypuri	10.7.63	—	?	?	San Diego 28.2.65
30	♀	India H	Deepali	1948	28.12.63	—	—	Washington 16.12.63
31	♀	Basle 5	Miris	12.6.64	—	Kaziranga 4	Kaziranga 5	W.-Berlin 6.7.65
32	♂	Hamburg 1	Gauhati	11.8.64	—	Kaziranga 4	Kaziranga 7	W.-Berlin 6.8.65

No.	Sex	Studbook name	Name	Date		Sire		Dam	Where kept / date
33	♂	Kaziranga 9	Mehan	?12.1.65	—	—	—	—	Delhi ?
34	♀	Basle 6	Nanda	28.8.65	—	Kaziranga 4	—	Basle 2	Stuttgart 29.5.68
35	♂	Assam 7	Herman	?	—	India D	—	India C	Los Angeles 8.3.66
36	?	Tokyo 1	—	20.6.66	—	—	—	—	Tokyo
37	♀	Nepal 1	Kanchi	?	9.1.67	—	—	—	E.-Berlin 6.8.66
38	♀	Hamburg 2	Shita	9.4.67	—	Kaziranga 8	—	Kaziranga 7	Hamburg
39	♂	Basle 7	Pandur	7.7.67	—	Kaziranga 8	—	Kaziranga 5	Hamburg 3.9.68
40	♀	Nepal 2	Kumari	5.67	—	—	—	—	E.-Berlin 1.8.67
41	♂	Basle 8	Puri	22.12.67	—	Kaziranga 8	—	Basle 2	Stuttgart 3.6.69
42	♂	Mysore 1	Mysore	13.2.68	—	Assam 1	—	Assam 6	E.-Berlin 24.4.71
43	♂	Kaziranga 10	Rengi	?28.3.68	—	—	—	—	Delhi ?
44	♂	Basle 9	Ruedi	27.4.69	9.2.71	Kaziranga 8	—	Kaziranga 5	Houston 6.10.70
45	♀	Basle 10	Randa	5.10.69	—	Kaziranga 8	—	Basle 2	Houston 6.10.70
46	♀	Assam 8	Rhadha	?	—	—	—	—	Brownsville 6.4.72
47	♀	Kaziranga 11	?	4.67	—	—	—	—	Los Angeles 29.11.69
48	♀	Assam 9	?	6.68	31.1.70	—	—	—	Los Angeles 30.11.69
49	♂	Nepal 3	Mohan	6.69	—	—	—	—	Omaha 1.70
50	♀	Nepal 4	Shanti	?	—	—	—	—	Crandon 23.4.70
51	♀	Dehli 1	Roopa	27.1.71	—	—	—	—	Florida/Crandon 12.6.70
52	♂	Milwaukee 1	?	30.1.71	—	Basle 1 ?	—	Whipsnade 1 ?	Whipsnade 6.2.73
53	♂	Mysore 2	?	16.4.71	—	Assam 1	—	Assam 6	Milwaukee
54	♀	Stuttgart 1	?	16.7.71	16.7.71	—	—	—	Mysore
55	♀	Basle 11	Tutuma	11.8.71	—	Kaziranga 8	—	Basle 6	Stuttgart
56	♀	Basle 12	Tanaya	24.8.71	—	Kaziranga 8	—	Basle 2	Antwerp 5.9.72
57	♂	Gauhati 3	Krishna	12.9.71	—	Kaziranga 8	—	Kaziranga 5	Basle
58	♂	Hyderabad 1	?	25.11.71	—	India F	—	India G	Gauhati
59	♀	Kaziranga 12	Rukmini	?28.1.71	—	—	—	—	Hyderabad
60	♂	W.-Berlin 1	Kumar	4.4.72	—	Kaziranga 8	—	Basle 5	Delhi 28.1.72 ?
61	♂	Kaziranga 13	Sonto	?	—	—	—	—	Amsterdam autumn 1973 / Gauhati 28.6.72

Key: (1) Kaziranga = animals born in Kaziranga Reservation; Assam = animals born in Assam, including the Kaziranga Reservation; Nepal = animals born in Nepal; India = animals born on the Indian subcontinent, including Nepal.

(2) The studbook-number indicates the sequence of arrival in captivity, whilst the studbook-name shows the name of the town where any animal was born in captivity. The number following the name of the town in the studbook-name indicates the sequence of birth or capture at that place.

For example: 8 ♀ Assam 3 is the eighth animal to be taken into captivity and the third to be caught in Assam.

CAPTIVE BREEDING POPULATIONS

Given one Indian rhino pair composed of animals of about the same age, and good luck, a breeding unit can be established. This has been proved in Basle. The ideal unit is a trio of one male and two females. Zoological gardens with enough room to keep larger breeding groups comfortably form the exceptions. Much could be achieved, however, if neighbouring gardens were prepared to work together. In this connection, I would like to recall the praiseworthy example of Berlin. When we lost our bull "Gadadhar" in 1964 there were only two specimens in Europe suitable to replace him, the roughly 7-year-old "Arjun" in the Berlin Zoo and a somewhat older bull in Rome. When the matter was put to him, Heinz Klos, the director of the Berlin Zoo, immediately recognized the necessity of continuing the Basle breeding group and convinced his Board that the bull "Arjun" should be placed at Basle's disposal. In return, we presented the young female to Berlin and made arrangements for a young male, which had been sired by our first bull and, in the meantime, delivered to Hamburg, to be transferred to Berlin. Thus another potential breeding unit was established.

We have made a point of selling Indian rhinos to zoos where they are kept in pairs. The first-born male "Rudra" went to Milwaukee with a female, born in Whipsnade. A calf produced by this pair was unfortunately stillborn (30 January 1967). As yet no further birth has been recorded. We have delivered young pairs to Houston, USA and Stuttgart, as well as partners for single animals in Hamburg-Stellingen, Berlin and Paris-Vincennes.

Zoological gardens should be aware of the responsibility they assume in keeping Indian rhinos. If we had room, we would install a second bull or even a second breeding pair. With only one bull available, the breeder always has the disconcerting feeling of standing on one leg! But the cooperative example set by Berlin Zoo is indeed very encouraging.

Within a span of 15 years, 12 Indian rhinos—with one male and one female during the first 5 years, then with one male and two females—have been born in Basle. In captivity, the Indian rhino has a life-expectancy of 40 years (Crandall, 1964). The gestation period lasts 478 days, which allows for one calf about every 2 years. With careful management, the present captive population (24, 20 in 25 zoos) could produce sufficient offspring to cover zoo requirements and for subsequent release in the wild. The preservation of this species would then be ensured for generations to come. An international studbook has now been established for the Indian rhinoceros, and this should be of great value in coordinating any long-term programme (see Table 1).

Breeding the Indian Rhinoceros at Delhi Zoological Park

C. L. Bhatia and J. H. Desai

The great Indian one-horned rhinoceros (*Rhinoceros unicornis*), the largest of all Asian animal species (see Prater, 1971), is commonly exhibited in the Zoological Gardens and Parks of the world. But like all rhinoceroses, the great Indian rhinoceros does not breed readily in captivity (see Crandall, 1964). Until recently, births of Indian rhinoceroses in captivity were very rare. Up to 1960, only five calves had been born in captivity. One reason for the rarity of rhino births in captivity might be the violent battles that take place between male and female, which discourage zoo authorities from keeping them together. Over the last 10 years, however, more Indian rhinos have been bred in captivity. According to the *International Zoo Yearbook* (Volume 10, 1970) there have been 12 births of Indian rhinoceroses in captivity during that time (see also Tong, 1960).

The Delhi Zoological Park obtained Mohan, a male great Indian rhinoceros, in December 1965. It was $3\frac{1}{2}$ years old when it came to the zoo. Later, in March 1968, a female rhinoceros Rongi of about 6 years of age was brought to the zoo from Gauhati, Assam.

The rhino enclosure at Delhi Zoological Park is an open-air enclosure of about one acre in area (Fig. 1). The enclosure has luxuriant growth of naturally growing trees and undergrowth of mesquite (*Prosopis juliflora*). In the centre of the enclosure, a muddy depression has been provided where the animals can wallow. The enclosure has a few cells and a large enclosed paddock where the animals may be kept separately if the need arises. Details of the diet are provided in Table 1.

Rongi, the female rhinoceros, arrived at the zoo in the evening of 28 March 1968, and was kept in the paddock. Mohan was at that time kept in the outer enclosure. It was observed that Mohan was very much interested in meeting Rongi, but she was not very keen and remained restless for the first few days. Later on, both animals began to sniff and to look at each other regularly. It was then decided to introduce the female to Mohan. However, this decision was not taken without apprehension, as it was known that rhinoceros do not readily live in captivity together. In fact, a pair at Whipsnade Zoo had fought and the female was eventually removed to Regent's Park, London. A pair at Chicago, USA, never became reconciled to each other.

Due precautions were therefore taken to avert any possible trouble. In the early morning hours of 14 April 1968, about 20 animal keepers and attendants were kept in readiness with loud explosive crackers, tin cans and bamboo sticks. The partition door between the paddocks and the main enclosure was gradually

FIGURE 1. Great Indian rhinoceros (male Mohan and female Rongi) in the large open-air enclosure at Delhi Zoological Park.

opened. At 7.00 a.m. Mohan and Rongi met for the first time in the middle of the enclosure. The male was interested in mounting, but the female kept him at a distance. She looked apprehensive, broke off and ran away several times. After about an hour, both settled down, the male went to the mud wallow and the female was seen eating green fodder given to her. Fortunately, there was no fighting and the two settled down together in the course of time.

The female came into oestrus on 4 January 1969 for the first time; but the male remained indifferent to her, and no mating took place. She came into oestrus again on 22 September 1969. This time, the male was seen continuously chasing the female in the enclosure and also in the water moat. The female, however, broke off and ran away several times. At about 1.00 p.m. a very fierce battle took place between the two. Both were mildly injured during the fight and, later on, the male was shut in the paddock as it was feared that one of them might be very seriously injured. Two days later the male was released again with due precautions and there was no fighting. Then again on 1 October 1969, hard blowing and shrill whistling noises were heard from the male as well as female. Both of them ran about in the enclosure and in the water moat. Several confrontations took place between the two, but this time it was not necessary to shut either of them inside. At 2.40 p.m. the first mating took place on hard ground.

TABLE 1. Diet of the Indian rhinoceros at Delhi Zoological Park, New Delhi.

Foodstuff	Quantity per animal per day	
Bananas	6	
Green fodder	150 kg	
Leaf fodder	40 kg	
Molasses	1 kg	
Green gram (*Phaseolus aureus*)	1 kg	
Rice	1 kg	Cooked together and mixed with one litre of mustard oil or any edible oil
Turmeric powder	100 g	
Linseed	100 g	
Common salt	100 g	

The whole act lasted for about 30 min. In the afternoon another similar mating was observed. No mating was observed from 2 October 1969 onwards and both animals became calm and quiet. It was hoped that successful mating had taken place, and in the late winter it became apparent that the female was pregnant.

The two rhinos were nevertheless kept together in the same enclosure till July 1970 when Mohan was shut in the paddock. The female was now definitely in calf. Her mammary glands increased in size and became active. She also stopped showing any interest in the male in the adjoining paddock.

On 27 January 1971, she took her usual food at 11.30 a.m. and retired into the bushes. At about 3.00 p.m. she became very restless and emitted bleating sounds from time to time and it was apparent that she was in labour pains. At 4.00 p.m. she went to the far corner of the enclosure, away from the public, and sat in a small wet depression. A watery discharge was seen from her vulva. She stood up at 4.15 p.m. when birth became imminent. The front legs and head of the infant were seen emerging while she was standing. At 4.20 p.m. she exerted herself a little and the calf was born. The mother was totally exhausted and sat down. She showed little interest in the calf for the first 5 min and then she started licking the baby. The duration of gestation in this case was 484 days, as calculated from the day of last mating to the day of birth.

The baby was pink in colour at birth. At 5.05 p.m. the calf made attempts to stand up but could not succeed. However, at 6.00 p.m. the baby was seen standing on all fours.

The last observation of the mother and calf was made at 7.00 p.m. on 27 January 1971 and by then she still had not nursed the calf. Next day, in the early morning hours, the calf was seen suckling. The vulva of the baby appeared very clearly and it was hence possible to sex her on 28 January 1971. The colour of the skin also appeared to be slightly darker than on the previous day. The mother was very protective of the calf and did not even come for feeding during the daytime. However, at about 7.00 p.m. she came for feeding along with the calf. She first made the calf sit down on the straw bedding in the enclosure and then went to be fed. This procedure was followed till the middle of February 1971. On 20 February, she came out of the bush with the baby in broad daylight at about 1.00 p.m. (see Fig. 2).

On 27 February, at 6.00 p.m. the calf was seen nibbling green fodder for the first time. She took some fodder leaves in her mouth and attempted chewing. She continued to play like this for about 15 min. However, since 17 March 1971, the calf has been observed to take and eat some green fodder. The calf and mother were kept together for almost 2 years in the large outdoor enclosure, and in February 1973 the calf was sent to Whipsnade Park in England.

On 15 March 1972, it was observed that the female was in heat. The male, who was still kept in the paddock, tried to join her and both adult animals became restive. The calf was separated from the mother on the 21 March 1972 and taken inside the cells. The calf, which apparently looked docile, became restless and both the mother and the calf went on calling to each other throughout the day and night of 21 March 1972. The mother did not even take food offered to her. Next day, however, both stopped calling to each other and ate their rations separately.

On 6 April 1972, the sliding door between the paddock and the main outdoor enclosure was opened at 8.30 a.m., but the male rhino did not come out. Repeated attempts to lure him out were made by offering him his favourite tit-bits. Fresh green fodder was put near the sliding door, but even that failed to bring him out. The female subsequently came near the door herself, and this also failed to bring him out. The female started eating the fodder. In course of time the two animals saw each other, but the female did not take any notice of the male. The male ventured twice to put his snout outside the sliding door but did not come out. The female did not go inside the paddock and after completing her feed went away to her favourite spot, the wallow pit, in the outdoor enclosure. The male remained seated in one corner of the paddock.

At sunset the sliding door between the paddock and the main enclosure was shut, but left unlocked, and three animal keepers were kept at the enclosure to keep an eye on the animal during the night. At about 9.15 p.m. the male rhino got up and opened the sliding door by pushing with his snout and came out into the main enclosure. He approached the female. Both sniffed each other and there was a short fight between them. The female kept chasing the male all around the enclosure. This went on for about half an hour and then both quietened down. During the night the male made two unsuccessful attempts to mount the female

FIGURE 2. Female Indian rhino Rongi with her captive-born calf on the straw bedding provided in the enclosure.

but she shrugged him off. The female was expected to come into heat during the next 10 days and it was thought that mating might take place then. In fact, matings were subsequently observed in November 1972 and again on 20 February 1973, and the latter mating seems to have been fertile.

Plans for Breeding Colonies of Large Mammals in India

C. D. Krishne Gowda

A NEW HOME FOR THE GREAT INDIAN RHINOCEROS

The great Indian rhinoceros (*Rhinoceros unicornis*), which comes next to the elephant in size and mass, occurs naturally in the forests of Assam and Nepal. In these areas, the numbers of rhinoceros have dwindled to such low levels that these animals will be threatened with extinction if proper care is not taken at once to ensure their protection and multiplication. Since the total population of Indian rhino in the two areas is estimated at only a few hundred, urgent measures must be taken to permit an increase in their numbers before it is too late. In order to avoid the possibility of unforeseen epidemics or other natural calamities, any protected colony of rhinos would necessarily have to be housed in one or more areas far away from the present natural abodes of Assam and Nepal.

The founding of a new colony of this kind is not an easy task, since adequate attention must be paid to the living conditions of these animals to encourage them to thrive in their new home. This requires a comprehensive study of the ecological conditions enjoyed by the rhinos in Assam, so that a comparable tract of forest can be located in South India. Since fossil remains of rhino have been found in the United Provinces, in the Narbada Valley and near Madras, it may be assumed that rhinos were common in these areas as well in prehistoric times. The Geological Survey of India has excavated skulls and skeletons of the rhino at a site near Gokak in the State of Karnataka. However, with the passage of time, it is likely that there has been considerable change in the climatic conditions and other aspects of the natural surroundings. Consequently, these areas cannot be assumed to provide suitable alternative homes for the rhino without careful consideration. This has naturally prompted a fresh attempt to locate an entirely new abode in South India with conditions suitable for rhinos.

In this connection, special mention should be made of the temperate climate prevailing in the State of Karnataka, where the rich forests are entirely adequate to provide a tract of the size required. Given the cooperation of the Karnataka State Forest Department, it should not be difficult to locate a suitable area of about 5000 acres of forest to act as the "Rhino Home". It should be noted that the Mysore Zoo in Karnataka State has successfully been able to breed the great Indian rhino, with two recorded births: one on 13 February 1968 and the other on 16 April 1971 (Figs. 1 and 2). Scrutiny of the records of other zoos in the world which have been able to breed this species shows that Mysore Zoo enjoys a special position. Only 25 zoos throughout the world at present have great Indian rhino on display, and the total captive population is 44. Of these 25

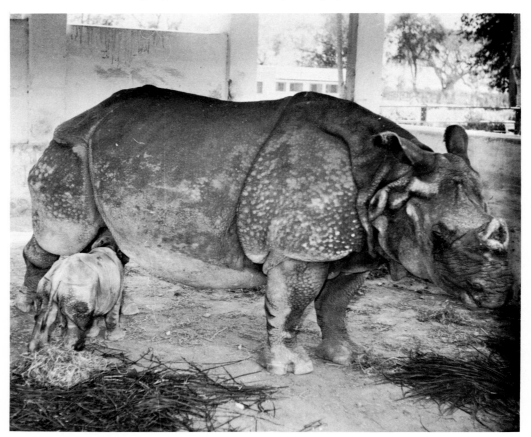

FIGURE 1. Female great Indian rhinoceros at Mysore Zoo with an infant born on 16 April 1971. The infant, here only a few weeks old, is seen in the typical suckling position.

zoos, only five have been able to breed Indian rhino in captivity: Basle Zoo; Whipsnade Park; Hamburg Zoo; West Berlin Zoo and Mysore Zoo. In having bred two calves, Mysore Zoo is prominent in this list, and this should provide encouragement for reaching a decision about plans to establish a new home for the rhinos in South India. The project could be effectively supervised by the authorities of the Mysore Zoo in conjunction with the officers of the Karnataka State Forest Department.

It is planned that an area of about 5000 acres in the forest, containing swamps, streams and extensive patches of elephant grass, would be set aside as the

"Rhino Home". Within this area, about 200 acres would be fully protected against external intervention of any kind, and an appropriate fence would be built. This core area would similarly need to contain swamps, pools, streams and patches of elephant grass, and it is in this area that a founding stock of two bulls and six cows would be initially housed and permitted to live in full freedom. The animals would be kept completely secluded from human beings in order to

FIGURE 2. Female and infant photographed at a later date. Note that there is still little sign of development of the horn in the offspring.

reduce their fear of the new surroundings, but a discreet watch would be kept on the progress of mating and other activity.

As the initial stock increases through fresh births, surplus calves would be unobtrusively channelled off into the remaining part of the 5000-acre forest area as soon as they become independent. However, the founding stock of eight animals would continue to be retained within the fenced core area.

A BREEDING ENCLOSURE FOR CARACALS

The caracal or desert lynx (*Caracal caracal*), one of the smaller members of the cat family, is an inhabitant of the forests of the Punjab, Rajaputana,

Uttarpradesh and the dry region of Central India. It preys upon birds, rodents, small deer and antelopes, and its habitat is desert terrain and scrub jungle. Sightings of the species are becoming increasingly uncommon, and this indicates that it may well be on the way to extinction. Immediate measures are therefore necessary to increase the numbers of caracal through breeding from the presently available captive stock under careful supervision. Ideally, any project should be set up in close proximity to the natural homeland of these animals, that is to say in North-West India.

An appropriate plan would be to establish a breeding enclosure in an area of about 25–50 acres on an island including burrows, hollow trees and rock crevices. The island should first be stocked with fair numbers of birds, rodents and deer to provide natural food. After the potential prey stocks have settled down well, a few caracal could be introduced to serve as a parent stock. In fact, the Mysore Zoo, which has been breeding this species regularly, is in a convenient position to spare a suitable parent stock for this purpose. Any offspring born and reared on the island could subsequently be moved to a suitable area of the natural habitat which is effectively protected against poaching.

As explained above, the island enclosure would have to be located in Rajaputana, the Punjab, Uttarpradesh or Central India. Therefore, this project could be conveniently supervised by the Jaipur Zoo authorities or the Delhi Zoo authorities in cooperation with the State Forest Departments.

A BREEDING PROGRAMME FOR HUNTING CHEETAH

The famous Indian hunting cheetah (a subspecies of *Acinonyx jubatus*) once reigned over the plains and hills of Northern and Central India, and their geographical range extended up to the Deccan Plateau and to Mysore. But the present picture of the status of this famous animal is a distressing one. For example, not a single cheetah has been sighted in the forests of India over the last few decades. It would seem that the species is extinct or almost extinct in India, and it is necessary to start at once on a programme for captive maintenance, breeding and reintroduction to suitable habitat areas. The only solution would seem to be the introduction of wild or captive-bred specimens of the African subspecies.

The cheetah, being an animal which moves very swiftly, requires a considerable area for the performance of its natural activities, preferably a flat forest area containing many rodents and birds. A suitable forest zone could be located in one of the two districts of Bellary and Tumkur in Karnataka State.

At this point, it should be emphasized that hunting cheetah have been bred only very rarely in captivity. Only two zoos, namely Whipsnade Park and Montpellier Zoo, claim the distinction of having bred the African subspecies of this animal in captivity.

Thus, it would seem that the most promising strategy for re-establishment of the cheetah lies in protection of a colony in a natural forest area. For this purpose, it is necessary to select and fence off about 100–200 acres to serve as a breeding area. The area would have to be stocked with various birds and rodents before the cheetah are introduced. After the rodents and birds have settled down well, a foundation breeding stock of two male and four female hunting cheetah could be introduced into the fenced area and provided with complete protection against external intervention of any kind. Even the officials involved in the breeding programme for these animals should reduce their visits to a minimum in order to avoid frightening the animals. The original foundation stock of the African subspecies of the cheetah could be obtained from the Mysore Zoo or directly from Africa. Given scope for unlimited movement and full protection against disturbance from outside, it is quite possible that the cheetah would breed well in the fenced area. Any offspring could subsequently be moved into the larger surrounding forest area to live in complete freedom, though protection against poaching would be essential.

This project could be supervised by the Forest Range officers with the guidance and cooperation of the Mysore Zoo authorities. Needless to say, all such projects depend on full and wholehearted cooperation from the Karnataka State Forest Department to ensure their success.

River Otters in Captivity: a Review

N. Duplaix-Hall

INTRODUCTION

Unlike other contributors to the Conference I have the dubious distinction of having had *no* first-hand experience of the animals discussed in this contribution. That is to say, I have never owned an otter, nor do I plan to. Instead I have gone from zoo to zoo, to make detailed observations, ask questions and learn everything that I could about otters. Although my observations focused mainly on behaviour, husbandry techniques began to fascinate me. One question was ever present: why is it that otters seldom breed regularly in zoos? After observing nearly 150 otters in 25 zoos and searching for an answer over the course of 8 years, I now believe that breeding success is linked to three factors: the enclosure, the diet and the otters themselves.* Time and time again it is one of these factors which is at fault and, most often, the otters are not to blame. The problem is one of basic human misconceptions—too often we presume that the captive conditions provided are adequate when actually they are not.

But first let us take a closer look at the otters themselves, in a brief introduction to the four species most commonly kept and bred in captivity:

First, *Amblonyx cinerea*, the Oriental small-clawed otter (Fig. 1); a tropical species which is hardy in palaearctic climates and breeds well in captivity when given the opportunity. It is social, and large groups of up to 12 can be built up, provided that new individuals are not added haphazardly to the close-knit captive unit. The alpha female rules the group while the dominant male (usually her consort) protects it from intruders. These otters, called *Fingerotter* in German, are delightfully dexterous and spend a great deal of time investigating shallow pools with their forepaws like diligent raccoons.

Lutrogale perspicillata, the Indian smooth-coated otter (Fig. 2) is a heavy-set animal, living in marshes and coastal areas in the Far East, where it is sometimes erroneously known as the "sea otter". Also a social species, it is a noisy extrovert and adapts extremely well to zoo life. The group is also dominated by a female with her male consort defending the territory. As in *Amblonyx*, the male/female relationship is a very close one and the male plays a prominent role in raising the cubs. A surprising trait, which we discovered quite by chance when designing

---

* See also: Duplaix-Hall, 1972.

an otter enclosure at Twycross Zoo, is *Lutrogale's* truly fossorial tendency. The female dug a long tunnel and lined the chamber with straw bedding. Soon

FIGURE 1. The Oriental small-clawed otter *Amblonyx cinerea*, kneading its fur with its forepaws, a grooming behaviour pattern. (Photo: Nicole Duplaix-Hall.)

afterwards, a cub was born. It is the first time that *Lutrogale* has ever bred outside the Far East! I believe that allowing this excavation to go on unhindered may have been partly responsible for the breeding success.

Lutra lutra, the Eurasian otter (Fig. 3) is shy, and probably the most delicate of all. It is usually nocturnal but becomes diurnal when it has settled down in captivity. Unlike the two species already considered, *Lutra lutra* is not social and the male does not participate in rearing the cubs—the female keeps him away from them in no uncertain terms. *Lutra lutra* has recently bred four times at the Norfolk Wildlife Park, and the number of times it has bred at all in captivity can be counted on two hands.

FIGURE 2. Indian smooth-coated otters *Lutrogale perspicillata*. (Photo: Michael Lyster.)

Lutra canadensis, the Canadian otter (Fig. 4), adapts well to captivity, much better than its European counterpart, and has bred a number of times both in America and in England. In fact, there is a recent record of a complete third generation birth which took place at Mole Hall, Widdington, Essex. I think that the breeding successes in most cases were due to the fact that the dens were reasonably isolated from the public, both visually and acoustically, or alternatively the births took place in private collections with virtually no disturbance at all.

REQUIREMENTS FOR CAPTIVE MAINTENANCE

Now let us look at the basic minimum requirements for an enclosure. Before building an enclosure, one must eradicate two preconceived ideas immediately: (*a*) that an otter needs as much water as a seal, and (*b*) that it can live quite cheaply on fish. An otter is an expensive animal to house and to feed if one is to succeed in keeping it alive, let alone breeding it.

Table 1 shows the really *minimum* requirements for *one pair*. It can be seen that, since *Amblonyx* fares better in groups, these figures should be considerably expanded. The most important points to remember are the land *v.* water proportions, the turf *v.* shrub ratio, the extent of areas available for grooming, and the smooth overhang. *Lutra lutra* is a very nimble climber and once on its

FIGURE 3. Eurasian otters *Lutra lutra* (female left, larger male right). (Photo: Nicole Duplaix-Hall.)

own in the zoo can be a menace to pinioned waterfowl. Zürich Zoo lost some flightless steamer ducks and the Bronx Zoo some James' flamingos to this dangerous epicure! Otters have another weak point—their fur. Keep that fur clean and waterproof and your otter will live! They possess a dense, water-resistant pelt which provides warmth, insulation and buoyancy; but it is extremely vulnerable. Rubbing and preening keep the guard hairs unmatted and dry. A poorly balance diet or prolonged contact with mud and excrement (as in cramped, damp enclosures) quickly reduces the water-resistant properties. The sea otter *Enhydra lutris* is the most fragile otter of all in captivity for precisely this reason. Until we can solve fur problems during transport completely, keeping sea otters in Europe is out of the question. But back to river otters. In extreme cases of loss of fur condition, the otter has difficulty in keeping afloat and often refuses to go into the water at all. Figs. 5–7 illustrate various coat conditions. The dry coat of a healthy *Lutrogale* looks fluffy (Fig. 5), while a good wet coat in *Lutra canadensis* shows how the guard hairs have formed regular

FIGURE 4. Canadian otter *Lutra canadensis*. (Photo: Nicole Duplaix-Hall.)

TABLE 1. Minimum accommodation requirements for one pair of otters in captivity.

	Size of enclosure (m)	Land/water ratio	Number of hollow logs	Turf/shrubs ratio	Fence (height) + 80 cm smooth overhang (m)
Amblonyx	10 × 6	5 or 6 : 1 + shallow pools	1	3:2	1·50
Lutrogale	15 × 10	4 : 1	2	3:1	1·80
L. lutra	15 × 10	4 : 1	2	1:3	1·80
L. canadensis	15 × 10	4 : 1	2	2:3	1·80

spikes. The water does not penetrate to the underfur, instead forming droplets on the surface which are shaken off with a toss of the head (Fig. 6). When an otter's fur is waterlogged, the guard hairs are clumped together and sometimes the white underfur shows through (Fig. 7). The slick smoothness of the guard hairs over the sacral region shows that they are soaked, clinging to the wet underfur. This is the danger signal indicating that the situation needs immediate attention. This case is probably the direct result of a lack of sufficient dry grooming areas, that is to say an area of turf in the summer or bristle-brush doormats in the winter. Rocks and hollow logs also provide rubbing areas. Sand, unless it is of a non-abrasive quality, is not recommended; builder's sharp sand is particularly dangerous, as it wears away the guard hairs. A diet low in unsaturated fats or vegetable oil is also often responsible for poor coat condition.

FIGURE 5. The dry coat of this Indian smooth-coated otter presents a healthy appearance; it is fluffy, smooth and the underfur does not show through. (Photo: Michael Lyster.)

Now for the dens (Table 2). I would like to stress again that the two most important attributes of the den are its quiet and privacy. To have at least two dry, draught-free dens per enclosure is an obvious requirement and providing dry bedding and a bristle-brush doormat inside is a good idea; thermostatically regulated underfloor heating to keep the den at 22°C in winter is as mandatory as in a bear den. Each den should have a separate access. A long, narrow, L-shaped tunnel, where the otter can squeeze the excess moisture from its fur, is advisable; furthermore a female with cubs can block the entrance to the male or another otter very easily. This artificial tunnel is, I believe, a convenient way of catering to the fossorial tendencies and also of giving the otters a sense of security . . . which may prove vital to the cubs' welfare during the first few weeks. One or two regular keepers, who become familiar to the otters, will ensure minimum disturbance factors when cleaning out the dens.

Provision of fish has been the most tenacious preconceived notion as far as the otter's diet is concerned. Feed an otter exclusively on fish, and the coat condition will disappear along with the otter. Table 3, which lists the ingredients of otter

FIGURE 6. Head of a Canadian otter, photographed just after emergence from the water. Note how the guard hairs form regular spikes, allowing the water to run off the surface and not reach the underfur. (Photo: Nicole Duplaix-Hall.)

diets, will give some idea of the variety and complexity of the daily requirements. One may well be a strong supporter of the Ratcliffe diet, but some additives are also necessary; that is, vegetable oils, bone meal, fresh fish and chicks. One must remember that otters can, and do, eat up to 20 per cent of their own weight daily. This is due to a high metabolic rate and a rapid digestion. Usually an adult eats no more than 500 g of food at a time, which is another reason why it is better to divide the quantity into two, preferably three, meals per day rather than let it turn sour in the sun. Although fish should never make up a major proportion of the diet, it is recommended as roughage along with day-old chicks. Both fish and chicks are best given first thing in the morning and should be absolutely fresh. Providing *live* small fish or eels is probably the safest way of making sure that they are just that.

We will now see how important the enclosures and diets can be, by looking at the results of 88 post mortems gleaned from the record cards of London, New York, Paris, Zürich and other zoos. These findings are separated into two tables, dealing respectively with infectious and non-infectious diseases. Some otters died from multiple causes. One is immediately struck by the high incidence of viral and bacterial deaths (Table 4). Pneumonia is a very loose term which is not, I think, always a primary cause of death but rather a secondary one. Most of these

FIGURE 7. The wet fur of these two *Lutra canadensis* is in poor condition. The guard hairs are clumped and do not form regular spikes; the white underfur shows through. The smooth fur on the back indicates that both the guard hairs and the underfur are saturated. (Photo: Michael Lyster.)

otters probably died from the consequences of the coat losing its waterproof qualities, as a result of a bad diet or a bad enclosure, or a combination of both. It is worth drawing attention to fungal infections. Otters which are kept on damp concrete floors are prone to these tenacious infections, which usually start on the interdigital webbing but may soon spread to other areas, particularly axillary regions. Deaths from panleucopenia, distemper and leptospirosis are equally alarmingly high. Like other mustelids, otters appear to be particularly vulnerable to feline enteritis. Imported animals should receive the necessary inoculations on arrival and be quarantined before being mixed with other otters in any collection. Enteric diseases of various kinds are numerous. Once the mucous lining of the otter's fragile intestines (probably a protection against fish bones) is

TABLE 2. Minimum den accommodation requirements for one pair of otters.

	Size (cm)	Heating (22°C) thermostat	Access diameter (cm)	Bedding (dry)	Mats
Amblonyx cinerea	60 × 60 × 50	Autumn-spring	15	+	+
Lutrogale perspicillata	75 × 75 × 50	Autumn-spring	Tunnel 20	+	+
Lutra lutra	75 × 75 × 50	Winter + Cubs	Tunnel 18	+	+
Lutra canadensis	75 × 75 × 50	Winter + Cubs	22	+	+

TABLE 3. Daily food requirements per otter per day.

	Amblonyx	*Lutrogale*	*Lutra lutra*	*Lutra canadensis*
Chopped raw beef or horse meat	1000 g	1850 g	1250 g	1500 g
Dog meal	100 g	250 g	150 g	200 g
Osteo-calcium	$\frac{1}{4}$ tablet	1 tablet	$\frac{1}{2}$ tablet	$\frac{1}{2}$ tablet
Halibut liver oil	2 drops	5 drops	4 drops	4 drops
Soluble multi-vitamins	2 drops	4 drops	3 drops	3 drops
Bone meal	20 g	50 g	30 g	50 g
Bran	20 g	50 g	30 g	50 g
Raw carrot	20 g	50 g	30 g	50 g
Vegetable oil or margarine	20 g	50 g	30 g	50 g
Day-old chicks	2	5	3	4
Fish (6–10 in.)	1	3	2	3
or eels	2	4	3	4

TABLE 4. Infectious diseases of otters in captivity.

Fungal	Viral		Bacterial		Parasitic	
Pedal mycosis 3	Panleucopenia	18	Tuberculosis	4	Microfilaria	6
	Distemper	2	Jaundice	2	Trypanosomiasis	1
	Hepatitis (leptospirosis?)	6	Pneumonia	31	Nematodes	4
			Septicaemia	4	Trematodes	4
			? dental abscess	11	Cestodes	1
			Endocarditis	2		

Total: 88 post mortems

sloughed off, enteritis takes a very firm hold and death can, and often does, occur within 24 hours.

Non-infectious diseases are relatively uncommon in comparison (Table 5). Dental disease is one of the common hazards because of the peculiar molar

TABLE 5. Non-infectious diseases of otters in captivity.

Dietary		Neoplastic		Others	
Dental disease	11	Lymphosarcoma	1	Drowning	4
Renal calculi	5	Sarcoma ?	2	Injury	5
Osteomalacia	3			Poisoning	3
Hypovitaminosis					
AEB	6			Foreign body	4
				Degenerative	
				joint disease	1

Total: 88 post mortems

construction of the Lutrinae. The molars have become enlarged sideways disproportionately in relation to the length of the palate, particularly in crustacean-loving *Amblonyx*. Peridontal disease may perhaps be linked with a soft diet, which is why I advise feeding fish and day-old chicks. But it is not for me to reason why, as I am not a veterinarian; I only wish to point out that this condition is relatively frequent under captive conditions.

BREEDING IN CAPTIVITY

Now that we have considered the means of keeping otters in the pristine conditions they demand, let us consider breeding (Table 6). Mating is very rarely observed. In over a thousand observation hours, I have only witnessed mating three times; it is about as depressingly infrequent as in gorillas. Social species have a higher incidence of sexual activity than non-social ones. To placate your fears, may I say that once mating takes place, otters become extremely single-minded and mate a number of times during the day. Mating may begin on land but is usually completed in the water. *Amblonyx* and *Lutrogale* are said to mate on land occasionally but *Lutra* species seem to be strictly aquatic as far as this activity is concerned.

Only *Lutra canadensis* is not polyoestrous, but its South American conterparts are. Oestrus takes place in most species every 20–30 days. The vulva swells and there is a discharge between the 25th and 28th day. Urination, a form of marking, becomes more frequent. During this time, nipples may swell slightly, raising the hopes of many zoo men that their otter is pregnant when, in fact, she is not. *Lutrogale* females at this time may be particularly belligerent, which is a convenient sign to look for. *Amblonyx* females chase the male and attempt to initiate sexual behaviour, often unsuccessfully.

TABLE 6. Comparison of reproductive cycles and gestation periods.

	Oestrus	Signs of oestrus	Gestation period (days)	Signs of imminent birth	Post-partum oestrus	Necessary to remove male?	Cubs removed after
Amblonyx	Monthly 24–30 days	Female friendly towards male. Swollen vulva, nipples	60–64	Nest-building	?	No	6 months
Lutrogale	Monthly	Female friendly towards male. Female aggressive towards keeper. Swollen vulva, nipples	62	Excavating; swollen nipples	Yes	No	?
Lutra lutra	Monthly 24–28 days	Vulva swollen, discharge	60–62	♂ rejected	?	Yes	5–6 months
Lutra canadensis	Oct–May	Vulva swollen, discharge, male and female aggressive	245–365 (delayed implantation)	Nest-building, swollen nipples. ♂ rejected	Yes	Yes	6 months

Signs of imminent birth are difficult to detect. For instance, nest-building is a frequent activity in *Amblonyx* whenever new bedding material is supplied and does not necessarily represent pre-partum behaviour. *Amblonyx* females seem to sleep more and engage in fewer agonistic social encounters. In *Lutra*, the female rejects the male forcibly at this time, not allowing him to enter the den. *Lutra* males are best removed at such times. For this reason, it seems a good idea to

FIGURE 8. The male *Amblonyx* is carrying his cub on his forepaws while walking bipedally (tracing from photograph).

have one breeding pair and several extra females. When mating has been observed, the male can be removed and another female introduced to the male, thereby increasing the chances by taking advantage of the polyoestrous cycle. This is the technique that Philip Wayre of the Norfolk Wildlife Park has used with *Lutra lutra*, with great success. On the other hand, *Amblonyx* and *Lutrogale* males play an important part in rearing the cubs. They change the bedding and retrieve cubs that have strayed by carrying them under their chins back to the nest (Fig. 8).

In conclusion, I would simply like to say that, once we have understood the basic specific differences and met the necessary requirements, otters should not be difficult to breed regularly. Whether we can ever envisage the breeding of other species, such as the Brazilian giant otter *Pteronura brasiliensis*, in sufficient numbers to save it from extinction borders on the fairy tale. But then so many zoo breeding successes have started with "Once upon a time this animal was thought impossible to breed . . ." that perhaps we can and will breed *Pteronura*, and even the sea otter. Why not? I sincerely hope so.

Breeding Tigers as an Aid to their Survival

A. C. V. van Bemmel

Without any trace of a doubt, the tiger (*Panthera tigris*, Fig. 1) is an endangered species and zoos can make a real contribution to the survival of this species. The total population of the Indian tiger has decreased to perhaps 2000 specimens in the wild. As for Indo-China, we do not have the slightest idea how many tigers are still left there, but we can assume that the war in that part of the world represents a serious threat to every wild species, the tiger included. In Sumatra the total population of tigers has been estimated at some hundreds. In Java not more than 13 tigers seem to be still surviving. In Bali tigers are extinct. The total population of the Siberian tiger can be estimated at not more than 250. In Fukien (China) only a few tigers are still left. The Caspian tigers have decreased to less than 50 in number.

In all, 248 Siberian tigers, 62 Sumatran tigers and four Chinese tigers are kept in zoos at present. So at least in the case of the Siberian tigers the total population present in zoos outnumbers the population in the wild. It is impossible to say how many Indian tigers are kept in captivity at present, because many specimens, labelled as "Bengal tiger" are in fact hybrids between the Indian tiger and some other subspecies.

Lions have been bred regularly in zoos for a hundred years, and the zoos at Dublin and Leipzig have particularly impressive records in this respect. However, tigers have proved to be much more difficult to breed. There were only a few records of tiger births in captivity 50 years ago, and those that were born seldom lived to maturity. There must be some biological reason for this striking difference in breeding results. Lions are social animals, tigers are more or less solitary in the wild. Although a lioness seeks privacy and leaves her pride some weeks before giving birth, staying away from the pride till her offspring is 6 weeks old, in captivity this privacy during the critical weeks of pregnancy and the first weeks of the new-born cub's life nevertheless seems less important to the lioness than to the tigress.

The old-fashioned, traditional carnivore houses, such as those in which Dublin and Leipzig zoos achieved their breeding records, had small sleeping dens which provided the lioness with some privacy; but even these were barely isolated from the noise and disturbance caused by the public. Possibly, the lioness felt secure

FIGURE 1. (*above*) Female Sumatran tiger "Doutchska" at Whipsnade Zoo. (Photo: London Zoological Society.) (*below*) Female Sumatran tiger "Katrina" with two 6-week-old cubs born 15.4.72 at Whipsnade. (Photo: London Zoological Society.)

enough under these circumstances to rear her cubs, whereas the tigress did not. Other factors may well be involved as well: possibly the need for vitamins and minerals, now considered essential for any breeding success, is less pronounced in lions than in tigers. Certainly, many lionesses over the years have raised their cubs successfully on a diet of lean horse meat and milk, though tigresses have rarely done so. Another possible reason for the difference in breeding records is that lions and tigers have different mating patterns. Even in the small cages of the old, traditional carnivore houses, lions mated freely. But a pair of tigers, kept together for a long time in such a small cage and living without conflict, hardly ever consummated their marriage. If we consider the copulatory sequence of tigers, as depicted in the excellent drawings illustrating the paper by Sankhala (1967), we can see that there is an important behavioural difference as compared with the mating pattern of lions. After mating, the male tiger is thrown off by the female and he then tries to get out of her reach as quickly as possible. In the small cages of the old-fashioned carnivore houses, the male was unable to get away from the female, who often attacked him fiercely. After having been mauled in such a way by his loving wife, the male tiger will, in many cases, never try to mate with her again.

At this point, I should like to turn to the experience that I have gathered during my time in the Rotterdam Zoo, where there was (and still is, as far as I am aware) a very good breeding record (see van Bemmel, 1968). Between 1949 and 1969, just over 200 tiger cubs were born there, and 75 per cent of this number were raised. This does not mean that Rotterdam Zoo had developed the very best system for tiger breeding. But the system developed at Rotterdam has worked quite well, and perhaps others will be able to find in this system a solution for problems that have arisen under different zoo conditions.

One important thing seems to be access to *fresh air*. None of the tiger dens and enclosures at Rotterdam Zoo was ever heated, even during a winter with heavy frost (though "heavy frost" in the Netherlands involves temperatures less than minus 20°C). The majority of our tigers were kept in cages made from wire-netting and measuring 8 × 4 m. They were floored with sand and only protected by a roof of glass, which covered half of the cage (Fig. 2). In wintertime, rush-mats were put up along the side of each cage to protect the animals from the prevailing wind. The den consisted of a wooden box (Fig. 3), just large enough for the animal to stand and lie down comfortably. The front of the den had a sliding door of iron bars, which permitted access to fresh air day and night. The animals were shut in during the night. In summertime, this den was strewn with sawdust, but in wintertime the animals were provided with a thick bed of straw. Because the walls of the dens were double and well insulated, the animals were able to keep themselves warm during the night. We measured the temperature in the box during a night in which the outside temperature dropped to minus 15°C; the temperature in the box with the sleeping tiger remained at plus 7°C! All tigers kept in this way, even the Sumatran tigers, grew heavy coats in wintertime. We never had any cases of pneumonia or other diseases of the lungs.

The tigers were kept in these cages in pairs or groups consisting of a male and two or three females. As a rule, every animal had its own sleeping box. If the group consisted of more than a pair, the wire-netting cages were interconnected with sliding doors, so that a group could use two or three enclosures at once.

Any female tiger was considered to be pregnant if she did not come into heat 1 month after mating. After 2 months of pregnancy, the tigress was isolated, sometimes in her own enclosure but usually in a special breeding den inside the carnivore building. The breeding dens there were completely isolated from the

FIGURE 2. Tiger enclosures at the Royal Rotterdam Zoo.

public, both visually and acoustically. Nobody had access to the breeding dens, except the keeper. Inside the breeding den, which measured 2×4 m and was only lit by a skylight, there was a low, open box, filled with straw. Some tigresses liked the straw, others threw it out. The tigress was kept in this den till the cubs were 6 weeks old. Mother and cubs were then moved to an open-fronted cage at the back of the building. After 2 weeks, the family had settled down and the public was allowed to view the cubs in the open-fronted cage. During the night, however, this front was covered up with shutters.

The cubs remained with the mother until they were 4–5 months old. They were weaned in a special building and, if they were not sold immediately, they were transferred to the wire-netting cages after 4 weeks. The cubs were inoculated against panleucopenia at 6 weeks, 3 months, 5 months and 6 months of age. In the Netherlands, this inoculation is essential since feline enteritis (feline distemper) is widespread in domestic cats.

The tigers are fed on beef, sometimes mutton and, if possible, lean pork. Horse meat is rarely available. Pregnant females and growing cubs were fed regularly with freshly-killed rabbits, guinea pigs or young goats. Extra vitamins and a mineral mixture (Carnicon B) were included in the diet. The amount of meat fed to full-grown animals is less than is usually given in zoos; according to size and condition every animal receives between 4 and 7 kg of meat daily. They

FIGURE 3. Sleeping boxes provided in the tiger enclosures at Rotterdam.

are fed every day, with no fast day. (See Vaneysinga, 1969 for further comments on tiger diet.)

Rotterdam Zoo started by breeding Bengal tigers of unknown origin. After some years, the male died and was replaced by a male from Indo-China. This group was followed by a group of imported Sumatran tigers, originating from Deli (North Sumatra). There proved to be no more difficulty breeding from jungle-born animals than from zoo-born individuals. Nearly all cubs were reared by their mothers; only very few had to be hand-reared.

From 1956 onwards, Siberian tigers were also kept and soon afterwards the Zoo stopped breeding with the Bengal tigers of unknown origin. Only five jungle-born animals have been used for breeding, all others were zoo-born. Among those used for breeding there were no hand-reared animals.

As a rule, the breeding groups consisted of one or two males and two or three females. During the years between 1957 and 1967, 14 litters of Sumatran tigers have been born. Six litters consisted of three cubs, four litters of two cubs, four litters of only one cub. Litters consisting of a single cub were all born to old tigresses. The youngest Sumatran tigress to give birth was born on 23 October 1963 and produced a litter of three cubs on 22 January 1967. The oldest female bore her last single cub at the age of at least 17 years. This single cub, a female, was then left with her mother until she became pregnant herself.

Our famous "Bengal" tigress Suleika (a former circus artist), which reared 26 cubs, was born in 1941 and gave birth to her last single cub in 1958. She reared this cub herself.

The group of Siberian tigers reared 13 litters of cubs over a period of 8 years: five litters consisted of four cubs, three litters of three cubs, and five litters of two cubs. A female, born in April 1959, gave birth for the first time in July 1962. She did not rear this litter herself, but reared all her subsequent litters.

One may now ask: 'Does this list of conditions provide the whole secret of rearing so many tigers?' I think the answer is "No". For breeding tiger mothers, privacy is important and so is the space available in the cages. A variety of food and plenty of fresh air are important, but most important is the human factor: an experienced keeper who knows the requirements and peculiarities of each specimen in his care, who knows the moment to change the diet, the moment to change the amount of food given to a certain animal, who knows which female requires privacy and which can be left in her own quarters to give birth. During the period covered by this report, the tigers were looked after by one and the same keeper. But is this human factor not the most important thing in every zoo?

I am not a veterinarian, but I would nevertheless like to mention the ailment described by Veselovsky (1967), in which animals grow thin, vomit regularly and digest their food badly. This ailment has never occurred in our group of Siberian tigers, but two Sumatran tigers showed these symptoms. One, a female, was jungle-born, the other, a zoo-born male. We tried to cure the animals by feeding small amounts of lean pork twice a day and by giving antibiotics. They never quite recovered, but this did not prevent the female from rearing three flourishing litters of two cubs herself. The cubs were, and stayed, completely normal.

More important in my opinion is another question: if a zoo wants to breed endangered animal species, to further their survival, it is not enough to obtain one pair, start breeding, sell the male offspring and keep one or two of the female offspring. This will not only lead to inbreeding, but if something un-expectedly goes wrong, the whole attempt will be in vain. Breeding endangered animals means that one will have to build up a healthy breeding group, carefully selected from other breeding groups and, if possible, include a few jungle-born animals of precisely known origin. Zoo people will have to proceed just as breeders of thoroughbred horses or dogs do: selecting, interchanging bloodlines, keeping files and studying the ancestry of their animals and the breeding results of the different combinations. The aim should be, not to rear as many animals as is possible, but to breed perfect animals. That also means that we have to dispose of weak or abnormal animals and that we will have to select the right type of the subspecies we are breeding. Now let us look at the lions in zoos, bred for more than a hundred years, with hardly any fresh blood ever brought in and consisting of a mixture of several different subspecies. Most zoo lions clearly show the signs of domestication: short heads, short legs and very reduced brain weight. The gene-pool of the various subspecies of tigers at present available in our zoos is very limited indeed. We will need all the skill of true breeders to exclude abnormal, inbred animals and animals which clearly show signs of domestication. We have to select animals to meet the highest standard of type and quality. And it would be better to kill animals of poor quality, rather than sending these to small zoos, for they may be used for breeding there and thus spoil the overall results. My ideal would be to collect all specimens of endangered species into international pools, and to keep them out of animal trade. They would then be distributed to good breeders, rather than to wealthy zoos or collectors of rare animals. If we really want to further the survival of endangered species, we will have to take action in the right way, or we will merely waste both time and effort.

Captive Breeding of Cheetahs

V. J. A. Manton

The British orientalist and jurist Sir W. Jones (1746–94) wrote that the use of the cheetah for hunting originated with Hushing, King of Persia in 856 B.C. So popular did their use for this sport become with the Mongol emperors that many of the latter kept thousands of cheetah, all trained to the leash. Despite this long association with man and his success with other animals, it is surprising to read a report by the English naturalist W. I. Blandford, in 1888, that the cheetah had not been known to breed in captivity. This may in part be related to the methods of obtaining and training the animals. All were picked up at an "early age" and hand-reared in an atmosphere where man was the dominant factor.

Again in 1950 Dr. Hediger listed the cheetah as a non-breeder in zoological gardens. However, 6 years later the pair of animals at Philadelphia gave birth to three youngsters which unfortunately were not reared. Some 13 months later they produced a second litter whch were reared by hand but died from "distemper" at 3 months of age. In April 1960 the pair at Krefeld unexpectedly gave birth to four youngsters. All were unfortunately dead within 4 months and although a single birth occurred later this was "unsuccessful". In 1959 or 1960 and again in November 1962 two young were born in Oklahoma City, but all attempts to rear them failed and the longest survivor only lived 10 days. In January 1966, following the loan of two of Rome Zoo's males for mating, a tame female belonging to Signor Spinelli gave birth to a single youngster, and to three in December of the same year.

September 1967 saw the first of Whipsnade's four litters to date (1/2, 1/2, 1/1 and 0/3), of which only two females in the first litter have not been reared to maturity by the mother (see Fig. 1). Montpellier produced three young in December 1968 and four in May 1970, while the latest birth appears to be that of four young in Toledo Zoo, Ohio. Young have also been reported at Arnhem Zoo and at Longleat, but they either did not survive for long or were stillborn.

To summarize: over a period of 15 years, 43 young (19 males, 13 females and 11 of unidentified sex) have been born in nine collections to nine females. The question we should be asking ourselves is how and why. Firstly, I have searched all the available records for common factors. Age of the parents does not seem to play a part once the cheetah are sexually mature. The Philadelphia pair had an age disparity of about 4 years—the male probably being the older. At Krefeld the female was about 5 or 6 years old and the male 4 or 5 at the time of birth of the infant. Signor Spinelli's female was just under 4 years old and the males were about 9. Whipsnade's female was just over 3 years old at the time of the first litter and the male was about 5. At Montpellier the female was 4 and the male 5, while at Toledo both parents were only $2\frac{1}{2}$–$3\frac{1}{2}$ years old.

The time of year does not seem to be important, since with 14 litters, births

FIGURE 1. The female cheetah Juanita with her first litter of three cubs (born 19 September 1967). This was the first litter of cheetah cubs born in the United Kingdom and one of the offspring was reared to maturity.

occurred in every month except June, August and October. Generally speaking, litters result from animals kept as pairs although Spinelli's female was introduced to two males and the Montpellier female was with a second barren female at the time of breeding. Size of cage does not appear to be important. The Philadelphia pair bred in small dens of 7·5 sq. m (though the proximity of the male may have adversely affected the rearing in this case), the Krefeld pair bred in a pen of 90 sq. m, Signor Spinelli's pen was 150 sq. m, Whipsnade's was 800 sq. m, Montpellier's three pens each covered 1200 sq. m, while the pen at Toledo covered about 1625 sq. m.

It is highly probable that improvement in the standard of diets, and knowledge of suitable nutrition gained since Ratcliffe (of Philadelphia) and Wackernagel (of Basle) highlighted the unsuitability of the diets initially provided, has helped the species towards a fit breeding state in captivity. However, it is very hard to obtain detailed information on diets fed at cheetah breeding establishments. The recognition that carnivorous animals in the wild seldom feed entirely, or even mainly, on red meat (Ca: P ratio at least 1 : 12) has reminded cheetah keepers that small prey when caught live is often consumed entirely, thus ensuring a correct Ca: P ratio, plentiful supplies of vitamin A (or at least carotinoids) and the B complex vitamins. Instead of feeding whole or (from the animals' point of view, better still) live prey, supplementation is required and necessary for complete breeding and rearing success. At Philadelphia, the animals received horse meat varied with whole chickens or pigeons, but Ulmer (1957) states "it is doubtful if this helped for, in India, their (cheetah) owners have been feeding them natural (sic) food for centuries without any breeding taking place". This was altered shortly after the female arrived in the zoo to a compounded diet consisting basically of raw ground horse meat, powdered skim milk, a protein, mineral and vitamin B supplement, salt and a multivitamin powder. Oklahoma fed "mainly horse meat", while Krefeld fed horse meat and occasionally freshly killed rabbits. Here, however, 4 months before the first birth both parents received daily "20 cb (sic)" of a vitamin preparation containing 1 million i.u. vitamin A, 100,000 i.u. vitamin D_3 and 40 mg vitamin E per c.c. Signor Spinelli's female Beauty was fed apparently on donkey meat; the first youngster was also eating chicken heads at 4 months of age. All Whipsnade's cheetah were fed mainly on beef fit for human consumption dusted with steamed bone flour and alternating as often as possible (several times a week) with whole poultry and rabbits. They now receive on 3 lb of meat a 15 g supplement containing 20,000 i.u. vitamin A, 750 i.u. vitamin D_3, 40 i.u. vitamin E, 30 mg vitamin B_1, 45 μg vitamin B_{12}, 0·1 mg iodine, 4 g calcium and 2 g phosphorus (these last two as calcium dihydrogen phosphate). Montpellier feeds "meat" sprinkled "periodically" with powdered milk, brewer's yeast or vitamin mineral salts and a weekly whole chicken. Toledo feeds horse meat sprayed with vitamin supplements 6 days a week, with a whole rabbit once a week.

It is very difficult to discover the history of each breeding animal to ascertain if it was hand-reared from an early age or caught wild as an adult. Certainly the Oklahoma cheetahs were reasonably tame at the time of breeding since both were harnessed and exercised on a leash 3 days a week. The Krefeld animals do not appear to have been handled, whereas Signor Spinelli's Beauty was so tame that he "had prepared the teats for suckling . . . by sucking them in his mouth . . ." and after 2 weeks from the birth visitors were accepted by her into the den, though only "one at a time". At Whipsnade the female was never tamed and had always resented the too close approach of any human even to the wire of her quarantine quarters. She had been rescued from an attack by cape hunting dogs when two-thirds grown and artificially fed from then on, spending 18 months on her own before meeting any other cheetahs. The sire was "leash tame", having been hand-reared in Nairobi. The Montpellier animals were imported young although both were over 1 year old. No record of tameness is available. The Toledo animals arrived in Ohio when between 2 and 3 years old, 5 months prior to breeding.

It is interesting to note that the sire at Philadelphia had been "observed to mate on several occasions" with a previous mate with whom he had lived for 4 years. Yet Ulmer (1957) felt that "psychological factors can be ruled out". Despite this, the close proximity of the male at parturition apparently caused unease in the female, who attacked and killed her offspring. At Oklahoma the male "ate the first cub" and was therefore removed. The same happened with the first litters at Krefeld. Spinelli's dam was kept separate, as was Whipsnade's (although by mistake the second litter was born not only in the presence of the sire but in a spare hut, on a busy weekend). At Montpellier the sire and the barren female were removed at the "moment of birth". In Ohio the female was separated and put into a run of some 46 sq. m where supplementary heating and observation windows were available. Joy Adamson, in "The Spotted Sphinx", quotes an area of 63 square miles covered by Pippa and her three cubs and if this example is typical of the wild, then wild-caught adults are not used to the close proximity of unrelated animals, except at breeding time. Indeed what zoo, or even safari park can hope to imitate the wild in keeping cheetah in this sort of area? I believe it is very important to realize that if males and females only come together for mating and the females only share a territory with a maturing family at other times, then pairs should not be kept together in the same enclosure throughout the year. Indeed one of the most obvious common factors amongst zoos who have successfully bred cheetah is the separation of the breeding pairs and the bringing together of animals only when mature. Breeding occurred at Philadelphia 6 months after a second female was obtained for the male. Oklahoma's animals were removed from the pens frequently for exercise, although it is not known if the animals were exercised separately. Krefeld's pair were not put together until less than 9 months before the birth. Signor Spinelli's female of course lived on her own and was introduced to the male at the onset of oestrus. At Whipsnade oestrus and/or mating has been recorded on four occasions and each time between 10 and 14 days of the reintroduction of the male to the female. Within 12 months prior to the births at Montpellier the breeding pair were selected after some "violent battles" and left alone. A similar selection took place at Toledo from four adult imports. In most of these cases, at least one parent was an adult or late juvenile import and not a youngster hand-reared with the rest of the litter or a group of animals of similar age.

Another factor which I believe to be important is the siting of the cheetah pen. These animals are well known for their ability to focus on objects in the distance even when tame and on a leash. Spinelli's pen is on a hill facing the sea, which is about 15 kilometres away. At Krefeld the pen, although at ground level, allows very good vision across the zoo paddock in which there is plenty of activity. At Whipsnade free-flying peafowl (*Pavo cristatus*) and turkeys (*Meleagris gallopavo*) often land in or near the breeding pen, while free-roaming Bennett's wallabies (*Protemnodon rufogrisea*) and muntjac (*Muntiacus* spp.) frequently pass close to the pen on either side. Being on a slightly higher contour line, there is a good view across the main elephant lawn, the African buffalo (*Syncerus caffer*) and musk ox (*Ovibos moschatus*) paddocks in which there is plenty of movement. At Toledo, a paddock nearly 70 m long gives a good view beyond each end.

It is interesting to note that although Joy Adamson feels that cheetah are "not built for climbing" but only acquired this habit when "driven by man from . . . open plain, and forced into wooded country", and young animals at Whipsnade were seen climbing up a tree without the mother first setting an example, at three zoos symptoms of leg weakness have occurred. R. Bigalke, lately of Pretoria Zoo, found it common in young wild-caught cheetah that he had attempted to rear. At Philadelphia the cubs of the second litter developed, prior to 12 weeks of age, "some weakness in the carpal region of the forelegs". This apparently resolved without treatment. At Montpellier the four youngsters in the second litter (after being vaccinated for the first time against Carré's disease, leptospirosis and infectious hepatitis) became lame but the symptoms rapidly regressed on treatment with an "anti-rachitic vitamin (Sterogyl 15)". With the first litter at Whipsnade one cub was reported to be "carrying a hind leg" on 21 November when 2 months old. Careful observation showed the condition to clear up without treatment and no abnormalities could be felt when the cubs were handled for vaccination 6 days later. However, on 9 January 1968 a severe electrical black-out coupled with cold weather forced us to move the mother and her family to new quarters where an alternative form of heating could be supplied. They were all very nervous and highly suspicious of this new house, very different from the small dark kennel in which they were born. Ten days later the youngster already mentioned above was reported to be weak in her hind legs. When the animal was X-rayed at Regent's Park under phencyclidine sedation the picture revealed a "healing osteodystrophia, evidence of earlier calcium deficiency in the skeleton" and a healed fracture of the lower third of the left tibia. This latter could well have been a "greenstick" fracture and present on 27 November. Accepted back by her mother, this animal did not appear to recover completely from the sedation and collapsed and died (possibly after an epileptiform fit) on 10 February. The other two animals, having been seen to be "weak on their hind legs" since 1 February, were transferred to Regent's Park hospital on 12 February where their hind limb weaknesses were much exaggerated. The female youngster having died, the male was returned to Whipsnade on 23 April 1969, where he made a slow and prolonged but almost complete recovery. Indeed, when the female from the 1970 litter (see Fig. 2) with which he lived came into season in March 1972 he made two very concerted efforts and nearly served her, so strong are his hind legs now.

On reflection I cannot help feeling that the double disturbance in the life of this litter played a more important part in our failure to rear them than the level of nutrition or the lack of experience on the part of the dam with her first litter. However, experience at the other zoos confirms that rapidly growing young

FIGURE 2. Juanita with two cubs born on 20 February 1970 (her third litter), photographed at about 8 weeks of age. One cub is half-hidden but can be identified by the wet tail lying across the mother's right forelimb.

cheetah may be very susceptible to slight deficiencies or imbalances in their diet when it comes to the calcification of bones.

Any attempt to provide guidelines for an ideal cheetah breeding and maintenance programme makes one realize the depths of one's ignorance. It would seem that accommodation standards are not of overriding importance, but that the provision of dry bedding out of the wind and away from human interference is. Paddocks (see Fig. 3) should have a good view, preferably with plenty of

FIGURE 3. The new cheetah enclosure at Whipsnade Zoo (approximately 50 ft long and 32 ft deep). This is not a breeding enclosure and no cubs have been born in it so far (up to September 1974).

movement in the middle to far distance. The diet should certainly be as near as possible to that obtained by the animals in the wild and based on complete carnivore foods or whole animals. I would advise strongly against handling or attempting to tame any cheetah which is destined for breeding and the most important factor of all is to keep separating and reintroducing sexually mature animals, which should otherwise be kept in isolation (both from sight and sound) from one another, but still with good "views". Any house should be well ventilated to limit upper respiratory infections, but be free of draughts. I believe annual vaccination against feline infectious enteritis to be desirable, using a 3 ml dose.

I do not believe our knowledge extends to making proposals for a viable breeding unit, but a spare male should always be kept and young females should be retained to replace an older breeding animal. Once into the F_2 generation, dispersal of the group is an excellent idea provided that the new location understands cheetah husbandry. No thought should be given to sending captive-born stock back to the wild until at least six breeding units have progressed into the F_2 generation and cross-breeding has been satisfactorily carried out.

ACKNOWLEDGMENTS

I would like to thank Head Keeper F. Hughes of the Carnivore Section, without whose conscientious record keeping much of this information would be lost and Senior Keeper G. Lucas of the same section who acted on his own initiative to obtain some interesting information concerning other collections.

My thanks also go to Mr. Larry Hicks, B.S., Mr. Philip Skeldon, Dr. Charles Vallet and Mr. M. Jollet for personal communications essential to the preparation of this paper.

A New Building for Small Cats

W. P. Crowcroft

The subject of this paper is a new installation for housing smaller members of the cat family, constructed by the Chicago Zoological Society. Dr. Paul Leyhausen, the well-known authority on cats, has been acting as consultant in the design of the new building.

FIGURE 1. Mother and infant Pallas cat (*Felis manul*) at Brookfield Zoo. This species breeds even under the present conditions of maintenance and four were born in 1973. (Photo: Leland La France.)

At Brookfield Zoo near Chicago, as in various other zoos, we have a number of small cats pacing backwards and forwards in boxes which bear a general resemblance to public conveniences. Despite the fact that many of these cats such as the Pallas cat, *Felis manul* (Fig. 1) do in fact breed under these conditions (see Table

1), some species do not. In any event, we have taken exception to this low standard of accommodation. Our interest in replacing these cages with a more amenable habitat is, I confess, more concerned with bringing them into more pleasing surroundings than with improving the breeding performance, but the two are not irreconcilable. Indeed, we are aiming to achieve a number of potentially conflicting goals at the same time. We are in a very difficult position in attempting to cater for all of the various zoo requirements at once, but we believe that the new building provides a fairly good compromise solution.

The Chicago Zoological Society, which manages the Brookfield Zoo for Cook County (the actual owners of the zoo) has unexpectedly been provided with a handsome amount of money. To cut a long story short, the Society is embarrassed by the presence of some millions of dollars which must be spent intelligently on improving the zoo. This is only a minor embarrassment, since I can guarantee from bitter experience that it is not as uncomfortable as being frustrated by lack of funds.

TABLE 1. Breeding record of small species of cats for 1973 at the Chicago Zoological Park, Brookfield, Illinois.

Leopard cat (*Felis bengalensis*)	4
Pallas cat (*Felis manul*)	4
European wildcat (*Felis sylvestris*)	5
Margay (*Felis wiedii*)	2
Lynx (*Lynx canadensis*)	2
Sand cat (*Felis thinobia*)	6

Brookfield Zoo once enjoyed a reputation as an innovative zoo. When it was built, it was thought to be rather *avant garde*, but it is now, of course, somewhat old-fashioned, and we would very much like to be *avant garde* again. But this means trying to break away not only from the old physical structures, but also from the old fixed ideas, because it is mainly the ideas and attitudes that are in fact binding us to our present state. So we sat down and tried to formulate a plan to keep the cats in a much better way for all concerned—better for the visitors, better for the cats, better for the keepers, and better for the money at the gate. We decided after a great deal of discussion and deliberation that we really needed to build a *theatre*, rather than a cage. We have designed a building which is something like a sound stage at a film studio. In this theatre, we will attempt to present the habitats and habits of the smaller cats (Fig. 2).

Basically the structure consists of a great big box which is divisible into four levels. The basement level is intended for all mechanical devices, electrical equipment, compressed air and other apparatus. Incidentally, the mechanical devices will be fairly sophisticated because we wish to manipulate the cats into sitting where the public can see them most of the time. For example, if there is a spot in a corner where an animal tends to sit and the public cannot see it, we will direct a gentle breeze on to the animal to make it mildly uncomfortable, and if

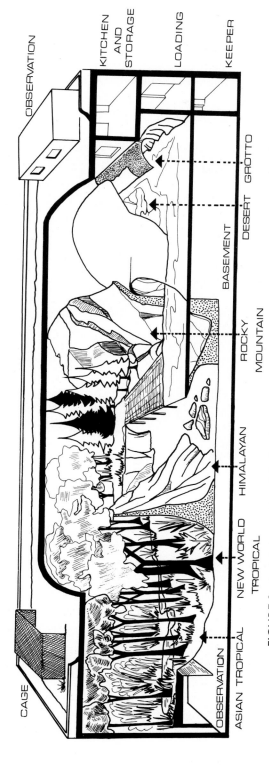

FIGURE 2. Artist's impression of the interior of the new building for small cats planned for Brookfield Zoo.

there is a particular place where we want the animal to sit we shall slightly warm it so that it is somewhat more comfortable and attractive. Enough is known about these animals for this kind of manipulation to be possible. All that is necessary is to take the attitude that it is desirable to do these things.

The next level above is the visitor level, where the visitors will proceed along a walkway through four large habitat exhibits. The third level is for the keepers, who will actually walk on the roof of the visitors' walkway. Finally, on the level

FIGURE. 3 Persian sand cat (*Felis thinobia*) at Brookfield Zoo. In the new building, it is proposed to keep this species under desert conditions. (Photo: Leland La France.)

above that (the roof itself) there will be open-air cages for the cats and nobody else. The public will not be allowed on to the roof; there will be access only to the cats and their keepers and research workers. So in its conception, as indicated above, this new house for small cats is rather out of the ordinary, but we are hoping that it will work out very well. The overall size of the building is about 150 × 50 ft. This means that a pair of cats in this house, instead of having about 50 sq. ft as available in the usual installations, will have about 1000 sq. ft of simulated habitat.

The various cats are now in preparatory training for the new building. We are proposing to have sand cats (*Felis thinobia*—Fig. 3) in simulated desert conditions. We also have fishing cats from South-East Asia, which at the present time at Brookfield Zoo catch their fish at 11.00 a.m. and 3.00 p.m. daily. The goldfish are released into the pool, a little bell is rung and (just as in the text books) the cats come out, wade in, catch the fish and eat them in front of a delighted small group of the public. One or two fish lovers have objected. In our new house, there will be a permanent stream and pool and the fish will be there in abundance for the cats to feed themselves.

The other idea we wanted to get away from was that people coming to the zoo are entitled to see everything on every visit. These cats in the new building are going to be available to the public for approximately 4 h in the afternoon every day, from 1.00 p.m. to 5.00 p.m. They are nocturnal animals, but instead of doing a 12-h direct inversion of the light schedule, we will give them a stretched twilight between 1.00 p.m. and 5.00 p.m., which means that the public will see them at their most active. The animals will have the morning in the outside cages and their day will just be staggered by half of the normal amount. The inside enclosures will literally have "cat walks" leading to the roof, and the cats will come and go as they please between the outside and inside cages for all of the day except the 4 h when the house is open to the public. The cages on the roof will provide accommodation for more cats than are exhibited at any one time, which means that some of them can be kept under different conditions if necessary, while some of them can be alternated in display.

It is worth mentioning that these same principles are being adopted in our new Ape House, to be called The Tropic World. The apes will have private rooms where they will spend their nights, and there will be duplicate animals for switching of animals on display. The building shell itself has been designed by an architect, as we had to make sure that it would stand up. But we have carefully kept the architect from any involvement in the design of the exhibits. Whilst not wishing to hurt anybody's feelings, I must declare that estimation of architects does not rank highly in the zoo profession, because there is something about zoos that seduces architects into losing all sense of proportion. The architects that we are using have had no previous experience in zoo work, so we can brainwash them for ourselves. We hope that, by combining structural necessity with our own exhibit design based on the natural habitats, the new building will provide an environment which is more attractive and more conducive to regular breeding in captivity.

Breeding Sloth Bears in Amsterdam Zoo

E. F. Jacobi

INTRODUCTION

In an earlier article on breeding facilities for polar bears in captivity (Jacobi, 1968), I made the following statement, which in fact applies to a number of other mammals as well: "In Nature the pregnant female finds a concealed place where she feels safe and undisturbed to give birth to and care for her young." Certainly, all bears give birth in a concealed place. Under natural conditions, the female makes or chooses a suitable retreat; in captivity *we* have to make the arrangements, and our choice is usually quite limited. Problems arise when the facilities provided do not satisfy the pregnant animal, and it is then necessary to determine what changes are necessary. If the facilities are not acceptable, we usually have to try to find more suitable conditions by trial and error, as good information about dens under natural conditions is seldom available. What is accepted by a particular female depends to some extent upon the species, but individual characteristics may be more important. A tame female is easier to accommodate than a shy, fearful female, and an animal which has had a normal upbringing with her mother and other young is better prepared than a bottle-fed, isolated female. Food must of course, contain adequate nutrients, vitamins and minerals.

In most cases, a zoo has to solve its problems with incomplete information about the natural situation. We are now quite well informed with respect to the difficulties encountered with polar bears in captivity; brown bears readily accept the standard zoo accommodation for bears, but we know little or nothing about sloth bears and they rarely breed in captivity.

For polar bears, the temperature (even severe frost) is not important if the animals are not disturbed. If there is electric heating to keep the cub warm when the mother leaves the den for short periods, disturbance will not be harmful.

BREEDING OF SLOTH BEARS

Although sloth bears (*Melursus ursinus*) are not at present in direct danger of extinction, information gained from our experience with them in captivity may prove to be of value in other cases.

We received the parent animals (one male and three females) in May 1965 from Calcutta Zoo. They were 5–6 months old, and were supposedly taken from the wild. They were very tame on arrival, and this tameness has persisted. Accommodation was provided specially for the sloth bears in summer 1970, in cages built during the reconstruction of an old building in the zoo. The space provided is very limited, but it does allow for breeding facilities for three females. In the inside enclosure each female has an enclosed breeding den together with an open cage as the "outside world", where food and water are supplied. The facilities for the three females are made up as follows (see Fig. 1):

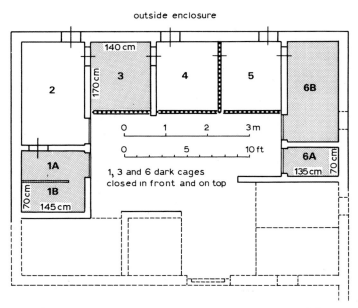

FIGURE 1. Plan of the inside enclosures used for the sloth bears.

1st female: Covered breeding den in cage 1 (overall dimensions: 150 × 150 cm), divided in summer 1971 into two sections. Connecting open enclosure in cage 2 (250 × 150 cm).

2nd female: Covered breeding den in cage 3 (175 × 140 cm). Connecting open enclosure in cage 4 (175 × 150 cm).

3rd female: Covered breeding den in cages 6A and 6B (135 × 70 cm and 250 × 125 cm, respectively). Connecting open enclosure in cage 5.

(Normally, cages 6A and 6B provide accommodation for cheetahs, but they can also be used as breeding dens for the bears when necessary.)

Heating and ventilation is ensured by means of heated air currents, which maintain the temperature at 15°–20°C. All cages are provided with heated floors, and straw bedding has been provided in the breeding dens (though it was not actually used by the animals).

In 1970, the breeding den cages (1, 3 and 6) were not closed over on top, and a front shutter of cage 3 did not fit properly. At that time, the three female sloth bears were separated in cages 1 + 2, 3 + 4 and 5 + 6, whilst during the night the male sloth bear was shut in cage 5 with a pair of sun bears (*Helarctos malayanus*). In 1971 (summer), cages 1, 3 and 6 (the breeding dens) were closed over on top in order to darken them, and all of the front shutters were fitted properly. Cage 1 was divided into two equal sections (1A: 75 × 150 cm; 1B: 75 × 150 cm), and the male sloth bear and the sun bears were moved to other quarters (see Fig. 1 for the detailed layout of the cages.)

CASE HISTORIES

In 1970, mating attempts involving all three females were seen between 23 June and 10 July. These were followed by three births on 28 November (cage 1), 29 November (cage 3) and 9 December (cage 6A), giving a maximum gestation period of 169 days. At the time of these births the three adult females were about 6 years old.

The females were separated for the births, and they were very nervous and restless. After the young had been born, they stayed in the breeding den cages most of the time.

One dead cub was found in cage 1 three days after birth, and it was found that it had not been suckled. It is possible that a second cub had been born and subsequently eaten. If this was the case, then all three mothers had produced two infants. In cage 3, the two cubs similarly survived for only 3 days, and they had not been suckled. Since these first two mothers went out with the other bears on 2 December, following the unsuccessful births, and since cage 4 remained empty, the situation was much better for the third female in cages 5 + 6A + 6B. This female selected the smallest inside cage available (6A: 70 × 140 cm) to give birth. Her infants survived for 7 and 9 days, respectively, after which they disappeared (presumed eaten).

In 1971, when the above-mentioned changes were made to the cages, better breeding results were obtained. Mating attempts were observed from 3 May to 12 June, and two births were recorded on 5 December and 26 December. Thus our data so far do not permit a definite statement about the gestation period. These dates indicated a *minimum* gestation period of 176 days for 1971, whilst the *maximum* gestation period indicated for 1970 was 169 days.

As from 11 November 1971, the three female sloth bears had all six cages entirely to themselves, and they no longer went out. They spent most of the time together in cages 4 and 5. As one female was seen in cage 2 on 18 November, it was decided that she preferred this area, and she was accordingly separated in cages 1 + 2. The two other females remained together in cages 3 + 4 + 5 + 6A + 6B (cages 3 and 6 being kept dark).

The female in cages 1 + 2 gave birth on 5 December in cage 1A or 1B. She ate little food for the first few days, and from 10 December she stopped eating entirely. From then on, she only drank milk (1 litre per day) which was provided instead of water. At 71 days after birth, the mother began to take food again, but feeding remained irregular for some time. On 10 December, the decaying body of a dead cub was removed from cage 2, and it was not until 13 December that it was possible to make an inspection of the breeding dens (cages

FIGURE 2. Female sloth bear and her infant coming out of the den into the outside enclosure.

1A and 1B). On that date, a healthy cub was seen on the bare floor of cage 1A; the straw bedding had been moved to the sides. The cub was seen in cage 2 for the first time on 9 February, at the age of 66 days. The mother and cub went out into the outside enclosure for the first time on 14 March, when the cub was 94 days old.

With the other two females, which retired together to cage 3, young were born on 26 December. Both females took very little food in the 2 days following birth, and they then ceased to take anything other than milk until 2 February, 38 days after the birth. Thereafter, feeding remained irregular for some time. On 1 January, a female was seen in cage 4 carrying a live cub in her

FIGURE 3. Young sloth bear riding jockey-style on the female's back.

mouth, and on 2 January a female was seen there carrying a dead cub, which she left in cage 4. On 21 February, a cub was seen moving unaided in cage 4 for the first time, at 57 days of age, and it then appeared that there was only one surviving cub. (It is not clear whether one or both females had given birth.) On 16 March, the two females and the cub went out into the outside enclosure, and on 17 March all three female sloth bears and the two young were together in the outside enclosure, though they were separated again for the night. From 18 March onwards, all of the sloth bears were kept together day and night, and it was observed that one female nursed two young.

ADDITIONAL OBSERVATIONS

The young sloth bear is protected by being placed between the hind legs of the mother, whilst it is transported on her back. When being carried in this way, the young bear holds on with its mouth and claws to the mother's long hair (see Figs. 2 and 3).

It is important to note that, when infants survived, the female sloth bears did not take solid food for 1–2½ months after the birth. A breeding den of 70 × 140 cm is apparently quite big enough for this animal, despite its relatively large body size; indeed, there is some indication that the pregnant sloth bear actually prefers small breeding dens. It is apparently preferable to darken the breeding den areas to provide the mothers with sufficient seclusion.

NORMAL DAILY DIET OF SLOTH BEARS

Doko (mixture of meat, oils, vitamins, minerals)	1500 g per animal
Vegetables	500
Apples	500
Carrots	500
Whiting (fish)	500
Ground meat	1000
Bread	300

The females with young only took 1 litre of milk a day till the time when the young were about 2–3 months old.

Experimental Embryology as a Tool for Saving Endangered Species

R. T. Francoeur

Artificial insemination (see Hafez, 1968) is widely used throughout the world in the breeding of domestic animals. Why should not this technique be adapted and applied to build up populations of rare and endangered species?

In 1776 Abbé Lazzaro Spalanzani, an embryologist-priest, artificially inseminated the eggs of 165 female frogs, and 4 years later he successfully inseminated a canine bitch. In 1799 Dr. Home, a British physician, artificially inseminated the first woman. In the 1890s English dog breeders tried their hands at artificial insemination. In 1899 E. I. Ivanoff was asked by the chief of the Royal Russian Stud Farm to explore the uses of artificial insemination to improve the Russian horse stock. Ivanoff went on to inseminate cattle, sheep and birds successfully, in each case improving on the natural conception rate. The first cooperative organized to take advantage of the efficiency of artificial insemination came in 1936 in Denmark. Two years later the Holstein breeders in New Jersey formed the first American cooperative for artificial insemination.

Since the late 1950s we have been able to freeze semen in straws and store it for 10 years, if not indefinitely, without genetic deterioration (e.g. see Roussel and Austin, 1967). The breeding of domesticated animals with frozen semen and artificial insemination is now an impressive and profitable business. (In 1971 sperm banks for frozen human semen were opened as commercial ventures in several American cities.) One recent farm census indicates that 59 million cows, 47 million ewes, 1 million sows, 125,000 mares and 56,000 goats were artificially inseminated in a single year. In some countries 99 per cent of all calves born are the product of artificial insemination. In the United States each year over 4 million turkey hens are artificially inseminated. The resultant accelerated reproduction and economy have led to this extensive use of artificial insemination, but beyond the domesticated ungulates and turkey this technique has found little use among the 4000 existing species of mammals, and even less with other animals.

Considering the long-standing concern of many ecologists, zoo managers, environmentalists and naturalists around the world, I find it incredible and disturbing that so little attention has been given to the possible uses and advantages of artificial insemination in the attempt to save endangered animal species from extinction (see also Francoeur, 1972). The National Academy of Medicine, in a literature search of its computer memory bank (MEDLARS) undertaken at my request, turned up only three experiments with the artificial insemination of non-human primates between 1 January 1970 and 1 October 1971, and revealed less than a dozen reports of artificial insemination being attempted with semi-domesticated or wild hoofed animals: the water buffalo, alpacas and some African antelopes. Nothing could be found on the artificial insemination of birds, reptiles or fish. There has been an occasional experiment in academia, as for instance, Cade's insemination of a red-tailed hawk at Cornell University, and probably some work at various game reserves and primate centres, but these do not turn up in the MEDLARS bibliography (see Temple, 1972).

At the same time, natural environments and reserves everywhere are being invaded and destroyed by man, driving more and more wild populations to the verge of extinction. In captivity, many of these animals refuse to breed unless they have benefited from watching mating behaviour of conspecifics during infancy in the wild and/or unless a close imitation of their natural environment, food, light, temperature, space and population size can be knowingly provided by their captors. But with our limited knowledge of these animals and their behaviour and requirements in the wild, the task of developing a quasi-natural captive environment is an almost impossible challenge, a groping-in-the-dark effort rarely rewarded with success. Natural reserves are disappearing, breeding in captivity is often limited to adults imported from the wild, nations are placing embargoes on the capture and export of many species, and we are left with dwindling zoo populations scattered haphazardly among hundreds of zoos and game reserves around the world.

My impressions from general reading and from a discussion of this problem with John Perry, assistant director of the National Zoological Park (Washington DC) and secretary of the Wild Animal Propagation Trust, confirm my suspicion that with many endangered species we have neither the time nor the captive populations to continue the tedious groping search for simulated natural breeding facilities. Radical as it may sound to some naturalists, the best hope lies in the suggestion I put forward in 1970 in *Utopian Motherhood* (see Francoeur, 1974), and more recently in an article for *Catalyst for Environmental Quality*. I proposed the establishment of a consortium, a research team composed of zoo managers, experts in animal behaviour and husbandry, reproductive physiologists and experimental embryologists. Each would bring his or her own expertise to a carefully planned project to experiment with artificially inseminated captive stock. Frozen semen, drawn from a cooperative breeding pool, would be supplied by the participating institutions. Breeding females would be committed by the participating zoos and maintained wherever the best facilities could be found. Finances would be handled jointly.

A dozen scientists and naturalists, I feel, could handle this project, drawing where necessary on the experience and expertise of scientists around the world. We have the manpower, the basic knowledge and the raw material to launch this venture. The question is whether the right people can be convinced of the advantages of using artificial insemination to preserve some endangered species.

The obstacles are not insurmountable if the expertise of experimental embryologists, animal behaviour specialists and reproductive physiologists can be called upon. Methods will have to be developed to determine, control and perhaps even induce oestrus in females, and to collect and freeze the semen, while equipment and techniques for insemination itself will have to be found. Zoos and reserves will have to be convinced that it is in their best interests to contribute to the sperm banks and loan their females to the project, and finance will have to be sought.

The first attempts at artificial insemination of exotic species might be made either with species which, though not rare themselves, are closely related to rare forms, or with species which are closely related to domesticated forms where artificial insemination has been extensively proven. In both cases, species should be chosen which can be handled with a minimum of risk arising from physical restraint or drug immobilization, a risk which varies and is often an unknown quantity in the rarer species. A good subject for an early experiment could be the pair of bongos in the Milwaukee Zoo where the male is too lame to service the female and there is little chance of obtaining another male. The knowledge gleaned from many successful cases of artificial insemination of domesticated hoofed mammals could be applied to these bongos with a minimum of risk. In another area, if experiments with the commoner marmosets proved successful, artificial insemination might be tried with the golden lion marmoset. A considerable amount of work has already been conducted with non-human primates, so much useful information is available (see Bennett, 1967a, b; Dede and Plentl, 1966; Dukelow, 1970 and 1971; Fussell, Roussel and Austin, 1967; Gilman, 1969; Kraemer and Vera Cruz, 1969; Lang, 1967).

Another technique in experimental embryology might also be worthwhile considering: artificial inovulation or embryo transplantation to a surrogate mother of another closely related species after test-tube fertilization of eggs from a superovulated rare female. Embryo transplants with bovine and sheep embryos are about 75 per cent successful. At present there are only 44 Indian rhinoceroses in 25 zoos and only eight births have been reported since 1964, five of them at Basle. Is it too far-fetched to suggest inducing superovulation of a single female with hormones, collecting the eggs non-surgically, fertilizing them *in vitro* and then implanting the resultant embryos in the wombs of more common black rhinoceroses which have been synchronized in their oestrous cycle? The same technique might be used with the more common marmosets serving as surrogate mothers for the rare golden lion marmoset, or the common American bison assisting as a prenatal wet nurse for the European bison.

The techniques are available and have been proven with extensive experience among domesticated and human animals (see also Gregoire and Mayer, 1965). The question is whether those concerned with preserving our endangered species are interested in exploring some new avenues.

Captive Propagation: A Progress Report*

J. Perry, D. D. Bridgwater and D. L. Horsemen

The first zoo to propagate a species in captivity earns a mark of distinction. In recent years, there have been fewer such events than in the past. Many species once thought impossible to breed in captivity have been bred. Others that reproduced rarely now do so more often.

On balance, zoos are still consumers rather than producers of wildlife. A few zoo directors have protested this statement, but available vital statistics confirm it. A typical report from a leading zoo shows:

	Births and hatchings	Deaths	Net
Mammals	156	178	− 22
Birds	252	433	− 181
Reptiles, Amphibians, etc.	0	318	− 318

Further, births and hatchings are not evenly distributed over the species in a collection. Among the birds, for example, a few species usually account for most hatchings.

A few zoos are net producers. By and large, these have specialized in their collections. Game parks, game farms, and establishments devoted to breeding waterfowl or upland game birds usually produce annual surpluses.

That zoos might become survival centres for endangered species is not a new idea. Proposing that a national zoo be established, in 1889, Smithsonian Secretary Samuel P. Langley declared it would be "a home and a city of refuge for the vanishing races of the continent". As more and more species approach extinction, interest in survival centres has increased. Citing the Przewalski horse and wisent as examples, some zoo directors assert that captive breeding will be the last hope for many species.

It seems timely to consider what has been accomplished thus far. Because the preceding table is typical, we have limited this review to mammals. The IUCN *Red Data Book* lists 291 mammal species and subspecies as rare or endangered. In 1962, the *International Zoo Yearbook* (IZY) undertook the first of its annual

* This paper is reprinted from *Zoologica*, vol. 57, pp. 119 *et seq.* (1972), and permission for reproduction of the text is gratefully acknowledged.

censuses of rare species in zoos. Since that time, 162 of the 291 species and subspecies have been represented in collections. IZY reports of births indicate that 73 of these produced offspring at least once in the 10-year period.

To simplify analysis, we chose two base years, 1962 and 1965, and from the 73 species and subspecies selected those with captive populations of ten or more in either year. This is a crude method of choice; a herd of eight could be a good breeding base, while two dozen widely scattered would not be. However, on reviewing the species and subspecies thus eliminated, we saw no serious omissions for purposes of this study.

There were 41 mammal species and subspecies with base-year populations of ten or more. The 1971 IZY Census showed population increases for 36 of them. This is not, in itself, evidence of breeding success, since the IZY Census does not report acquisitions from the wild. Further, the number of zoos reporting to IZY increased.

IZY does report the numbers of captive-born individuals within each year's totals. When this data is assembled, there are strong indications of whether a captive population is self-sustaining.

(In the following tables, a blank for 1962 may mean zero response. However, some species and subspecies have since been added to the Census list.)

TABLE 1. Zoo populations of rare and endangered species: 1962–71.

	1962	1965	1971	Captive-born No.	Per cent
MARSUPIALIA					
Yellow-footed Rock Wallaby					
(*Petrogale xanthopus*)	4	52	46	42	91
Long-nosed Rat Kangaroo					
(*Potorous tridactylus*)	5	13	23	8	35
White-throated Wallaby					
(*Macropus parma*)	—	19*	180	70	39
* Not reported by IZY in 1965. Data for 1966.					
PRIMATES					
Black Lemur					
(*Lemur macaco*)	32	25	73	28*	38
Red-fronted Lemur					
(*Lemur fulvus rufus*)	3	10	43	15*	35
* Number of captive-born not reported by Tananarive.					
Mongoose Lemur					
(*Lemur mongoz mongoz*)	22	59	167	64	38
Red Uakari					
(*Cacajao rubicundus*)	8	32	38	4	11
Goeldi Monkey					
(*Callimico goeldii*)	—	10**	16	6	38
** Not reported by IZY in 1965. Data for 1967.					

	1962	1965	1971	Captive-born No.	Per cent
Golden Lion Marmoset					
(*Leontopithecus rosalia*)	—	72***	76	39	51
*** Not reported by IZY in 1965. Data for 1966.					
Orang-utan					
(*Pongo pygmaeus*)	205	349	539	152	28
Bonobo Chimpanzee					
(*Pan paniscus*)	9	22	21	4	19
CARNIVORA					
Maned Wolf					
(*Chrysocyon brachyurus*)	7	11	65+	22	34
Spectacled Bear					
(*Tremarctos ornatus*)	13	43	85+	16	19
Brazilian Otter					
(*Pteronura brasiliensis*)	10 min	10 min	15	3	20
Brown Hyena					
(*Hyaena brunnea*)	5	32	49	17	35
Asiatic Lion					
(*Panthera leo persica*)	3	37	66+	22+	33
Siberian Tiger					
(*Panthera tigris altaica*)	—	120	296+	153+	52
(Includes Korean form)					
Sumatran Tiger					
(*P. t. sumatrae*)	—	23	78+	59+	76
North China Leopard					
(*Panthera pardus japonensis*)	—	29	51+	44+	86
Snow Leopard					
(*Panthera uncia*)	22 min	54	98	31	32
PERISSODACTYLA					
Przewalski Horse					
(*Equus przewalskii*)	85 min	121 min	182	181	99
Onager					
(*Equus heminonus onager*)*	62	113	139+	75	53
* Including animals reported as *E. h. heminonus*. This combination was initiated by IZY in 1966.					
Indian Wild Ass					
(*E. h. khur*)	3	11	11	1	9
Nubian Wild Ass					
(*Equus asinus africanus*)	7	16	17	17	100
Hartmann Mountain Zebra					
(*Equus zebra hartmannae*)	54	72	91+	37+	41

TABLE 1.—*continued*

	1962	1965	1971	Captive-born No.	Per cent
Baird Tapir (*Taipirus bairdii*)	6	11	12 +	2	17
Great Indian Rhinoceros (*Rhinoceros unicornis*)	26	39	45 +	16	36
Black Rhinoceros (*Diceros bicornis*)	119	124	128 +	28	22
ARTIODACTLYA					
Pygmy Hippopotamus (*Choeropis liberiensis*)	49	85	128 +	58 +	45
Vicuña (*Vicugna vicugna*)	—	72	69	57	83
Burma Brow-antlered Deer (*Cervus eldi thamin*)	13	11	37	5	14
Thailand Brow-antlered Deer (*C. e. siamensis*)	—	12*	10	9	90

  * Paris Zoo herd identified as *C. e. eldi* in IZY 1965.

	1962	1965	1971	Captive-born No.	Per cent
Tule Elk (*C. canadensis nannodes*)	—	14	32	17	53
Formosan Sika (*C. nippon taiouanus*)	—	306	374 +	336 +	90
Père David Deer (*Elapharus davidianus*)	130	436	550	550	100
Anoa (*Anoa depressicornis*)	—	23	24	7	29
Wisent (*Bison bonasus*)	132	234 min	303 +	232 +	77
Arabian Oryx (*Oryx leucoryx*)	5	27	75 +	49 +	65
Scimitar-horned Oryx (*Oryx tao*)	18	23	141	101	72
Addax (*Addax nasomaculatus*)	20	63	142	116	82
Arabian Gazelle (*Gazella gazella arabica*)	—	10 min	44 +	19 +	43

Ovis orientalis is omitted because of apparent changes in subspecies identification.

These 41 cases include a wide range of situations. The Przewalski horse story is familiar. At the other extreme, the Brazilian otter is obviously insecure. In between are a number of species which show promising trends but, as yet, provide more reason for hope than confidence.

Our purpose was to identify those situations where zoo propagation has been sufficient to give reasonable assurance that a species can be permanently maintained without further acquisitions from the wild. As a beginning, we chose two arbitrary factors: a 1971 captive population of 100 or more, and at least half of these captive-born. While these factors alone could not guarantee long-term security, it is unlikely that anything less would.

Using these two factors as a screen, only eight species or subspecies qualified: the Siberian tiger, Przewalski horse, onager, Formosan sika, Père David deer, wisent, scimitar-horned oryx and addax. The mongoose lemur (*Lemur mongoz mongoz*) is a possible candidate for this list; of the two principal collections, one did not report, while the second did not report numbers of captive-born.

1. SIBERIAN TIGER	1964	1965	1966	1967	1968	1969	1970	1971
No. zoos reporting	36	41	49	50	51	66	71	77
Total population	104	116	149	162	191	224	248	296
Captive bred	73	66	87	109	140	161	192	253
Per cent captive bred	70	57	58	67	73	72	77	85
Births (surviving)	21	28	28	43	58	59	75	—*
Individuals per collection	3	3	3	3	4	3	3	4

* IZY reports births for the year preceding the Census.

The number of individuals per collection remained almost static during the years the population increased by 185 per cent. The number of births increased slightly more rapidly than the total population.

In the years shown, 312 successful births were reported. The total population increased by 192, the population of captive-born individuals by 180. The number of wild-caught individuals increased from 31 to a peak of 63 in 1969, and has since declined to 43. The apparent birth rate has increased.

2. PRZEWALSKI HORSE	1964	1965	1966	1967	1968	1969	1970	1971
No. zoos reporting	24	29	33	35	40	41	43	42
Total population	118	121	149	147	157	160	161	182
Captive bred	116	120	148	146	156	159	160	181
Per cent captive bred	98	99	99	99	99	99	99	99
Births (surviving)	18	12	18	19	19	14	27	—
Individuals per collection	5	4	5	4	4	4	4	4

This species is often mentioned as a prime example of survival in zoos. The total population has shown a slow but steady increase. The number of zoos having the species has also increased The average number of individuals per collection remained constant.

3. ONAGER*	1964	1965	1966	1967	1968	1969	1970	1971
No. zoos reporting	26	33	38	39	32	37	43	44
Total population	89	113	135	150	118	132	145	139+
Captive bred	34	34	61	76	65	56	77	74
Per cent captive bred	38	30	45	51	55	42	53	53
Births (surviving)	6	18 min	15	14	13	14	14+	—
Individuals per collection	3	3	4	4	4	4	3	3

* Includes animals once reported as *E. h. heminonus*.

An apparent population decline occurred in 1968. While there were reporting inconsistencies, losses were also indicated, and the population total has not yet regained its 1967 peak, nor has the total of captive-born individuals.

The average number per collection has remained almost static, as has the apparent birth rate. Of the 44 collections reporting in 1971, 11 had only one sex.

The onager position is not yet secure, though there is no immediate reason for alarm.

4. FORMOSAN SIKA	1964	1965	1966	1967	1968	1969	1970	1971
No. zoos reporting	21	33	32	29	26	26	24	30
Total population	135	306	260	327	420	414	539	374
Captive bred	113	189	209	234	233	248	361	336
Per cent captive bred	84	62	80	72	55	60	67	90
Births (surviving)	49	46	65	70	38	52 min	68	—
Individuals per collection	6	9	8	11	16	16	22	12

There appear to be problems of subspecies identification here. Mountain Home (Texas), a private game ranch, reported 105 *Cervus nippon taiouanus* in 1970, none in 1971. However, it reported 60 *C. n. mantchuricas*, all captive-born, in 1970 and an estimated 200 in 1971. The total population shown for 1971 was further affected by lack of a report from Taipeh, which had reported an estimated 150 in 1970.

Total population in all other collections increased by 90 from 1970 to 1971. The average number per zoo declined from 15 to 12; the number of collections increased from 22 to 30.

This subspecies appears to be in a strong position for long-term survival in captivity.

5. PÈRE DAVID DEER	1964	1965	1966	1967	1968	1969	1970	1971
No. zoos reporting	43	44	45	49	51	54	60	63
Total population	410	432	436	452	485	497	525	550
Captive bred	410	432	436	452	485	497	525	550
Per cent captive bred	100	100	100	100	100	100	100	100
Births (surviving)	97	87	104	120	102	27	99	—
Individuals per collection	10	10	10	9	10	9	9	9

The apparent decline in births for 1969 was caused by a lack of report from Woburn.

IZY now reports only totals for this species, not individual zoo data, which is available from the studbook. In 1968, last year for the individual reports, 60 per cent of the population was at Woburn.

This species appears to be in a reasonably secure position.

6. WISENT	1964	1965	1966	1967	1968	1969	1970	1971
No. zoos reporting	45	58	64	61	70	82	74	76
Total population	177	234	248	258	249	281	283	303
Captive bred	146	145	154	182	192	193	212	232
Per cent captive bred	82	62	62	71	77	69	75	77
Births (surviving)	24 min	31	34	30	47	51	44	—
Individuals per collection	4	4	4	4	4	3	4	4

The total population has increased, the average per collection remaining static. Though the population increase has been slow, the species seems secure.

7. SCIMITAR-HORNED ORYX	1964	1965	1966	1967	1968	1969	1970	1971
No. zoos reporting	7	11	9	10	14	18	23	25
Total population	11	23	22	27	53	92	125	141
Captive bred	8	16	16	15	14	44	73	101
Per cent captive bred	73	70	73	56	26	48	58	72
Births (surviving)	4	4	8	5	26	23	29	—
Individuals per collection	2	2	2	3	4	5	6	6

The captive population of the scimitar-horned oryx has increased almost explosively since 1967, leaping from 27 to 141 individuals. From 1967 to 1968, the wild-caught population increased from 12 to 39, reaching a peak of 52 in 1970. Since 1968, the number of captive-bred individuals has risen from 14 to 101, and the percentage of captive-bred individuals has been rising rapidly. The average number of individuals per collection has also increased. If the trends continue, this species will be in a strong position for the future.

8. ADDAX	1964	1965	1966	1967	1968	1969	1970	1971
No. zoos reporting	12	17	18	19	17	21	24	27
Total population	59	63	55	72	75	93	126	142
Captive bred	30	42	32	42	31	58	81	116
Per cent captive bred	51	67	58	58	41	62	64	82
Births (surviving)	8	16	15	18	24	29	29	—
Individuals per collection	5	4	3	4	4	4	5	5

The reported wild-caught population has fluctuated from year to year, reaching a peak of 45 in 1970, declining to 26 in 1971. The captive-bred population has increased rapidly since 1968. While this species has not yet attained the total numbers of the wisent or Père David deer, the position is becoming stronger.

In seven of these eight cases, captive breeding seems to have established reasonable security for the species, or nearly so. It is interesting that seven of the eight are hoofed animals, which require more zoo space than most smaller mammals.

When the zoo-by-zoo data is analysed, it appears that the collections with the largest numbers of a species tend to produce disproportionately large shares of the births. One reason for this is that the general averages are depressed by the number of collections having only one sex. In a number of cases, an increase in the number of collections is accompanied by an apparent decline in the average birth rate. This may be because a collection just acquiring the species may not have both sexes or it may have acquired a pair not yet of breeding age.

Among the 33 other species in the initial table, a number show promising population increases. Five have total populations of more than 100. For nine others the percentage of captive bred exceeds 50. We have chosen nine additional cases from the 33, not by formula but because of their special interest:

1. GOLDEN MARMOSET	1964	1965	1966	1967	1968	1969	1970	1971
No. zoos reporting	ND	ND	23	27	28	24	23	20
Total population	ND	ND	72	99	102	96	84	76
Captive bred	ND	ND	6	8	19	22	34	39
Per cent captive bred	ND	ND	8	8	19	23	40	51
Births (surviving)	5 min	7	5	10	10	18	11	—
Individuals per collection	ND	ND	3	4	4	4	4	4

ND = No data available.

The population has decreased since 1968. While the percentage of captive-bred individuals has risen sharply, this is not in itself a hopeful sign. Since imports of new stock have been cut off, this percentage could rise to 100 per cent while the number in captivity approached zero.

2. ORANG-UTAN	1964	1965	1966	1967	1968	1969	1970	1971
No. zoos reporting	96	107	120	141	120	119	117	128
Total population	278	349	389	438	434	455	469	539
Captive bred	37	44	46	55	68	81	112	152
Per cent captive bred	13	13	12	13	16	18	24	28
Births (surviving)	6	9	21	19	28	28	30	—
Individuals per collection	3	3	3	3	4	4	4	5

The apparent population increase of 70 in 1971 was largely caused by reporting incongruities.

The percentage of captive-born individuals has been rising slowly, as has the number of births. The apparent birth rate has remained relatively stable since 1966.

Many wild-caught orang-utans were acquired within a few years preceding 1967. The wild-caught population outside Indonesia reached a peak in 1967 and is now slowly declining. Thus far, captive births have more than offset this decline, but it will be several years more before the likelihood of survival in captivity can be assessed.

3. SUMATRAN TIGER	1964	1965	1966	1967	1968	1969	1970	1971
No. zoos reporting	20	11	27	34	30	30	28	29
Total population	44	23	50	86	66	65	62	78
Captive bred	24	5	24	42	42	42	48	59
Per cent captive bred	55	22	48	49	64	65	77	76
Births (surviving)	1	6	7	18	12	9	12	—
Individuals per collection	2	2	2	3	2	2	2	3

While there have been reporting inconsistencies, the population decline following the 1967 peak seems to be real. The wild-caught total has declined from a peak of 44 to 19. The number of births has not significantly increased. The apparent birth rate over 7 years has been substantially below that of the Siberian tiger.

4. SNOW LEOPARD	1964	1965	1966	1967	1968	1969	1970	1971
No. zoos reporting	27	28	28	33	39	42	39	44
Total population	49	54	54	64	90	96	93	98
Captive bred	8	4	3	15	15	20	29	31
Per cent captive bred	16	7	6	23	17	21	31	32
Births (surviving)	3	1	6	15	7	10	7	—
Individuals per collection	2	2	2	2	2	2	2	2

The population of this species has increased chiefly through acquisitions from the wild. Only a modest increase has occurred since 1968. The number of births does not show an upward trend. The average number per collection has remained static, at two. Of the 44 collections, 11 had only one sex in 1971.

5. HARTMANN MOUNTAIN ZEBRA	1964	1965	1966	1967	1968	1969	1970	1971
No. zoos reporting	21	20	22	28	28	33	34	29
Total population	80	72	78	86	81	94	84	91 +
Captive bred	21	24	32	35	36	38	42	37 +
Per cent captive bred	26	33	41	41	44	40	50	41
Births (surviving)	9	7	14	10	9	9	10	—
Individuals per collection	4	4	4	3	3 min	3 min	2	3

Total population has fluctuated only slightly during this period. The captive-bred numbers have changed only slightly since 1967. Of the 29 collections, ten have only one sex. While 68 successful births were reported, the captive-born population increased by only 16.

6. BLACK RHINOCEROS	1964	1965	1966	1967	1968	1969	1970	1971
No. zoos reporting	63	66	72	68	67	72	71	65 +
Total population	113	124	132	126	126	136	130	128 +
Captive bred	18	16	23	21	21	24	27	28
Per cent captive bred	16	13	17	17	17	18	21	22
Births (surviving)	2	6	1	3	6	7	9	—
Individuals per collection	2	2	2	2	2	2	2	2

Total population fluctuated only slightly during the period. There was a modest increase in the number and percentage of zoo-born individuals. While 34 successful births were reported, the zoo-born total increased by only ten. The average number per collection remained static. Of the 65 collections reporting in 1971, 25 had only one sex.

7. PYGMY HIPPOPOTAMUS	1964	1965	1966	1967	1968	1969	1970	1971
No. zoos reporting	31	33	38	43	43	47	46	48
Total population	80	85	99	103 +	108	124	126	128 +
Captive bred	35	38	42	45	44	55	50	58 +
Per cent captive bred	44	45	42	44	41	44	40	45
Births (surviving)	6	12	7	3	11	5	8	—
Individuals per collection	3	3	3	2	3	3	3	3

This species came close to the arbitrary selection factors: 100 or more individuals, 50 per cent or more captive-born. In the period shown, the captive population increased by 48, the captive-born total by 23. The number of births reported during the period was 52.

The percentage of captive-born individuals remained remarkably static. Births averaged 7·4 per year, the actual number fluctuating from year to year. The apparent birth rate tended to decline. The average number per zoo remained static.

8. VICUÑA	1964	1965	1966	1967	1968	1969	1970	1971
No. zoos reporting	28	32	ND	ND	23	20	22	22
Total population	69	72	ND	ND	64	70	70	69
Captive bred	34	38	ND	ND	43	53	44	57
Per cent captive bred	49	53	—	—	67	76	63	83
Births (surviving)	7	4	7	4	10	3 min	5	—
Individuals per collection	2	2	—	—	3	4	3	3

ND = No data available.

The percentage of captive-bred individuals has risen, but total population has not increased. The number of births has fluctuated from year to year. Nine of the collections have only one sex.

9. ARABIAN ORYX	1964	1965	1966	1967	1968	1969	1970	1971
No. zoos reporting	4	4	5	5	6	5	4	4
Total population	27	27	39	49	44	48	58	75
Captive bred	2	7	10	9	9	18	18	49
Per cent captive bred	7	26	26	18	20	38	31	65
Births (surviving)	2	3 min	3 min	1	5	4	6	—
Individuals per collection	7	7	8	10	7	10	15	19

The increase from 1970 to 1971 in the number of captive-bred individuals is distorted by the report from Qatar, which failed to report this item in 1970, but reported 21 captive-bred animals in 1971. The significant increase is in the captive-bred totals for Phoenix and Los Angeles: from 18 in 1970 to 28 in 1971. For these two collections alone, the percentage of captive-bred individuals was 62 in 1970, 74 in 1971.

The total captive population has increased rapidly, with a significant increase in the average number per collection. Births show an upward trend.

On the record to date, zoos have not become a significant resource in the preservation of rare or endangered mammals. Seven species or subspecies endangered or extinct in the wild appear to have reasonably secure captive populations with potential for reintroduction. In a few other cases, favourable trends give promise of security in the near future. While these are important contributions, their number is small by comparison with IUCN's long and growing list.

The data also indicate that zoos can become a more significant resource. The chief deficiency is managerial, not scientific. Zoos have learned, over the years, how to keep most species alive and healthy in captivity, and how to breed them. Many of these species would undoubtedly multiply to satisfactory numbers if adequate breeding groups were brought together under proper conditions. While some species now present special problems, such as inadequate second-generation reproduction, most should be responsive to concerted efforts.

The troublesome problem is that many species which reproduce adequately under good management do not have self-sustaining captive populations.

That many zoos report only single males or single females is only part of the problem. A zoo with one of each does not necessarily have a breeding pair. The problem centres in the zoos that do the best job of propagation but, for lack of space, are compelled to dispose of offspring. Too often these offspring are sent to zoos with lesser resources and qualifications, zoos that may wish to have them only for exhibition.

A breeding pair may produce offspring for several years. Then, if the male or female is lost, no replacement may be readily at hand. Further, many zoo directors report difficulty in finding takers for their surplus. They might prefer to send their animals to excellent zoos that emphasize breeding, but such discrimination may not be possible. One zoo deliberately prevented matings of an endangered species because its pens were overcrowded by the previous year's surplus.

The capacity of zoos is limited, and most still emphasize diversity in collections. A random selection of ten leading zoos shows an average number of individuals per mammal species of 3·9, the range being from 3·1 to 4·6. Since this average includes over-age individuals, non-breeders, and juveniles, there are, inevitably, many situations without breeding potential.

Increased propagation of endangered species is feasible, but it may be stifled or become futile unless progeny can be accommodated in their natal zoos or in others willing and able to undertake further propagation. Room for growing numbers must be found, either by displacing more common species or by establishing rural survival centres.

A Cautionary Note on Breeding Endangered Species in Captivity

M. A. G. Warland

INTRODUCTION

Although I hesitate to throw cold water on the good intentions expressed at the Conference, I feel that it is necessary to take a careful look at the idea of breeding endangered species in captivity with a view to returning them subsequently to the wild. Certainly, if we judge by what has been achieved so far in this field, there is no room at all for complacency, and it may even be that breeding endangered species in captivity from this point of view is not particularly productive. With this somewhat subversive statement, I do not intend to imply that the Conference served no good purpose, nor that we should abandon our efforts at this stage, since we are in fact at least beginning to breed many of the species that were originally regarded as the most difficult. I have been asked to provide an outline of the policy of the Survival Service Commission of IUCN as far as the captive breeding of endangered species is concerned, and this is what I shall try to do in what follows. I shall examine the idea of captive breeding programmes in order to see to what extent conservation of the species in the wild state may benefit from them, and it should emerge from this that some of those concerned with conservation in the natural habitat may justifiably be rather sceptical about the present prospects of restocking areas which have been depleted of their natural fauna.

FUNCTIONS OF CAPTIVE BREEDING PROGRAMMES

Apart from providing a basis for biological studies under carefully controlled conditions, captive breeding programmes in general have as a main function, as Gerald Durrell has pointed out, the accumulation of a reservoir of material which is available either for exchange or sale purposes or for reintroduction into the wild.

At the present time, one of the most important practical contributions that zoos and other breeding centres can make to conservation is the establishment of captive stocks of endangered species for sale or exchange to other zoos, in order to reduce consumer demand on ever-decreasing stocks. For years now, the

Survival Service Commission (SSC) has been freely used by many zoos and other institutions to help them obtain specimens of endangered species, supposedly as a contribution to conservation. I feel that this can no longer be considered acceptable and the keeping of captive stock *per se* should not be considered as a vindication for the continued acquisition of specimens of endangered species from the wild. On balance, zoos are still undoubtedly consumers rather than producers of wildlife.

In summary, then, captive breeding of endangered species may reduce the demand on wild stock, increase the chances of success of husbandry techniques and provide a gene pool where measures taken to preserve the species in the wild have failed or are unable to be implemented in the foreseeable future.

THE SURVIVAL OF ENDANGERED SPECIES IN THE WILD

In my view, too little is known of the practical problems of returning animals to the wild, for this to be, currently, an important function of captive breeding programmes for endangered species. Furthermore, the original habitat remains more often than not totally unstable, both ecologically and politically, and this is usually the prime reason for the scarcity of attempted reintroduction schemes. This is an aspect which is naturally of tremendous concern to the Survival Service Commission of IUCN.

The policy of this Commission is to prevent the extinction of species and ultimately to rebuild their wild populations to a level at which they can once more play their natural roles in the habitats or ecosystems of which they form a part. This, by definition, implies the support of appropriate protective laws and regulations, preservation of habitat and the maintenance of genetic diversity. Captive breeding therefore may at times be found necessary to implement this policy in order to prevent the loss of genetic material and to rebuild wild populations, whilst the necessary field action is being taken.

In most cases, however, captive breeding can only be considered a complement to broader conservation measures—a kind of insurance policy. It is also a means of restoring those species whose response to other measures has been inadequate for them to survive—a last resort measure. Accordingly, captive breeding itself is only *one* part of a larger operation of capture, breeding and return to the wild, and it is therefore incomplete without the third element. I therefore submit that any captive breeding programme should be accompanied by concomitant and parallel programmes for the rehabilitation of the natural habitat, both ecologically and politically.

In view of the *kudos* and profit which zoos and related institutions obtain for exhibiting endangered species, I do feel that they should be prepared to play some part in contributing financially to the action taken to prepare these habitats for the return of the surplus stock built up, or to improve the habitat for the remaining stock. It is because of this lack of attention to preparation of the habitat that precious little has been achieved in successfully restoring stocks of endangered species to their original biotopes.

To date, breeding programmes for endangered species in captivity have resulted in only a few successful reintroductions; the Hawaiian goose, Swinhoe's and Cheer pheasants, certain New Zealand island birds and the European bison may be cited as the chief examples. Furthermore, some endangered species can be bred only with the greatest difficulty under captive conditions, because we lack knowledge of their social and environmental requirements. It is recognized, however, that the captive breeding of endangered animals has proved more successful in recent years and it does provide a means of improving this knowledge which, in turn, will increase the chances of success in larger-scale captive breeding programmes.

LONG-TERM IMPLICATIONS OF CAPTIVE BREEDING UNDERTAKINGS FOR ENDANGERED SPECIES

Let us see how, in the future, we can best use all our resources, on a thoroughly coordinated and cooperative basis, for promoting the long-term survival of species in the wild, which, after all, is (or certainly should be) the main concern of the participants of the present Conference. It has been suggested that serious attempts at captive breeding and rehabilitation programmes should be coordinated by a central body. In fact IUCN, through its SSC, is probably the central body at present best equipped to deal with this problem, but it should then either be the only operator in this field, or at least be able to coordinate the activities of others.

What are the basic requirements of a captive breeding programme for endangered species? Above all, the greatest possible care should always be taken to preserve the species in a form as near to its wild state as possible and to maintain those characteristics which particularly fit it for life in the wild.

Sir Otto Frankel, an eminent Australian geneticist, has stated that "wild species can only be preserved in the context of communities within their natural habitats. By way of contrast, botanical or zoological gardens provide habitats akin to domestication with a crucial difference that wild animals and plants in captivity are deprived of the range of genetic variation which the breeder provides under domestication. Hence, even botanical or zoological gardens with semi-natural conditions cannot provide for more than relatively short term survival of wild species". He went on to state that any restriction of variation tends to restrict evolutionary potential. We would do well to mark these words and to remember that captive breeding is in fact a relatively short-term solution, or only the first phase of a solution. We cannot continue captive breeding through successive generations indefinitely, if we wish to return to the wild an animal that closely resembles its forebears.

Captive breeding programmes of course usually require heavy investment in special facilities and trained personnel. Some animals are unlikely to breed in the confines of a cage, and conditions that more nearly resemble their natural habitats may have to be provided. Too little remains known of the social, psychological and habitat requirements of many captive animals. Moreover, captive stock should be distributed amongst a small number of captive breeding centres to minimize the risk of a catastrophe befalling the entire stock. One-third of the herd of Arabian oryx in Qatar has died from an epidemic. This would of course have been disastrous if the surviving stock were to be found only in Qatar, but fortunately there are two more herds elsewhere.

CRITERIA FOR INCLUSION IN SCC-SUPPORTED PROGRAMMES FOR CAPTIVE BREEDING OF ENDANGERED SPECIES

In summary, the SSC, in a recent policy statement on the subject, has stated that the following conditions should be fulfilled by any sound captive breeding programme:

(i) captive breeding is essential for obtaining information which may further the survival of the species, or necessary for finding out how to perpetuate a vanishing form in its natural habitat;

(ii) the effects of the capture operation on the total wild population have been assessed;

(iii) capture follows the principles expressed in the SSC's policy statement "The capture of rare or endangered animals", published in September 1970;

(iv) the professional competence of the individual in charge of husbandry and the skill of the auxiliary staff are exceptional;

(v) the physical facilities, including special requirements for housing, exercise, observation, record-keeping and veterinary treatment, are of a sufficiently high standard;

(vi) there is evidence that the programme will not be discontinued prematurely for lack of funds or other reasons;

(vii) terms can be agreed upon for the number of captive animals to be maintained, for the distribution of surplus animals, and for the numbers (in proportion to captive-bred stock) that should be made available for reintroduction purposes;

(viii) provision has been made for an effectively planned studbook;

(ix) cooperation in efforts to improve the original habitat prior to the return of surplus animals is reasonably assured.

Most of the programmes concerned are being, or would be, undertaken by zoological gardens and it is within the context of the SSC Zoo Liaison Group that I believe such coordination should take place. With our present very limited resources, however, this is clearly impossible. A project has been elaborated by SSC which allows for the expansion, reorganization and coordination of the Zoo Liaison Group of SSC. The objective is to promote more active participation by zoos in conservation work. We hope to be able to employ a full-time coordinator for the Zoo Liaison Group, and amongst his numerous functions would be the coordination of captive breeding programmes for certain species, including the selective allocation of breeding nuclei to specialist zoos. In other words, for an SSC-sponsored breeding programme, certain zoos would be selected which have proved themselves to be the most expert in raising a particular species, or a closely related taxon. The coordinator would also be responsible for monitoring the disposal of the offspring from the programme and helping in arrangements for the re-establishment of the animals in the wild and for coordinating the placing and acquisition of individual animals, especially endangered species, in zoos which request them.

We believe that this is a real breakthrough as far as coordinating the conservation efforts of zoos is concerned, and we hope very much that the Conference participants will be sufficiently interested to participate in this scheme.

I hope that this statement will provide food for thought, and that it will ultimately contribute to the survival of some of our most critically endangered species—a survival which all the conference participants have close to their hearts, and towards which we are all working in the long run.

ADDENDUM

The Survival Service Commission of IUCN is still in the process of formulating its policy with respect to the breeding of endangered species in captivity. Those interested in obtaining more recent information should write to: *The Survival Service Commission, International Union for Conservation of Nature*, 1110 *Morges, Switzerland.*

Conclusions

Peter Scott

In summing up the proceedings of this first international conference on the breeding of endangered species in captivity, I should like to start by referring to two symbols. One is the dodo, symbol of the Jersey Wildlife Preservation Trust, and the other is the oryx, emblem of the Fauna Preservation Society. Aptly enough, the first is an animal which has gone for ever, whilst the second is an animal which is in very great danger. If we can prevent the second joining the first before *both* become symbols of extinction, then we have been carrying out part of our overall task.

In one of the contributions to the meeting, we had a very controversial comment made by the Secretary of the Survival Service Commission (Moira Warland), indicating that she had yet to be convinced that we are not wasting our time. Of course, we must recognize that we have to maintain some kind of continuing dialogue between a number of people with somewhat extreme views at both ends of the scale. At one end are the extreme conservationists who simply claim that zoos are a drain on wild populations and that they have not so far managed to maintain their captive animal stocks without repeated replenishment from the wild. They maintain that there is no real evidence that zoos can breed animals and return them to the wild, and that their managers are mainly concerned about conservation because it is the fashionable thing to be concerned about. At the other end of the scale you find a certain number of zoo people claiming that the conservationists are a collection of cranks who are only out to interfere with their business, and proclaiming that zoos should have nothing to do with them. But there is a middle line along which I am sure we can achieve a real measure of cooperation between zoos and conservationists and also, of course, a measure of cooperation between one zoo and another, because this is one of the important requirements that was repeatedly emphasized during the Conference.

I was delighted, as I am sure many people were, with the high quality of the papers presented to the Conference. I believe that it has been positively and quite convincingly established that wild animals *can* be bred in captivity and that more and more species will be bred in the future. Captive breeding is therefore a practical tool for the conservation of endangered species and one of the most hopeful features about it is to realize how many of the species discussed in detail at the Conference were thought to be impossible to breed until a few years ago.

Flamingos provide just one example; although possibly none of the species is threatened with extinction immediately, they are all vulnerable because they are so specialized, and ten years ago it was widely held that it would never be possible to breed flamingos in captivity. To date, four out of the six world species have been bred in captivity and we hope that we shall soon be able to breed the other two as well. This shows what can be done, and every success represents another advance in the field of captive breeding. John Perry has quoted the example of the passenger pigeon with the sad observation that it actually bred freely, or could be persuaded to breed freely, in captivity; but nobody cared at the time and so it disappeared. But now the climate of opinion has changed very sharply. A lot more people now feel very strongly about preserving species and preventing extinction.

At this stage, I feel it might be helpful to consider some of the basic principles. To my mind, there are four essential principles, which can perhaps be taken in the following order of priority. The first is to prevent extinction at all costs; the second is to know how to release rare animals back into the wild; the

FIGURE 1. A Caribbean flamingo chick (*Phoenicopterus ruber ruber*) taking food when a few days old. This chick was hatched at Slimbridge in June 1968 and was the first flamingo to be successfully reared in Britain. (Photo: J. A. Middleton.)

third is to reduce the present drain on wild populations; and the fourth is to educate the public. With respect to captive maintenance itself, I would like to enumerate four additional principles which were put forward by Dr. Brambell as a basis for breeding of all wild animals in captivity: "Breeding of wild animals in captivity depends on: (1) understanding the biology of the species; (2) having enough animals of suitable age and sex; (3) providing sufficient space, facilities and management; (4) re-distributing stock to ensure continual mixing of the gene pool". The latter point is one which was not discussed to any great extent, but it is surely an important one to bear in mind. These principles, which emerged at various points in the Conference, would seem to summarize the general feelings of the participants.

There were some very good examples of how important specialists can be and of the fact that when those concerned really set their minds to it in nearly every case they discover suitable methods. I was greatly impressed with Christian Schmidt's report on the survival of young vicuñas in captivity, which apparently substantially exceeds the survival of young wild vicuñas. But of course in every situation there is the problem of priorities and the problem of money. Money is itself a question of priority, because for conservation money is very short. It is just a question of what we think the highest priorities are and there will be continuous argument between those who feel that the money is best spent in the field protecting the natural habitat and those who feel that we would be best advised to concentrate on captive breeding. But I think that when there are good cases for maintenance in captivity there should be applications to the various conservation organizations, including the World Wildlife Fund. Such projects should be put forward for support, though I am hoping very much that the zoos themselves will feel it is worth contributing in a fairly big way to these programmes so as to be able to produce animals suitable for eventual return to the wild. I am sure we need more breeding groups of most of the species discussed than exist at present, and I would like to suggest that we should not really be happy about the situation until there are separate colonies of each species established in at least five places and preferably ten.

Some discussion was held on the question of whether it was worth spending much time on subspecies, as opposed to full species, and indeed Mr. Watt referred particularly to this topic. It is, perhaps, an ivory tower, but I think that many of us feel a certain reverence for the processes of evolution. A subspecies is, after all, an incipient species, the birth of a new species, and to me it is very important to preserve it. If we can preserve subspecies, I think we should do it even at the expense of the love-life of unfortunate hybrid orang-utans in captivity. I feel that it is important to establish this as a matter of policy.

Now I believe that we ought to try to establish more specialist zoos of the kind that has been founded in Jersey, because this is a specialist zoo for endangered species. There may be other zoos that could be specialists on certain subjects. One example is Great Witchingham; the Pheasant Trust has had tremendous success with pheasants. The Wildfowl Trust at Slimbridge has also achieved a certain amount with ducks and geese. These are the kinds of specialist zoos which I think should be set up in greater numbers, and I think the public will demand to have more of such zoos and rather less of the comprehensive zoos, which have to have one of each of everything that they can get their hands on. I think another equally important thing is *continuity*. It has to be assured that any programme is taken up in a way which will guarantee that it is going to continue for a reasonable number of years. This will immediately encourage scientists to become involved in the programmes and, incidentally, it will also encourage finance towards the projects because they have guaranteed continuity.

I was going to devote some space to discussing the public's attitude to zoos and to safari parks, which was briefly discussed during the Conference. However, I am not sure that I should really spend much time on this topic, except to say that I did not wholeheartedly agree with Dr. Crowcroft's comments about what the motivations should be and what is respectable in terms of zoos or safari parks. I feel that the primary motivation should concern the welfare and husbandry of the animals; any zoo which does not go along with this is courting trouble from the public, who demand high standards in this respect. Of course it is very rash and difficult to try to discover other people's motivations; they are very deep down and may start by being one thing and change to another. Some people may start by going into the zoo business purely for the money and come out devoted to animals, so one cannot really tell how things are going to turn out; but I think that the first thing to create is a heaven for the animals. I say a "heaven" rather than a "paradise" because, as is common knowledge, the origin of the word paradise lies in a Persian word meaning "a hunting park". I think, then, that creating a heaven for the animals is the first priority. Of course, animals do not really associate bars with prisons and they are quite happy as long as there is something nice to walk or climb on, for they do not really notice that the environment is artificial. Nevertheless, the visitors immediately equate bars with a prison, and therefore one has to take special measures to try to avoid this impression. There is, of course, the well-known line of Robert Burns: "A robin redbreast in a cage sets all heaven in a rage"; but robins live longer in cages than they do anywhere else and they are probably perfectly happy. The trouble about alternatives to cages is that they are only occasionally possible and almost always they are extremely expensive. The moat system, which is wonderful for hoofed mammals, large predators, etc., is all very well; but it does cost a great deal of money to install.

It was mentioned during the Conference by Bob Martin that breeding in captivity is a pretty good yardstick for the well-being of animals, and I think he is probably right. Of course, especially among the primates, one cannot entirely dismiss the possibility that they breed because they are *bored* and therefore there should probably be a good deal more study on boredom than is being conducted at the present time. Information on this would be useful for human animals as well as for the higher apes.

There are those who believe that the days of zoos may well be numbered except in the context of the plans discussed at the present Conference, once three-dimensional colour television comes in. If one can look at an animal on the "telly" at home, seeing it in 3-D and colour in its wild habitat in perfect reproduction, this will always be considerably better than seeing the animal in any kind of a cage. But finally one is left with the one basic fact that 3-D television animals cannot be bred, and this vital function remains for the zoos. There is just one further point about cages in a zoo, or captivity as such, which is that in many cases confinement may be necessary for the safety of the animal. The animal may be at such risk where it is, for example in a place where the forest is being cleared, that captivity is actually the best thing for its safety, quite apart from the question of rehabilitating it afterwards.

Various points were raised in discussions about returning to the wild animals which are too inexperienced to survive, as might be the case with large cats lacking experience with natural prey. I think there is one other vital point which was only covered to some extent (in the Hawaiian goose paper by Janet Kear) and that is the return to the wild of animals which are too tame, which are too familiar with human beings and are no longer frightened of them, which they ought to be in order to survive.

This brings me to the ways in which we can perhaps profit from the dialogue conducted at the Conference. At the meeting of the Survival Service Commission which was held just before the Conference, there was discussion of a new project for the coordination of a Zoo Liaison Group of the Survival Service Commission. Dr. Brambell, in his paper, suggested the formation of a pragmatic group not afraid to say where any particular animal should go to increase breeding prospects. I think that a group of this kind is precisely what is needed, though it is obvious that this kind of group can never succeed unless it has the wholehearted trust and cooperation of both sides in the equation.

One other element in the communication and coordination field is, naturally, the *International Zoo Year Book*. Its Editor, Nicole Duplaix-Hall, has played an active part in the Conference and she is an extremely dynamic young lady who plans to make the *Year Book* a really good means of communication between all concerned on both sides of the discussions involving conservation and captive breeding.

It is necessary to mention something about the politics of these plans for captive breeding. If we only had to breed animals and to discover how best to do this, we would not have any troubles at all. All of our troubles really stem from people, and when one gets down to basic facts it is always a question of politics at some level. It may be international politics or national politics or local politics or personal politics or simply practical politics, but at any rate there is always some kind of political problem to overcome and this is what has to be achieved somehow in every case. This is brought out by one of the suggestions which was made, by Christian Schmidt, during the closing session of the Conference.

There is a case in point to bring together the rare cranes dispersed in European zoos. These single birds are not serving any purpose, and they are a blight on the landscape of a conservation-conscious zoo. Larger groups would allow these singletons to choose a mate, and the pairs could then be returned to the collections which contributed their stock originally.

This is a clever idea for a particular case, where you lend your bird and just wait for it to pair up, so that everybody benefits eventually. But it is a situation where the political problems must be solved along with the biological ones.

On another tack, Bob Martin pointed out the need for an experiment, and produced a recommendation which can be dealt with as an in-house recommendation within the conservation movement:

> In order to test the practical value of returning captive bred stocks to the wild it is proposed that a pilot experiment should be set up as soon as possible to expand on information available from reintroductions which have already been carried out. The project should involve animals of a suitable species, not necessarily one which is at present under threat of extinction, which could be marked, released and intensively observed over a long period in a suitable area incorporating the natural habitat conditions of that species. The experiment would require continuous supervision from ecologists, geneticists and other specialist observers in order to monitor the long term consequences and level of success of return of a captive colony to the wild. In view of the great importance of such an experimental project the Conference is invited to recommend that high priority should be given in the allocation of funds to such a venture.

I feel that this is a very important suggestion, though I am not too sure how highly one should rate the priority of such a plan in comparison with measures to protect an animal species actually on the verge of extinction. This is certainly something that we ought to consider very seriously and I would like to put this forward as an in-house resolution to IUCN. and to the World Wildlife Fund.

I should like to refer very briefly to the message sent to the Jersey Conference by Dr. Maurice Strong, the Secretary-General of the Stockholm Conference held in June 1972, since it should be made clear how important and significant this is. The Stockholm Conference on the Human Environment was an inter-governmental conference attended by political leaders from countries all over the world, and many people regard it as being one of the most important conferences ever held for the future of mankind. To have an expression of opinion from the Secretary-General of that conference on our particular subject of breeding endangered species is a sort of opening of the door. The door is slightly ajar for us and we should be able to follow this up and get the door a little wider open.

It has been suggested, specifically by Gerald Durrell, that there should be a repeat of the Jersey Conference in 2 or 3 years' time. I am not sure of the general feeling about the optimum interval that should elapse between conferences. My personal view is that the interval should be 3 or 4 years, and I think that possibly a gap of less than 3 years might be a mistake.

Finally we come to the main Conference resolution, the Jersey Declaration, which was submitted to the participants at the closing session for discussion and amendment. It brings together the important principles which have been accepted by those who took part in the first international conference of the breeding of endangered species in captivity:

The Jersey Declaration
on Breeding Endangered Species
as an Aid to their Survival

The Conference on Breeding of Endangered Species as an Aid to their Survival, held in Jersey from 1 to 3 May 1972, DECLARES THAT:

1. The breeding of endangered species and subspecies of animals in captivity is likely to be crucial to the survival of many forms. It must therefore be used as a method of preventing extinction, alongside the maintenance of the wild stocks in their natural habitat.

2. The techniques must be learnt, improved, extended and published.

3. All who keep endangered species have a responsibility to carry out breeding programmes and to cooperate both with other zoos or collections for this purpose and with conservationists in returning them to the wild.

4. Such programmes will reduce the demands being made currently on wild populations and may serve to re-inforce them, or, if they have disappeared in the wild, to re-establish them.

5. Even if reintroduction ultimately proves to be impossible, maintaining a captive population is obviously superior to the irrevocable alternative of extinction.

6. As an additional point we urge that wherever possible breeding programmes be encouraged and supported in habitats or regions natural to the endangered species. This does not in any way imply a desire to supplant those programmes that are currently under way, but there are important reasons for carrying out such programmes in the natural areas of distribution. One important consideration is the education of the indigenous population, who otherwise may not completely understand the significance, the requirements, or the future of the animals, upon which they themselves will depend.

References

ADAMSON, J. (1969). "The Spotted Sphinx." Collins & Harvill, London.

ANDREYEVA, E. G. (1939). Analiz struktury kostnoj tkani v poljarizovanom svete na primere izučenija pjasti lošadi Przevalskogo. *Trudy Inst. evoljuc morfol.* **2**, 23–37.

ATKINSON, I. A. E. (1964). Feeding stations and food of North Island saddleback in August. *Notornis* **11**, 93–97.

ATKINSON, I. A. E. (1966a). Feeding stations and food of North Island saddleback in May. *Notornis* **13**, 7–11.

ATKINSON, I. A. E. (1966b). Identification of feeding stations of forest birds in New Zealand. *Notornis* **13**, 12–17.

ATKINSON, I. A. E. and CAMPBELL, D. J. (1966). Aspects of the habitat of saddlebacks on Hen Island. *Proc. N.Z. Ecol. Soc.* **13**, 35–40.

BATES, H. W. (1864). "The Naturalist on the River Amazon." John Murray, London.

BAUDY, R. E. (1970). In quest of *Geochelona radiata*. *Int. Turt. Tort. Soc. J.* **4**, 19–23, 27.

BEMMEL, A. C. V. VAN (1968). Breeding tigers at Rotterdam Zoo. *Int. Zoo Yearb.* **8**, 60–63.

BENNETT, J. P. (1967a). The induction of ovulation in the squirrel monkey (*Saimiri sciureus*) with pregnant mare's serum (PMS) and human chorionic gonadotrophin (HCG). *J. Reprod. Fert.* **13**, 357.

BENNETT, J. P. (1967b). Artificial insemination of the squirrel monkey. *J. Endocrinol.* **37**, 473.

BEVERIDGE, W. I. B. (ed.) (1972). "Breeding Primates." Karger, Basel.

BLACKBURN, A. (1964). Some observations on behaviour of the North Island saddleback in August. *Notornis* **11**, 87–92. *

BLACKBURN, A. (1966). Notes on the breeding behaviour of North Island saddleback. *Notornis* **13**, 185–8.

BLACKBURN, A. (1967). Feeding stations and food of the North Island saddleback in November. *Notornis* **14**, 67–70.

BLANCHARD, F. N. and FINSTER, E. B. (1933). A method of marking live snakes for future recognition, with a discussion of some problems and results. *Ecology* **14**, 334–47.

BOWMAN, R. I. (1960). "Report on a biological reconnaissance of the Galápagos Islands during 1957." UNESCO Report, Paris.

BRAZAITIS, P. (1969). The determination of sex in living crocodilians. *Brit. J. Herpetol.* **4**, 54–58.

BRUCE, H. M. (1963a). Olfactory block to pregnancy among grouped mice. *J. Reprod. Fertil.* **6**, 451–60.

BRUCE, H. M. (1963b). A comparison of olfactory stimulation and nutritional stress as pregnancy-blocking agents in mice. *J. Reprod. Fertil.* **6**, 221–7.

BUSTARD, H. R. (1969). Tail abnormalities in reptiles resulting from high temperature egg incubation. *Brit. J. Herpetol.* **4**, 121–3.

BUSTARD, H. R. (1971). Temperature and water tolerance of incubating crocodile eggs. *Brit. J. Herpetol.* **4**, 198–200.

CALABY, J. H. (1971). Kangaroos and men. *Austral. Zool.* **16**, 17–31.

CARR, A. (1952). "Handbook of Turtles: The turtles of the United States, Canada and Baja California." Cornell University Press, Ithaca.

CHABRECK, R. H. (1967). Alligator farming hints. *Publ. Louisiana Wildlife and Fisheries Comm.* 1–21.

CHABRECK, R. H. (1971). Management of the American alligator. *Spec. IUCN Publ., n.s., suppl.* **32**, 137–44.

CHARLES-DOMINIQUE, P. and HLADIK, M. (1971). Le *Lepilemur* du Sud de Madagascar: écologie, alimentation et vie sociale. *Terre et Vie* **25**, 3–66.

CHRISTIAN, J. J. (1950). The adreno-pituitary system and population cycles in mammals. *J. Mammal.* **31**, 247–59.

CHRISTIAN, J. J. (1963). The pathology of overpopulation. *Milit. Med.* **128**, 571–603.

COIMBRA-FILHO, A. F. (1969). Mico-leao, *Leontideus rosalia* (Linnaeus, 1766), Situaco actual da espercie no Brazil (Callithricidae—Primates). *An. Acad. brasil. Ciênc.* **41** (suppl), 29–52.

COLLINS, L. R. (1973). "Monotremes and Marsupials: a reference for zoological institutions." Smithsonian Institution (Washington) Publication 4888.

CONAWAY, C H. and SORENSON, M. W. (1965). Reproduction in tree shrews. *In* "Comparative Biology of Reproduction in Mammals", I. W. Rowlands (ed.). Academic Press, New York and London.

CORBET, P. S. (1959). Notes on the insect food of the Nile crocodile in Uganda. *Proc. Roy. Ent. Soc., Lond. A.* **34**: 17–22.

COTT, H. B. (1961). Scientific results of an inquiry into the ecology and economic status of the Nile crocodile (*Crocodylus niloticus* L.) in Uganda and Northern Rhodesia. *Trans. Zool. Soc. Lond.* **29**, 211–356.

CRANDALL, L. S. (1964). "Management of Wild Animals in Captivity." University of Chicago Press, Chicago.

D'SOUZA, F. and MARTIN, R. D. (1974). Maternal behaviour and the effects of stress in tree shrews. *Nature, Lond.* **251**, 309–11.

DEBLOCK, R. (1973). "Crâniometrie comparée de *Pan paniscus* et *Pan troglodytes*." Doctoral thesis, University of Lille.

DEDE, J. A. and PLENTL, A. A. (1966). Induced ovulation and artificial insemination in a rhesus colony. *Fert. Steril.* **17**, 757.

DELACOUR, J. (1951). "The Pheasants of the World." Country Life, London.

DELACOUR, J. (1954, 1956, 1959, 1964). "The Waterfowl of the World." (4 vols.). Country Life, London.

DUKELOW, W. R. (1970). Induction and timing of single and multiple ovulations in the squirrel monkey (*Saimiri sciureus*). *J. Reprod. Fert.* **22**, 303.

DUKELOW, W. R. (1971). Semen and artificial insemination. *In* "Comparative Reproduction of Laboratory Primates." Hafez, E. S. E. (ed.). C. C. Thomas, Florida.

DUPLAIX-HALL, N. (1972). Notes on maintaining river otters in captivity. *Int. Zoo Yearb.* **12**, 178–81.

EIBL-EIBESFELDT, I. (1959). Survey on the Galápagos Islands. *UNESCO Mission Reports* **8**, 1–31.

EIBL-EIBESFELDT, I. (1961). "Galápagos—Noah's Ark of the Pacific." Doubleday, New York.

ENCKE, W. (1960). Birth and rearing of cheetah at Krefeld Zoo. *Int. Zoo Yearb.* **2**, 85.

EPPLE, G. (1970). Maintenance, breeding and development of marmoset monkeys (Callithricidae) in captivity. *Folia primat.* **12**, 56–76.

ERICKSON, R. C. (1968). A federal research programme for endangered wildlife. *Trans. N.A. Wildlife Nat. Res. Conf.* **33**, 418–433.

ERNST, C. H. (1971). Observations on the egg and hatchling of the American turtle *Chrysemys picta*. *Brit. J. Herpetol.* **4**, 224–8.

FIEDLER, W. and WENDT, H. (1967). *In* "Grzimeks Tierleben." **10**, *Säugetiere* 1. Kindler Verlag, Munich.

FLORIO, P. L. and SPINELLI, L. (1967). Successful breeding of cheetah in a private zoo. *Int. Zoo Yearb.* **7**, 151.

FLORIO, P. L. and SPINELLI, L. (1968). Second successful breeding of cheetahs. *Int. Zoo Yearb.* **8**, 76.

FRANCOEUR, R. T. (1970). "Utopian Motherhood." Doubleday, New York.

FRANCOEUR, R. T. (1972). Experimental embryology and endangered animal species. *Bull. Atom. Sci.* **28**, 11.

FRANCOEUR, R. T. (1974). "Utopian Motherhood: New Trends in Human Reproduction." (2nd ed.) A. S. Barnes, Perpetua, New Jersey.

FRANKLIN, W. L. (1969). "Peru's New Vicuña Laws and Their Significance." (Manuscript).

FUSSELL, E. N., ROUSSEL, J. D. and AUSTIN, C. R. (1967). Use of the rectal probe method for electrical ejaculation of apes, monkeys and a prosimian. *Lab. Anim. Care* **17**, 528.

GANDRAS, R. and ENCKE, W. (1966). Case histories of a breeding group of cheetahs. *Int. Zoo Yearb.* **6**, 275.

GILMAN, S. C. (1969). Relationships between internal resistance stimulation voltage, and electroejaculation in the pigtail monkey (*Macaca nemestrina*): a preliminary report. *Lab. Anim. Care* **19**, 800.

GOIN, C. J. and GOIN, O. B. (1962). "Introduction to Herpetology." Freeman Co., San Francisco.

GREGOIRE, A. T. and MAYER, R. C. (1965). The impregnators. *Fert. Steril.* **16**, 130.

GRIMWOOD, I. R. (1963). Operation Oryx. *Anim. Kingd.* **66**, 115–21.

GRIMWOOD, I. R. (1967). Operation Oryx: The three stages of captive breeding. *Oryx* **9**, 110–18.

GRIMWOOD, I. R. (1969). Notes on the distribution and status of some Peruvian mammals, 1968. *N.Y. Zool. Soc., Spec. Pub.* **21**.

GROEBEN, G. VAN DEN (1932). Das Zuchtbuch. *Ber. d. Internat. Ges. z. Erhalt. d. Wisents* **5**, 7–50 (Berlin).

HAFEZ, E. S. E. (1968). Animal reproduction and artificial insemination. *Science* **162**, 703.

HAMPTON, J. K. Jnr., HAMPTON, S. H. and LANDWEHR, B. T. (1966). Observations on a successful breeding colony of the marmoset *Oedipomidas oedipus*. *Folia primat.* **4**, 265–287.

HARRISSON, B. (ed.) (1971). Conservation of non-human primates in 1970. *Primates in Medicine* **5**. Karger, Basel.

HEDIGER, H. (1942). "Wildtiere in Gefangenschaft." Benno Schwabe, Basel.

HEDIGER, H. (1950). "Wild Animals in Captivity." Butterworths, London.

HEDIGER, H. (1962). Tierpsychologische Beobachtungen aus dem Terrarium des Zürcher Zoos. *Rev. Suisse Zool.* **69**, 317–24.

HEDIGER, H. (1965). Environmental factors influencing the reproduction of zoo animals. *In* "Sex and Behaviour." Vol. 2, pp. 319–54, Beach, F. A. (ed.). John Wiley, New York.

HENDRICKSON, J. R. (1966). The Galápagos Tortoise, *Geochelone* Fitzinger 1835 (*Testudo* Linnaeus 1758 in part). *Proc. Symp. Galápagos Int. Sci. Proj.*, 252–7. University of California Press, Berkeley.

HENDRICKSON, J. R. and WEBER, W. A. (1964). Lichens on Galápagos giant tortoises. *Science* **144**, 1463.

HILZHEIMER, M. (1926). "Natürliche Rassengeschichte der Haussäugetiere." Berlin and Leipzig.

HOLST, D. VON (1969). Sozialer Stress bei Tupajas (*Tupaia belangeri*). *Z.f. vergl. Physiol.* **63**, 1–58.

HOLST, D. VON (1972a). Renal failure as the cause of death in *Tupaia belangeri* exposed to persistent social stress. *Z.f. vergl. Physiol.* **78**, 236–73.

HOLST, D. VON (1972b). Die Funktion der Nebennieren männlicher *Tupaia belangeri*. *Z.f. vergl. Physiol.* **78**, 289–306.

HOLST, D. VON (1974). Social stress in the tree shrew (*Tupaia belangeri*), its causes and physiological and ethological consequences. *In* "Prosimian Biology." Martin, R. D., Doyle, G. A. and Walker, A. C. (eds.). Duckworth, London.

HONEGGER, R. E. (1970a). Beitrag zur Fortpflanzungsbiologie einiger tropischer Reptilien. *Freunde Kölner Zoo* **13**, 175–9.

HONEGGER, R. E. (1970b). Beitrag zur Fortpflanzungsbiologie von *Boa constrictor* und *Python reticulatus* (Reptilia, Boidae). *Salamandra* **6**, 73–79.

HONEGGER, R. E. (1970c). "Red Data Book. 3: Amphibia and Reptilia." IUCN, Morges.

HONEGGER, R. E. (1971). Zoo breeding and crocodile bank. *Spec. IUCN. Pub., n.s., suppl.* **32**, 86–97.

HONEGGER, R. E. and HEUSSER, H. (1969). Beiträge zum Verhaltensinventar des Bindenwarans (*Varanus salvator*). *Zool. Gart.* (N.F.) **36**, 251–60.

HONEGGER, R. E. and SCHMIDT, C. R. (1964). Beiträge zur Haltung und Zucht verschiedener Reptilien. *Aquar. Terr. Z.* **17**, 339–42.

HOUSE OF REPRESENTATIVES COMMITTEE ON WILDLIFE CONSERVATION (1971). Interim report: Conservation and Commercial Exploitation of Kangaroos. Parliamentary Press, Canberra.

HÜBSCH, I. (1970). Einiges zum Verhalten der Zwergschimpansen (*Pan paniscus*) und der Schimpansen (*Pan troglodytes*) im Frankfurter Zoo. *Zool. Gart.* (N.F.) **38**, 107–32.

HUEY, W. S. (1963). New Mexico ducks return, *New Mexico Wildlife* **8**, 18–19.

HYDE, D. O. (1968). "Sandy." Dial Press, New York.

IPPEN, R. (1965). Reptilienerkrankungen. *7. Int. Symp. Erkrankungen Zootiere, Zürich and Basel* 66–71. Akademie-Verlag, Berlin.

IPPEN, R. (1967). Die Krankheiten des Verdauungsapparates der Reptilien. *9th Int. Symp. Erkrankungen Zootiere, Prague* 33–42. Akademie-Verlag, Berlin.

IPPEN, R. (1968). Die Erkerankungen des Respirationsapparates bei Reptilien. *10th Int. Symp. Erkrankungen Zootiere, Salzburg* 37–44. Akademie-Verlag, Berlin.

IPPEN, R. (1971). Zur Problematik des Parasitenbefalls bei Reptilien. *13th Int. Symp. Erkrankungen Zootiere, Helsinki* 173–86. Akademie-Verlag, Berlin.

JACKSON, M. M., JACKSON, C. G. and FULTON, M. (1969). Investigation of the enteric bacteria of the Testudinata-I: Occurrence of the general *Arizona, Citrobacter, Edwardsiella* and *Salmonella. Bull. Wildlife Dis. Ass.* **5**, 328–29.

JACKSON, C. G. and JACKSON, M. M. (1971). The frequency of *Salmonella* and *Arizona* microorganisms in zoo turtles. *J. Wildlife. Dis. Ass.* **7**, 130–2.

JACOBI, E. F. (1968). Breeding facilities for polar bears, *Thalarctos maritimus* (Phipps 1774) in captivity. *Bijdr. t. Dierk.* **38**, 39–46.

JOANEN, T. and McNEASE, L. (1971). Propagation of the American alligator in captivity. *Proc. 25. Conf. S.E. Assoc. Game Fish Comm.* 1–23.

JONES, M. L. (1972). "Preliminary Studbook for the Golden Lion Marmoset (*Leontopithecus rosalia*)." (Manuscript: American Association of Zoological Parks and Aquariums.)

JOSHI, P. N. (1967). Reproduction of *Python sebae. Brit. J. Herp.* **3**, 310–11.

JUNGIUS, H. (1971). The vicuña in Bolivia: the status of an endangered species, and recommendations for its conservation. *Z. Säugetierkd.* **36**, 129–46.

JUNGIUS, H. (1972). Bolivia and the vicuña. *Oryx* **11**, 335–46.

KASTLE, W. (1964). Verhaltensstudien an Taggeckonen der Gattungen *Lygodactylus* und *Phelsuma. Z.f. Tierpsychol.* **21**, 486–507.

KAUFFELD, K. (1969). The effect of altitude, ultra-violet light, and humidity. *Int. Zoo Yearb.* **9**, 8–9.

KENDRICK, J. L. (1964). Observations on the song of the North Island saddleback. *Notornis* **11**, 98–99.

KINGSTON, W. R. (1969). Marmosets and tamarins. *Lab. Anim. Handbook* **4**, 243–50.

KINGSTON, W. R. (1970). On the breeding of marmosets and tamarins. *Lab. Prim. Newsl.* **9**, 9–10.

KINZL, H. (1970). Bedrohte Natur in den peruanischen Anden. *Colloq. Geogr.* **12**, 253–270.

KIRCHSHOFER, R. (1962a). Beobachtungen bei der Geburt eines Zwergschimpansen (*Pan paniscus* Schwarz 1929) und einige Bemerkungen zum Paarungsverhalten. *Z.f. Tierpsychol.* **19**, 597–606.

KIRCHSHOFER, R. (1962b). The birth of a dwarf chimpanzee, *Pan paniscus* Schwarz 1929, at Frankfurt Zoo. *Int. Zoo Yearb.* **4**, 76–78.

KIRSCHE, W. (1967). Zur Haltung, Zucht und Ethologie der griechischen Landschildkröte (*Testudo hermanni hermanni*). *Salamandra* **3**, 36–66.

KLÖPPEL, G. (1971). Amoeben-Dysenterie bei Menschenaffen. *13th Int. Symp. Erkrankungen Zootiere, Helsinki* 111–13. Akademie-Verlag, Berlin.

KOFORD, C. B. (1957). The vicuña and the puna. *Ecol. Monogr.* **27**, 153–219.

KOURANY, M., MYERS, C. W. and SCHNEIDER, C. R. (1970). Panamanian amphibians and reptiles as carriers of *Salmonella. Amer. J. Trop. Hed. Hyg.* **19**, 632–58.

KRAEMAER, D. C. and VERA CRUZ, N. C. (1969). Collection, gross characteristics and freezing of baboon semen. *J. Reprod. Fert.* **20**, 345.

KRASIŃSKI, Z. (1967). Free living European bison. *Acta theriol.* (Bialowieża) **12**, 391–405.

KRASIŃSKI, Z. and RACZYŃSKI, J. (1967). The reproduction biology of European Bison living in reserves and in freedom. *Acta theriol.* (Bialowieża) **12**, 407–44.

KRYSIAK, K. (1963). News of the European Bison in Poland. *Oryx* **7**, 94–96.

KUHN, H. J. and STARCK, D. (1966). Die Tupaia-Zucht des Dr. Senckenbergischen Anatomischen Institutes. *Natur u. Museum* **96**, 263–77.

Kuschel, G. (1971). Entomology of the Aucklands and other islands south of New Zealand. *Pacific Insects Monograph* **27**, 242.

Lang, C. M. (1967). A technique for the collection of semen from squirrel monkeys (*Saimiri sciureus*) by electroejaculation. *Lab. Anim. Care* **17**, 218.

Lang, E. M. (1960). The rhino house at Basle Zoo. *Int. Zoo Yearb.* **2**, 15.

Lang, E. M. (1961). Beobachtungen am indischen Panzernashorn. *Zool. Gart. (N.F.)* **25**, 369.

Lang, E. M. (1967). Einige biologische Daten vom Panzernashorn. *Rev. suisse Zool.* **74**, 603.

Laszlo, J. (1969). Observations on two new artificial lights for reptile display. *Int. Zoo Yearb.* **9**, 12–13.

Lederer, G. (1942). Fortpflanzung und Entwicklung von *Eunectes notaeus* Cope (Boidae). *Zool. Anz.* **139**, 162–76.

Lederer, G. (1944). Nahrungserwerb, Entwicklung, Paarung und Brutfürsorge von *Python reticulatus* (Schneider). *Zool. Jb. (Anat.)* **68**, 331–440.

Lederer, G. G. (1956). Fortpflanzungsbiologie und Entwicklung von *Python molurus* (Linné) und *Python molurus bivittatus* (Kuhl). *Aquar. Terrar. Z.* **9**, 243–48.

Legler, J. M. (1956). A simple and practical method of artificially incubating reptile eggs. *Herpetologica* **12**, 290.

Legler, J. M. (1960). Natural history of the ornate box turtle, *Terrapene ornata ornata* Agassiz. *Univ. Kans. Pub., Mus. Nat. Hist.* **11**, 527–669.

Lucas, J. and Duplaix-Hall, N. (eds.) (1972). *Int. Zoo Yearb.* **12**, 406–7.

Lynn, W. G. and Ulrich, M. C. (1950). Experimental production of shell abnormalities in turtles. *Copeia* **1950**, 253–62.

MacFarland, C. G. and Black, J. (1971). The Law and the Galápagos. *Int. J. Turtle Tortoise Soc.* **5**, 36–37.

MacFarland, C. G., Villa, J. and Toro, B. (1974a). The Galápagos giant tortoises (*Geochelone elephantopus*). Part I: Status of the surviving populations. *Biol. Cons.* **6**, 118–33.

MacFarland, C. G., Villa, J. and Toro, B. (1974b). The Galápagos giant tortoises (*Geochelone elephantopus*). Part II: Conservation methods. *Biol. Cons.* **6**, 198–212.

MacKinnon, J. R. (1971). The orang-utan in Sabah today. *Oryx* **11**, 141–91.

Mallinson, J. J. C. (1972). Observations on the breeding of red-handed tamarin, *Saguinus* (= *Tamarin*) *midas* Linnaeus 1758, with comparative notes on other species of Callithricidae (= Hapalidae) breeding in captivity. *Ann. Rep. Jersey Wildl. Pres. Trust* **8**, 19–31.

Mangili, G. and Baschieri-Salvadori, F. (1970). Kasuistik und Ergebnisse der Verwendung einer Kombination aus Perphenazin und Piperidin als Neuroplegikum und Schlafmittel bei der Immobilisierung von Tieren im zoologischen Garten von Rom. *Zool. Gart. (N.F.)* **38**, 297–309.

Manton, V. J. A. (1970). Breeding cheetahs at Whipsnade Park. *Int. Zoo Yearb.* **10**, 85.

Manton, V. J. A. (1971). A further report on breeding cheetahs at Whipsnade Park. *Int. Zoo Yearb.* **11**, 125.

Marlow, B. J. (1968). "Marsupials of Australia." Jacaranda Press, Brisbane.

Martin, R. D. (1966). Tree shrews: unique reproductive mechanism of systematic importance. *Science* **152**, 1402–4.

Martin, R. D. (1968). Reproduction and ontogeny in tree-shrews (*Tupaia belangeri*), with reference to their general behaviour and taxonomic relationships. *Z. f. Tierpsychol.* **25**, 409–532.

MARTIN, R. D. (1972*a*). A laboratory breeding colony of the lesser mouse lemur. *In* "Breeding Primates", pp. 161–71, Beveridge, W.I.B. (ed.). Karger, Basel.

MARTIN, R. D. (1972*b*). A preliminary field study of the lesser mouse lemur (*Microcebus murinus* J. F. Miller 1777). *Z.f. Tierpsychol.* Beiheft **9**, 43–89.

MARTIN, R. D. (1972*c*). Adaptive radiation and behaviour of the Malagasy lemurs. *Phil. Trans. Roy. Soc. Lond. B.* **264**, 295–352.

MARTIN, R. D. (1973). A review of the behaviour and ecology of the lesser mouse lemur (*Microcebus murinus* J. F. Miller 1777). *In* "Comparative Ecology and Behaviour of Primates", 1–68, Michael, R.P. and Crook, J. H. (eds.). Academic Press, London and New York.

MAYNES, G. M. (1972). Age estimation in the parma wallaby, *Macropus parma* Waterhouse. *Austr. J. Zool.* **20**, 107–118.

MAYNES, G. M. (1973). Reproduction in the parma wallaby *Macropus parma* Waterhouse. *Austr. J. Zool.* **21**, 337–51.

MAYNES, G. M. (1974). Occurrence and field recognition of *Macropus parma*. *Austr. Zool.* **18**, 72–87.

MAYR, E. (1963). "Animal Species and Evolution." Harvard University Press, Cambridge, Mass.

MERTENS, R. (1950). Über Reptilienbastarde. *Senckenbergiana* **31**, 121–44.

MERTENS, R. (1956). Über Reptilienbastarde—II. *Senck. biol.* **37**, 383–394.

MERTENS, R. (1964). Über Reptilienbastarde—III. *Senck. biol.* **45**, 33–49.

MERTENS, R. (1968). Über Reptilienbastarde—IV. *Senck. biol.* **49**, 1–2.

MERTON, D. V. (1965). Transfer of saddlebacks from Hen Island to Middle Chicken Island, January 1964. *Notornis* **12**, 213–22.

MERTON, D. V. (1966*a*). Some observations of feeding stations, food and behaviour of the North Island Saddleback on Hen Island in January. *Notornis* **13**, 3–6.

MERTON, D. V. (1966*b*). Foods and feeding behaviour of some forest birds on Hen Island in May. *Notornis* **13**, 179–84.

MERTON, D. V. (1970). The rehabilitation of Cuvier Island. *Wildlife 1970—A Review*; *N.Z. Wildlife Service* **2**, 5–8.

MILLER, J. C. (in press). The importance of immobilizing wings after tenectomy and tenotomy. *Veterinary Medicine, Small Animal Clinician.*

MOHR, E. (1959). "Das Urwildpferd, Equus przewalskii Poljakoff 1881." Ziemsen, Wittenberg Lutherstadt.

MOLL, E. O. and LEGLER, J. M. (1971). The life history of a neotropical slider turtle, *Pseudemys scripta* (Schoepf), in Panama. *Bull. Los Angeles Co. Mus. Nat. Hist., Sci.* **11**.

MONACHON, G. (1973). Sterilizing goose egg-shells with ultra-violet light. *Int. Zoo Yearb.* **13**, 95–97.

MOYNIHAN, M. (1970). Some behaviour patterns of platyrrhine monkeys. II: *Saguinus geoffroyi* and some other tamarins. *Smithson. Contrib. Zool.* **28**, 1–77.

MULLER, P. (1970). Einige Beobachtungen zur Fortpflanzungsbiologie bei Riesenschlangen im Zoologischen Garten Leipzig. *Aquar. Terrar. Z.* **17**, 162–4.

NOACK, T. (1902). *Equus przewalskii. Zool. Anz.* **25**, 135–45.

PAWLEY, R. (1969). Observations on the reaction of the Mata Mata turtle, *Chelys fimbriata*, to ultra-violet radiation. *Int. Zoo. Yearb.* **9**, 31–32.

PAWLEY, R. (1971). A convenient system for housing "off-exhibit" reptiles in Brookfield Zoo, Chicago. *Brit. J. Herpetol.* **4**, 210–13.

PERRET, M. (1974). Variations of endocrine glands in *Microcebus murinus*. In "Prosimian Biology." Martin, R. D., Doyle, G. A. and Walker, A. C. (eds.) Duckworth, London.

PERRY, J. (1971). The golden lion marmoset. *Oryx* **11**, 22–24.

PERRY, R. (1970). Tortoise rearing in the Galápagos Islands. *Zoonooz* **42**, 8–15.

PETERS, U. (1969). Some observations on the captive breeding of the Madagascar tortoise, *Testudo radiata*, at Sydney Zoo. *Int. Zoo Yearb.* **9**, 29.

PETTER, J.-J. and PEYRIERAS, A. (1970). Observations éco-éthologiques sur les lémuriens malgaches du genre *Hapalemur*. *Terre et Vie* **24**, 356–81.

PETTER, J.-J., SCHILLING, A. and PARIENTE, G. (1971). Observations éco-éthologiques sur deux lémuriens nocturnes: *Phaner furcifer* et *Microcebus coquereli*. *Terre et Vie* **25**, 287–327.

PETTER-ROUSSEAUX, A. (1962). Recherches sur la biologie de la reproduction des primates inférieurs. *Mammalia* **26**, Suppl. 1, 1–88.

PETTER-ROUSSEAUX, A. (1970). Observations sur l'influence de la photopériode sur l'activité sexuelle chez *Microcebus murinus*. *Ann. Biol. anim. Bioch. Biophys.* **10**, 203-8.

PETTER-ROUSSEAUX, A. (1972). Application d'un système semestriel de variation de la photopériode chez *Microcebus murinus*. *Ann. Biol. anim. Bioch. Biophys.* **12**, 367–75.

PETZOLD, H. G. (1969a). Zur Fortpflanzungsbiologie asiatischer Kobras (*Naja naja*). *Zool. Gart.* (*N.F.*) **36**, 133–46.

PETZOLD, H. G. (1969b). Zur Haltung und Fortpflanzungsbiologie einiger kubanischer Schlangen im Tierpark Berlin. *Salamandra* **5**, 124–40.

POOLEY, A. C. (1962). The Nile crocodile, *Crocodylus niloticus*: notes on the incubation period and growth rate of juveniles. *Lammergeyer* **2**, 1–55.

POOLEY, A. C. (1971). Crocodile rearing and restocking. *Spec. IUCN Pub., n.s., suppl.* **32**, 104–30.

POOLEY, A. C. (ed.) (1972). *IUCN/SSC Crocodile Group: Newsletter No. 3.*

POUGH, F. H. (1971). Bioenergetic aspects of lizard herbivory (Abstract). *Herp. Rev.* **3**, 107.

PRATER, S. H. (1971). "The Book of Indian Animals." Bombay Natural History Society, Bombay.

PROGSCHA, K. K. and LEHMANN, H. D. (1970). Angeborene Missbildung in einem Wurf von *Sanzinia madagascariensis*. *Salamandra* **6**, 108–14.

REICHENBACH-KLINKE, H. H. (1963). "Krankheiten der Reptilien." Fischer, Stuttgart.

REID, B. and RODERICK, C. (1973). New Zealand scaup and brown teal in captivity. *Int. Zoo Yearb.* **13**, 12–15.

RIDE, W. D. L. (1957). *Protemnodon parma* (Waterhouse) and the classification of related wallabies (*Protemnodon, Thylogale* and *Setonix*). *Proc. Zool. Soc. Lond.* **128**, 327–46.

RIDE, W. D. L. (1970). "A guide to the Native Mammals of Australia." Oxford University Press, Melbourne.

RIPLEY, S. D. (1973). Saving the wood duck through captive breeding. *Int. Zoo Yearb.* **13**, 55–58.

ROHR, W. (1970). Die Bedeutung des Wärmefaktors für Fortpflanzungsperiodik und Eiablageverhalten sudeuropäischer Landschildkröten im Terrarium. *Salamandra* **6**, 99–103.

ROUSSEL, J. D. and AUSTIN, C. R. (1967). Preservation of primate spermatazoa by freezing. *J. Reprod. Fert.* **13**, 333.

SANKHALA, K. S. (1967). Breeding behaviour of the tiger. *Int. Zoo Yearb.* **7**, 133–47.

SAVAGE, C. D. W. (1969). Wildfowl Survey in South-west Asia: progress in 1968. *Wildfowl* **20**, 144–7.

SAVAGE, C. D. W. (1970). Marbled teal project at Lal Suhanra, West Pakistan. *Wildfowl* **21**, 88.

SCHAEFER, W. H. (1934). Herpetological notes: Diagnosis of sex in snakes. *Copeia* **1934**, 181.

SCHENKEL, R. and LANG, E. M. (1969). Das Verhalten der Nashörner. *Handbuch der Zoologie.* Walter de Gruyter and Co. Berlin.

SCHERPNER, C. (1967). Extension for the anthropoid ape house at Frankfurt Zoo. *Int. Zoo Yearb.* **7**, 47–50.

SCHIRNEKER, B. (1921). "*Equus przewalskii* Poliakoff." Thesis, Halle-Wittenberg.

SCHWEIZER, H. (1965). Ei-Zeitigung, Aufzucht und Entwicklung einer Strahlen-Schildkröte (*Testudo radiata*). *Salamandra* **1**, 67–73.

SELYE, H. (1950). "The Physiology and Pathology of Exposure to Stress." Acta, Montreal.

SHAW, C. E. (1963). Notes on the eggs, incubation and young of some African reptiles. *Brit. J. Herp.* **3**, 63–70.

SHAW, C. E. (1967). Breeding the Galápagos tortoise—success story. *Oryx* **9**, 119–26.

SHAW, C. E. (1970). The hardy and prolific soft-shelled tortoise. *Int. Turt. Tort. Soc. J.* **4**, 1.

SIMPSON, G. G. (1940). Mammals and land-bridges. *J. Wash. Acad. Sci.* 30, 137–63.

SIMPSON, G. G. (1952). Probabilities of dispersal in geologic time. *Bull. Amer. Mus. Nat. Hist.* **99**, 163–76.

SLEVIN, J. R. (1959). The Galápagos Islands: A history of their exploration. *Occ. Pap. Calif. Acad. Sci.* **25**, 1–150.

SNOW, D. W. (1964). The giant tortoises of the Galápagos Islands. Their present status and future chances. *Oryx* **7**, 277–90.

SOLA, R. DE (1930). The Liebespiel of *Testudo vandenburghi*, a new name for the Mid-Albemarle Island Galápagos Tortoise. *Copeia* **1930**, 79–80.

SPRANKEL, H. (1959). Die Aufzucht von Tupajas—wird sie gelingen? *Freunde Kölner Zoo* **2**, 20–21.

SPRANKEL, H. (1961). Über Verhaltensweisen und Zucht von *Tupaia glis* (Diard, 1820) in Gefangenschaft. *Z.f. wiss Zool.* **165**, 186–220.

STEMMLER, O, (1971). Gefangenschaftsnachzucht von *Epicrates cenchria maurus* × *Epicrates cenchria cenchria* (Reptilia, Boidae). *Aquar. Terrar. Z.* **18**, 415–20.

SWEDBERG, G. E. (1967). "The Koloa." Division of Fish and Game, Hawaii.

SWEIFEL, R. G. (1961). Another method of incubating reptile eggs. *Copeia* **1961**, 112–13.

SZIDAT, H. (1968). Eine Methode zur Erkennung des Geschlechtes bei Squamaten. *Zool. Gart.* (*N.F.*) **35**, 282–7.

TEMPLE, S. (1972). Artificial insemination with imprinted birds of prey. *Nature* **237**, 287.

THORNTON, I. (1971). "Darwin's Islands: A Natural History of the Galápagos." Natural History Press, New York.

THROP, J. L. (1969). Notes on breeding the Galápagos tortoise, *Testudo elephantopus*, at Honolulu Zoo. *Int. Zoo Yearb.* **9**, 30–31.

TONG, E. H. (1960). The breeding of the Great Indian Rhinoceros at Whipsnade Park. *Int. Zoo Yearb.* **2**, 12–15.

TOWNSEND, C. H. (1925). The Galápagos tortoises in their relation to the whaling industry. A study of old logbooks. *Zoologica, N.Y.* **4**, 55–135.

TROUGHTON, E. (1965). "Furred Animals of Australia." Angus and Robertson, Sydney.

TURBOTT, E. G. (1947), Birds of Little Barrier Island. *New Zealand Bird Notes* **2**, 98.

TURKOWSKI, F. J. and MOHNEY, G. C. (1971). History, management and behaviour of the Arabian Oryx herd. *Arizona Zool. Soc. Bull.* **2**, 1–36.

TURKOWSKI, F. J. and TINKER, T. L. (1972). Project 129: Arabian oryx—breeding herd at Phoenix Zoo, Arizona. *World Wildlife Yearb.* **1972**, 135–8.

ULMER, F. A. (1957). Cheetahs are born. *America's First Zoo* **9**, 7.

ULRICH, W. (1971). "Wilde Tiere in Gefahr." Urania Verlag, Leipzig.

US DEPARTMENT OF THE INTERIOR (1968). Rare and endangered fish and wild-life of the United States. *Bureau of Sports Fisheries and Wildlife Resource Publication, Washington, D.C.* **34**.

VALLAT, C. (1971). Birth of three cheetahs at Montpellier Zoo. *Int. Zoo Yearb.* **11**, 124.

VAN DEN BERGH, W. (1966). The Congo peacock in the Antwerp Zoo. *Peacock Annual* **3**.

VAN DENBURGH, J. (1914). The gigantic land tortoises of the Galápagos Islands. *Proc. Calif. Acad. Sci. ser. 4*, **2**: 203–374.

VANEYSINGA, C. R. (1969). The dietary requirements of lions, tigers and jaguars when kept outdoors during winter months. *Int. Zoo Yearb.* **9**, 164–6.

VERHEYEN, W. N. (1965). "Der Kongopfau." (Die Neue Brehm Bücherei—Heft 351.) A. Ziemsen, Wittenberg Lutherstadt.

VERHEYEN, W. N. *et al.* (1962). Monographie du paon congolais *Afropavo congensis* Chapin 1936. *Bull. sci. Soc. Roy. Zool. d'Anvers* **26**.

VESELOVSKY, Z. (1967). The Amur tiger in the wild and in captivity. *Int. Zoo Yearb.* **7**, 210–15.

VOLF, J. (1967). Der Einfluss der Domestikation auf die Formentwicklung des Unterkiefers beim Pferd. *Equus* **2**, 401–406.

VOLF, J. (1970). "Generální plemenná kniha koní Przevalského" (General Pedigree Book of the Przewalski Horse). Zoological Gardens, Prague.

WACKERNAGEL, H. (1966). Feeding wild animals in Zoological Gardens. *Int. Zoo Yearb.* **6**, 23.

WALLACH, J. D. (1969). Medical care of reptiles. *J. Amer. Vet. Med. Ass.* **155**, 1017–34.

WALLIS, R. L. and MAYNES, G. M. (1973) Ontogeny of thermoregulation in *Macropus parma* (Marsupialia: Macropodidae). *J. Mammal.* **54**, 278–81.

WAYRE, P. (ed.) (1959). "Ornamental Pheasant Trust Annual Report, 1959." Norfolk Wildlife Trust, Norwich.

WAYRE, P. (1970). "A Guide to the Pheasants of the World." Country Life, Middlesex, England.

WEBER, D. (1971). Pinta, Galápagos: Une île à sauver. *Biol. Conserv.* **4**, 8–12.

WILKINSON, A. S. and WILKINSON, A. (1952). "Kapiti Bird Sanctuary." Masterton Printing Co., New Zealand.

WODZICKI, K. A. and FLUX, J. E. C. (1967). Re-discovery of the white-throated wallaby, *Macropus parma* Waterhouse 1846, on Kawau Island, New Zealand. *Austr. J. Sci.* **29**, 429–30.

WOLFE, L. G. *et al.* (1972). Breeding and hand-rearing marmosets for viral oncogenesis studies. *In* "Breeding Primates" (Beveridge, W. I. B., ed.), 145–57. Karger, Basel.

WOODBURY, A. M. (1951). A snake den in Tooele County, Utah. Introduction: A ten year study. *Herpetolog.* **7**, 4–14.

YNTEMA, C. L. (1960). Effects of various temperatures on the embryonic development of *Chelydra serpentina*. *Anat. Rec.* **136**, 305–6.

YANGPRAPAKORN, U., McNEELY, J. A. and CRONIN, E. W. (1971). Captive breeding of crocodiles in Thailand. *Spec. IUCN Pub., n.s., Suppl.* **32**, 98–101.

ŻABINSKI, J. (1957). The progress of the European Bison. *Oryx* **4**, 184–8.

ŻABINSKI, J. (ed.) (1966). "Pedigree book of the European Bison, 1947–1966." The International Society for the Protection of the European Bison, Warsaw.

ŻABINSKI, J. (ed.) (1971). "European Bison Pedigree Book, 1965–1969." Polish Scientific Publishers, Warsaw.

ZEHR, D. R. (1962). Stages in normal development of the common garter snake, *Thamnophis sirtalis sirtalis*. *Copeia* **1962**, 322–9.

ZINGG, A. (1968). Zur Fortpflanzung von *Dispholidus typus* (Reptilia, Colubridae). *Salamandra* **4**, 37–43.

ZUCKERMAN, S. (1932). "The Social Life of Monkeys and Apes." Kegan Paul, Trench & Trubner, London.

ZWEIFEL, R. G. (1961). Another method of incubating reptile eggs. *Copeia* **1961**, 112–3.

Index

Numbers in italic indicate pages which carry illustrations

A

Abidec, *see* dietary additives
Abijan Zoo, 245
Abortion, 220, 256, 257, 258
    spontaneous, 219, 225, 226
Accipiter, 129
    gentilis, 130
acclimatization, 68, 93, 238, 298
acetylamino-nitrothiazole, 95
Acinonyx jubatus, 312
Acrobates pygmaeus, 176
Addax (*Addax nasomaculatus*), 364, 365, 367
addled eggs, *see* eggs
Adelaide Zoo, *175*, 245
adrenal glands, 161
Aegolius funereus, 130
Aepyprymnus rufescens, 175
Afropavo congensis, *76*, *84*, 87
age 121
aggressive behaviour, 82, 93, 105, 106, 181, 194, 196, 197, 228, 229, 232, 246, 258, 266, 277, 296, 297
    redirection, 211
agonistic encounters (*see also* fighting), 32, 327
Aix sponsa, 50
Alberta game farm, 277, 283
Alectoris, 87
alligator (Chinese), 45
alpaca, 358
Amazona v. vittata, 99
Amblonyx cinerea (*see also* otter), 315, *316*, 318, 323, 324, 325, *326*, 327
Ammospiza maritima nigrescens, 99
    maritima mirabilis, 99

amoebiasis, 11
amoebic dysentery, 250
amphibians, 361
Amsterdam Zoo, 245, 274, 277, 279, 283, 293, 351
anaemia, 190
Anas
    aucklandica chlorotis, 50
    platyrhynchos wyvilliana, 50
    platyrhynchos diazi, 50
Anatidae, 115
anatum peregrine, *see* falcon
Animal and Bird Protection Board of Tasmania, 183
annual cycles, 152, 153 (*see also* breeding season)
annual distribution of births, *see* birth season
Anoa (*Anoa depressicornis*), 364
anoestrus, 149, 168, 169
Anoplocephala gigantea, 297
Antechinomys, 181
    spenceri, 178
    laniger, 178
Antechinus, 181
    apicalis, 177
    bellus, 177
    flavipes, 177
    godmani, 177
    macdonanellensis, 177
    maculatus, 177
    minimus, 177
    stuarti, 177
    swainsonii, 177
antibiotics, 96, 110, 195, 199, 216, 334
antihelminthic preparations, 57, 266

antiseptic solutions, 110
Antwerp Zoo, 75, 85, 245, 274, 277, 279, 283
aorta, rupture of, 195
apes, 349, 382 (*see also* chimpanzee, gorilla, orang-utan)
Arkansas National Wildlife Refuge, 113
Arnhem Zoo, 300, 337
artificial insemination, 107, 137, 356, 358
artificial selection, 236, 243, 255, 260
Ascaris, 77
Asio otis, 130
Askania Nova, Soviet Acclimatization Station, 263
aspergillosis (*Aspergillus fumigatus*), 53, 60, 75, 76, 95
ass
   Indian wild, 363
   Nubian wild, 363
   Tourkmenian wild, 267
Assam, 309
Athene noctua, 129
atherosclerosis, 76
atresia, *see* ovary
avian tuberculosis, 90
aviary, *see* cage
Aythya novaeseelandiae, 50

B

bacteria, 10 (*see also* disease, parasites, pathology)
   symbiotic, 238
bacterial infections, 216, 323
bandicoot, 180
   long-nosed, 177
   pig-footed, 177
   rabbit-eared, 177
   short-nosed, 177
   spring, 182
Bangkok crocodile farm, 44, 45
Barcelona Zoo, 245, 279
Basle Zoo, 279, 293, *294*, 295, 296, 300, 301, 338, 359
bat, 73, 172
bear, 351
   brown, 351
   polar, 351
   sloth, 351, *352, 354, 355*
   spectacled, 363
   sun, 353

bedding (*see also* nest facilities), 306, 320, 323, 327, 352
behaviour, 100, 229, 346
   distortion, 206
   factors, 188, 257
   observations, 145
   studies, 144, 211
Berlin Zoo, 245, 275, 293, 295, 300, 301, 302, 310
Betsy Island, *64*, 73
Bettongia, 180
   gaimardi, 175
   lesueuri, 175
   penicillata, 175
   tropica, 175
Bialowieża Primaeval Forest, 253, *254*, 257, 261
Big Chicken Island, 66, 68
Big South Cape, *64*, 71
Big Stage Island, 72
birds of prey, 125, 129, 131, 133, 144
birth
   abnormal, 228
   in captivity, 190, 233, 246, 268, 290, 353, 365, 366, 367
   premature, 256
   rate, 241, 366, 368, 369, 370
   season, 269, 277, *279, 280*
   signs of, 325
   unsuccessful, 353
Bison bonasus, 364
Bison
   American, 253, 360
   European, 253, *254, 257, 258*, 360, 375
Black Forest, 129
blindness, 282
blood testing, 57
boa (*see also* snakes), 2
Boa constrictor, 6, 7
bobwhite, masked, 99
bone meal, 321
bongo, 182, 359
bonobo (*see also Pan paniscus*), 245, *247, 248*, 363
boodie, 173
boredom, 382
botulism, 60
brachiation, 236

brain weight, reduction of, 335
branches, *see* cage furniture
Branta
    canadensis leucopareia, 50
    sandvicensis, 50, 115
Brasschaat Zoo, 277, 279, 283
breakdown in parental behaviour (*see also* tree shrews, mouse lemurs, "cannibalism"), 139
breeding (*see also* inbreeding, outbreeding, generation)
    captive, 302, 311
    centres, 20, 28, 34, 35, 36, 253, 261, 262
    conditions, 49, 52, 208
    control, 58
    difficulties, 146, 149
    failure, 13, 18, 43, 145, 158, 178, 193, 197, 199, 202, 209, 315, 327, 329, 337, 361, 373
    farms 11,
    group, 46, 58, 96, 242, 250, 255, 256, 260, 292, 302, 311, 313, 334, 358, 371
    long term, 211
    pairs, 163, 327
    pens, *137, 215, 287,* 352, 356
    poodles, 236
    population, 19, 30, 34, 35, 47, 302, 311
    potential, 131, 250
    principles, 143, *et seq.*, 165
    programme, 19, 30, 34, 35
    records, 78, 116, 125
    stock, 35, 46, 85, 131
    season, 20, 21, 22, 29, 58, 115, 144, 152, 169, 187, 256, 270, 277, 338
    success, 20, 34, 40, 41, 59, 77, 95, 96, 116, 120, 135, 137, 158, 167, *176,* 178, 189, 190, 193, 194, 195, 196, 199, 203, 205, 213, 228, 233, 241, 245, 246, 263, 270, 274, 283, 285, 293, 303, 310, 312, 316, 329, 331, 338, 339, 345, 353, 361, 362, 365, 366, 371, 373, 375, 380
    systems, 255
brooding, *27* (*see also* incubation)
Brookfield Zoo, Chicago, 291, *345,* 346, *348*
Brownsea Island, 90
Bubo bubo, 125
Bureau of Sport Fisheries and Wildlife, 99, 114
Burramys parvus, 171, 173, *176,* 181, 176
burrows, 5, 180, 181

C

Cacajao rubicundus, 362
caecal worms, 119 (*see also* parasites)
caecum, 198, 199, 238
cage (*see also* enclosure, nest, rest facilities), 208, 382
    aviary, 130, 183, 189, 194, 195, 197, 205, 208, 214, *209,* 236, 249, 338
    construction, *239*
    furniture, 20, 21, 39, 75, 130, 149, 184, 189, 190, 194, 201, 213, 226, 230, *240,* 249, 275, 382
    groups, 162, 163, 168, 189, 218, 246, 332
    outdoors, 28, 49
    size (*see also* enclosure size)
Cairina scutulata, 50
calcification, 343
calcium (*see also* diet, dietary additives), 108, 109, 110, 111, 339
    deficiency, 45, 341
    eggs, 8
    phosphate, 6
Calcutta Zoo, 352
Callaeas cinerea, 61
Callimico goeldi, 362
Callithrix
    argentatus, 213, *219,* 219, 220
    jacchus, 213, 215, *217, 218,* 219, 220
Callitrichidae, 203, 213, 221
Caloprymnus campestris, 175, 180
Canadian Wildlife Service, 133, 114
cancer, 190
Candida, 77
Canis familiaris, 172
"cannibalism", 130, 158, 159, 162, 163, 184, 353
Capillaria obsignata, 75, 76, 80
Caprimulgus noctitherus, 99
captive breeding, *see* breeding (*see also* population)
caracal (*Caracal caracal*), 311
carbohydrate, 56, 57, 296,
    excess of, 298
carnivore houses, 329
carrying cases, 68, 72, 104
Catreus wallichi, 91, 94
cats, 16, 19, 345, 383
    "eastern native", 183, 185
    European wild, 346

cats—(contd.)
  fishing, 348
  leopard, 346
  lynx, 346
  Margay, 346
  Pallas, *345*, 346
  sand, 346, *348*
Cebuella pygmaea, 213, 221
cellulose, digestion of, 238
census in zoos, 362
Cercatetus
  concinnus, 176
  nanus, 176
  lepidus, 176
Cérélac, *see* dietary additives
Cervus
  eldi siamensis, 364
  eldi thamin, 364
  canadensis nannodes, 364
  nippon mantchuricas, 366
  nippon taionanus, 364, 366
cestodes, 11 (*see also* parasites)
Chaeropus ecaudatus, 177
Chamaeleo tigris, 3
chameleon, *3*, 4
Charles Darwin Research Station, 13, 19, 20,
    22, 23, 24, *26*, 27, 28, 29 30, *31*, 35,
    37
cheetah, 337, *338*, *342*, 352
  enclosure, *343*
  Indian hunting, 312
Cheirogaleus, 192
  major, 192
  medius, 192
Chelydra serpentina, 9
Chelys fimbrimata, 6
chemical residue, *see* pesticides
Chetwode Islands, 73
Chicago Zoo (*see also* Brookfield Zoo), 300
Chicago Zoological Society, 345, 346
chimpanzee (*see also* Pan paniscus), 241, 242
  common, *249*
  pygmy, 245 et seq., *249*
Choeropis liberiensis, 364
chronic stress, *see* stress
Chrysemys, 1
Chrysemys pieta, 8, 9
Chrysocyon brachyurus, 363

cleaning, 46, 52, 56, 95, 153, 189, 213, 226,
    229, 232, 321
climatic conditions, 33, 34, 49, 50, 51, 270
  changes in, 172, 309
cloacal opening, 23
clutch (*see also* litter-size), 21, 23, 25, 28, 29, 52,
    123
  repeat, 116
  replacement, 58
Coccidia, 282
coccidiosis, 76, 96, 119
coccidiostats, 95, 110
Coenocorypha aucklandica iredali, 71, 72
Colchicus, 90
cold
  common, 242
  sensitivity to, 195
Colinus virginianus ridgwayi, 99
Cologne Zoo, 223, 224, 274, 275, 276, 293
Columba inornata wetmorei, 99
Commelina diffusa, 20
compounds, *see* enclosure
condor, Californian, 99
conservation, 10, 13, 87, 88, 114, 115, 131, 133,
    144, 145, 171, 172, 173, 221, 235, 236,
    271, 292, 309, 373, 375, 379, 380, 383
  habitat, 35, 173
  projects, 61
  prospects, 251
conservationists, 172, 379
constipation, 225
cooperation
  between zoos, 36, 41, 85, 86, 242, 253, 263,
    283, 359, 362, 379, 382, 385
coot, 52
coprophagy, 10
copulation, *see* mating, mating behaviour
Coquerel's mouse lemur (*see also* lemur, *Microce-
    bus*), 190, *191*
Cornell University, 135, 137, 358
Coryza contagiosa equorum
Coturnix, 87
courtship, 49, 51
cranes, 383
  sandhill, 99, 100, *102*, 107, 113
  whooping, 99, 100, *101*, *103*, *104*, 107, 112,
    113
crickets, *see* diet

crocodiles (*see also Crocodylus*), 2, 4, 6, 43, *44,* 47
   New Guinea freshwater, 46
   saltwater, 46
Crocodylus
   novaguineae, 9, 46
   porosus, 43
   siamensis, 46
cropping, of birds, 73
cross-breeding (*see also* generations), 253, 274, 276, 344
   inter-specific, 14
Crossoptilon crossoptilon, 94
Crossoptilon manchuricum, 94
crow, 52
   rare wattled, 61
cuscus, 175
Cuvier Island, 68
cycles, physiological, 187, 189 (*see also* daylength, photoperiod)
Cyclura, 4

D

Dactylopsia, 181
   trivirgata, 176
Dallas Zoological Gardens, 75, 85
Dasycercus, 181
   cristicauda, 177
dasyurids, 180
Dasyuroides, 181
   byrnei, 177
Dasyurus (Satanellus), 181
   geoffroyi, 177
   hallucatus, 177
   maculatus, 177
   viverrimus, 177, 183, 185
Daubentonia madascariensis, 201
day length (*see also* photoperiod), 49–52, 56, 58, 152, 153, 187, 188
   manipulation of, 139
DDT (*see also* pesticides), 126, 178
death (*see also* mortality), 23, 30, 159, 166, 172, 174, 216, 227, 246, 324
   accidental, 195, 282, 297
   causes of, 161
   viral, 322
deer
   Burma brown antlered, 364

Père David, 235, 364, 365, 366, 368
   Thailand brown-antlered, 364
deficiency (*see also* diet), 166
   calcium, 45, 150
   protein, 195
deformation, of embryos, 166
dehydration, 6, 10, 216
   treatment of, 199
Delhi Zoo, 301, 303, *304*, 305, 312
Dendroaspis, 5
Dendrolagus, 180
   bennettianus, 175
   lumholtzi, 175
dens (*see also* cage furniture), 5, 320
dental disease, 324
depletion of wild populations, 374
desert, 173, *348*
Deutscher Naturschutzring, 128
diarrhoea, 199, 227
Diceros bicornis, 364
diet
   in captivity (individual species), 29, 39, 45, 46, 56–58, 78, 95, 107, 108, 109, 116, 130, 149, 150, 167, 180, 182, 189, 190, 198, 201, 208, 215, 225, 226, 241, 249, 296, 303, 305, 315, 321, 323, 331, 338, 339, 341
   in captivity (general), 34, 49, 66, 93, 117, 249, 287, 298
   bark, 201
   change of, 184, 225, 238, 334
   change with age, 96, 107, *108*, 109–111
   deficiencies, 45, 150, 166, 194, 195, 343
   deleterious effects of, 166
   effects of, 151
   experimentation with, 205
   importance, 322
   in natura, 180, 192, 194, 196, 197, 201, 208, 215, 238, *343*
   insects, 194, 238
   number of meals, 321
   Ratcliffe diet, 321
   variety, 192
dietary additives (*see also* dietary constituents, antibiotics), 111, 150, 356,
   Abidec, 150
   bone meal, 321, 323
   calcium, 108, 109, 110, 182, 289, 323, 339
   Cérélac, 150

dietary additives—(*contd.*)
  fat, 108, 109, 110, 296
  folic acid, 108, 109, 110
  minerals, 79, 96, 109, 182, 276, 289, 296, 333,
      339, 351, 356
  niacin, 108, 109, 110
  phosphorus, 108, 109, 110, 182, 339
  protein, 39, 95, 108, 109, 110, 296, 339
  riboflavin, 108, 109, 110
  salt, 182, 276, 339
  trace elements, 182
  vegetable oils, 95, 321, 323
  vegetable protein, 208
  Vionate, 150, 276
  vitamins, 6, 45, 79, 96, 108, 109, 110, 150,
      181, 182, 189, 194, 195, 196, 208, 216,
      238, 249, 250, 276, 296, 323, 333, 339, 341,
      351
  Yeastmin, 150
dietary constituents, 20, 31, 181, 238
  crickets, 150
  eels, 56, 57
  fat, 269
  fish, 56, 57
  fresh fruit, 20, 31, 150
  Gaine's dog meal, 31
  grape sugar, 250
  green food, 31, 58, 167
  insects, 150, 181
  leaves, 225, 226
  live food, 321
  locusts, 150, 215
  mealworms, 78, 96, 150, 181, 215
  meat, 150
  monkey biscuits, 195, 215
  natural food, 20, 31, 296
  oil, 56, 57, 58, 96
  pellets, 56, 58, 107, 150, 238, 276, 288, 296
  protein, 56, 57, 58, 96, 215, 249, 250, 296
  roughage, 45, 58, 321
  seeds, 57
  sprats, 56
  termites, 181
digestive disturbance, 30, 289
dingo, 172
discharge, vulval, 305
disease (*see also* parasites, pathology), 52, *53*, 57,
    58, 76, 108, 154, 166, 216, 287, 290, 331

  avoidance of, 56, 85, 117
  Carré's, 341
  degenerative, 56, 58
  dental, 324
  enteric, 322, 343
  epidemic, 85, 183, 376
  eye, 5
  hazards of, 153, 285, 333
  infectious, 275, 282, 323
  intestinal, 30
  non-infectious, 324
  nutritional, 241
disinfectants, 214
disinfection, 57, 105, 107, 110
disruption of behaviour
  maternal care, 157, 159, 163
  mating, 157
distemper, 322, 323
  feline, 333
distribution of stock, 292, 376
disturbance, 7, 68, 80, 118, 162, 311, 313, 317,
    329, 339, 341, 351
  effects of, 130, 184, 190
  in fertilization, 257
  of nests, 27, 52
  in oestrus, 260
  protection from, 332, 334
dodo, 379
dogs, 16, 34
domestic animals, 357, 359, 360
domestication, 257, 335, 375
  of wild horse, 267, 270
dominance, 168, 194, 196, 246, 289, 315
donkeys, 16, 19
Dorset Naturalists' Trust, 90
Dracaena, 4
drain, *53*
drainage, 56
drowning, 282
  danger of, 236
drugs
  anti-blackhead, 95, 96
  immobilization, 359
Drymarchon, 5
Dublin Zoo, 329
ducklings, *55*
ducks (*see also* teal, waterfowl), 49, 115, 381
  blue, 58

Hawaiian, 50, *118*
mallard, 60
Mexican, 50
muscovy, 116
North American wood, 50
torrent, 58
white winged wood, 49, 50, *55*
Duisburg Zoo, 245
Duke University, 199
dwarf lemurs, 192

E

eagles
golden, 137, 138
monkey-eating, 138
Southern bald, 99
ear-marking (*see also* identification), 278
ear-slits, 277, *278*
ear-tags, 277
echidna, 171, 172, 174, 178
Echymipera, 181
rufescens, 177
ecological
balance, 179, 374
factors, 257
mechanisms, 255
rehabilitation, 374
relationships, 145
requirements, 61, 126
ecologists, 235, 383
ecology, 66, 73, 94, 99, 173, 309
ecosystem, 71, 74, 173, 235, 374
change of, 72
ectoparasites, 11
Ecuador, 19, 36, 37
Ecuadorian National Park Service, 35
eczema, 227
education
of public, 35, 380, 385
educational advantages of zoos, 144
eels, 56, 57
egg
binding, 58
candling, 25
collectors, 128
covering, 22
fertility, 41, 107, 116
laying, 22, 39, 56, 58, *77*, 85, 107, 115

loss, 16, 22, 23, 27, 103
removal, 103
rotation, 105
weight, 123
eggs, *7*, 25, 27, 49
collection of, 35, 95
dummy, 52
handling, 23
turning, 23, 24, 28, 29, 52
unfertilized, 80
Elaphae oxycephala, 7
Elapharus davidianus, 364
elk, Tule, 4, 364
embryo, 184
loss, 23, 24, 25, 28, 29
transplantation, 359
embryo resorption, *see* resorption
embryology, experimental, 357
emperor tamarin (*see also Saguinus*), *206*
Enamphimerus, 77
enclosure (*see also* cage), 255, 265, 287, 317, 322, 323
arrangement, 35, *275*, 315, *332*, *333*
outdoor, 32, *209*, *237*, *240*, *286*, *295*, 296, 303, *304*, 306, 348, 352, 354
plan, 237, 239, *265*, 352
size, 20, 21, 23, 43, 93, 95, 130, 148, 167, 183, 184, 263, 274, 276, 283, 287, 289, 298, 319, 331, 352
endangered species, 16, 20, 34, 35, 36, 329
Endangered Species Facility, Alberta, *137*
Endangered Wildlife Research Programme, 99, 114
endometritis, 297
enema, 225
Enhydra lutris (sea otter), 318
enteritis, 324
feline, 322, 333
enterocolitis, 246
epidemics, 85, 183, 309, 376
epileptiform fit, 341
epizootics, 173
Equus
asinus africanus, 363
hemionus onager, 363
hemionus khur, 363
hemionus hemionus, 363, 366
hemionus kulan, 267

Equus—(*contd.*)
  przewalski, 363
  zebra hartmannae, 363
Escherichia coli, 77
Espanola Island, 17, 18, 19
Eunectes notaeus, 4
European bison pedigree book (*see also* stud book), 253
evolution, 14, 144, 173, 375, 381
excess of vitamin A, 166
exercise, 39, 41, 184, 206, 208, 287, 339
extinct species, 13, 15, 16, 117, 167, 174, 175, 177, 178, 183, 312
extinction, 14, 61, 72, 73, 99, 123, 173, 235, 253, 312, 358, 361, 374, 379, 380, 385
  danger of, 87, 309, 351

F

faeces, checking of, 11, 39, 106, 119, 266, 275
Falco
  novaseelandiae, 65
  peregrinus (*see also* falcons, tundra race), 130, 135
  sparvinus, 131
  tinnunculus, 129
falconers, 125, 133
falcons, 129, 133, *137*
  anatum race, 135, *136*
  Peale's peregrine, 135
  peregrine, 130, 135, 137, 140
  prairie, *134*, 135, 137, *138*, 139, 140
  tundra race, 135, 139
family groups, 194, 211, 276, 283
Fanel Island, 68
fat, 108, 109, 110, 111, 269, 296
fat
  deposits, 166
  storage, 189, 192
Fauna Preservation Society, 235, 285, 379
fear, of human beings (*see also* visitor effect), 196
fecundity, 47, 116, 259
  decrease of, 260
feeding (*see also* diet), 147, 266, 276
  station, *288*
Felis
  bengalensis, 346
  manul, *345*, 346
  sylvestris, 346

  thinobia, 346, *348*
  wiedii, 346
Fernandina Island, 16
ferret, black-footed, 99
fertility, 23, 24, 25, 27, 28, 29, 34, 58, 107 116, 123, 259, 260
  low, 114, 116
fertilization, disturbances of, 257
field studies, 5, 13, 35, 116, 140, 145, 163, 187, 190, 197, 236, 309
fighting, 93, 130, 168, 192, 201, 211, 289, 303, 304, 340
fights, 197, 236, 305, 307
financial support, 97, 381
fire alarm bell, 164
firebacks, 95
flamingos, 380
"Flehmen" (lip curl), 297
foetal heart rate, 241
folic acid, 108, 109, 110
food pellets, *see* diet
food requirements, *see* diet
foraging, 33, 151, 266, 238
foreign body, 324
forest destruction, 87
fork-crowned lemur, 193
Fort Wayne Zoo, 245
fossorial tendency, 316, 321
foster
  mother, 52, 116
  parents, 95, 96, 140, 241
founder populations, 144
fracture, 341
  of long bones, 166
Francolinus francolinus, 87
Frankfurt Zoo, 245, 275, 277, 279, 283, 293
Frankfurter Zoologische Gesellschaft, 37
free ranging, 253, 255, 257, 260, 261, 262
fresh air, 331, 334, 352
fresh fruit, *see* diet
frost, 331, 351
fumigation, of incubators, 110
fungal infections, 322, 323
fungus, 8

G

Galápagos Islands, 13, 23, 28, 34, 35
Galápagos National Park Service, 13, 19, 20, 37

Galápagos tortoise, 35, 36, 39, *40*
Gallirallus australis, 73
Galloperdix, 87
game
    birds, 361
    farms, 361
    ranch, 366
Game Research Association, 91
Gazella arabica, 364
gazelle (Arabian), 364
geckos, 4, 5
Gekko gekko, 4, 5
gene
    flow, 14
    pool, 13, 35, 236, 242, 335, 374
generation, 268
    second, *178*, 212, 217, 344, 371
    third, 212, 218, 317
genetic
    considerations, 35, 100, 112, 144, 236, 380
    diversity, 374
    drift, 100, 35
    traits, 236
    variability, 35, 36, 144
geneticists, 375, 383
gentle lemur (*see also Hapalemur*), 195
    broad-nosed, 197, *198*
Geochelone
    abingdoni, 17, 18, 20, 35, 36
    chathamensis, 17, 18, 20, 29, 32
    darwini, 17, 18, 19, 20, 28, 29, 30, 32
    elephantopus, 13, 14, *15*, 17, 22, 34
    elephantopus becki, 16–20
    elephantopus guntheri, 14, 17, 18, 20
    elephantopus microphyes, 16, 17, 18, 19, 20
    elephantopus vandenburghi, 14, 17, 18, 19, 20
    elephantopus vicina, 14, 17, 18, 20, 31, 32, 36
    ephippium, 17, 18, 20, 22–30, *31*, 32, 33, 36
    hoodensis, 17, 18, 20, 21–25, 27, 29, 30, 32, 35, 36
    porteri, 17–20, 22, 23, 24, 26, 27, 28, 29, 30, 31, 32, 33
Geoffroy's tamarin (*see also Saguinus*), *207*
geographical range, *249*
gestation, 150, 163, 184, 211, 216, 227, 228, 241, 297, 305, 332, 351, 356
    delayed, 169
    diagnosis, 332

period, 169, 211, 228, 256, *257*, 277, 302, 325, 353
Gila monster, 2
glaciation, 173
glycosuria, 190
goats, 16, 18, 19
golden eagles, *see* eagles
golden lion marmoset, *see* marmoset
goose
    Aleutian Canada, 50
    Hawaiian, 47, 50, 56, 58, *59*, 115, *117, 118, 119, 120*, 144, 383
    light-bellied Brent, 51
    kelp, 58
gorilla, 238
goshawks, *see* hawks
goslings, 57, 118
grape sugar, 250
grazing activity, 39
great apes, 154 (*see also* chimpanzee, gorilla, orang-utan)
grooming, 232, 316, 318, 320
groups (*see also* cage groups, social groups), 153, 276, 318
    dispersal, 33
    in captivity, 180, 266, 267
grouse, 87
growth, 184, 185
    curve, *31, 217*, 217, 218, *219, 281*
    rate, 28, 30, 31, 32, 57, 58, 279
    retardation, 161
Grus americana, 100
Grus canadensis (*see also* cranes), 99
guanacos, 277
guineafowl, 87
Gymnobelideus, 181
    leadbeateri, 176
Gymnogyps californianus, 99

H

habitat, 16, 90, 91, 179, 223, 346, 374
    destruction, 16, 87, 90
    improvement, 376
    preferred, 66, 88
    preservation, 100, 374
    simulation, 348
    suitability, 121, 126
"hacking", 125, 139, *140*

haemorrhaging, 166, 227
Halenkala National Park, 118, 122
Haliaectus leucocephalus, 99
Hamburg Zoo, 293, 295, 300, 301, 302, 310
handling, 34, 186, 217, 343
hand-rearing, *53*, 147, 154, *155*, 158, 186, 190, 211, 216, 241, 281, 333, 339, 340, 351
Hapalemur
  griseus, 195, 197, *198*
  simus, 197, *198*
Hapalidae, *see* Callitrichidae
hardening of the arteries, 58
Harris hawk, *see* hawk
hatching, 23, 25, 27, 41, *77*, 85, *104*, 105, 109
  decrease in, 80
  "hatchability", 107, 123
  period, 30
  success, 23, 24, 28, 29, 34
hatchlings, 16, 18, 20, 29, 30, 31, 78, *117*
Hauraki Gulf, *63*
Hawaiian Board of Agriculture and Forestry, 116
Hawaiian goose, *see* goose, *Branta*
Hawaiian Islands, *121*
Hawaiian Island Agencies, 122
hawks, 125, 129
  goshawks, 130, 137, 138
  Harris, 137
  red-tailed, 137, 140, 358
  Swainson's, 140
Hawk Trust, 133
hay-belly, 289
Healesville Sanctuary, 167
health, 123, 150, 167, 187, 215, 219, 260, 295
heating (*see also* temperature), 25, 29, 43, *53*, 56, 95, 181, 201, 226, 320, 351, 352
  additional, 51
  therapeutic effect of, 216
Helarctos malavanus, 353
Heloderma, 6
Hemibelideus lemuroides, 176
Hen Island, 62, 65, 66, 68
hepatitis, 323
  infectious, 341
herbivore, 150, 198, 199
Heterakis gallinae, 77
Heteralocha acutivostris, 61
hippopotamus, pygmy, 364, 370
home-range, 148, 149

Honolulu Zoo, 28, 31, 36, 39, 42, 122
hoofed mammals, 359, 368, 382
hormone
  deficiency, 250
  disturbance, 246
horns, rubbing of, 295
horses, Przewalski, 263, *264*, 268, 269, 283, 361, 363, 364, 365
Houston Zoo, 302
huia, 61
human activity, 173
human exploitation, 15, 18, 19
human factor, 334
humidity, 25, 41, 52, 75, 106, 107, 238, 285
  humidification, 105
  rainfall, 45, 151, 152, 188, 192, 193, 195, 199
  relative, 4, 8
hunting, 91, 115, 173, 271, 337
  instinct, 125
Hyaena brunnea, 363
hybrids, 10, 242, 256, 283, 381
  fertile, 253
hyena, brown, 363
hygiene, 46, 153, 290
Hymenolepis, 77
hypersexuality, 270
hypovitaminosis, 324 (*see also* vitamins)
Hypsiprymnodon moschatus, 173, 175, 180

I

ibis, 52
identification, 4, 58, *59*
  individual, 277, *278*, 290
  of eggs, 23
iguana, 2
immunity, natural level, 58
imprinting, 113, 137, 138, 154, 156, 169
inbreeding, 35, 47, 58, 96, 112, 116, 173, 260, 334, 335
incompatibility, 131
incubation, 1, 20, 25, *27*, 28, 29, 34, 45, 52
  artificial, 8, 24, 34, 41, 52, 95
  of eggs, 43
  natural, 52, 58, 72, 105
  period, 8, 25, 26, *27*
incubators, *9*, 23, 25, *26*, 35, 45, 105
  fumigation of, 110
  temperature of, 27, 107

individuals per collection, 365–371
Indri indri, 201
infant (*see also* mortality), 300, 354
  development of, 211, 230
infection, *see* disease, parasites
infertility, 24, 27, 51, 258, 259, 260
  in the wild, 27, 28
inflammation of kidneys, 75
infra-red lamps, 105, 205, *210*
inhalation of diet, 216
injury, 305
Inner Chetwode Island, 72, 73
inoculation, 250, 322, 332
insecticides, *see* pesticides
insemination, 357
  artificial, 107, 137, 356, 358
instinctive traits, 113
interbreeding, natural, 14
International Council for Bird Preservation, 91
International Zoo Yearbook, 2, 36, 203, 293, 361,
  362, 363, 365, 367, 383
intolerance, 194
introduced species, 65, 172, 173, 174, 303
  artificial, 16
Isabela Island, 14, 15, 17, 19, 39
island community (*see also* population), 14, 173
isolation, 195, 241
  auditory, 49
  from public, 317
  geographic, 14
  visual, 49
Isoodon
  auratus, 177
  macrourus, 177
  obesulus, 177
IUCN (International Union for the Conservation
  of Nature) (*see also* Survival Service
  Commission), 97, 262, 271, 273, 374,
  383
  Red Data Book, 115, 361, 371, 375

J

Jaipur Zoo, 312
Jersey Declaration, 384, 385
Jersey Wildlife Preservation Trust, 94, 205,
  379
Jersey Zoo, 85, *147*, 158, *206*, *207*, 208, 381
Johannesburg Zoo, 279

K

Kaimohu Island, *64*, 72, 73
kangaroo, 171, 174, 180
Kapiti Island, 62, 65
Karnataka State Forest Department, 310, 313
Kawau Island (New Zealand), 167, 174
kestrels, 129, 137
  American, 131
kidney damage (*see also* inflammation of kidneys,
  renal calculi), 56
  failure, 57
King's College Bird Club, 74
koala, 177
kokako, *see* crow, rare wattled
Kowari, 177
Krefeld Zoo, 337, 338, 339, 340

L

labour pains, 305
lactation (*see also* suckling), 150, 162, 241, 260
  failure, 163
  inadequacy, 280
Lagorchestes, 180
  asomatus, 174
  conspicillatus, 174
  hirsutus, 174
  leporides, 174
Lagostrophus, 180
  fasciatus, 174
Lama
  vicugna, 271
  vicugna mensalis, 282
  vicugna vicugna, 282
langur (*see also* *Pygathrix nemaeus*), 159, 223,
  224
  new-born, 229, *231*
Lasiorhinus, 181
  barnardi, 177
  gillespiei, 177
  latifrons, 177
laying season, 51,
  fertile eggs, 52
  time, 24
lead, 60
learning
  to kill, 125, 128, 129
  to mate, 241
leaves, 225

leg bands, 58
leg weakness, *see* limb weakness
Leipzig Zoo, 329
Lemur, 187, 193, 194, 195, 196, 197
    catta, 187, 193, 194
    fulvus, 193, 194, 362
    macaco, 362
    mongoz, 193, 362
lemur, 146, 151, 152, 187 *et seq.*
    avahi, 199
    aye-aye, 210
    black, 362
    broad-nosed gentle, 197, *198*
    Coquerel's, 190, *191*
    dwarf, 192
    fork-crowned, 193
    gentle, 195
    indri, 201
    mongoose, 193, 194, 362, 365
    mouse, 146, *148*, 152, 162, 163, 187, 188
    red-fronted, 362
    ringtail, 187, 193, 194
    sifaka, 199, *200*
    sportive, 150, 197
    variegated, 193, 194
Leontideus, 213
    rosalia, 213
Leontopithecus rosalia, 363
leopard
    North China, 363
    snow, 363, 369
Leopoldville Zoo, 245
Lepilemur mustelinus, 197
leptospirosis, 322, 341
lifespan, average, 280
light-schedule, 29, 152
    inversion of (*see also* photoperiod, day length), 349
limb weakness, 56, 57, 341
lions, 329, 335
    Asiatic, 363
Lisbon Zoo, 245
litter-size, 144, 219, 221, 334, *338*, 353
Little Barrier Islands, 62, 65
lizards, 1, 5
London Zoological Society, 85, 158, 201, 236, *237*, *239*, *240*, 241, 242, 275, 279, 285, 293, 304, 322, *330*

longevity, 16, 58, 112, 144, 178, *179*, 190, *207*, 219, 221, 223, 258, 280, 302
Longleat, 337
Lophophorus
    lhuysi, 94
    sclateri, 94
Lophura, 95
    edwardsi, 94
    imperialis, 94
    swinhoei, 88, 94
Los Angeles Zoo, 292, 371
Lutra
    canadensis (*see also* otter), 317, 319, 322, 323, 324, 325, 327
    lutra, 317, *318*, 323, 324, 325, 327
Lutrogale perspicillata (*see also* otter), 315, 316, *317*, 322, 324, 325, 327
Lynx canadensis, 346
lynx, desert, *see* caracal

M

macaques, 195
Macropus
    agilis, 174
    antilopinus, 174
    bernadus, 174
    dorsalis, 174
    eugenii, 174
    fuliginosus, 174
    giganteus, 174
    irma, 174
    parma, 167, 169, 174, 362
    parryi, 174
    robustus, 174
    rufogrisea, 174
Macrotis, 181
    lagotis, 177
    leucura, 177
Malagasy lemurs, *see* lemur
mallard, *see* duck
mammals, 16, 143 *et seq.*, 166, 172, 351, 357, 361, 362, 372
mammary gland, 305
    reduction of, 162
mange, 282
Marchena Island, 19
Margalla Hills, 91

marking
  behaviour, *147*, 153, 154, 162, 190, 192, 206, 214, 324
  scent, *147*, 162, 206
  urine, 190, 297, 324
Marking for identification, *see* indentification
Marmaronetta augustirostris, 50
marmosets, 213, *219*, 359
  cages, *209*, *210*, *214*
  golden-lion, 205, 359, 360, 363, 368
marsupial mice
  long legged, 178
  narrow footed, 177
  numbat, 178
marsupial mole, 178, 180
marsupials (Metatheria), 167, 171, 172, 174, 180, 183
  pouch, 184
mata-mata, 6
maternal behaviour (*see also* lactation), 232, 241, 306, 351
  disruption of, 157, 159
  of tree shrews, 149, 157
maternity area, 290, *291*
mate selection, 106, 112, 218
mating, 18, 49, 168, 183, 184, 241, 246, 250, *257*, 279, 287, 297, *299*, 304, 305, 324, 340, 353
  failure, 20, 257
  fertile, 307
  free, 261
  neck grip, 184
  pattern, 331
  prelude, 298, *298*, 299
  prevention, 372
  season, 257
  stimulation of, 296
  urge, 298
mating behaviour, 4, 7, 40, 161, 227, 296, 331, 358
  disruption of, 157
Maui, 117, 120, 121, 122
Maui Electric Co., 122
meal worms (*see also* diet), 78, 96, 150, 181, 215
Megaleia rufa, 174
Melbourne Zoological Gardens, 167, 183
Melursus ursinus, 351

menstruation, 241
mercury components (*see also* pesticides), 126
Mexico City Zoo, 245
Microcebus
  coquereli, 190, *191*
  murinus, 146, *148*, 152, 162, 163, 187, 188
Middle Chicken Island, 66, 67, 68
migrating experience, 113
Milwaukee Zoo, 302, 359
minerals, 79, 264, 276, 331, 333, 339, 351
miscarriage, *see* abortion—spontaneous
mist-net, 66, 71
mites, 297
mixed species, in cages, 276
moat
  dry, 275
  wet, 275, 295, 304
mocking birds, 22
Monash University, 167
mongoose lemurs, 193, 194
monitor, *see Varanus*
monitoring, of populations, 133
monkey biscuits (*see also* diet), 195, 215
monkey-eating eagles, *see* eagles
monotremes (Prototheria), 171, 172, 174, 178
Montpellier Zoo, 312, 337, 338, 339, 340, 341
mortality (*see also* death), 28, 30, 34, 58, 123, 165, 195, 197, 274, 283, 361
  differential, 151
  of eggs, 16, 71
  following release, 128
  of infants, 16, 18, 20, 211, 233, 280, 337, 353, 354, 355
motor disturbance, 192
moult, 50, 51, 56
Mountain Home (Texas), 366
Mount Bruce Native Bird Reserve, 66, 67
mounting, *see* mating
mouse lemur, 146, *148*, 152, 162, 163, 187, 188
  cage groups, 162, 163
  hand rearing, 154
mulgara, 177
multivitamins, *see* vitamins, dietary additives
Munich Zoo, 245, 277, 279, 283
Mustela nigripes, 99
mustelids, 322
muttonbirds, 71

Myrmecobius, 181
   fasciatus, 178, 179
Mysore Zoo, 300, 301, *310*, 311, 312, 313

N

National Geographic Society, 37
national parks, 173, 293
National Parks Wildlife Service, 183
National Science Foundation, 37
National Taiwan University, 88
National Trust, 90
National Zoological Gardens, Pretoria, 85
National Zoological Park, Washington, 358
natural conditions, 52, 78, 99, 151, 197, 206
   destruction of, 374
   food, 117, 118
   habitat, 27, 32, 34, 35, 36, 141, 235, 236,
      242, 255, 285, 312, 373, 375, 381, 383,
      385
   imitation of, 358
   rehabilitation of, 374
"navel-ill", 290
nematodes, 11 (*see also* parasites)
nene, *see* Hawaiian goose
Nene Restoration Programme, 118
Nepal, 309
nephritis (*see also* stress, pathology, disease), 76,
   80, 190
nervous tics, 196
Nesomimus parvulus, 22
nest-building, 45, 324
   destruction, 16, 19
   interference, 23
   protection, 19
   robbery, 58
   site, 21, 49, 52, 58, 60
   use, 52
nest facilities, 20, 21, 149
   nest-box, 60, 76, 130, 149, 157, 158, 184,
      189, 196, 197, 201, *210*, 213, *214, 215*,
      216
   nests, 26, 27, *28*, 29, 41, *80*, 126, 327
   nest size, 189
   number of, 22, 24, 121, 149
nesting
   artificial sites, 21, 23, 221
   grounds, 18, 19, 24, 25, 33, 34, *103*
   material, 52

   season, 20, 21, 24, 25, *27*
   success, 21
nestling, *136*
New South Wales, 167, 183
New York Zoo, 36, 37, 322
New Zealand, 168
   birds, 375
   Islands, *see* South Muttonbird Islands
   Native Bird Protection Society, 62
   Wildlife Service, 61
niacin, 108, 109, 110, 111
nocturnal activity, 152
nocturnal animals, 5, 349
noises, 156, 163, 165, 192
non-infectious disease, 324
Nordiska Museet, 125
Norfolk Wildlife Park, 126, 127, 128, 129, 130,
   317, 327
Notoryctes, 181
   typhlops, 178
Notoryctidae, 178
numbat, 178, *179*, 180
Numidinae, 87
nutrient intake (*see also* diet,) 107
nutrition (*see also* diet), 100
nutritional requirements, 223
   conditions, 270
Nyctea scandiaca, 130

O

obesity, 298
oestrus, 162, 163, 168, 188, 227, 241, 257, 266,
   324, 325, 327, 331, 340
   disturbance of, 260
   post-partum, 216, 219, 296, 297, 304, 306,
      307, 325
oestrous cycle, 168, 169
   induction of, 259
   synchronization of, 359
oil (*see also* diet, dietary additives), 56, 57, 58,
   95, 96
okapi, 182
Oklahoma City Zoo, 337, 339, 340
olfactory
   communication, 190
   investigation (*see also* marking behaviour), 303,
     306
omnivores, standard food mixture, 249

onager, 365, 366
Onychogalea, 180
  fraenata, 174
  lunulata, 174
  unguifera, 174
Opuntia, 20
orang-utan, 151, 171, 235, *237, 239, 240*, 363,
  368, 369
  Bornean, 242
  hybrids, 242, 381
  Sumatran, 242
Oribatidae, 297
Ornithological Society of New Zealand, 74
Ornithorhynchus anatinus, 174
oryx, 379
  Arabian, 235, 285, *286, 287, 288, 291*, 364,
    371, 376
  Scimitar-horned, 364, 365, 367
Oryx leucoryx, 364
  tao, 364
osteodystrophia, 341
osteomalacia, 208, 324
otters
  Canadian, 317, 319, 321
  Eurasian, 317, *318*
  giant Brazilian, 327, 363, 364
  Indian smooth-coated, 315, *317, 320*
  oriental small clawed, 315, *316*
  sea-otter, 318
out-breeding, 47, 116
ovary, atresia of, 161
over-stocking, 34
Ovis orientalis, 364
owls, 126
  barn, 129, 130
  eagle, 125, 126, *127*, 128
  little, 129
  snowy, 130
  tengmalm's, 130
  young, 125

P

Pademelons, 174
Pampa Galeras National Park, 283
Pan paniscus, 245, *247*, 363
Pan troglodytes, *249*
panic in captive animals, 80
panleucopenia, 322, 323, 332

Panthera
  leo persica, 363
  pardus japonensis, 363
  tigris sumatrae, 363
  tigris, 329
  tigris altaica, 363
  uncia, 363
pantothenic acid, 108, 109, 110, 111
paralysis, 192
parasites, 10, 50, 58, 80, 108, 119, 190, 271,
  275, 282, 297, 323
  Capillaria, 75, 76
  Coccidia, 282
  Prosthenorchis elegans, 215
  Spirocerca, 195
  Strongyloides, 282
  Trichostrongylus, 282
  Trichuris, 282
  water-borne, 57
Parc Zoologique de Clères (France), 85, 96
parental training, 113
Paris Zoological Gardens, 201, 245, 277, 279,
  283, 302, 322
parma wallaby, *see* wallaby
parrot (Puerto Rican), 99
parturition, 216, 228, 246, 266, 297
paternal behaviour, 230, 233, 315, *326*
pathogenic organisms, *see* parasites
pathology (*see also* stereotypy, pelage condition),
  56, 75, 80, 100, 109, 149, 208, 227, 246,
  250, 282, 322, 341
  symptoms of, 154, 166, 190, 192, 195,
    199
Patuxent, *see* U.S. Fish and Wildlife Service
  Wildlife Research Centre, 99, *101*, 103, 104,
    107, 112, 113, 131
peacock, 90
  Congo, 75, *77, 76, 80, 81*, 82, *84*, 87
Peale's peregrine, *see* falcon
pecking preference, 57
Pekin Zoo, 94
pelage, 150
  care of, 267
  condition of (*see also* dietary deficiency, health),
    192, 193, 225, 318, *320, 321*
pellets (food), 56, 58, 107, 150, 238, 276, 288,
  296
Peradorcas concinna, 174

Perameles, 181
  bougainvillei, 177
  eremiana, 177
  gunni, 177
  nasuta, 177
Perdix, 87
peregrine, *see* falcon
peregrine survey, 135
perphenazin, 282
pest, 172, 179, 180
  control, 173
pesticides, 6, 126, 133, 135, 178
Petaurus
  australis, 176
  breviceps, 176
  norfolcensis, 176
Petrogale, 180
  brachyotis, 174
  penicillata, 174
  purpureicollis, 174
  xanthopis, 174, *175*, 362
Phalanger, 181
  arboreal, 179
  maculatus, 175
  orientalis, 175
Phaner furcifer, 193
Phascogale, 177, 181
  calura, 177
  tapoatafa, 177
Phascolarctos cinereus, 177
Phasianus, 88
pheasants, 87, 91, 96, 381
  bar-tailed, 94, 96
  Blyth's tragopan, 94
  Bornean peacock pheasant, 94
  brown-eared, 94
  Cabot's, 94
  Cheer, 91, *92*, 94, 375
  Chinese monal, 94
  common, 90
  Edward's, 94, 96
  Elliot's, 94, 96
  Hume's, 96
  Imperial, 94
  Mikado, 90, *90*, 94, 96
  Palawan peacock pheasant, 94
  Sclater's monal, 94
  Swinhoe's, 88, *89*, 90, 94, 96, 375

  Western tragopan, 94
  white-eared, 94
Pheasant Trust, 88, *89*, 90, 91, *92*, 93, 95, 96, 97, 381
Philadelphia Zoological Gardens, 85, 337, 338, 339, 340
Philesturnus carunculatus, 61
Phoenix Zoo, 285, *286*, 287, 290, *291*, 371
phosphorus, 108, 109, 110, 111, 339
photoperiod (*see also* day length), 139
  inversion of, 349
  variation of, 107
photoperiodicity, 50, 56
physiological cycles, *see* cycles
physiological factors, 270
pigeon, Puerto Rican plain, 99
Pinta Island, 17, 18, 19
Pinzón Island, 17, 18, 19, 27, 32, 33, 34
placenta, 159, 228, 229, 233, 279
Planigale, 181
  ingrami, 171, 177, *178*
  subtilissima, 177
  tenuirostris, 177
platypus, 172, 174, 178
play behaviour, 228, 249, 267, 306
pneumonia, 246, 322, 323, 331
poaching, 18, 36, 312, 313
Pohakuloa, Hawaii, 116, *120*, *121*
poison, 19, 60
poisoning, 324
  symptoms of, 166
pollution, 173
polyoestrous condition, 324, 327
Polyplectron emphanum, 94
  malacense (schleiermacheri), 94
Pongo pygmaeus, 363
poodle breeding, 236
pool, heated, 295
population
  apparent increase, 369
  decline, 18, 115, 133, 369
  decline in wild, 20, 173
  density, 149
  density in captivity, 168, 366
  depletion, wild, 374
  estimates, 17
  fluctuation, 173
  increase in captivity, 367, 368

size, 16, 358
survey, 133
survival, 18
population: captive, 32, 126, 235, 262, 274, 273, 292, 302, 310, 329, 358, 362, 365, 367, 370, 371
island, 177, 179
natural/wild, 13, 15, 18, 19, 21, 23, 126, 255, 271, 283, 285, 293, 309, 312, 329, 358, 374
sustaining 371
total, 369, 370, 371
possum
brush-tailed, 171, 175, 180
gliding, 176
honey, 176
Leadbeater's, 176
mountain pygmy, 173
pygmy, 176, *176*
ring-tailed, 171, 175, 180
scaly-tailed, 175
post-mortem examination, 282, 324
Potorous, 181
platyops, 175
tridactyius ,175, 362
pouch young (*see also* marsupial), 169
Prague Zoological Garden, 263, *264, 265*
predation, 18, 32, 87, 88, 196
predators, 16, 17, 20, 52, 73, 95, 112, 115, 119, 120, 123, 382
absence of, 61
control of, 19, 123
pregnancy, *see* gestation
pregnant females, 228
premature birth, 163, 227, 256
pre-partum behaviour, 327
Pretoria Zoo, 85, 275, 341
preventive medical treatment (*see also* inoculation, vaccination), 10, 241, 250, 266, 290, 297
prey, 312, 339
primate centres, 358
primates (*see also* individual species), 382
primiparous females, 216
Propithecus verreauxi, 199, *200*
protein (*see also* diet, dietary additives), 39, 57, 58, 95, 108, 109, 110, 111, 296, 339
prothrombin time, 166
Przewalski horse, *see* horse

Pseudemys, 1
scripts, 6
Pseudoaspidodera, 77
Pseudocheirus peregrinus, 175
psychological effects, 250
of cage transfer, 154
factors, 270
Pternistis, 87
Pteronura brasiliensis, 327, 363
puberty, 217
Pukaweka Island, *64,* 71
pulmonary oedema, 190
damage, 195
Pygathrix nemaeus, 223 *et seq.*, *224*
Python
molurus, 48
reticulatus, 47, 78
python (*see also* snakes), 2, 8

Q

Qatar, 376
quail, 87
quarantine, 10, 117, 226, 322, 339
facilities, 11, 290
stations, 255
quokka, 173

R

Rabida Island, 16
race, *see* subspecies
rail, Yuma clapper, 99
rain, 6, 20, 34, 51, 288
protection from, 238
rainfall, 172, 173, 264, 266
rainy season, 152
Rallus longirostris vumanensis, 99
rank-order, 194, 289
Raptor Research Foundation, 133, 141
raptorial birds, *see* birds of prey
rat kangaroo, 175, 179
long-nosed, 362
musk, 173, 179, 182
Ratcliffe diet, 321, 338
rearing, 52, 58, *77,* 327
artificial, 280
centre, *120*
"reassuring", 153, 154
receptivity, 40, 246

record forms, 84
    system, 60, 85
records of zoos, 310
Red Data Book (IUCN), 115, 174, 262, 361, 371
Red Mercury Island, 68, *69, 70*
red-tailed hawk, *see* hawk
refusal to eat, 216
regular keepers, 321
regulation of numbers, 255
reintroduction to the wild, 19, 32, 34, 35, 36, 49, 51, 65, 67, *69, 70,* 73, 74, 88, 90, 91, 100, 112, 113, 116, *121,* 122, 125, 126, 128, 131, 139, 151, 242, 250, 267, 312, 344, 373–377, 380, 382, 383, 385
    experimental, 143
    potential, 371
    procedure, 91
rejection of male, 327
release methods, 113
    pen, 118
relic fauna, 173
renal calculi (*see also* kidney), 324
repair, 156
reproductive biology, 267
    cycle, 325
    dynamics, 255, 258
    isolation, 13
    potential, 34, 255, 259
    problems, 34
    seasonality, 256
    stimulation (*see also* breeding seasonality), 107
reptile, 1 *et seq.,* 43, 45, 361, 358
    eggs, 9
reserves, 18, 358
    area, 173, 256, 267
    natural, 73, 91, *92,* 144
resorption of embryos, 162, 163
restocking (*see also* reintroduction to wild), 19, 20, 35
restraint, 186
retreat, 331, 351
retrieval of cubs, 327
reunification of group, 232
rhinoceros
    black, 359, 364, 370
    Indian, 293, *294, 295,* 296, *298, 299,* 303, *304,* 307, 309, 310, 311, 359, 364

Sumatran, 182
white, 144, 296
Rhinoceros unicornis, 293, *294,* 303, 309, 364
riboflavin, 108, 109, 110, 111
Richardson's merlin, 135
rickets, 217, 241, 341
ring-tailed lemur, 187, 193, 194
Riyadh Zoo, 287, 290
rodents, 165, 172
Rome Zoo, 302, 337
Rotterdam Zoo, 345, 331, 332, *333*
roughage (*see also* diet), 39, 45, 321
Royal New Zealand Air Force, 74
Royal New Zealand Navy, 71, 74
Royal Russian Stud Farm, 357
Royal Zoological Society Antwerp, 75, 85
rut, 257, 266

S

saddleback, 61, *69,* 70, 71
    North Island, 62, 66, 73
    South Island, 62, 73
safari parks, 340, 381
sale of wild animals, 255
salmonellosis, 109
salt (*see also* diet, dietary constituents), 264, 276, 339
San Antonio Zoo, 277
San Cristóbal, 17, 19
San Cruz, 17, 18, 19, 20, 21, 27, 32
San Diego Zoo, 22, 23, 28, 29, 36, 37, 245, 246, 274, 275, 277, 292, 296
Santa Fé, 19
San Pasqual Zoo, 296
San Salvador, 17, 19
Sanzinia madagascariensis, 10
Saguinus
    geoffroyi, 207
    illigeri, 213
    imperator, 206
    midas, 204
    nigricollis, 213, *219,* 221
    oedipus, 213, 218, 219, *219,* 220
Salmonella, 11
sarcoma, 324
Sarcophilus harrisii, 177
Scaup, New Zealand, 50
scent-marks, *see* marking behaviour

Schoinbates volans, 176
"sea-otter", *see* otter, Indian smooth-coated
seasonality of breeding, *see* breeding
seclusion, 356
second generation reproduction, *see* generations
security, 10, 210
sedation, phencyclidine, 341
Select Committee on Wildlife Conservation (Australian House of Representatives), 172
selection,
    artificial, 236, 243, 260
    of males, 58
semen
    collection of, 58, 107, 359
    frozen, 358, 359
    sample, 51
    storage of, 357
semi-domesticated animals, 358
senescence, 100, 219
sense of security, 321
septicaemia, 323
Sernylan, 282
Setonix brachyurus, 173
sex
    determination of, 4
    ratio, 85, 100, 258, 280
sexing techniques, 1
sexual
    activity, 267
    dimorphism, 1, 82
    display, 51
    drive, 267
    interest, 277
sexual maturity, 58, 82, 144, 170, 209, 211, 217, 267, *268*, 270, 280, 337, 353
    delay in, 161
sexual skin, 227, 246
shelter, 20, 130, 181, 238, 331, 351
shock (*see also* stress), 72
shy, *see* timid
sika, Formosan, 364, 365, 366
Simla, 91, *92*
single specimens, 366, 368, 369, 370, 371, 383
skin condition (*see also* health, pelage), 295
sleeping box, 186, 331, 332, *333*
Slimbridge (Wildfowl Trust), 47, 50, 51, *53, 54, 55,* 58, *59,* 116, *117, 118,* 119, 122, 123, 381

"slipped wing", 57
Smardzewice reserve, 256
Sminthopsis, 181
    crassicaudata, 177
    froggetti, 177
    granulipes, 177
    hirtipes, 177
    leucopus, 177
    longicaudata, 177
    macroura, 177
    murina, 177
    nitela, 177
    psammophila, 177
    rufigenis, 177
snakes, 1, 2, 4, 5, 6, 52
snipe, 72
snowcocks, 87
social
    behaviour, 236, 246, 292, 317, 329, 375
    conditions, 197
    environment, 151, 318
    groups in captivity, 218, 276, 315
    groups *in natura*, 194, 196, 201
    hierarchy, *see* dominance
    relationship, 270
solar radiation, *see* sunshine
Solomon Island, *64*, 71
Southern Muttonbird Islands, *64*
sparrow
    cape sable, 99
    dusky seaside, 99
sperm (*see also* semen), 51, 116, 357
spermatogenesis, arrest of, 161
Spilotes, 5
Sporting Shooters Association, Victoria, 167
sportive lemur (*see also* lemur), 150, 197
sprats, 56
spurfowls, 87
SSC Vicuña Group, 283
Stage Island, 73
stereotypy
    behaviour patterns, 215
    of movement, 196, 274
sterility, 161, 298
sterilization agents, 19
Steward Island, *64*, 71
stillbirth, 257, 258, 280, 302, 337

stock distribution, 292

Stockholm Conference, 384

stomach, ulceration of, 190

stress, 68, 138, 139, 154, 163, 184, 190, 196, 197, 198, 211, 225, 226, 227, 241, 334, 341

    chronic, 159

    environmental, 163

    physiological measures of, 161

    social stress, 159

    stressors, 154

    symptoms, 196

    tail-ruffling, in tree-shrew, 160, 161

"stress syndrome", 154

Strongyloides, 282

stud book, 47, 236, 273, 283, 335, 367, 376

    European bison pedigree book, 253

    international, 300, 302

Stuttgart Zoo, 295, 302

subileus, 246

subspecies, 13, 14, 71, 171, 175, 242, 282, 312, 313, 335, 371, 381

suckling (*see also* lactation), 216, 246, 279, 280, 306, 339, 355

    difficulties, 159, 353

    position

    rhythm, tree-shrew, 157, *158*, 161, 164

sunshine, 25, 28, 30, 32, 49, 51, 58

    lack of, 31

supplement, *see* diet dietary additives

survival

    centres, 361, 372

    in captivity, 35, 366, 368

    information, 376

    potential, 13

    rates, 30, 34

    in wild, 18

Survival Service Commission (SSC—IUCN), 373, 374, 375, 379, 383

    policy statement, 376

Swainson's hawk, *see* hawk

swan, 49, 56

    Trumpeter, 113

Syrmatieus

    ellioti, 94

    humiae, 94

    mikado, 91, 94

T

Tachyglossus aculeatus, 174

tagging, 60

tail ruffling, *see* tree-shrew

Taiwan (Formosa), 88, *89*, *90*, 91

tamarin, 203, 213, *et seq.* 219

    red handed, *204*

tame animals, 186, 196, 339, 351

taming, *see* hand rearing

tapeworm, 77, 297

tapir

    Baird, 364

Tapirus bairdii, 364

Taronga Zoo, 171, *176*, *178*, *179*, 181

Tarsipes spencerae, 176

Tasmania, 173, 177, 178, 184

Tasmanian Devil, 177

tattoos, 277

taxonomy, 171

teal

    brown, 50, 52

    marbled, 50

    New Zealand brown, *54*

temperature (*see also* incubation), 4, 5, 6, 9, 25, 26, 27, *28*, 41, 43, 45, 51, 58, 75, 81, 104, 105, 106, 151, 152, 172, 188, 193, 197, 201, 205, 216, 226, 238, 264, 266, 320, 331, 351, 352, 358

Tenebrio mollitor, *see* meal worms

Terrapene, 1

    ornata, 8

terrarium, 4

territory, 45, 66, 67, 129, 181, 210, 315, 340

territorial, 49, 276

    call, 66

    security, 213

testes, descent of, 161

test-tube fertilization, 359

Testudo carbonaria, 9

    graeco, 5

    hermanni, 5, 9

    marginata, 5

    radiata, 3, 5

    vicina, *40*

Tetraoninae, 87

Tetroagallus, 87

thiaminase, 56, 57

thiamine, 111

Thylacinus, 173
  cynocephalus, 178
Thyogale
  billardierii, 174
  stigmatica, 174
  thetis, 174
tiger, 329
  Bengal, 333
  Caspian, 329
  Chinese, 329
  Indian, 329
  Siberian, 329, 333, 334, 363, 365, 369
  Sumatran, 329, *330*, 331, 333, 334, 363, 369
Toledo Zoo, 337, 338, 339, 340, 341
tooth development, 185
tortoise, 29, 30, 35, 215
  Galápagos, 39, *40*
  giant, 13, 14
  Mediterranean, 5
  radiated, *3*, 5
  raising centre, 35
toxicosis, 199
toxoplasmosis, 195
Tragopan, 95, 97
  blythi, 94
  caboti, 94
  melanocephalus, 94
tranquillizer, 282
transfer (of endangered species), 62, 71, 72
transport, 34, 199
  method, 68
  of eggs, 23, 24, 25, 28, 34
tree kangaroo, 175, 180
tree-shrews (*see also Tupaia*), 146, *147*, *157*, 161, 163, 164, *164*
  disruption of behaviour, 159
  hand rearing, 154, *155*
  marking, 162
  maternal behaviour of, 149, 153, 157
  stress in, *160*
  suckling rhythm, 157, *158*, 161, 164
Tremarctos ornatus, 363
Trichostrongylus, 282
Trichosurus
  caninus, 175
  vulpecula, 175
Trichuris, 282
trumpeter swans, 113

Tsimbazaza Zoo, 200
tuatara, 2
tuberculosis, 109, 242, 282, 323
  avian, 57, 90
  BCG vaccination, 250
Tupaia belangeri, *see* tree shrew
tundra peregrine, *see* falcon
turtles, 1, *2*
  red-eared, 6
twilight, 349
Twycross Zoo, 316
Tyto alba, 129

U

Uakari, red, 362
ultra-violet light, 5, 205
U.S. Fish and Wildlife Service, 122
  Research Laboratory, 135
umbilical cord, 159, 228
University of Western Australia, 182
unsaturated fats, 320
urination, 20
  increase, 297
urine marking, *see* marking behaviour

V

vaccination, 57, 341, 343
Varanus, 4, 9
Varecia, 193, 194
variegated lemurs, 193, 194
vegetable oils, 320, 321
vegetable protein supplement (*see also* dietary additives), 280
Verreaux's sifaka, *200*
veterinary problems (*see also* parasites, pathology), 34, 45
  medicine, 100
Vicugna vicugna, 364
vicuña, 271, *272*, *273*, *274*, *275*, 276, *278*, *279*, *280*, 364, 370, 381
Vienna Zoo, 293
Vietnam, 96
Vionate, *see* dietary additives
viral disease (*see also* parasites), 323
visitor effect, 156
vitamins (*see also* diet, dietary additives), 45, 79, 249, 276, 331, 333, 341, 351
  A, 79, 108, 109, 110, 111, 166, 339

vitamins—(*contd.*)
  B group, 57, 79, 108, 109, 110, 181, 192, 339
  C, 79, 250
  D, 181, 216, 217
  D₃, 79, 108, 109, 110, 111, 208, 339
  E, 108, 109, 110, 111, 182, 339
  K, 108, 109, 110, 111, 166
  deleterious effects of, 166
  hypovitaminosis, 324
  multivitamin powder, 339
Vombatus ursinus, 177

W

Wallabia bicolor, 174
wallaby, 149, 168, 174, 179
  yellow-footed rock, *175*, 182
  hare, 174
  large, 174
  nail-tailed, 174, 182
  rock, 174
  small, 174

wallow, 306
water buffalo, 358
waterfowl, 49, 115, 361
  Arctic, 57
  longtails, 58
  scoters, 58
waterlogged fur, 319
water supply, 29, 53, 56, 60, 95, 151, 189, 226,
    238, 276, 352
wattle-bird family, 61
weaning, 332
weka, 73
whip-poor-will,
  Puerto Rican, 99
Whipsnade Park Zoo, 242, 300, 302, 304, 306,
    310, 312, *330*, 337, 338, 339, 340, *342*, *343*
Whooping Crane Advisory Group, 113
Wild Animal Propagation Trust, Honolulu, 39,
    41, 42, 358
wildfowl, 49
  tropical, 51